Mothers, Mothering, and COVID-19

Dispatches from a Pandemic

Edited by Andrea O'Reilly and Fiona Joy Green

DEMETER

Mothers, Mothering, and COVID-19
Dispatches from a Pandemic

Edited by Andrea O'Reilly and Fiona Joy Green

Copyright © 2021 Demeter Press

Demeter Press
2546 10th Line
Bradford, Ontario
Canada, L3Z 3L3
Tel: 289-383-0134
Email: info@demeterpress.org
Website: www.demeterpress.org

Demeter Press logo based on the sculpture "Demeter" by Maria-Luise Bodirsky www.keramik-atelier.bodirsky.de

Printed and Bound in Canada

Cover artwork: *Taming the Virus,* Catherine Moeller
Cover design and typesetting: Michelle Pirovich

Library and Archives Canada Cataloguing in Publication
Title: Mothers, mothering, and COVID-19 : dispatches from a pandemic / edited by Andrea O'Reilly and Fiona Joy Green.
Names: O'Reilly, Andrea, 1961- editor. | Green, Fiona J., editor.
Description: Includes bibliographical references.
Identifiers: Canadiana 20200374176 | ISBN 9781772583434 (softcover)
Subjects: LCSH: Working mothers. | LCSH: Stay-at-home mothers.
| LCSH: Motherhood. | LCSH: COVID-19 (Disease)—Social aspects.
| LCSH: Telecommuting—Social aspects. Classification: LCC HQ759.48.
M68 2021 | DDC 306.874/3—dc23

To all mothers living through Covid.

Acknowledgments

Our respect and gratitude to each and every one of the contributors cannot be overstated. For mothers to write and create work during the chaos, fear and uncertainty as humanity transitioned, pivoted, recalculated and adjusted time and time again to the unprecedented reality of the global pandemic is unfathomable. They worked within unimaginable situations, including without many hours of sleep, and the emotional and physical toll of caring for children and other family members under lockdown and the closures of schools and care homes. They sacrificed their own self-care and took time, attention, and care away from family to work and engage in the emotional and intellectual labour necessary to write and create the pieces showcased here. We offer you our deepest admiration and appreciation.

We want to express our appreciation to Catherine Moeller for creating and contributing her stunning embroidery art piece "Taming the Virus" featured on the cover of the book. Thank you, Catherine, for exploring and bravely sharing your fears of COVID-19 in this way.

Thanks also to Jesse O'Reilly-Conlin, the most extraordinary Copy Editor we've worked with. His proficient skills and attention to detail, along with his kind approach to asking questions and offering suggestions throughout the editing process are rare and greatly appreciated. Thank you, Jesse. Deep gratitude as well to Demeter's type setter and designer Michelle Pirovich who once again created order from the chaos, under impossible deadlines, and always with impeccable skill and generous grace. And thank you to Demeter's new proof reader Jena Woodhouse who bravely and skillfully took on the formidable task of proofing this massive manuscript. Thank you Jena for joining the Demeter team!

Fiona would also like to take this opportunity to thank the intrepidly daring and formidable Andrea O'Reilly for both spearheading this important project and for inviting her to join Andrea as co-editor in the ambitious feat of assembling this most needed and timely collection in the first year of the global COVID-19 pandemic. Andrea's drive, experience, wisdom and no-nonsense attitude made working together intensely rewarding. Thank you, Andrea. It's been an honour.

And as always, Fiona is deeply grateful for her life partner Barry Edginton, who ensures she is able to take on this work by caring for and supporting her in ways that only he can.

Andrea would also like to thank Fiona Joy Green for co-editing this volume with her. When I decided to take on what seemed to be a near impossible undertaking—doing a book on mothers and COVID-19 in a pandemic—I knew I could not do it alone, and would need someone with the skill, smarts, grit, grace to keep me and the book on track. One name immediately came to mind—Fiona a brilliant scholar and one of my closest friends and colleagues. This book could not, would not have happened without Fiona. From the writing of the CFP, the selection of the chapters, the endless readings and revisions of the chapters, the compilation of the manuscript, and writing of the book's introduction, you were always one step ahead of me with your insights and ideas. Thank you for making what would have been an arduous journey alone so joyful in our partnership.

And always, my deepest gratitude to my life partner Terry Conlin, who has always been there for and with me for every book I have written, and particularly for this one as he tolerated my endless rants and ruminations on mothers and COVID-19 under pandemic lock down and isolation in the bush on the shores of Peter Lake.

Contents

CONTENTS

Introduction

Andrea O'Reilly and Fiona Joy Green

We finished writing this introduction to *Mothers, Mothering, and COVID-19: Dispatches from a Pandemic* on January 11, 2021, ten months after The World Health Organization (WHO) declared the novel coronavirus (COVID-19) outbreak a global pandemic on March 11, 2020. Today, January 11, 2021, 1,944,951 people have been infected by the virus, and 90,783, 838 have died. In these ten months, countries have moved in and out of lockdown. Schools have closed, reopened, and then closed again. Countless people have lost their jobs, and innumerable businesses have closed. Families have been separated, travel has ended, and the rituals of community and family life—weddings, birthdays, funerals, and holiday celebrations—have gone virtual. Work and schooling for many are now remote, and the mental health of many has been deleteriously affected by the social isolation, stress, and losses of the pandemic. Words and concepts not even imaginable a year ago— physical distancing, social bubbles, lockdown, shelter in place, mandatory masking, flatten the curve, community spread, acute respiratory stress syndrome (ADRS), contact tracing, herd immunity, PPE (personal protective equipment), self-quarantine, WFH (working from home), and super spreader events—are now common terms in our social lexicon. The recent discovery and current distribution of a vaccine offers hope that by the end of 2021, the pandemic will be behind us. But even when this virus is finally under control, our lives will be forever changed by COVID-19.

This book explores the impact of COVID-19 on mothers' employment, carework, and wellbeing and health. The central directive of the COVID-19 pandemic has been conveyed in two words: stay home. However, throughout the pandemic, there has been little mainstream media coverage, public policy, or social research on how families are managing under social isolation and pandemic protocols. Few have acknowledged, let alone sought to support, the crucial work mothers are doing as frontline workers to keep families functioning in these times of increasing uncertainty. Many of the posts on Andrea's Facebook newsfeed have been by mothers who are exhausted, overwhelmed, panicked, and terrified. They share stories of guilt, self-blame, and despair at not being able to manage or cope, and they are also often shamed and judged by others for their failures caused by the pandemic. One particularly heartwrenching post from April 2, 2020, in the early days of the pandemic, was by a single mother who was bullied and harassed when she took her children with her to shop for needed groceries:

If anybody has ever wondered what defeat looks like, here it is folks. This is the look of a single mom during a pandemic. The look of a single mom who hasn't left the house except for a grocery order pickup since they called the State of Emergency. A grocery order which had 100$ worth of items that wasn't available, but that I still needed even though it wasn't available. The look of a single mom who decided to pack up the children to go to Costco to pick up a prescription and to hopefully get the rest of the things I needed to be able to stay home for a few weeks at least. Because my options are a) get a babysitter which I'm not allowed to do b) leave the kids home alone which I'm not allowed to do or c) get someone to pick up my stuff which by the way equaled 300$. So this is the look of a single mom who was rudely told by not 1, not 2, but 3 Costco employees that it is the last time I will be able to bring in my children, and overheard 2 employees rudely point at me and say "yeah are we putting up signs about children because clearly they're not gonna listen until we do." Most employees were amazing, smiling, and friendly, but I'm guessing a few stressed ones took it out on me. You're looking at the face of a single mom who can't ship their kids off to their dads and have a break. A single mom who's been trying to follow the rules, who has been trying my best at working from home with an 8 year old and a 4 year old who fight and scream and need to eat and are bored just like every other kid. And the look of a single mom who came out of Costco with tears streaming down her face to hear that I will now have to add homeschooling to the mix.

Andrea shared the post with these comments:

The current situation of forced social isolation for single mothers is not sustainable. Governments and communities must act now to provide support for mothers in such impossible situations. While I applaud the Canadian government for all they are doing for those in paid labour—Canada Emergency Relief Benefit, wage subsidies, and so forth—why are mothers in their homes doing the impossible as frontline workers in this pandemic not likewise entitled to and deserving of our respect and support?

Although most of the many comments on Andrea's post supported this single mother's untenable situation, a few said that what she did was still wrong or wondered why she did not have anyone to help her. However, and as Andrea responded, "Under the rules of social distancing, no one can be in her home other than those that reside there; no family, babysitter etc. can give a single mother even an hour of respite. No one can live like this for weeks let alone the now proposed several months." As another single mother commented:

I have emotional resources to draw on, people to FaceTime, and only 1 toddler—who doesn't have additional needs—but I have been REALLY challenged by the isolation. I can't imagine what it'd be like to have compounding factors making things harder AND to be facing months and months alone. It is a massive reminder that we are NOT designed to mother alone, it's completely unnatural.

Indeed, the situation is completely unnatural and unsustainable, but why is no one talking about this in the mainstream media? And why is there no public policy being developed or research undertaken to support mothers in this pandemic?

As mothers' stories filled Andrea's Facebook newsfeed, another story was being told in mainstream news media. Commercial after commercial and news story after news story were acknowledging and giving thanks to frontline workers of the pandemic; first, it was doctors and nurses, but the list soon expanded to include personal support workers (PSWs), retail workers, truck drivers, transit workers, firefighters, letter carriers, restaurant staff, pharmacists, first responders, and sanitation workers. We were rightly honouring the essential services of many in the public service who are keeping us safe and cared for, but no one in the countless commercials or news coverage seen throughout this pandemic has publicly thanked mothers or acknowledged, let alone honoured, the essential work mothers are doing in their homes to keep families safe and cared for. Jackie Dunham argues that "There's this idea that we're all in this together, but in many ways, it certainly is not an equal-opportunity pandemic.... The people that are impacted most will always be the most marginalized ... that includes all women, but especially those women who are from racialized groups, newcomer communities, Indigenous women, and those with disabilities." We suggest that it is more specifically mothers who are most impacted by the pandemic because it is mothers who are doing the necessary and arduous carework to sustain our families and communities. However, few are recognizing, let alone supporting, mothers as frontline workers or acknowledging and appreciating what mothers are managing and accomplishing in their homes under unimaginable circumstances. Indeed, as Claire Gagne asked early in the pandemic: "Why is no one talking about how unsustainable this is for working parents?" Gagne further stresses the following:

> While it seems like every day, we hear of new funding for businesses, support for students and money for the unemployed (all necessary and worthwhile of course), I haven't heard a damn thing about a solution for parents who've suddenly had all their supports—school, childcare, extended family—ripped away, and then been expected to carry on with their full-time jobs.

When there is no separation between work, family, and home, pressure inevitably builds, and we need to be asking what toll this is taking on mothers and how as a society we can support mothers and their essential service of caregiving. Indeed, as Farhad Majoo wonders in her June article "Two Parents. Two Kids. Two Jobs. No Childcare": "How could anyone think this is sustainable. Attempting to work full time while rooming with, feeding, and educating one or more children during the pandemic?"

In April, Andrea felt increasingly frustrated and angered by the deafening silence concerning mothers and mothering in the pandemic. She decided that one way both to learn about what mothers were experiencing in the pandemic and to provide support to mothers was through creating a mothers and COVID-19 Facebook group as well as an accompanying website. The group aimed to inform, support, and empower mothers through and after the pandemic. The Facebook group—called simply Mothers and COVID-19—was established May 1, 2020. In twenty-four hours, the group had two hundred members, and at the time of writing this introduction, ten-plus months later, 1,429 mothers have joined. The website, mothersandcovid.com, was launched a week later. The instant and ardent interest in the Facebook group confirmed the urgent need for a book on the topic of mothers, mothering, and COVID-19. So, in May 2020, Andrea and Fiona wrote the call for proposals for this collection, and by July, we had received over one hundred abstracts, more than any submitted for a previous Demeter book collection. From these abstracts, we developed a special double issue of the *Journal of the Motherhood Initiative* on academic motherhood and COVID-19, with eighteen articles (published December 2020: http://journalofmotherhoodinitiative.org/product/academic-motherhood-and-covid-19/), and this book *Mothers, Mothering, and COVID-19: Dispatches from a Pandemic*, containing forty-five chapters. With this book, we seek to address the disconnect between what is happening in homes across the world and what is being reported in the media. We want to ask why motherwork, even during a pandemic when it is so crucial, remains so devalued and invisible. Finally, and most urgently, we want to explore how mothers are managing and what can be done to better support them in this pandemic.

This is the first book on the impact of COVID-19 on mothers and mothering. Mothers do the bulk of domestic labour, childcare, and elder care. And with the implementation of social isolation and pandemic protocols, the burden of their carework has increased exponentially in both time and concern as mothers are running households with little or no support, under close to impossible conditions, and while often engaged in wage labour. "Despite the mass entry of women into the workforce during the 20th century," writes Helen Lewis, in her article "The Coronavirus is a Disaster for

Feminism," "the phenomenon of the 'second shift' still exists." She continues: "Across the world, women—including those with jobs—do more housework and have less leisure time than their male partners." One Canadian study reports that men spent an average of thirty-three hours of caregiving per week before the pandemic and forty-six hours during the pandemic. Women spent an average of sixty-eight hours before the pandemic and ninety-five hours after (Gregory). The pandemic has particularly compounded what we call the "third shift"—the emotional and intellectual labour of motherwork. Such labour also mirrors what philosopher Sara Ruddick has termed "maternal thinking": the organizing, remembering, anticipating, worrying, and planning that mothers take on for the family. As well, with COVID-19, many mothers are working in what may be termed the "fourth shift"—that is, the homeschooling of children. A *New York Times* survey found that 80 per cent of mothers said they were picking up most of the responsibility for homeschooling, whereas only 3 per cent of women said that men were doing more (Daniel). Although schools and childcare centres are reopening in some countries, their capacity is gravely limited because of pandemic protocols, the hybrid format (in class and remote) of many schools, the likelihood of closures, and children having to return home to self-isolate due to exposure. As well, despite the gradual reopening of economies, mothers still have little respite from their motherwork, as they continue to do the bulk of the caregiving work. "School closures and household isolation," Lewis writes, "are moving the work of caring for children from the paid economy—nurseries, schools, babysitters—to the unpaid one." Lewis goes on to ask: "What do pandemic patients need? Looking after. What do self-isolating people need? Looking after. What do children kept home from school need? Looking after. All of this looking after—this unpaid caring labor—will fall more heavily on women, because of the existing structures of the workforce." Add income or employment loss, financial or housing instability, food insecurity, single parenting, new immigrants, mothering in abusive situations, and the stress is amplified. Indeed, as Sara Petersen notes in her July *YahooStyle,* article: "The burden of unpaid labor in the home has always fallen disproportionally on mothers, but the pandemic has shone a glaring light, neon light into a situation that has always been impossible." "As this pandemic unfolds" as noted by Soraya Chemaly, "the caregiver second shift is becoming a third and fourth shift. Children are home from school, partners are home from the office, and elderly parents are at high risk of COVID-19 infection." The unequal distribution of unpaid work in the home and the increased burden of care throughout the pandemic has been particularly detrimental for mothers in the paid labour force.

The November 2020 United Nations *Whose Time to Care* report found that women were taking on more household tasks than men throughout the pandemic and were more likely to leave the workforce (Cassidy, Braithwaite, and Diab). Worldwide at the end of the second quarter of 2020, 1.7 times as many women as men were outside the labour force (321 million women comparted to 182 million men). The U.S. Bureau of Labor, similarly, reported in October 2020 that 80 per cent of the nearly 1.1 million workers who left the workforce in September were women: 865,000 women compared to 216,000 men (Ebbert). A report from the Center for American Progress estimates the cost of mothers leaving the workforce or reducing their hours to take on unpaid work to be $64.5 billion a year in lost wages, which will, in turn, affect future earnings, career advancement, and retirement savings (Magnus). The pandemic has also resulted in a decline of women attending postsecondary education: an Australian study revealed that there were 86,000 fewer women enrolled to study in May 2020 than in May 2019, compared with just over 21,000 fewer men (Churchill). The biggest decline in tertiary education was among women over the age of twenty-five. This sharp decline in female enrolment suggests it was likely because of caring responsibilities— leading to not only reduced employment opportunities but reduced future income for these mothers. Interestingly, for men over twenty-five, there were significant increases in university enrollment from 2019 to 2020 (Churchill). Another Australian article reported that "[with] 80% of all Australian female businesses owned by mothers and with pandemic restrictions the burden of arranging childcare, homeschooling, sourcing supplies, taking care of elderly parents and relatives and ensuring adequate hygiene has fallen squarely onto the shoulders of women. This has translated into mothers sacrificing time on their businesses" (Bowie). UN Women's Deputy Executive Director Anita Bhatia emphasizes that the "coronavirus pandemic could wipe out 25 years of increasing gender equality" and that the care burden poses a "real risk of reverting to the 1950s gender stereotypes" (qtd. in Lungumbu and Butterfly). The disproportionate effect of COVID-19 on working women has been so great that the current pandemic recession is being called a "she-recession." Before 2020, as Titan Alon and colleagues note "All previous recessions were either mancessions or they depressed women's and men's employment roughly equally. In contrast, in the 2020 recession, job losses are much higher for women. At the highest peak of the disparity, women's unemployment had risen by 2.9 percentage points more than men's unemployment. Indeed, as Canadian doctor Nathan Stall emphasizes, "All of us are being affected by this, but I always think it's important to recognize that women during a pandemic are really bearing the brunt of all this and I think that should not be ignored" (qtd. in Dunham). Or more precisely, in the words of the title of Brandie Kendrick's article, the 2020 pandemic has meant "the death of the working mother."

The pandemic has resulted in a greater appreciation for the work of many, which before the pandemic was little valued and poorly paid, such as PSWs and retail workers. As a result, there have been calls for increased wages, more respect, and better working conditions, but this sadly has not been the case for mothers and motherwork. While there has been increased attention to the pandemic's effect on rising inequality (Bloom) as well as COVID-19's devastating toll on women (Gogoi), governments still have not provided the same support for carework as they have for waged work, nor has mainstream media truly acknowledged or discussed how in 2020, to borrow journalist Tracey Clark-Fiory's words "everything collapsed on moms." Despite the cataclysmic upheavals of the pandemic, one fact remains unchanged: Motherwork remains invisible, devalued, and taken for granted. Indeed, as Andrea Flynn observes: "The coronavirus has laid bare many divisions in our society. And, like any serious crisis does, it has elevated the extent to which structural sexism permeates our lives: impacting the gendered division of labor within the home and also shaping what is possible for women, and particularly mothers, in the public sphere." Relatedly, the pandemic has also revealed what has been termed a crisis in social reproduction—that is, the failure to recognize the value of motherwork and carework more generally. As Liza Featherstone elaborates, "While capitalist profit-making is completely dependent on the essential work of caring for people, of keeping them alive and healthy, the processes of lifemaking is also completely at odds with this labor."

This collection asks questions still largely ignored in public policy, social research, and media coverage. Why are most forms of frontline work being acknowledged and appreciated while motherwork is not? Why is no one asking mothers how they are managing as is regularly done with other frontline workers? Why are our governments not discussing, let alone implementing, public policies to support motherwork? Why is the care and crisis of mothers during the COVID-19 pandemic being completely ignored? Why are so few people talking about any of this? We suggest it is because motherwork does not, in the words of Marilyn Waring, "count." But as the chapters in the collection make compellingly and cogently visible and apparent, mothering, in the words of Meg Luxton, is "more than a labour of love." And, indeed, in this pandemic, motherwork is not just labour; it is more precisely a frontline essential service.

Mothers, Mothering, and COVID-19: Dispatches from a Pandemic draws upon the experience, knowledge, and wisdom of mothers to give voice to mothers' frontline work of caring for families during the first year of the pandemic. The compilation embraces diverse voices from a variety of global locations. These include those of Indigenous mothers, grandmothers, and daughters living on Turtle Island as well as the voices of mothers living in Australia, Brazil, Canada, India, Korea, Mexico, Spain, South Asia, the United Kingdom, and the United States. Using feminist standpoints, seventy authors and artists engage with historical, cultural, semiotic, philosophical, intersectional, and sociological perspectives to reflect upon the associated gamut of emotions and experiences of mothers during these COVID-19 times. Their contributions expose what has been made invisible and to render audible what has been silenced. They explicitly name, document, and articulate the crisis of motherwork as Indigenous mothers, as racialized mothers, as queer mothers, as mothers with neurodiversity or disabilities, as mothers caring for children and others who are neurodiverse or living with cognitive challenges or physical disabilities, and as mothers working within the arts, law, and academia. They offer the lessons they learned while mothering through a pandemic and offer possible ways to move forwards.

The aim of this book is to create and hold space for mothers who are on the frontline of parenting and who are providing for families during the first year of the pandemic. This collection wishes to detail the realities of self-isolation, physical distancing, as well as stay-at-home directives and their effect on families, mothers, and children. Publishing the experiences of mothers within the first year of the pandemic is crucial, as it captures and documents some of the ways in which the COVID-19 pandemic has drastically changed the way of life for mothers, children, and other family members. The often raw, passionate, and moving reflections reveal how the unprecedented changes have included the need to respond to family dynamics that are under unparalleled stress and anxiety. Along with scholarly research, these works point to the ability of mothers to recalibrate their life, relationships, and responsibilities in ways that adapt to a rapidly evolving new normal. Moreover, the collection explores how mothers are coping with their own physical, mental, and emotional health, as well as that of other family members during 2020. When there is no separation between work, family, and home, pressures rise exponentially, with added concern, work, stress, and anxiety. The contributors are well aware of these pressures, challenges, and tensions. They speak candidly and honestly about the toll this pressure is taking on mothers and families. They provide answers to important questions. What are the implications of being a mother in a stay-at-home family during a pandemic? How can we provide help for mothers? How do we develop social strategies, policies, and provisions to better support mothers as they perform the essential work of caregiving?

The importance of this book cannot be overstated. Little research on the specific impact of the COVID-19 pandemic on mothers and motherwork exists at the time of writing. This collection is the first to explore the impact of the pandemic on mothers' care and wage labour in the context of employment, schooling, communities, families, and the relationships of parents and children. This volume speaks with a global perspective and presents mothering experiences from a variety of standpoints, including single, partnered, queer, racialized, Indigenous, economically disadvantaged, disabled, and birthing mothers. This book also examines the increasing complexity and demands of childcare, domestic labour, elder care, and homeschooling under the pandemic protocols; the intricacies and difficulties of performing wage labour at home; the impact of the pandemic on mothers' employment, maternal health, and wellbeing; and the strategies mothers have used to manage the competing demands of care and wage labour, or loss thereof. In offering a record of the firsthand experiences and research directly focused on what maternal experiences are like during a global pandemic, *Mothers, Mothering and COVID-19* offers an invaluable contribution to scholarly and activist endeavours. It provides a rich resource to look back on and to learn from. Historically focused and aware, these diverse voices, along with their rich experiences and knowledge, establish a foundation for further research and activism.

The collection is divided into three sections: 1) Wage Labour, 2) Carework, and 3) Maternal Health and Wellbeing. Each section incorporates scholarly writing and creative works—whether in the form of drawings, paintings, photography, poetry, or prose. These various approaches offer diverse perspectives and insights into the realities of mothering during the COVID-19 pandemic.

The first section, titled "Wage Labour," highlights the many and varied conditions and challenges facing employed mothers throughout the pandemic. Many mothers engaged in paid labour, whether outside or inside the home, are also responsible for their children's education, as daycare and schools open and close according to local and ever-changing pandemic orders, and mothers are required to homeschool their children through remote learning. The section opens with a painting and a poem that honour the caring labour of mothers in the work force, and the following ten chapters examine the pandemic's impact on mothers' wage labour and carework as well as how mothers have responded to these challenges. Attention is paid to various employment sectors and experiences of working for pay. For instance, the experiences of mothers working in "caring" or "pink collar" industries draw attention to the persistence of gendered carework and the realities of employment disruption and/or loss for women and mothers during the first wave of COVID-19. Moreover, positioning the pandemic in the context of increased visibility of anti-Black racism, as well as the heightened effects of poverty, enables an assessment of the pandemic's effects on mothers from an intersectional lens. Artist testimonials, coupled with sector data, reveal how the pandemic has exposed existing systemic barriers to mothers working in professional dance in Canada. Focusing on postsecondary institutional responses to COVID-19 and attending to the challenges of academic mothers, of Mexican scientific mothers, and of the impact of remote course delivery on neurodiverse students and their caregivers provide a rich analysis of the unequal opportunities and harsh realities for mothers in academia as they juggle work and mothering through the early lockdown days of the pandemic.

Research with academic mothers in the United States unearths the gratitude and grace with which the mothers often met those overwhelming challenges. The way in which a Canadian law firm responded to the challenges, shifting visibilities, and new realities presented by COVID-19 in a manner that fostered diversity and inclusion reveals the normalization of flexible work, thus, enabling the legal profession to become a more workable economic sector for mothers in the long term. In exploring the reproduction of individual and structural gender inequalities of the pandemic in South Asia, coping mechanisms to mitigate this burden are uncovered, as are elements of a grassroots feminist movement in South Asia. Furthermore, the COVID-19 crisis may also open space for a new paradigm, inspired by feminist politics, to influence labour and economic policies that support workers.

The second section of the book, titled "Carework", explores the ways in which mothers engage in carework. The eleven chapters, one poem, and several art pieces in this section address how motherwork intensified for mothers when support systems and relational connections dwindled or stopped completely due to the restrictions imposed by pandemic protocols. Not only did intensive mothering become more intense, but it also became unsupported and more isolating. Although social media has become an invaluable source of social support for some, for others, its hyperconnectivity has created greater demands of intensive mothering with new forms of emotional and digital labour. COVID-19 carework has expanded for single mothers, bringing new layers of risk, stress, and joy. It has also brought invisibility for lone mothers, especially when considering that some county-level data on single parents are not delineated by race and gender.

Invisibility and isolation are compounded for mothers caring for themselves and children who live with neurodiversity or with disabilities as well as for mothers in the sandwich generation who are caring for their children as well as their own mothers or elderly relatives, who themselves may be in lockdown. Nonmonogamous mothers must deal with restrictions that expose neoliberal strategies for the management of vulnerability and care through the nuclear family. Spanish mothers working from home and Korean immigrant mothers with few English language skills living in the USA experience isolation and increased responsibilities of motherwork. Carework has also intensified for racialized mothers, particularly for Black and interracial families who may also draw upon their Black cultural values while homeschooling. Author Zaje Harrell concludes the section on carework with a Black feminist perspective on nurturing during the pandemic. Her analysis of domestic labour and health disparities in the early months of the crisis frame an understanding of the uprising following the murder of George Floyd in Minneapolis.

The third and final section of the book, titled "Maternal Health and Wellbeing," continues to showcase diverse experiences and perspectives—whether they be those of maidens, mothers, crones, grandmothers, sisters, daughters, friends, or professionals from around the globe. Using creative works such as embroidery, sketches, poetry, photovoice, livestream performances and photography, as well as interviews, reflections and research—contributors address the impact of and importance of maternal health and wellbeing while adjusting to and coping with the restrictions imposed by the pandemic.

This section opens with images addressing the sense of fear due to the inability to see COVID-19 as well as the feelings of helplessness and anxiety of mothers who are unable to protect or visit the elderly and vulnerable during the initial lockdown. The following chapters address the lived experiences of those who are preparing for birth, who are birthing, who are supporting birth, or who are caring for children during the first wave of the pandemic. They articulate the importance of attending to reconstructed meanings of pregnancy, birth, parenthood, and motherhood for those birthing and for people supporting those who birth. In one case, this means addressing the need for Australian medical professionals to develop nonessentialist biological understandings of birthing persons, including folks who identify as nonbinary or transgender, and the related ethical, mental health, and medical practices associated with this shift. In others, it means attending to the importance of access to midwifery expertise in the United Kingdom at a time when parents are experiencing higher levels of fear, uncertainty, and social isolation. And for others still, it means revealing the struggles Brazilian professionals have in relating to the seriousness of their own limitations in ensuring human rights to birthing citizens and full access to humanized obstetric care while managing their mental health and their risk of infection.

The wisdom of mothers, grandmothers, crones, as well as daughters and maidens highlights the ever-present responsibility, burden, and, at times, lightness and creativity that comes with attending to the mental and physical health of self, children, and elders during shelter-in-place orders. These reflections, whether alone or with friends, through text or art, continue to underscore the relentless and harmful expectations of intensive mothering that leave mothers feeling inadequate and unsupported, particularly for those already on the edge of mental health.

Being present to their children's development—as students studying in school, as they explore their gender identity, or as they progress through adolescence—allows some mothers to expand and enrich their relationships with their children and with others. Engaging with their children in play and yoga or in other activities, such as photography, art production and cooking, offers ways to talk with each other about their relationship and to challenge obligations of mothers and the expectations of patriarchal family structures. An Anishinaabeg ceremony of smudging, for instance, illustrates how an Indigenous maternal approach assists in dealing with the isolation, effects, and experiences of living through the COVID-19 pandemic. And the storytelling narratives shared among a group of Indigenous mothers and friends reflect how self-care practices and elements of being compassionate towards themselves and their immediate family members help alleviate pandemic induced stress.

The section concludes with a reminder of the social expectation that mothers have a public duty to place family above all else, particularly during a pandemic. Assumptions about the role of mothers during COVID-19 are not new; rather, these assumptions have their antecedents in the Australian public health response to the 1918 flu pandemic, which idealized the good mother who took care of her family as a public duty. This expectation of mothers performing their public duty through their parenting is clearly seen in the poignant drawing that concludes the collection, which illustrates the feelings of invisibility, isolation, and exhaustion felt by those with children sequestered at home as they struggle to—in the words Dr. Bonnie Henry's much-echoed mantra—"Be Calm. Be Kind. Be Safe."

Conclusion

In "If We Had a Panic Button, We'd Be Hitting it Right Now," Rachel Thomas, CEO of Lean In, asserts that we have never seen so many women exiting the labour force as we have in this pandemic, which will likely have long-term consequences for their own professional and financial goals (qtd. Vesoulis). *Mothers, Mothering and COVID-19: Dispatches from a Pandemic* offers insight into ways to move forwards, out of, and beyond the crisis of COVID-19 for mothers and families. It begins the discussion regarding policy development related to work, family, childcare, as well as the mental health and wellbeing of mothers and children. Many feminist and social justice researchers and activists see the COVID-19 crisis as opening space for a coalition movement for workplace justice and for the reevaluation of carework as an essential part of an economic agenda. This collection dispatches the maternal visions and voices for this necessary and long-overdue conversation on, and action towards, empowered social change. Indeed, the book confirms, in the words of the title of Sara Petersen's article, how, and why "after the pandemic, we'll finally have to address the impossible state of motherhood."

Works Cited

Alon, Titan, et al. "The Shecession (She-Recession) of 2020: Causes and Consequences." *VOX*, 22 Sept. 2020, voxeu.org/article/shecession-she-recession-2020-causes-and-consequences. Accessed 4 Jan 2021.

Bloom, Nicholas. "Stanford Professor on the New Remote Economy: A 'Productivity Disaster' and 'Ticking Time Bomb for Inequal-ity.'" *Stanford,* 7 Oct. 2020, siepr.stanford.edu/news/stanford-professor-new-remote-work-economy-productivity-disaster-and-ticking-time-bomb. Accessed 4 Jan. 2021.

Bowie, Courtney. "Mother, Wife or Boss? The Impact of COVID-19 on the Modern Woman." *Smart Company*, 1 June 2020, www.smartcompany.

com.au/people-human-resources/impact-onworking-mothers-during-covid-19/. Accessed 5 June 2020.

Cassidy, Amy, Sharon Braithwaite, and Sarah Diab. "Covid Pandemic Disproportionately Hurting Women, UN Warns." *CNN*, 26 Nov. 2020, www.cnn.com/2020/11/26/world/covid-gender-quality-un-scli-intl/index.html. Accessed 4 Jan. 2020.

Brendan, Churchill. "No One Escaped COVID's Impacts, but the Big Fall in Tertiary Enrolments Was 80% Women. Why?" *The Conversation*, 22 Nov. 2020, https://theconversation.com/no-one-escaped-covids-impacts-but-big-fall-in-tertiary-enrolments-was-80-women-why-149994#:~:text=Ersin%20Tekkol%2FShutterstock-,No%20one%20escaped%20COVID's%20impacts%2C%20but%20big%20fall,tertiary%20enrolments%20was%2080%25%20women. Accessed 4 Jan 2020.

Clark-Flory, Tracey. "The Year Everything Collapsed on Moms." *Jezebel Magazine*, 30 Dec. 2020, jezebel.com/the-year-everything-collapsed-on-moms-1845937124. Accessed 4 January, 2021.

Chemaly, Soraya. "Coronavirus Could Hurt Women the Most. Here's How to Prevent a Patriarchal Pandemic." *NBC News*, 10 Apr. 2020, www.nbcnews.com/think/opinion/coronavirus-could-hurt-women-most-here-s-how-prevent-patriarchal-ncna1186581. Accessed 5 June 2020.

Daniel, Zoe. "How Coronavirus Has Changed the Roles in the Family Home." *ABC News*, 13 May 2020, www.abc.net.au/news/2020-05-13/coronavirus-has-changed-roles-in-familyhome/12239542?fbclid=IwAR1PRqB8h_4M0XGbulzpGjUN5Z g89IXHavtHyRAC0trw4AV mckwG9DPyhVM. Accessed 5 June 2020.

Dunham, Jackie. "Women Disproportionately 'Bearing the Brunt' of Coronavirus Crisis, Advocates Say." *CTV News*, 22 Apr. 2020, www.ctvnews.ca/canada/women-disproportionately-bearing-the-brunt-of-coronavirus-crisis-advocates-say-1.4907309. Accessed 5 June 2020.

Ebbert, Stephanie. "Women Are Leaving the Workforce in Droves." 2 Oct. 2020, *Boston Globe*, 2 Oct, 2020, www.bostonglobe.com/2020/10/02/metro/women-are-leaving-workforce-droves/ #:~:text=The%20latest%20data%20from%20the,women%2C%20compared%20to%20216%2C000%20men. Accessed 4 Jan. 2020

Featherstone, Liza. "The Pandemic Is a Family Emergency: How the Coronavirus Exposes a Crisis of Care Work." *New Republic*, 7 May 2020, www.newrepublic.com/article/157528/coronavirus-pandemic-family-care-work-crisis-social-reproduction-theory. Accessed 5 June 2020.

Flynn, Andrea. "The 'All-Consuming' Emotional Labor Caused by Coronavirus—and Shouldered by Women." *Ms.*, 31 Mar. 2020, msmagazine.com/2020/03/31/op-ed-the-all-consuming-emotional-labor-caused-by-coronavirus-and-disproportionately-shouldered-by-women/. Accessed 5 June 2020.

Gagne, Claire. "Why Is No One Talking How Unsustainable This Is for Working Parents?" *Today's Parent*, 24 Apr. 2020, www.todaysparent.com/blogs/opinion/why-is-no-one-talking-about-how-unsustainable-this-is-for-working-parents/. Accessed 5 June 2020.

Gogoi, Pallavi. "Stuck-At-Home Moms: The Pandemic's Devastating Toll on Women." *NPR*, 28 Oct. 2020, www.npr.org/2020/ 10/28/928253674/stuck-at-home-moms-the-pandemics-devastating-toll-on-women. Accessed 4 Jan. 2021.

Greggory, Laurel. "Mothers Taking on 'Shocking' Number of Hours Caring for Children during Pandemic: Study." *Global News*, 20 Oct. 2020, globalnews.ca/news/7408226/mothers-hours-child-care-pandemic-study/. Accessed 4 Jan. 2021.

Kendrick, Brandie. "2020 Will Be The Death Of The Working Mother." 23 July 2020, *ScaryMommy*, www.scarymommy.com/2020-will-be-the-death-of-the-working-mother/. Accessed 4 Jan. 2021.

Lewis, Helen. "The Coronavirus Is a Disaster for Feminism." *The Atlantic*, 19 Mar. 2020, www.theatlantic.com/international/archive/2020/03/feminism-womens-rights-coronavirus-covid19/608302/. Accessed 5 June 2020.

Lungumbu, Sandrine, and Amelia Butterfly. "Coronavirus and Gender: More Chores for Women Set Back Gains in Equality." *BBC News*, 26 Nov. 2020, www.bbc.com/news/world-55016842. Accessed 4 Jan. 2021.

Luxton, Meg. *More Than a Labour Of Love: Three Generations of Women's Work In The Home*. Women's Press, 1997.

Majoo, Farhad. "Two Parents. Two Kids. Two Jobs. No Childcare." *New York Times*, 22 Apr. 2020, www.nytimes.com/2020/04/22/opinion/coronavirus-parenting-burnout.html. Accessed 5 June 2020.

Magnus, Amanda, and Frank Stasio. "The Economy Has Never Worked for Mothers, And Covid-19 is Pushing More Women Out of Work." *The State of Things, Blue Ridge Public Radio,* 17 Nov. 2020, www.bpr.org/post/economy-has-never-worked-mothers-and-covid-19-pushing-more-women-out-work#stream/0. Accessed 4 Jan. 2021.

Petersen, Sara. "After the Pandemic, We'll Finally Have to Address the Impossible State of Motherhood." *YahooStyle*, 24 June 2020, ca.style.

yahoo.com/pandemic-ll-finally-address-impossible-193034205.html. Accessed 4 Jan. 2021.

Ruddick, Sara. *Maternal Thinking: Toward a Politics of Peace.* Beacon Press, 1989.

Waring, Marilyn. *Counting for Nothing: What Men Value and What Women are Worth.* University of Toronto Press, 1999.

Vesoulis, Ab. "'If We Had a Panic Button, We'd Be Hitting It.' Women Are Exiting the Labor Force En Masse—And That's Bad For Everyone." *Time Magazine*, 17 Oct. 2020, time.com/5900583/women-workforce-economy-covid/. Accessed 4 Jan. 2020.

Section I

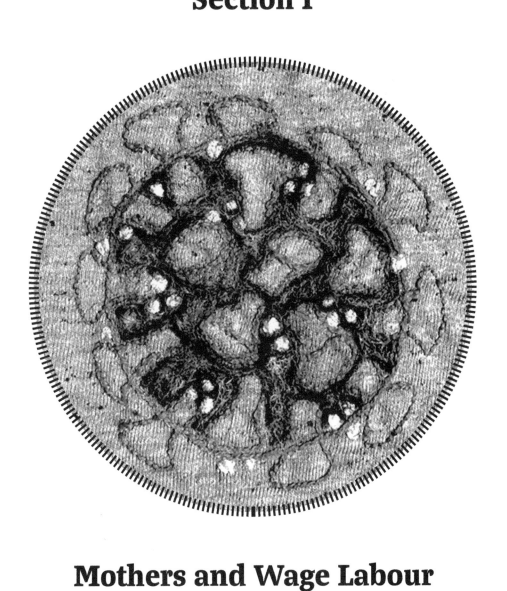

Mothers and Wage Labour

Chapter One

Thank You Heroes

Dara Herman Zierlein

Chapter Two

Women's Witness

Cali Prince

Who was it
during
the COVID-19 pandemic

who worked
day
until next dawn
at the hearth
of the kitchen table?

The women,
they said.

Who was it
who home-schooled
their daughters,
their sons?

Who quelled
the disorder
and alleviated
anxieties

as they toiled
together?

Not in solitude,
not in silence
or peace
not in purpose-built studies
but in the rubble
of breakfast dishes
and half-written sentences?

Not always,
but most often
it was the women,
they said.

And in the midst
of the pandemic
whose productivity
was compromised,
whose attention was
divided and split?

Not always,
but most often
it was the women,
they said.

And who was it
who worked the triple
or quadruple load?

Unable to catch
time
that from
the teat of mother
had been drunk?

Not always,
but most often
it was the women,
they said.

And who was it
who was
expected
to be available?

Not always,
but most often
it was the women,
they said.

And who was it
that prepared
fresh soups,
who baked
the extra tray of biscuits
and hand-delivered them
to the old ones?

Most often
it was the women,
they said.

And who was it who
was perceived
as a tortoise?

Yet more aptly
was a multitasking hare

or a triple headed
      - one hundred handed
goddess?

The women,
they said.

Chapter Three

"Certainly Not an Equal-Opportunity Pandemic": COVID-19 and Its Impact on Mothers' Carework, Health, and Employment

Andrea O'Reilly

In her *Guardian* article, Alexandra Topping explores the devastating effect COVID-19 has had on gender equality, which could set women back decades: "It has taken us 20 years to get this far on female participation in the workforce, but it could take only months to unravel." She discusses the long-term consequences of the pandemic under a range of key areas, including work, gender pay gap, maternity discrimination, childcare, violence against women, and politics. Significantly, and quite surprisingly, the article does not mention what for most women has been the greatest challenge of COVID-19—the simultaneous demands of carework and wage labour in a pandemic environment—and what has indeed caused the gender inequalities the article identifies. The pandemic has had a devastating impact on gender equality precisely because women, and in particular mothers, are overwhelmingly responsible for the carework of their homes and communities—childcare, elder care, and domestic labour—work that has increased exponentially under pandemic protocols. In other words, the gender inequalities in the public sphere we are now observing as COVID-19 unfolds are attributable to and caused by preexisting gender inequities in carework that the pandemic has now exacerbated. Jackie Dunham argues that "There's this idea that we're all in this together, but in many ways, it certainly is not an equal-opportunity pandemic.... The people that are impacted most will always be the most marginalized and that includes all women." I suggest, however, mothers are most affected because it is mothers who perform the necessary carework and are responsible for social reproduction to sustain their families and communities through and after this pandemic. Indeed, as noted by Francesca Donner in her *New York Times* article: "[Carework] underpins so many of the inequalities that women experience. These are hours that could be spent on income generation. It's at the heart of the motherhood penalty, wage inequality, structural biases in recruitment and promotion of women and jobs."

This article examines the pandemic's impact on mothers' wage labour and carework as well as how these mothers have responded to these challenges during the first four months of the pandemic through analyzing the emails of twenty-one mothers received between May 25 and June 5. On May 1, I established the Facebook group Mothers and COVID-19 (with 1,429 members as of January 11 2021), and I shared through this page and my personal Facebook page a call for participants to share their experiences concerning COVID-19 and its effects on their paid and unpaid work. The post was shared 150 times; more than forty women responded, and twenty-one women shared their experiences about the challenges the pandemic posed. The comments sent ranged from one hundred to five hundred words. Two of the participants identified as queer and in a relationship; five were single mothers, and several of the mothers were parenting children with disabilities. Only one participant identified her race and/or ethnicity, which was South Asian. They worked in a variety of different areas, including graduate study, academe, administration, running small businesses, communications, teaching, and social work. The mothers were from Argentina, Australia, Canada, England, Ireland, and the United States. The article first examines the mothers' comments under two sections—partnered and single mothers—and then explores three central themes of the mothers' commentary: their carework, their maternal health, as well as the long-term impact of the pandemic on their employment.

Partnered Mothers: "I Am Required to Make Big Changes and Lose My Freedom, While My Husband's Life Remains Unchanged"

A college professor of three young children became the primary caretaker of her three young children at the onset of the pandemic because her husband was a full-time student. After a week of trying to complete her paid work during the day while caring for the children, she realized it was not possible. She now does the bulk of her work after the children's bedtime and stays up to 2:00 a.m. to finish things. She comments: "It is extremely exhausting and very disruptive to my working progress." Another mother of a toddler also tried working while parenting, but it resulted in her not getting any work done and her toddler acting out due to her inattention. "The day," she says, "culminated with my two year old screaming while I cried back: 'I just have to write this email, please, please let me write this email.' It obviously wasn't working; my partner made arrangements to be at home on my work days." The mother was unable to work on a project, which resulted in her losing two paid days of work a week.

In another email, a lesbian mother in a partnered relationship with a six-year-old child began to work at home at the onset of the pandemic, whereas her partner worked full-time outside the home in essential service. During the pandemic, she attempted to mimic her usual routine, but it nearly broke her and her family: "We've piloted new schedules many, many times: our current approach is that we keep our son up very late so that I can get up very, very early and work while he is asleep. I also try to leave as much work as possible for the weekends when my wife is home and can take over childcare." Even though the mother recognizes that she is fortunate to have work and flexibility, she and her family still feel exhausted and live on a "priority by priority basis," which is unsustainable. A queer mother of two young children and a PhD student decided that because her partner made more money and had less job flexibility, she would take a leave of absence for the summer term to care for the children, planning to return in the fall when she is actually able to work. Due to the pandemic, this mother has been unable to deliver conference papers—a reality she fears that will negatively affect her CV and her position on the job market, which, she astutely observes "will, no doubt, be that much harder in a post-COVID recession when higher education is in crisis."

A teacher with a two-year-old discusses the overwhelming pressure she faces from people without children or older ones, who set virtual meetings at the start of her son's nap time: "I have been suffering from anxiety having to leave meetings early because my son woke up early and unexpected from a nap. I have been silently suffering while I'm video calling my students and can hear my son wanting my attention and crying for me in the room beside me." She goes on to say: "The pressure of caring for my one year old and working from home has been incredibly difficult.... The feeling of failing at work life and home life, despite best efforts, really takes a toll." Another mother, a professor with one young child, comments: "I have worked much more hours per day. But the worst are the constant distractions and multiplicity of tasks: make video classes, correct work, and Zoom meetings. [They leave me] feeling very scattered and feeling like I am 'putting out fires' all the time and [have] no time to study, read and write." She doubts she will complete a project by the deadline and will, thus, lose her research funding. Another mother who is a professor and mother of two young children shares childcare and domestic labour responsibilities with her husband. She works late into the night trying to complete her book manuscript by the deadline, but she worries she will soon have to ask for an extension. She emphasizes that it is not just the loss of time "but the physical and psychological exhaustion that makes it difficult to concentrate and complete my research." She often feels at the "point of breaking."

A graduate student—a mother of a young son and who is now caring for her mother-in-law at home due to the pandemic and whose husband works full-time outside the home—writes, "Suddenly I was a worker, a carer, working and trying to do my PhD all whilst at home." As a result of her duties, she has not worked on her thesis in months and feels guilty, but her priority now is "surviving, not striving for theoretical clarity." Another mother academic with one child comments that "It has been nearly impossible to meet deadlines while also homeschooling my child and managing never-ending domestic responsibilities." Since the start of the pandemic, she writes "I've been treading water." Another participant is an artist with three young children and whose husband is the sole breadwinner. She writes the following: "I'm often envious of my partner, because he is able to work without interruption. When the kids have an issue or a question or a comment, they come to me even if he's right there." A South Asian mother of one child who has also experienced discrimination as a result of COVID-19 no longer feels safe leaving her home for grocery shopping, and with her husband employed in essential services outside the home, she has become responsible for all childcare and domestic labour, which has resulted in her recently having to ask for an extension to complete her master's degree. An academic mother in a nontenure track position, with two young children and whose husband's income is twice hers, writes the following: "His job takes precedent and I am mostly with the children. I feel like a lot of mothers are making this decision; he makes more so I have to do the childcare." She is not able to do the necessary research and writing that would allow her to increase her own job security and scholarship. One mother has lost all of her work and income due to COVID-19, whereas her husband works full-time from home. She surveys her situation and poignantly and perceptively concludes: "I look ahead and see that my particular situation is not going to improve.... It feels that I am required to make big changes and lose my freedom, while my husband's life remains unchanged."

Single Mothers: "Extra Tough Being a Single Parent Right Now"

A doctoral student and artist living in a COVID-19 hotspot in the United States, and who shares custody of her special needs teenaged son with her former husband, became her son's caretaker when his boarding school closed at the onset of the pandemic. Because of her son's condition of enuresis and because she has no washing machine at home—the closest, unsanitary laundromat being a fifteen-minute walk away—she has been doing all the laundry by hand since the start of the pandemic, along with the housework, cooking, her graduate work, and organizing her son's increased therapy sessions and classwork. She comments: "We are not sure when my child can go back to school, even though his needs are such that the state agrees that they need round the clock support." She mentions that she has gained ten pounds in two months and always feels tired. A mother of an autistic child working in the violence against women sector feels "bitterly unsupported" by the management of her workplace. Her daughter's amplified depression and anxiety have resulted in additional appointments, calls, and visits to various specialists. A woman with young children was forced to return to her workplace in mid-May, although her work could have continued from home. At her workplace, no one was social distancing or wearing masks; many believed that COVID-19 was a hoax. She resigned the day she emailed her comments, explaining her decision in the following way: "I felt I had to choose my sanity and the safety of my children over work.... I do not have a backup plan.... I am afraid of what the next step will be.... I am jumping from the frying pan into the fire." A social worker and a mother of a special needs toddler now has her son back in his daycare, but with its reduced hours, she is now working an hour less every day and using her vacation time to cover the lost pay. With the daycare no longer providing meals, she now has to shop for, prepare, and pay for all of the lunches and snacks her son will need at daycare. She concludes her email by stressing how it is "extra tough being a single parent right now."

Discussion: Mothers' Carework: "It Has Taken a Global Pandemic of Epic Proportions to Draw Attention to the Value of the Caring and Household Work That Women Do"

In her article "The Coronavirus Is a Disaster for Feminism," Helen Lewis writes the following: "Despite the mass entry of women into the workforce during the 20th century, the phenomenon of the 'second shift' still exists. Across the world—women, including those with jobs—do more housework and have less leisure time than their male partners." Indeed, as evidenced in the emails discussed above, mothers do the bulk of domestic labour, elder care, and childcare, and with COVID-19, the burden of care work has increased exponentially. Mothers are running households with little or no support under close to impossible conditions, with the additional demands of homeschooling their children while doing paid labour from home. The pandemic has particularly compounded what I call the "third shift": the emotional and intellectual labour of motherwork. This idea is similar to what Sara Ruddick has termed "maternal thinking"—the organizing, remembering, anticipating, worrying, and planning that mothers take on for the family. Moreover, under COVID-19, many mothers now exist in what may be termed the "fourth shift"—that is, the homeschooling of children. A recent *New York Times* survey found that 80 per cent of mothers said they were mostly responsible for homeschooling. Only 3 per cent of women said that men were doing more (Daniel). As noted in a recent *Guardian* article: "The proportion of mothers who report being responsible for 90-100% of childcare has risen from 27% to 45% during the lockdown" (Sodha). The overwhelming majority of the participants were performing the second, third, and fourth shifts of carework, and most were doing so alongside the first shift of paid labour. Only two of the partnered mothers in this study said that the carework and domestic labour of their households were being shared equally with their partner. Concerning the other mothers, including the two queer partnered mothers, one person was shouldering most of the domestic labour and childcare even as they were working full-time at home. Many explained this situation as basic math—the other partner simply made more money.

For other mothers, the nature of their employment—teaching, administration, and operating small businesses—resulted in their work transitioning to home, whereas their partner's work did not, as they were engaged in essential services that remained in the public sphere and increased in hours. Mothers, thus, had to take on most of the carework and domestic labour, which became even more arduous and time consuming under pandemic protocols. For other mothers, their work granted more flexibility than that of their partners, allowing them to reduce or defer their work commitments Although it was not explicitly stated by the mothers, I believe the gendered nature of the mothers' work explains why they could transition to the home with greater flexibility: They are employed in professions designated as feminine, particularly teaching and social work. Indeed, as one participant comments, "If I had to be honest I will probably steer my two daughters away from work that is dominated by women." Significantly, most of the heterosexual mothers simply do not explain why they are doing the bulk of carework and domestic labour, even when both parents are working full-time from home, which suggests, I argue, how normalized gender inequities are in society—women's carework is simply a given. As noted by Dana Stefov, a women's rights policy and advocacy specialist with Oxfam Canada: "Carework has been so invisible, for so long, that it has taken a global pandemic of epic proportions to draw attention to the value of the caring and household work that women do" (qtd. in Jones).

Maternal Health: "This Unsustainable Hamster Wheel We're on Is Giving Rise to a Silent, Mental Health Pandemic"

Another central and deeply worrisome theme in both the single and partnered mothers' comments was the impact of the pandemic on their health. A recent Oxfam study of more than 6,300 men and women from five different countries found that 43 per cent of women are experiencing more anxiety, depression, fatigue, and isolation because of the pandemic; in Canada, the percentage is 71 (Jones). Nearly every mother in this study mentions exhaustion, burnout, anxiety, stress, overwhelming pressure, and silent suffering; they describe their life in the pandemic as "impossible," "taking its toll," "nearly breaking us," "simply surviving," "treading water," and "putting out fires." In the words of one single mother: "The stress from increasing juggling has been debilitating and my own mental health has suffered." Significantly, many mothers emphasize that their current situation is simply unsustainable: "[It is] definitely not sustainable for a long period of time"; "it can't be sustainable"; "I feel at the point of breaking"; and "I am jumping from the frying pan into the fire." Indeed, as Farhad Majoo asks, "How could anyone think [that] attempting to work full-time while rooming with, feeding, and educating one or more children during the pandemic [is sustainable]?" Likewise, the journalist and mother of three young children Lindsay Springer wonders, "How can I keep doing this? ... I, like many parents, am worn out and tired, and I fear this unsustainable hamster wheel we're on is giving rise to a silent, mental health pandemic."

The Long-Term Impact of the Pandemic on Mothers' Employment: "When Something Has to Give, It Is Very Often Women's Careers"

"Innovative," "resilient," and "resourceful" are some of many adjectives that could be used to describe the mothers' determination and resolve to keep working despite the near impossible conditions and challenges of the pandemic. They are working late into the night, devising creative scheduling, working while the children nap, managing to work amid the chaos, juggling homeschooling with their own work, deferring all but necessary work, using vacation pay to cover lost income, and negotiating temporary leave of absences or reduced work hours. But all of the mothers highlight that this juggling and coping cannot continue indefinitely and that for most of the mothers the pandemic already has had a substantial negative impact on their current and future employment prospects. Several of the graduate students have already applied for a leave of absence; many of the academic mothers have lost grant funding, have delayed or postponed research projects, and have missed deadlines for the submission of articles and manuscripts As one mother says, "If this continues and we do not have access to appropriate childcare or support, I may have to start delaying or deferring projects until I can focus my attention." Indeed, evidence suggests that women's research has plummeted during lockdown, but articles by men have increased (Fazackerley). Other mothers chose or were forced to reduce their paid hours, resulting in lost income and likely affecting their job security and/or future career advancement.

Other mothers have lost their jobs due to the pandemic. Single mothers are particularly vulnerable, as they have no choice but to work at great cost to their maternal and physical health. With schools and childcare centres closed or at reduced capacity for the foreseeable future, the situation will not improve any time soon for mothers. As well, there may not be work for mothers to return to, particularly in fields like higher education, in which staff numbers are being drastically reduced as universities transition to remote learning. As the sociologist Caitlyn Collins argues, "When something has to give, it is very often women's careers: their working hours, the expectations of what they are able to accomplish on the job, or the job itself" (qtd. in Kitchener).

Conclusion. A Perfect Storm: The Confluence of Gendered Carework and a Pandemic

A common refrain thoughout the pandemic has been that although we may be in the same storm, we are not in the same boat. Continuing with this metaphor, I suggest that it is mothers who are in the most turbulent of waters and that the pandemic has caused a perfect storm for their carework, health, and employment. The confluence of gendered carework and COVID-19 has meant that the devastating effects of the pandemic have been most fully and keenly felt by mothers. Although this study does not provide the depth and breadth of a full qualitative study, it does show it is women as mothers who have been the most negatively affected by the pandemic. Social research and public policy developed in response to the pandemic, thus, require not only a gendered lens but, more specifically and urgently, a matricentric[1] one in order to challenge and change normative motherhood, which has caused the gender inequities exacerbated by this pandemic.

Endnotes

1. In my book *Matricentric Feminism: Theory, Activism, Practice*, I define and develop the term "matricentric" to denote a mother-centred feminism that acknowledges and considers how and why the category of mother is distinct from the category of woman and that many of the problems mothers face—social, economic, political, cultural, psychological, and so forth—are specific to women's role and identity as mothers. Mothers are oppressed under patriarchy as women and as mothers. Consequently, mothers need a matricentric mode of feminism organized from and for their particular identity and work as mothers. Indeed, a mother-centred feminism is needed because mothers—arguably more so than women in general—remain disempowered despite forty years of feminism.

Works Cited

Daniel, Zoe. "How Coronavirus Has Changed the Roles in the Family Home." *ABC News*, 13 May 2020, www.abc.net.au/news/2020-05-13/coronavirus-has-changed-roles-in-family-home/12239542? fbclid= IwAR1PRqB8h_4M0XGbulzpGjUN5Zg89IXHavtHyRAC0 trw4AV mckwG9DPyhVM; Accessed 5 June 2020.

Donner, Francesca. "How Women are Getting Squeezed by the Pandemic." *New York Times*, 20 May 2020, www.nytimes.com/2020/05/20/us/women-economy-jobs-coronavirus-gender.html?fbclid=IwAR3zNs-5so qH0AmKPreyOAV5oVSugUgDXpmMkGGyZ1Z6709OVlBEbekrqg Accessed 10 June 2020.

Dunham, Jackie. "Women Disproportionately 'Bearing the Brunt' of Coronavirus Crisis, Advocates Say." *CTV News*, 22 Apr. 2020, www.ctvnews.ca/canada/women-disproportionately-bearing-the-brunt-of-coronavirus-crisis-advocates-say-1.4907309. Accessed 5 June 2020.

Fazackerley, Anna. "Women's Research Plummets during Lockdown—But Articles from Men Increase." *Guardian*, 12 May 2020, www.theguardian.com/education/2020/may/12/womens-research-plummets-during-lockdown-but-articles-from-men-increase, 12 May 2020; Accessed 12 May 2020.

Jones, Alexandra Mae. "7 Out of 10 Canadian Women Experiencing Anxiety Sue to Unpaid Care Work during Pandemic: Survey." *CTV News*, 18 June 2020, www.ctvnews.ca/canada/7-out-of-10-canadian-women-experiencing-anxiety-due-to-unpaid-care-work-during-pandemic-survey-1.4990812?cache=yes%3Fclipld%3D86116%3FautoPla y%3Dtrue. Accessed 20 June 2020.

Kitchener, Caroline. "'I Had to Choose Being a Mother': With No Child Care or Summer Camps, Women Are Being Edged Out of the Workforce." *The Lily*, 22 May 2020, www.thelily.com/i-had-to- choose-being-a-mother-with-no-child-care-or-summer-camps-women-are-being-edged-out-of-the-workforce/. Accessed 22 May 2020.

Majoo, Farhad. "Two Parents. Two Kids. Two Jobs. No Childcare." *New York Times*, 22 Apr. 2020, www.nytimes.com/2020/04/22/opinion/coronavirus-parenting-burnout.html. Accessed 1 May 2020.

O'Reilly, Andrea. *Matricentric Feminism: Theory, Activism, Practice.* Demeter Press, 2016.

Ruddick, Sara. *Maternal Thinking: Toward a Politics of Peace.* Beacon Press, 1989.

Sodha, Sonia. "Is the Pandemic Sending Us Back to the 1950s When It Comes to Taking Care of the Home?" *Guardian*, 21 June 2020, www.theguardian.com/commentisfree/2020/jun/21/is-the-pandemic-sending-us-back-to-the-1950s-when-it-comes-to-taking-care-of-the-home-?fbclid=IwAR0cwtxKCv3xgLIUi4Sk5lzOJa_faJXxsrPJZRK0 nIhpnozUYPfjANWlI3g. Accessed 20 June, 2020.

Springer, Lindsay. "Parents in Lockdown Are Quietly Falling Apart—I'm One of Them." *Today's Parent*, 12 June 2020, www.todaysparent.com/family/family-life/parents-mental-health-coronavirus/. Accessed 12 June 2020

Topping, Alexandra. "The Coronavirus Pandemic Is Having a Devastating Effect on Gender Equality and Could Set Women Back Decades." *Guardian*, 29 May 2020, www.theguardian.com/world/2020/may/29/covid-19-crisis-could-set-women-back-decades-experts-fear. Accessed 29 May 2020.

Chapter Four

Same Storm, Different Boats: Some Thoughts on Gender, Race, and Class in the Time of COVID-19

May Friedman and Emily Satterthwaite

In this chapter, the authors, one a professor of social work and the other a professor of tax law, explore the implications of current shelter-in-place provisions and the differential effect they have on various parents. Cognizant that we are presently in the midst of both a global pandemic and a heightened awareness of the impact of anti-Black racism, this chapter aims to explore the ways that the context of a global pandemic exposes the frailty of existing systems of child and home care and the persistent feminization and racialization of all kinds of caring labour. As the meme goes, although we are all in the midst of the same storm, we are emphatically not in the same boats.

Maternal labour is increasingly ignored and made invisible in the context of social distancing, yet motherhood, and especially Black motherhood, is hyperscrutinized. By exploring the gendered, raced, and classed ways in which motherhood is performed and experienced, we aim to consider the ways that the present context feels impossible for many of us while acknowledging that our circumstances are heightened by our exposure to sexism, racism, and economic injustice. This chapter explores the push and pull of family life and work life and argues that the context of social isolation exacerbates but does not invent tensions within and across households. Although this cursory examination of contemporary examples is not exhaustive, it, nonetheless, begins to paint a picture of the differential impact of COVID-19 across axes of gender, race, and class.

Where We Begin

We cannot explore the differential impacts of COVID-19 on motherhood without considering our own individual positionalities. I (May) am an Arab and Jewish brown cisgender woman born in Canada to immigrant parents. I work as a social work academic and parent my children, who presently span grades one through twelve. My experiences of this pandemic are uniquely affected by my positionality in a heterosexual (and, in many respects, hetero-normative) household; I have found the pandemic stretches the tensions around prioritizing competing work needs and competing cognitive loads in painful ways. These tensions are also mediated through my relatively able body as well as my experiences with mental health challenges. I teach about the welfare state, but it has been interesting and also harrowing to see its limitations so grossly exposed, especially in the moment of heightened attention to the effects on Black lives.

I (Emily) am a Jewish and Quaker white cisgender woman. I am the mother of two grade-school-aged children in Toronto. I work as an academic, focusing on tax law. Like May, my experiences of this pandemic also are affected by my positionality in a heterosexual two-parent household, my relatively able body, and my experiences with mental health challenges.

We are both mothers and academics, yet we are mindful of the diversity of our own experiences. COVID-19 has led to a heightened awareness of the ways that gender, race, and class interrupt or extend our experiences and observations of isolation and disruption. While acknowledging the ways that sexism, racism, and poverty interplay and also intersect with myriad other intersections, we focus here on each in order to tease out some of the unique effects of COVID-19 on mothers across these axes. In exploring the pandemic through these lenses, we hope to shed light on ways that COVID-19 has affected mothers while simultaneously acknowledging the deeply uneven experiences of these effects. The choice to foreground gender, race, and class may seem peculiarly old fashioned and out of sync with the current intersectional and nuanced realms in which we often position our work. We aim to acknowledge the complex interactions between these realms—and other aspects of lived experience—but also highlight the primacy of sexism, racism, and class warfare in the present moment.

Gender

It is impossible to consider the impacts of COVID-19 without referencing gender. Here, we do not mean to conflate motherhood and biology, as motherhood is achieved in a range of ways, and gender is elastic and continuous. At the same time, while maintaining a commitment to gender fluidity, the fact that caregiving labour is overwhelmingly performed by female-identified parents is being excised from many conversations about the effects of COVID-19 on parenting households. It is notable how easily "motherhood" gets subsumed under a blanket discussion of "parenthood." Although parents of all genders have been overwhelmed by school closures, the multiplicity of roles, and the anxieties of the present situation, there are unique implications for mothers who often disproportionately shoulder the burden of household responsibilities as well as the labour and emotional impact of decision making and planning. In part, this reality is due to the historic inequality posed by the patriarchal institution of motherhood. The different expectations placed on mothers and fathers allow for different responsibilities in the present moment; mothers may feel more keenly the impossibility of blending paid employment and homeplace responsibilities as well taking on more acutely fears for their children's emotional and physical safety.

The differing expectations and responsibilities for mothers have deep effects on self-esteem, stress, and mental health. Fathers who pitch in at this moment are valorized and celebrated; mothers may only be reminded of the ways they fall short. A May 2020 *New York Times* article—titled "Nearly Half of Men Say They Do Most of the Home Schooling. 3 Percent of Mothers Agree"—provides one case study showing the different ideologies at play (Cain Miller 1). What constitutes "homeschooling"? Is helping a child onto an online learning platform sufficient? Who is monitoring emails and phone calls from teachers? Who is ensuring that homework is complete or that lessons are understood? A recent study documents that measures of mothers' mental health have declined during the pandemic more than fathers' (Johnston Mohammed, and van der Linden 9). As with many parenting and household tasks, determining completion (or even adequacy) can be a moving target, and gender training may greatly affect expectations and experiences. As a result, paternal involvement may be reliably better than before while still being far outstripped by the work of mothers (United Nations Policy Brief 13). We are reminded, bleakly, of Marilyn Waring's insistence that "Men won't easily give up a system in which half the world's population works for next to nothing ... [and recognizes that] precisely because that half works for so little, it may have no energy left to fight for anything else" (qtd. in Gates 124). For mothers who were already trying to juggle unliveable demands in the realms of work and home, this sudden bolus of maternal labour is suffocating and unimaginable. The worries are infinite, and failure is a foregone conclusion.

There are very real implications to this divide. To speak from our own context, in the realm of academia, the outputs of female-identified academics with children plunged to a standstill, whereas, notably, male academics reported a surge of productivity (Viglione 365). This fact led to some journals taking the unprecedented move of halting all submissions unrelated to the COVID-19 pandemic to try to staunch the haemorrhage of inequality (ACME). Although these journals are to be commended, countless other publication venues, granting agencies, tenure committees, hiring committees, and other academic gatekeepers have offered no indication that the tangible impact on mothers' productivity will be addressed. At best, solutions are offered that aim to lessen expectations on women (extending tenure clocks, for example) without acknowledging that generations of academics will be skewed towards hyperproducing men who will dominate leadership and knowledge production roles. These implications are only made more dire for mother academics in the intersections of single motherhood, race, disability, sexual orientation, and/or other marginalized experiences.

Beyond the privileged halls of academia, of course, the situation is only more bleak. In dual earner households where one job must be forfeited, mothers are more likely to lose employment (Lemieux et al. 18). In low-earning households, work more often must be done onsite and, thus, is incompatible with homekeeping (Messecar, Morissette, and Deng 5). The disproportionate economic impact of COVID-19 on mothers of toddler or school-aged children (7 per cent employment decline) as compared to similarly-situated fathers (4 per cent decline) has led to the popularity of the term "shesession"; single mothers' employment has been even more staggeringly affected (12 per cent decline compared to 7 per cent among single fathers) (RBC 1). The current context for mothers feels like a game of musical chairs, in which many competing bottoms are being forced into too few seats. Someone must lose, and when the music stops, it is mothers who will have been overwhelmingly forced out of the workforce, pushed into anxiety and poverty. Without acknowledging the gendered impact of caregiving labour, layered over the already gendered landscape of racism, class, and other oppressions, mothers are being abandoned. Nancy Fraser writes that "Social reproduction is an indispensable background condition for the possibility of economic production in a capitalist society." (102) Capitalism has exploited caregiving responsibilities of women—for their own children and those of others, in both formal and informal arrangements—since its inception, and this pandemic is exposing the frailties of a system built on women's backs.

Race

We are in the midst of a shocking and unprecedented global crisis. Simultaneously, however, the deaths of George Floyd, Breonna Taylor, Regis Korchinski-Paquet, and so many others have raised awareness of the deadly impact of racism, specifically anti-Black and anti-Indigenous racism. Unlike COVID-19, this particular virulence is in no way unprecedented, although an awareness of its roots has begun to pervade mainstream consciousness. It is impossible to understand the impact of COVID-19 on motherhood without considering the unique implications for mothers of colour, especially given the gross overrepresentation of racialized bodies among COVID-19 cases and deaths (Ray 1).

Patricia Hill Collins reminds us that "Since work and family have rarely functioned as dichotomous spheres for women of color, examining racial ethnic women's experiences reveals how these two spheres actually are interwoven" ("Shifting" 46). The collapsing of paid and unpaid labour in the pandemic may, therefore, be much less surprising for mothers of colour, for whom these boundaries have always been blurred and porous. For mothers with less access to privileged spaces (racialized mothers and others), the extent to which COVID-19 has sidelined maternal autonomy and come at the expense of maternal capacity is a continuation of the status quo. At the same time, the heightened scrutiny paid to mothers of colour further exacerbates existing tensions. For example, the gross over-representation of Black and Indigenous families under child welfare scrutiny may be intensified as maternal resources wither in the present pandemic context (Pon, Gosine, and Phillips 387, 394-95).

One egregious example of this scrutiny was revealed in July 2020 in the story of Grace, a young Black teenager who was sent to juvenile detention for refusing to do her homework (Cohen1). The child of a single mother, Grace and her mother had, like many families, weathered a tumultuous adolescence but were beginning to knit their relationship back together. Nonetheless, Grace's experiences meant that when she, like teenagers and children across the globe, was unsuccessful at participating in online school, she was suddenly remanded into custody in a locked facility. The combination of her Blackness and her neuro atypicality (Grace was diagnosed with ADHD) led to a harsh punishment. Although Grace was the one being punished, it was her mother's behaviour that was being surveilled; like many Black mothers, her parenting was being judged as inadequate (Roberts 939, 941).

Although racism leads to poverty, class privilege does not guard against the effects of racism. An article authored by two Black mothers who are physicians explores the ways that racism and sexism converge to make them vulnerable:

As mothers we will naturally ask, "What will happen to my kids if something happens to me?" Particularly for Black mothers, we know we live in a world that can be so unkind to Black children. This internal discussion can be further compounded if we are pregnant. Black maternal mortality rates are higher than those of whites, regardless of education, insurance, or income. At baseline, the odds are not in our favor, and in the setting of a pandemic—now what? (Louisias and Marrast 1148)

All mothers are experiencing an absurd overtaxing of resources, but as Louisias and Marrast point out, when these resources are already besieged by the effects of racism, Black mothers find themselves at overwhelming levels of vulnerability. Hill Collins states that "Black mothers have been accused of failing to discipline their children, of emasculating their sons, of defeminizing their daughters, and of retarding their children's academic achievement." ("Black Women" 149) As she skilfully elucidates, however, such analyses invisibilize the great resources and resilience Black mothers must have to contend with the intersectional effects of racism and sexism in the midst of the overwhelming work of mothering. Centring the experiences of Black mothers must not only allow for an analysis of intersectional vulnerabilities—an analysis that is imperative at the present moment—but also highlight the hard-won skills and capacities of Black mothers. To do otherwise is patronizing and may enact a further layer of racism.

Class

The extent to which access to wealth has yielded differential effects on mothers through the COVID-19 crisis is staggering, and these effects are exacerbated by the raced and gendered landscape of poverty. For many educated and reasonably economically stable parents who may have the capacity to more often work from home, juggling care responsibilities with the demands of paid employment may feel exhausting. But what becomes of mothers who cannot work from home and for whom school closures translate wholly into the withdrawal of income?

In 1984, bell hooks wrote that "More than ever before, there is a great need for women and men to organize around the issue of childcare" (147). In prepandemic 2020 North America, having budgetary commitments to high-quality, community-based childcare programs that are available to and accessible by all parents felt more revolutionary than ever before. What about now, in the midst of the pandemic-induced recession/depression? Even though the pandemic lays bare the inadequacy of our public commitments to caring for children, surviving the pandemic economically—not to mention emotionally—is a full-time job. How is it possible to close daycare centres and schools without acknowledging it as a catastrophe for working-class parents, mothers in particular, as well as their children? How could such a closure occur without the urgent mobilization of other social infrastructure to support women who were already "parenting in isolation" (hooks 147) and living on the slimmest margin of resources of money and time? Fundamentally, the present pandemic exposes the extent to which the most economically vulnerable members of a society are left to drown as soon as the water begins to rise.

In a moment of prescience, Fraser reminds us that "The present strains on care are not accidental, but have deep systemic roots in the structure of our social order, which I characterize here as financialized capitalism... the present crisis of social reproduction indicates something rotten not only in capitalism's current, financialized form but in capitalist society *per se*" (100, emphasis in original). In other words, a system built on women's backs, and on the backs of mothers in particular, cannot be maintained when multiple competing demands are exposed.

Katie Smith writes personally about the impacts of mothering in poverty during COVID-19: "As a single mother of three who's fallen through Canada's safety net before, I spend a lot of time counting. Counting the money in my bank account, how much income I can expect—and how many days it will all last my family during this pandemic. I know it's only a matter of time before what comes in doesn't match what goes out." (1) Smith highlights the differential burden of anxiety as well as physical risk her household faces without the ability to accumulate private savings or rely on a public safety net. As we navigate challenging decisions about back-to-school plans, the illusory nature of these decisions for poor families come into focus. Risk eviction or risk COVID-19? Fear transmission or starvation? Such reckoning is far from hyperbolic: Mothers in poverty genuinely have no credible choices.

The rise in homelessness, evictions, and bankruptcies—coupled with the further eradication of social supports such as food banks and shelters—make the present moment unimaginable for working class and poor mothers. These losses, however, are not counted as COVID-

19-related outcomes for jurisdictions. The overall lack of support and care for people in poverty exposes the threadbare welfare state as fundamentally unconcerned about mothers and families, suggesting, once again, that neoliberal values of independence and self-reliance are preconditions for functional citizenship.

Conclusion

In this chapter, we have aimed to shed light on the deep inequalities that the COVID-19 pandemic exposes, forcing us to ask hard questions and avoid easy answers. We have many queries. During the early days of the pandemic, why did pointing out the practical impossibility of working and caring for children feel unpatriotic, tantamount to a betrayal of essential workers, who themselves are often racialized working mothers or others with caregiving responsibilities? Was the stripping away of even the most anemic public commitments to mothers and children framed as a nonissue to imply that it was anything less than reasonable for mothers to rely on those commitments in the first place? What portion of women's economic and social equality gains will be incinerated by this stripping away? How many mothers, including those pursuing entry-level qualifications, will have to put their educations or careers on hold to care for their children? How will the equity profiles of our workplaces—including legislatures, and the ranks of managers and the occupants of C-suites—change as a result? And how can this pandemic moment be understood as irreparably implicated in the war on Black bodies? How do we genuinely and wholeheartedly demand justice?

At the beginning of pandemic lockdown, scholar and visionary Sonya Renee Taylor noted on Instagram the following: "We will not go back to normal. Normal never was. Our pre-corona existence was never normal other than we normalized greed, inequality, exhaustion, depletion, extraction, disconnection, confusion, rage, hoarding, hate and lack. We should not long to return." Taylor reminds us that our despair can also ignite us and that we have an obligation to keep hoping and fighting, even while all evidence suggests that we do otherwise. We hope that by asking our questions we will continue to heed Taylor's entreaty that "We are being given the opportunity to stitch a new garment ... one that fits all of humanity and nature." We hope that this new garment will fit us equitably and will transform us towards a future of justice.

Works Cited

ACME Editorial Collective. "Pausing New Articles Unrelated to COVID-19 Pandemic-Related Issues." *ACME: An International Journal for Critical Geographies*, 1 May 2020, acme-journal.org/index.php/acme/announcement. Accessed 2 Jan. 2021.

Cain Miller, Claire. "Nearly Half of Men Say They Do Most of the Home Schooling. 3 Percent of Women Agree." *The New York Times*, 6 May 2020, www.nytimes.com/2020/05/06/upshot/pandemic-chores-homeschooling-gender.html. Accessed 2 Jan. 2021.

Cohen, Jodi S. "A Teenager Didn't Do Her Online Schoolwork. So a Judge Sent Her to Juvenile Detention." *Pro Publica*, 14 July 2020, www.propublica.org/article/a-teenager-didnt-do-her-online-schoolwork-so-a-judge-sent-her-to-juvenile-detention. Accessed 2 Jan. 2021.

Collins, Patricia Hill. "Shifting the Center: Race, Class, and Feminist Theorizing about Motherhood." *Mothering: Ideology, Experience and Agency*, edited by Evelyn Nakano Glenn, Grace Chang, and Linda Forcey, Routledge, 1994, pp. 45-65.

Collins, Patricia Hill. "Black Women and Motherhood." *Motherhood and Space*, edited by Sarah Hardy and Caroline Wiedmer, Palgrave, 2005, pp. 149-59.

Fraser, Nancy. "Contradictions of Capital and Care." *New Left Review* vol. 100, July-Aug 2016, pp. 99-117.

Gates, Melinda. *The Moment of Lift*. Flatiron Books, 2019.

hooks, bell. *Feminist Theory: From Margin to Center*. Boston: South End Press, 1984. Print.

Johnston, Regan M., Anwar Mohammed, and Clifton van der Linden. "Evidence of Exacerbated Gender Inequality in Child Care Obligations in Canada and Australia During the COVID-19 Pandemic." *Politics and Gender*, 3 Aug. 2020, 1-16, www.cambridge.org/core/journals/politics-and-gender/article/evidence-of-exacerbated-gender-inequality-in-child-care-obligations-in-canada-and-australia-during-the-covid19-pandemic/4E849E33B2F20D7C44A08B9FEA33CC2B. Accessed 2 Jan. 2021.

Lemieux, Thomas, et al.. "Initial Impacts of the COVID-19 Pandemic on the Canadian Labour Market." Working Paper Series, No. 26,

University of Waterloo, Canadian Labour Economics Forum (CLEF), Spring-Summer 2020.

Louisias, Margee, and Lyndonna Marrast. "Intersectional Identity and Racial Inequality During the COVID-19 Pandemic: Perspectives of Black Physician Mothers." *J Womens Health (Larchmt)*, vol. 29, no. 9, 2020, pp. 1148-49.

Messecar, Derek, René Morissette, and Zechuan Deng. "Inequality in the Feasibility of Working from Home During and after COVID-19." *Statistics Canada Catalogue No. 45280001*, 8 June 2020, www150.statcan. gc.ca/n1/pub/45-28-0001/2020001/article/00029-eng.htm. Accessed 2 Jan. 2021.

Pon, Gordon, Kevin Gosine, and Doret Phillips. "Immediate Response: Addressing Anti-Native and Anti-Black Racism in Child Welfare." *International Journal of Child, Youth and Family Studies*, vol. 3, no. 4, 2011, pp. 385-409.

Ray, Rashawn. "Why are Blacks Dying at Higher Rates from COVID-19?" *Brookings*. 9 Apr. 2020, www.brookings.edu/blog/fixgov/2020/04/09/why-are-blacks-dying-at-higher-rates-from-covid-19/. Accessed 2 Jan. 2021.

Roberts, Dorothy E. "Unshackling Black Motherhood." *Michigan Law Review*, vol. 95, no. 4. 1997, pp. 938-64.

Smith, Katie. "How I'm Dealing With Poverty In The Pandemic As A Single Parent." *HuffPost Canada*, 3 Apr. 2020, www.huffingtonpost.ca/entry/covid-19-poverty-single-mom_ca_5e8501f3c5b692780506e7db. Accessed 2 Jan. 2021.

Taylor, Sonya Renee [@sonyareneetaylor]. "There Can Be No Going Back to 'Normal'. *Instagram*, 31 Mar. 2020, www.instagram.com/tv/B-avtd KAXRh/. Accessed 2 Jan. 2021.

United Nations Policy Brief. "The Impact of Covid-19 on Women." *United Nations*, 9 Apr. 2020, asiapacific.unwomen.org/en/digital-library/publications/2020/04/policy-brief-the-impact-of-covid-19-on-women. Accessed 2 Jan. 2021.

Viglione, Giuliana. "Are Women Publishing Less during the Pandemic? Here's What the Data Say." *Nature*, vol. 581, 28 May 2020, pp. 365-66.

Chapter Five

"Who Cares?" Women's and Mothers' Employment in Caring Industries during the First Wave of COVID-19

Gillian Anderson and Sylvie Lafrenière

Introduction

These are undeniably trying times. The "stay home" directive issued during the COVID-19 pandemic was intended to contain the spread of the virus and ease the strain on public health services. However, in doing so, the order transferred the burden of care to informal networks, families, and mostly women. In this chapter, we use data from the Labour Force Survey to present a high-level overview of the intensification of women's caregiving labour amid the current pandemic, with a focus on the Economic Region (ER) of Vancouver Island-Coast in British Columbia. Our goal is to isolate the employment experiences of working mothers, specifically those in caring, or pink-collar industries in order to answer the following questions: amid the employment volatility and the economic repercussions of the pandemic, where are the mothers? And what caring work are they doing? We aim to draw attention not only to "who cares" (Ruderman et al.)—that is, who performs caring labour for a living—but to the persistence of gendered carework to better understand the shifts and changes to women's caring work in pandemic times.

Following a brief review of the literature and a presentation of our data, our analysis begins with an overview of employment in the ER of Vancouver Island-Coast, with a focus on women and mothers. Next, we examine the trends that have affected the female-dominated caring industries of health and social assistance, educational services, retail trade, and accommodation and food services. We show that mothers' caring labour has intensified since January 2020. We also hypothesize, but are unable to confirm, that mothers of young children have borne the brunt of this intensification. Further research is needed to address this concern. Finally, we argue that the affects of the pandemic on women, and mothers in particular, are hidden within official statistics, and we propose a continuation of our study to focus on more qualitative data.

Literature Review

The work of feminist political economists (FPE) is instrumental in understanding the gendered implications of mothers' COVID-19 experiences. FPE scholarship (Armstrong and Connelly; Bakker; Bezanson; Fox and Luxton) has long argued capitalist societies exploit women's role in social reproduction, including the unpaid physical, mental, and socio-emotional labour that women have traditionally performed in the private spheres of the home and family. Capitalism as an economic system does not attach monetary value to this work. It normalizes women's unpaid caring work as a "labour of love" (Luxton), constructing it as an individual or a familial responsibility rather than a matter of collective or public concern (Fox and Luxton), which contributes to the devaluation and invisibility of mothers' caring labour. It is "hidden in the household" (Fox). According to Nancy Fraser (2016), the system sees caring work as a "gift" and "takes it for granted."

These gendered relations of reproduction are not sustainable and have precipitated what Fraser (2016) terms a "crisis of care"—which is manifested in the ramping up of mothers' "double day," an additional "third shift" tied to the informal care of dependent, infirm, or elderly family members and a tightening of the "time bind" (Luxton; Hochschild). This crisis of care reinforces and at the same time downplays gender identities and inequalities, especially during the pandemic. It highlights the "dual process of both gender erosion and intensification" (Bakker 7; see also Brodie; Fudge and Cossman; Harder for discussions of the intensification and erosion of gender). To suggest that gender has been intensified and eroded is to say that gender has paradoxically become more and less salient. The erosion of gender is tied to the mainstream COVID-19 discourse that fails to recognize gendered aspects of caring labour. When calling on Canadians, British Columbians, and parents to do their part, there is little to no recognition that the burden falls mostly on women. However, previous research shows that women still bear the brunt of social reproduction in the household. More women than men participate in housework, and when men do participate, they spend less time at it than women (Moyser and Burlock).

Gender is also eroded in the discourse surrounding essential workers (e.g., nurses and care aides), which ignores the fact that upwards of 70 per cent of healthcare workers worldwide are women (Gupta). They tend to be over-represented in so-called caring profess-ions or the services-producing sector, such as healthcare, education, and accommodation. In 2015, 41 per cent of Canadian women compared to 13 per cent of men worked in these industries (Moyser).

Much has been learned from the previous Ebola, SARS, and HIV/ AIDS outbreaks, and organizations like Oxfam, CARE, the World Health Organization, and the United Nations have been instrumental in the development and promotion of guidelines and procedures aimed at facilitating gender-based analysis in the implementation of emergency responses to disease outbreaks. However, despite recognition that disease outbreaks affect women and girls differently than men and boys, responses to public health emergencies remain focused on urgency and on mitigating problems (Smith). Gender-based policies have yet to be implemented. In this unprecedented time, not only it is imperative then that we ask, "where are the women?" (Harman), but we also need, as Andrea O'Reilly states, a record of what "the mother experience is like during a global pandemic" (qtd. in Goodfellow Craig). Our research contributes to this larger historical narrative. By tracing the employment patterns of working women and mothers, specifically those employed in caring industries, we seek to better understand the shifts and changes to women's caring labour during the first wave of COVID-19.

Data

The data we present were obtained through Statistics Canada's custom tabulation service. We received rounded, unadjusted for seasonality, monthly employment data from the Labour Force Survey covering the period of January 2019 to August 2020. We present data for the ER of Vancouver Island-Coast, which in 2019, had an estimated population of approximately 870,297 (Statistics Canada).

We intended to undertake a macrolevel analysis of employment data to illustrate how many women were working during the pandemic, in what specific industries, and how many of them were mothers. To do so, we requested data that included the age of the youngest child, which would allow us to identify working mothers of young children— namely, those in need of child or substitute care.[1] We planned to present breakdowns of employed mothers with young children (those aged twelve and under) by industry.

However, the population size of the ER, and indeed at the provincial level, proved to be problematic due to Statistics Canada data suppression and quality guidelines. Instead, we present the available data for this ER and propose the need for further, more regionally based qualitative data in order to more fully identify the burden of care mothers experienced during the COVID-19 pandemic.

Findings and Analyses

In January 2020, prior to the official declaration of the pandemic, approximately 373,400 persons were employed in the ER of Vancouver Island-Coast. Chart 1 illustrates the year-over-year differences between 2019 and 2020, highlighting the significant loss of employment beginning in March 2020.

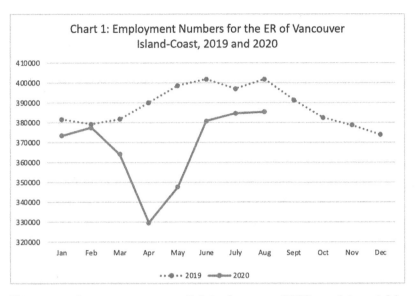

The unemployment rate was 5.9 in January 2020, and it quickly climbed to 12.9 in April, falling slightly to 10.5 in August 2020. Delving deeper into the data and in an attempt to identify the effects on women, Chart 2 shows that women were affected differently than men: women's employment numbers decreased sooner and faster.

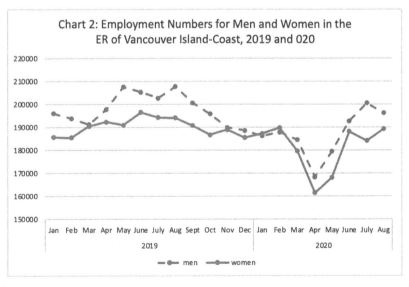

Our analysis points to the number of women rather than the proportion in order to draw attention to the hundreds of thousands of women who, we hypothesize, were burdened with managing the dual demands of paid and unpaid caring labour throughout the first wave of the pandemic.

Women's employment recovery has also been slower than men's, as evidenced in Chart 2. Men appear to have surpassed their January 2020 employment numbers in June, whereas it was not until August that women's employment numbers almost returned to what they were in January 2020. As of August 2020, women's employment remained below the 2019 levels. This finding is in line with previous research that indicates women workers often struggle to bounce back amid epidemics and other health emergencies, thereby potentially intensifying gender disparities in employment by undercutting women's financial and economic wellbeing (Smith). Julia Smith found although everybody's income was affected by the Ebola outbreak in West Africa, men's income returned to pre-outbreak levels faster than women's.

Our data also show that in January 2020, before the onset of COVID-19, the top ten industries employing approximately 80 per cent of all workers (women and men) in the ER of Vancouver Island-Coast were as follows: healthcare and social assistance; retail trade; accommodation and food services; construction; public administration; educational services; professional, scientific, and technical services; administrative and support, waste management and remediation services; other services (except public administration); and manufacturing. These ten industries employed 78 per cent of all men and 88 per cent of all women in the ER.

To highlight the employment experiences of mothers, we turn to the employment data for what Melissa Moyser characterizes as the "services-producing sector": health, education, and accommodation as well as food services. These industries are consistently gendered in the ER and include what are often characterized as caring professions or pink-collar jobs. We include retail trade among these caring occupations because it often involves attending to the needs of others and ensuring their comfort. Taken together, these caring industries represent four of the top six industries in the ER, and in January 2020, they employed 59 per cent of all women and 32 per cent of all men.

Chart 3 shows the impact COVID-19 had on employment numbers for women and men in all four of these caring industries from January to August 2020. It shows more women than men were employed in each of them, with healthcare and social assistance being the most pronounced. In fact, even at the lowest point in April 2020, there were almost four times as many women (40,900) employed in the healthcare industry than men (9,700), and more than twice as many women were employed in education than men (20,000 compared to 8,200 respectively).

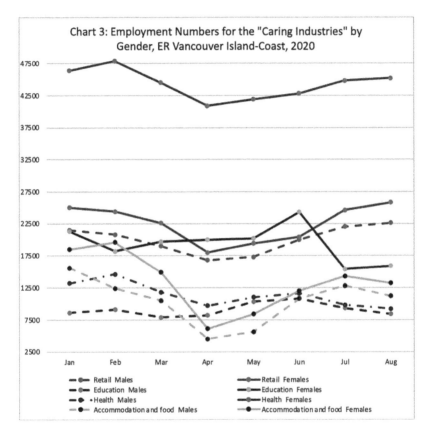

each of them, with healthcare and social assistance being the most pronounced. In fact, even at the lowest point in April 2020, there were almost four times as many women (40,900) employed in the healthcare industry than men (9,700), and more than twice as many women were employed in education than men (20,000 compared to 8,200 respectively).

Even at the height of the lockdown in April—when employment was at its lowest (Chart 1) and women were affected sooner and faster than men (Chart 2)—we see that in these caring industries, more women than men remained employed. Since past research indicates that women are also primarily responsible for undertaking most of the social reproduction and caring work in private households, we hypothesize that women in these industries are doing double duty—shouldering the brunt of the pandemic in both their work and personal lives.

Knowing there are more women than men employed in these caring professions, we then sought to identify mothers within these industries. We considered the variable "age of youngest child" broken down according to the different school milestones mentioned above. However, the variability of the estimates within said industries made this impossible at both the ER and provincial levels. Given this limitation, we are unable to isolate mothers in these sectors. We are, however, able to show that in January 2020, approximately 35 per cent of working women were mothers of children aged twenty-four or younger (Chart 4). In April, that percentage was 38 per cent, and in August, it was 36 per cent. Clearly, mothers continued to work throughout the first wave of the pandemic.

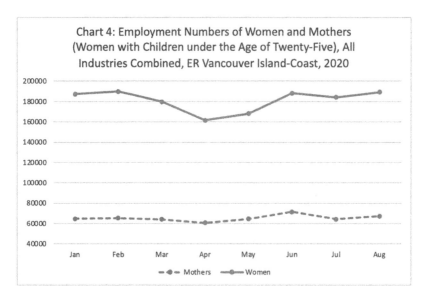

Chart 4: Employment Numbers of Women and Mothers (Women with Children under the Age of Twenty-Five), All Industries Combined, ER Vancouver Island-Coast, 2020

Furthermore, we tried to capture the breakdown of employed mothers by the age group of the youngest child. Chart 5 shows that in all industries combined, almost two-thirds of working mothers—61 per cent (N=39,700) in January 2020—had a child aged twelve or younger.[2] That proportion of working mothers remained relatively constant throughout the pandemic, despite the drop in total number of employed women. Regardless of industry, mothers of young children continued to work throughout the pandemic. They also likely did so while providing educational support (e.g., homework) as well as contending with the requirements of pandemic health regulations preventing children from attending school and daycares, playing in parks, or visiting friends. Moreover, younger children require a greater level of care, and existing caregiving arrangements were likely disrupted with the closure of schools and daycare centres. Given the gender gap in the division of unpaid household labour, these numbers point to a possible intensification of household stress upsetting any semblance of mothers' work-life balance.

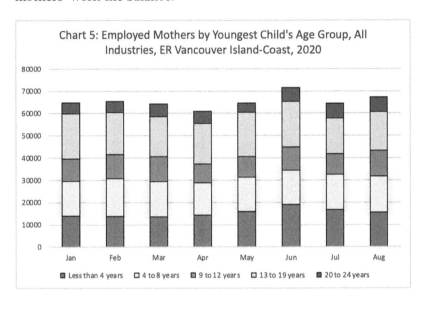

Chart 5: Employed Mothers by Youngest Child's Age Group, All Industries, ER Vancouver Island-Coast, 2020

These numbers do not tell us whether mothers potentially reduced their working hours from full- to part-time, used vacation, lieu time, or sick time in order to maintain their employment throughout the pandemic. Nor do they tell us if mothers quit a job during the pandemic and/or—for those who lost employment or were laid off—took on a new or less demanding job, one which may have allowed them to continue to work but also attend to their unpaid caregiving responsibilities. The Labour Force Survey data only begin to hint at what we hypothesize is happening with working mothers who bear the brunt of social reproduction, especially those working in caring industries. Unfortunately, due to the variability and volatility of the employment data collected during the first wave of the pandemic, when things were changing rapidly, we are unable to report the data related to age of the youngest child by caring industry. In fact, even at the provincial level, much of the data has high variability and cannot be presented.

COVID-19's effect on employment has amplified existing discrepancies between men and women as mothers of young children requiring more hands-on or specialized care. Those official statistics do not permit a detailed look at the impact of the disruptions experienced by mothers living in smaller coastal communities on Vancouver Island, such as Nanaimo, which obscures the difficulties mothers encountered and the added burden of care precipitated by the pandemic.

This is especially true within the caring industries. In this time of crisis, much of the essential work fell not only to those working on the front lines—such as doctors, nurses, and healthcare workers—but also to those working in the education and the food and service industries. The gendered nature of caring work is evident in these sectors of the ER, which implies that as the paid labour of working mothers within the caring sectors ramped up, so did the responsibilities within their own homes.

Healthcare and Social Assistance

The Healthcare and Social Assistance industry includes mothers employed as doctors, nurses, care aides, and support workers—paid caring labour that resembles much of the domestic work women have traditionally performed in the private spheres of home and family. Although the industry employs physicians and nurses, many jobs remain feminized, devalued, and underpaid.

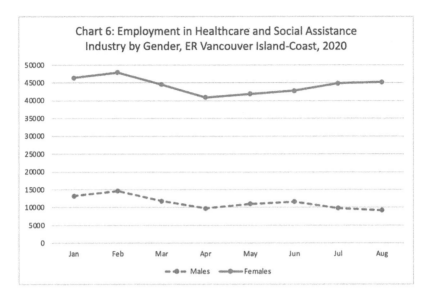

Chart 6: Employment in Healthcare and Social Assistance Industry by Gender, ER Vancouver Island-Coast, 2020

Employment numbers show the Healthcare and Social Assistance industry is female dominated (Chart 6). In January 2020, there were approximately 46,400 women employed compared to 13,200 men. Despite a dip to 40,900 and 9,700 for women and men, respectively, in April, employment remained fairly constant throughout the early months of the pandemic. This is to be expected, as those employed in the healthcare and social assistance industry continued working as essential workers, whereas other sectors experienced a more pronounced shutdown. Not only were women on the frontlines engaged in service delivery and care provision tied to their paid employment, but some were also undoubtedly mothers who were responsible for ensuring the emotional, physical, and social wellbeing of their children and families. We expect that mothers working in this industry had to care for children with the added worry and stress about the possibility of bringing the virus home.

Educational Services

The Educational Services industry includes women and mothers employed as teachers, educational or teaching assistants and school clerical workers. Not only does Chart 7 indicate that the industry is female dominated, but it also shows fluctuations in the employment trends for women and men. We do not believe these fluctuations are related to the pandemic, since with the exception of a slight drop in February 2020, employment trends in 2020 mirror those of 2019.[3]

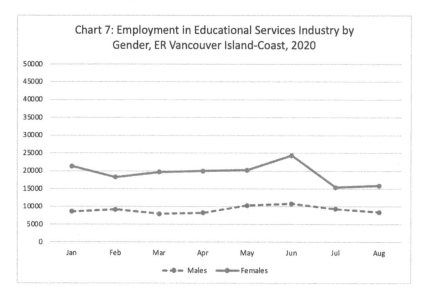

Chart 7: Employment in Educational Services Industry by Gender, ER Vancouver Island-Coast, 2020

This relative stability is unsurprising. Although schools were closed mid-March, teachers transitioned to online communication and learning for the remainder of the 2019-2020 school year with a few exceptions. There was a voluntary return to a modified and shortened version of in-class, face-to-face instruction in June. Moreover, some schools continued to operate as learning centres (grades K-7) for children of essential workers. In April 2020, Nanaimo Ladysmith Public Schools Deputy Superintendent, Tim Davie, characterized these learning centres as "a civic responsibility": "We deem we are also providing an essential service to meeting the needs of all families and whether that be through the continuity of learning plan or whether that be providing these centres, we want to take care of our students and recognizing that these times aren't normal for anybody" (qtd. in Yu).

This quote exemplifies how in the public discourse, the gendered nature of caring labour is eroded, favouring instead the gender-neutral characterization of essential service, with an eye to helping children, parents, and families cope in these unprecedented times. Essential workers are rendered genderless, obscuring identities and overlooking home lives. They may be the heroes that we, as a country are relying on, yet there is no mention or recognition of who is doing the work—that is, the workers staffing these centres. That said, we expect that it is working women, many of whom themselves may be mothers, who have been publicly shouldering the burden of care and social reproduction.

Services: Retail Trade and Accommodation and Food Services

Lastly, we consider the Retail Trade industry and the Accommodation and Food Services industry together because they reveal many similarities. Although there are slightly more women than men in both sectors, Charts 8 and 9 show the employment trends for both have been similar throughout the pandemic. These industries include women employed in public-facing jobs in grocery stores and, following stage two of the provincial economic restart plan, in clothing stores, restaurants, bars, and hotels. Ironically, some of these often poorly paid jobs were deemed essential during the pandemic (e.g., grocery store workers).

Chart 8: Employment in Retail Trade Industry by Gender, ER Vancouver Island-Coast, 2020

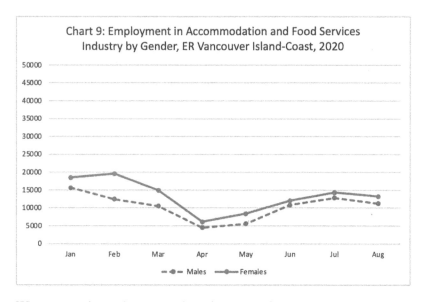

Chart 9: Employment in Accommodation and Food Services Industry by Gender, ER Vancouver Island-Coast, 2020

Women and mothers employed in retail may have seen their employment affected not only by closures but also by an increase in online shopping during the pandemic, whereas those in the hospitality industry were likely affected by closures, reductions in hours, layoffs, and travel restrictions. Hospitality workers employed in banquet halls and conference facilities that typically serve groups over fifty in size would have been directly affected by restrictions in gathering size, health and travel restrictions, and a decline in tourism. The slight uptick in employment numbers in May 2020 may be indicative of the gradual move to stage three as part of the provincial restart plan and an announcement at the end of June encouraging British Columbians to travel within the province during the summer.

Conclusion: Looking Ahead

Getting at the numbers of mothers' paid carework has been challenging, and the numbers we present here do not tell the whole story. Although we were able to show how the pandemic has caused disruptions to the work lives of mothers in four caring industries and that almost two-thirds of working mothers had a child aged twelve or younger, we could not breakdown the caring industries by children's age groups. Given the persistence of gendered divisions of household labour, we hypothesize that because of economic hardship resulting from continued employment in caring industries, as well as employment loss or reduction, mothers have experienced an intensification of the process of social reproduction typically associated with gender inequities in our homes and society. Moreover, we anticipate that this hardship will continue in the fall of 2020 amid the emergence of the second wave. In addition, our data only tell us the status of women's paid employment—that is, whether or not they were employed. It does not tell us whether their employment was full- or part-time, permanent or contract-based, nor does it tell us if mothers were making enough money to support their families or to pay their rent or mortgage. We do not know if their working hours allowed them to look after their children, if they had benefits that covered prescriptions, or if they needed to look for another job. Although this data may have been available from different sources, we decided to focus on the employment numbers because, in this first part of our study, we lay the foundation, with numbers, for the qualitative analysis to follow.

The next phase of our research involves the collection of qualitative and quantitative information from mid-Vancouver Island mothers. Through this next step, we hope to highlight the challenges and successes of working mothers and to contribute to the policy discussions surrounding health emergencies.

Endnotes

1. The children's age groups reflect school age milestones, including under four years, four to eight years, nine to twelve years, thirteen to nineteen years, twenty to twenty-four, and twenty-five or older or no children.

2. At twelve years old, children in British Columbia begin middle school, and they can legally be left alone at home. We assume it is the age at which they begin to show a degree of independence and require less care than younger children.

3. Some of the numbers in Chart 7 may reflect seasonal employment loss on the part of women working as support staff as well as teaching or educational assistants employed on a contract basis, whose employment would cease with the annual onset of summer holidays.

Works Cited

Armstrong, Pat, and M. Patricia Connelly. "Feminist Political Economy: An Introduction." *Studies in Political Economy*, vol. 30, no. 1, 1989, pp. 5-12.

Bakker, Isabella . *Rethinking Restructuring: Gender and Change in Canada*. University of Toronto Press, 1997.

Bezanson, Kate. *Gender, the State, and Social Reproduction: Household Insecurity in Neo-Liberal Times*. University of Toronto Press, 2006.

Brodie, Janine. *Politics on the Margins: Restructuring and the Canadian Women's Movement*. Fernwood Publishing, 2000.

Fox, Bonnie. *Hidden in the Household: Women's Domestic Labour under Capitalism*. Women's Educational Press, 1980.

Fox, Bonnie, and Meg Luxton. "Conceptualizing Family." *Family Patterns & Gender Relations*, edited by Bonnie Fox, Oxford University Press, 2009, pp. 3-20.

Fraser, Nancy. "Capitalism's Crisis of Care." *Dissent*, vol. 63, no. 4, 2016, pp. 30-37.

Fudge, Judy, and Brenda Cossman. "Conclusion: Privatization, Polarization and Policy: Feminism and the Future." *Privatization, Law, and the Challenge to Feminism*, edited by Judy Fudge and Brenda Cossman, University Toronto Press, 2002, pp. 403-20.

Goodfellow Craig, Ashley. "Mothering through a Pandemic: COVID-19 and the Evolving Role of Mothers." *YFile*, 2020, yfile.news.yorku. ca/2020/04/08/mothering-through-a-pandemic-covid-19-and-the-evolving-role-of-mothers/. Accessed 2 Jan. 2021.

Gupta, Alisha Haridasani. "Why Women May Face a Greater Risk of Catching Coronavirus." *New York Times*, 12 Mar. 2020, www.nytimes. com/2020/03/12/us/women-coronavirus-greater-risk.html. Accessed 2 Jan. 2021.

Harder, Lois. *State of Struggle: Feminism and Politics in Alberta*. University of Alberta, 2003.

Harman, Sophie. "Ebola, Gender and Conspicuously Invisible Women in Global Health Governance." *Third World Quarterly*, vol. 37, no. 3, 2016, pp. 524-41.

Hochschild, Arlie R. "The Third Shift." *Family Patterns & Gender Relations*, edited by Bonnie Fox, Oxford University Press, 2001, pp. 338-52.

Hochschild, Arlie Russell. *The Time Bind: When Work Becomes Home and Home Becomes Work*. Vol. 2. Macmillan, 2001.

Luxton, Meg. "Taking on the Double Day Housewives as a Reserve Army of Labour." *Atlantis: Critical Studies in Gender, Culture & Social Justice*, vol. 7, no. 1, 1981, pp. 12-22.

Luxton, Meg. *More Than a Labour of Love: Three Generations of Women's Work in the Home*. Vol. 2. Canadian Scholars' Press, 1980.

Moyser, Melissa. "Women and Paid Work", chapter 10 in *Women in Canada: A Gender-Based Statistical Report*, Seventh Edition, Statistics Canada catalogue number 89-503-X (2018).

Moyser, Melissa, and Amanda Burlock. "Time Use: Total Work Burden, Unpaid Work, and Leisure," chapter 14 in *Women in Canada: A Gender-Based Statistical Report*, Seventh Edition, Statistics Canada catalogue number 89-503-X (2018).

Ruderman, Carly, et al. "On Pandemics and the Duty to Care: Whose Duty? Who Cares?" *BMC Medical Ethics*, vol. 7, no. 1, 2006, pp. 1-6.

Smith, Julia. "Overcoming the 'Tyranny of the Urgent': Integrating Gender into Disease Outbreak Preparedness and Response." *Gender & Development*, vol. 27, no. 2, 2019, pp. 355-69.

Statistics Canada. "Population Estimates, July 1, by Economic Region, 2016 Boundaries." *Statistics Canada*, 2020, www150.statcan.gc.ca/t1/tbl1/en/tv.action?pid=1710013701. Accessed 2 Jan. 2021.

Yu, Karl. "Nanaimo-Ladysmith School District Operating Learning Centres for Children of Essential Service Workers. SD68 to Provide More Information This Week on a Continuity of Education Plan for Other Students." *Nanaimo Bulletin*, 13 Apr. 13, 2020, www.nanaimo bulletin.com/news/nanaimo-ladysmith-school-district-operating-learning-centres-for-children-of-essential-service-workers/. Accessed 2 Jan. 2021.

Chapter Six

Workplace and Social Justice: A New Feminist Movement for Labour and Love

Jennifer L. Borda

The COVID-19 pandemic has wrought a public health crisis compounded by an economic collapse on a global scale. In the United States (U.S.) and various other Westernized nations, COVID-19 has magnified the corollary pandemic of inhumane free-market capitalist policies being prioritized over social welfare ones; the few are being prioritized over the many. These coalescing crises expose the failures of neoliberal, individualist, and market-driven decision making, which has afflicted the professional and personal lives of people around the world. Meanwhile, in the U.S., nationwide protests have recentred calls for racial justice, highlighting how the effects of four centuries of systematic oppression and inequality have become embedded in American political, economic, educational, and cultural institutions. Then, in September 2020, public discourse commemorating the exceptional career of Supreme Court Justice Ruth Bader Ginsburg following her death was a cogent reminder that gender inequality also persists across the spheres of education, labour, the home, and the economy. This critical juncture of racial, gender, and economic injustice constitutes a humanitarian crisis, now compounded by a public health crisis that magnifies systemic inequalities, with COVID-19 affecting Black Indigenous people of colour (BIPOC) and poor communities in far wider numbers than white Americans of privilege. The COVID-19 pandemic requires a rededication towards collective feminist politics, through which we can unite diverse political coalitions and intersectional movements that seek emancipation by "embracing the common circumstances of precariousness, as against the unequal fate of precarity" (Butler qtd. in Kasmir 3).

And, so, I choose to write this chapter in a spirit of optimism, proposing new feminist imaginaries and exploring how we may "build back better" (to borrow from U.S. President-elect Joe Biden's campaign theme). Sonia Shah argues that how we talk about the COVID-19 pandemic matters: "Paradigms—the obscure, unspoken conceptual frameworks that shape our ideas—are powerful. They bring order and understanding to our observations about the messy, changing world around us." But they can also blind us, "elevating certain narratives and serving particular interests, often to our peril." However, Shah proposes that if we can change the narrative and write a new story for this pandemic, "we can emerge as the makers of our own destiny who can rebuild the postpandemic world anew." To this end, I embrace feminist rhetorician Cheryl Glenn's insistence that feminist rhetorical scholars "meditate on hope, to keep alive a tempered hope for the future in light of our present political moment" (4). My feminist hope is that by building back from the cultural and economic devastation wrought by COVID-19, we may create a new paradigm, inspired by feminist politics and imbued with the immanent values of equity, diversity, and inclusion. We can rebuild for the common good. From this framework, I argue that we have the potential to collectively refashion a socially just economy and usher in radical social trans-formations in gender—and human—equality. Achieving this end will require coalition building, political will, and innovative economic policies, which recognize the necessary contributions of women and marginalized workers, elevate economies of care, and enforce workplace justice

To this end, this chapter addresses the inexorable intersections of free market capitalism, the politics of work, and the overlooked and undervalued intersectional workers undergirding economies of care in the U.S. I contextualize this case study in scholarship examining gender, work, work-life conflict, and economic inequality to demonstrate how the current care burdens brought on by COVID-19 have further intensified the failures of the neoliberal paradigm while most severely impacting working women and mothers at the intersections. In a spirit of hope, I argue that burgeoning efforts towards supporting values that prioritize gender, egalitarianism, an ethics of care, and the common good will help to reframe gendered cultural norms to foster a stronger economic reality fuelled by the work of women and caregivers. I conclude that, by reimagining gender equality as a convergence of class consciousness, egalitarian social relations, racial justice, and workplace reform, the advancement of family-friendly policies and the revaluation of carework could become pandemic opportunities for radical social change.

Neoliberal Politics of Work and Working Women at the Intersections

As a feminist rhetorical scholar—who studies public discourse and contested ideologies at the intersections of gender, race, class, power, and women's labour, including how they are deliberated in the public sphere—I am concerned with ongoing efforts to bolster women's rights while strengthening American families. In October 2016, Justice Ginsburg wrote an op-ed for the *New York Times*, in which she references the ongoing struggle for women's equality at work and at home:

> Earlier, I spoke of great changes I have seen in women's occupations. Yet one must acknowledge the still bleak part of the picture. Most people in poverty in the United States and the world over are women and children, women's earnings here and abroad trail the earnings of men with comparable education and experience, our workplaces do not adequately accommodate the demands of childbearing and child rearing, and we have yet to devise effective ways to ward off sexual harassment at work and domestic violence in our homes. I am optimistic, however, that movement toward enlistment of the talent of all who compose "We, the people," will continue.

Yet we find ourselves in a time that does not promote optimism. For "We, the people" of the U.S., every day verifies the threats under which we exist—from COVID-19 and the consequent public health crisis to the hierarchy of values that drive our current political strategy and policy decisions. The convergence of prolonged political, economic, and cultural crises reveals strategic efforts to undermine progressivism and civil rights and to prioritize the social and economic agendas of only those whom the patriarchal political culture deems worthy of value: white, heterosexual, and cisgender men of economic privilege.

Despite these prioritizations, the last fifty years have demonstrated the value women bring to the economy in terms of their labour participation and domestic work. The contributions of women to American economic prosperity persist in the face of ongoing challenges of integrating care and paid labour. Beginning with Arlie Hochschild's 1989 landmark study, *The Second Shift*, sociologists and economists have focused on the legacies and limitations of second-wave feminism in terms of the intersecting relationships between motherhood, work, and family, both inside and outside of the home. Critical analyses of the price of motherhood, both financially and culturally (Crittenden)— including the challenges of trying to combine a professional career with motherhood (Slaughter; Swinth) and how various economic, legal, social, political, and familial institutions contribute to work-family conflict (Hochschild; Hesse-Biber and Carter)—have revealed how the overlapping constructs of a patriarchal workplace culture and uncompromising household politics reinforce gender subordination. It is clear that women's material gains in the economic realm have outpaced progress towards strengthening women's rights and achieving gender equality across the public and private spheres.

A limitation of early scholarship exploring gender, work, and family was a lack of concerted attention to the substantive ways in which motherhood is interpreted and experienced through racialized and class differences. Consequently, as Danielle Fuentes Morgan argues, "Black women are often told to ignore the reality of their experiences in the interstice in favor of a universal notion of the woman and the mother that is insufficient in its articulation" (857). Considerations of motherhood as universal put overt focus on women of the professional working class, and since both the labour and women's rights movement were built on the exclusion of BIPOC, the lives and experiences of these mothers and women remain outside theorizations about working motherhood. To expand understandings of maternal theory at these intersections, Black feminist theory has more fully interrogated the complexities of work, family, and Black women's oppression (Collins), reproductive politics and medical racism as systems of injustice (Davis), as well as the possibilities of Black maternal politics. "It is in this cultural moment," Jennifer Nash argues, "in which black motherhood is both the space of crisis and loss as well as the space of redemption" that Black maternal politics emerges as "a powerful and densely loaded site of political meaning" (703). Only very recently have scholars and activists begun to recognize—and practice—intersectionality as central to feminist politics. Catherine Rottenberg clarifies the potential of the "wave of mass feminist militancy" that emerged in the wake of Donald Trump's presidency in this regard:

> What is particularly striking about these mass demon-strations—as well as the grassroots activists who helped organize them, such as the new movement Feminism for the 99 percent—is they very consciously (if not always successfully or unproblematically) attempt to include and address inequalities that expand, in significant ways, the single analytic frame of gender. (173-74)

Expanding the Gender Frame to Include Differences That Matter

Cecilia Ridgeway has argued that the reason for the stalled gender revolution is the persistent use of gender as a framing device that "spreads gendered meanings, including assumptions about inequality embedded in those meanings, to all spheres of social life that are carried out through social relationships" (7). Ridgeway further explains that gender inequality "persists partly because everyday reliance on the gender frame in social relations has embedded beliefs about gender status and difference in established institutions of work and family that powerfully control access to resources and power" (185). Consequently, she argues that "cultural beliefs about gender *lag* changes in material circumstances between men and women" (185). Although white, professional working women made clear gains in the workforce during the 1960s, 1970s, and 1980s, by the turn of the twenty-first century, many scholars had declared the successes of the women's revolution stalled or greatly exaggerated. Ridgeway likens the process through which "material conditions erode and reshape cultural beliefs about gender" to the metaphor of waves moving a sandbar: "A single wave has little effect, but a repeating, pounding of waves utterly transforms the sandbar. The key, however, is that the waves of material change keep pounding despite the resistance of lagging beliefs" (Ridgeway 197-98).

Over the last two decades, sociologists, political theorists, and gender scholars have sought to, in Joan Williams's words, "jumpstart the stalled gender revolution" ("Jumpstarting" 1,283) by exposing how such lagging cultural beliefs about gender have undermined women's material change in terms of their positional status, agency, and power in the economic realm. Scholars have produced critical analyses of the economics of gendered labour; the normative functions of white, professional working class and neotraditional family arrangements; and the incompatibility of ideal-worker expectations and career ambition combined with intensive-mothering ideologies (Williams, Unbending; Hirshman; O'Brien Hallstein; Hays). Work-life scholars, in particular, have begun to intervene into gendered ideologies in ways seeking to reimagine more equitable gender politics and greater social power for working women and families across the socioeconomic spectrum. Williams's theory of "reconstructive feminism," for example, suggests that changes in gender talk can restructure the design of paid and family work, eliminate the gender wars, and formulate coalitions that could reorganize work around our collective social values (Reshaping). Whereas Williams focuses mainly on gender and socioeconomic class differences, emerging feminist theorizing and activist coalitions must also account for BIPOC workers and those in marginalized and impoverished communities as well as new political imaginaries that cross differences and divides. The unique circumstance of the COVID-19 pandemic has revealed the intersecting futures of race, gender, health, and economic equality, illuminating "how precariousness may be shaping emerging, future class formations" (Kasmir, 10).

Yet it remains to be seen how the progress toward a more egalitarian economic future for a diversity of women now eroded by the COVID-19 crisis might still produce social and political reform. Will more gender egalitarian social norms be established through this shared crisis, or will the modest material changes towards gender equality of the last few decades be further washed away? We know that women have made material gains over the last decade. Women pulled the economy out of the 2008 recession; the prepandemic years witnessed the rise of breadwinning moms, with 41 per cent of mothers being sole or primary breadwinners and an additional 23.2 per cent being cobreadwinners (Glynn). By February 2020, American women had hit a milestone— they comprised more than half of the civilian nonfarm labour workforce. What has not yet changed is the idealized, and masculinized, version of American workers—who can easily demarcate work boundaries from life boundaries—and attendant cultural norms that place responsibilities for making it all work on individual workers, especially working mothers. The COVID-19 pandemic is a crisis framed by gender, which has demonstrated that despite recent gains for women, the failures of U.S. neoliberal economic policy agendas are evident. Such policies normalize individualism, privilege a hollow moral framework of family values, and undermine gender equality.

COVID-19 and the Expanding Care Burden

Although women's relationship to work has changed in complex ways over the last half century, cultural beliefs have not evolved to reflect women's transformed roles in their professional and family life. Women (single, married, white, BIPOC, and from every class) continue to face a lack of options about how to make it all work. Kathleen Gerson draws on interviews with Gen X and millennial children of the gender revolution that represent a broad range of racial, ethnic, and class backgrounds, whose upbringing and current lives demonstrate that "changing lives are colliding with resistant institutions" (12). She argues that their hopes and dreams for a more egalitarian family life and prosperous future expose the tensions between the ideal of gender flexibility and the constraints of gendered breadwinning and caretaking roles. Gerson notes that this tension "involves more equal sharing and more fluid boundaries for organizing and apportioning emotional, social, and economic care" (10) and fallback positions, which constitute fewer desirable options and a retreat to traditional gendered roles to offset "time-demanding workplaces, unreliable partners, and a dearth of caretaking supports" (12). As Jocelyn Elise Crowley explains, both mothers with many resources and those with too few are required to exercise personal autonomy over the structure of their work and family lives. Yet Crowley asserts that it is public decision making that truly expands and contracts the scope of agency and power that mothers have over the nature of their paid work, as well as the range of workplace flexibility options that are available to them. Most policies promised by both political parties prioritize choices for working families while conveniently overlooking constraints. As I (and others) have written elsewhere, rhetorics of choice correspond to rhetorics of individual responsibility that lead to mother blame if intractable work-life family dynamics cannot be successfully navigated by working women alone (Borda).

Before the pandemic, work-life economist Heather Boushey argued for the need to shift from an economics based on individuals to one focused on families, for "if we start with *the individual,* not the family, we don't see how the changes in the divide between time for work and time for life have affected *family* economic security" (my emphasis, 14). Not only does addressing a range of workplace flexibility and family-friendly policies affect the quality of workers' and their families' lives outside of the workplace, which has societal impacts, but it also bolsters the national economy. Boushey argues that work-life policies are crucial to ensuring economic wellbeing and that "addressing sources of anxiety *inside* the home has a profound impact on what happens *outside* the home, including in the larger economy" (2).

Perhaps in no other time in recent American history has the anxiety inside the home been more acute, or more acutely intertwined with what is happening outside the home. Helen Lewis observes that during the COVID-19 pandemic, these rhetorics of individual choice have fallen indiscriminately on women, with dire consequences, predicting that "across the world, women's independence will be a silent victim of the pandemic." Lewis explains the following:

> At an individual level, the choices of many couples over the next few months will make perfect economic sense. What do pandemic patients need? Looking after. What do self-isolating people need? Looking after. What do children kept home from school need? Looking after. All this looking after—unpaid caring labor—will fall more heavily on women, because of the existing structure of the workforce.

In just eight months, the COVID-19 pandemic has caused a measurable erosion of women's power and agency in the professional realm as a result of an economic recession combined with women's overdetermined care economies, leading to no-choice choices. The economic impacts are grim and untenable.

As of October 2020, the U.S. Bureau of Labor Statistics monthly jobs report shows merely half of the 22.2 million jobs lost due to COVID-19 have returned. Women have lost nearly 5.8 million jobs, accounting for 53.9 per cent overall (Ewing-Nelson). More troubling data now show that over 1.1 million workers left the labour force. Of those job leavers, 865,000 (80 per cent) were women, including 324,000 Latinas and 58,000 Black women (Ewing-Nelson). According to a working paper from the National Bureau of Economic Research, the current recession is tougher on women than past economic downturns. The study also reports that among the 44 per cent of married, full-time employed couples with children, mothers provide 60 per cent of the childcare. However, those hit hardest by the crisis include the fifteen million single working mothers for whom options for supplemental childcare were already lacking, resulting in an increased likelihood—and danger—of those women leaving or being pushed out of the workforce (Karageorge).

Although my own COVID-19 experience reflects my economic and racial privilege, I also have experienced the burden of navigating professional work and carework with a lack of good choices during this time. Like most Americans, the added demands of living and working during a pandemic have left me feeling exhausted and frustrated. I have spent the last eight months in a maelstrom of professional, psychological, domestic, and care labour. From March 12, 2020, onwards, I have emotionally, psychologically, and, at times financially, supported my husband, whose small physical therapy practice incurred a brief shutdown and then ongoing financial struggles due to COVID-19. Simultaneously, I oversaw my fourth-grade daughter's transition to remote learning through the spring. I also felt the relentless—and logistically impossible—burden of caring from a distance for my elderly, widowed, and cancer-survivor father, who lives four hundred miles south in a state much harder hit by COVID-19. By mid-June, my daughter's typical schedule of enrichment camps and playdates had dissolved into long, nondescript summer days. My own frazzled, summer days were split between work responsibilities and efforts to make sure she remained physically active, emotionally nourished, and socially engaged. I arranged COVID-19 bubbles and childcare swaps with a few trusted and politically likeminded friends, an exercise initially fraught with relational landmines and risk-reward equations. I rationalized that the communal rewards of emotional and moral support far outweighed the discomfort and risks.

Concurrent to all of this carework, my unrelenting, professional labour as a college professor drained me of a much-needed presence of mind, particularly as I served as department chair through July, witnessing the pandemic-induced higher education crisis firsthand. Summer months involved hybrid course planning and concern about how our university could possibly reopen and how that decision would affect faculty, staff, contingent employees, and all of our families (especially the most vulnerable among us). By August, my energy had shifted to the battles being waged in our small, rural community regarding remote learning vs. in-person school. I agonized over how we could possibly choose when all of the choices seemed equally bad. Indeed, all choices a mother, or a family, may make (whether private tutor, co-op homeschool, nanny, or remote pods) correlated to enhanced feelings of guilt about perpetuating existing inequalities, anxiety about how to keep our children both safe and educated, struggles to manage outsized work-family obligations, and general resentment over how each of these individual choices felt as if they also undermine communitarian solutions.

Infectious disease physician and public health researcher, Dharushana Muthulingham, accurately describes the precarity of the present socioeconomic situation for mothers in a *New York Times* interview: Women are the "shock absorbers of our system, and the poorer and more precarious you are, the more shock you're expected to absorb" (qtd. in Grose). Women's employment is more concentrated in industry sectors greatly affected by the crisis (retail, service, hospitality, and healthcare) as well as those considered essential jobs (e.g., grocery store workers, health aids, and teachers). Even prepandemic, gig economy workers doing "precarious work—part-time and temporary, independent contractor work—increased dramatically for both men and women" (Kessler-Harris qtd. in Scutts), but the proportion of women is double that of men, and often mothers are responsible for the care of small children

All of the challenges that working women and mothers faced prepandemic—including the gender wage gap, gender segregated jobs, the double binds of women's leadership, job instability, the mommy penalty, the domestic chore burden, and the demands of intensive motherhood—have been exacerbated by the now completely unsustainable integration of professional obligations and immense childcare needs. The Women in the Workplace 2020 report reveals the following:

> As a result of these dynamics, more than one in four women are contemplating what many would have considered unthinkable just six months ago: downshifting their careers or leaving the workforce completely. This is an emergency for corporate America. Companies risk losing women in leader-ship—and future women leaders—and unwinding years of painstaking progress toward gender diversity.

These accumulated liabilities for women, as well as the attendant consequences for women's mental health and wellbeing, are exposing the fissures of an economic system built on several centuries worth of gender exploitation—a system never built to last.

Reimaginings: A Movement for Gender, Human Equality, Labour, and Love

The COVID-19 pandemic has shown that even the reality of women's equal representation in the U.S. labour force will not alter gender inequalities unless economic and business policies are reframed to reflect the realities of workers' lives and livelihoods. A twenty-first-century movement for feminist equality requires a reimagined economy that works for everyone and for all families, equally. Rather than rhetoric upholding profits over people, politics over people, and political freedom over the public good, we need to refashion our economic policies around the value of all people who work. As Alice Kessler-Harris has proposed, we should be "asking for fair human rights, what the Swedish call jämställdhet—a concept that imagines not just women equal to men, but gender equality as the basis for human equality" (quoted in Scutts). We need to design intersectional economic policies that accommodate a diverse and profitable workforce constituted across gender, socioeconomic classes, race/ ethnicity, sexuality, changing family structures, and differing demands for household and caregiving labour.

If human equality is the goal, whose stories do we need to be listening to during this economic and public health crisis? How do we shift the conversation from personal responsibility and individual choices to collective decisions made for the public good and to an economy that ensures the collective health of the nation? Perhaps the exigence of an economy that cannot get back to work without the work of women will call forth a new and inclusive structural paradigm featuring gender flexibility in both the workplace and the home. We no longer need to find a place for women in the world of work, as women have been reshaping the workforce for decades. Transforming workplaces for the postpandemic economy must centre egalitarianism as the paradigm to address all other inequalities. Already, the revitalized women's movement has begun to integrate a labour-feminist agenda. As Dorothy Sue Cobble explains, "The burdens that once bore down largely on working-class women—long hours, the incompatibility of parenting and employment, the lack of societal support for caring labor—are increasingly the problems of everyone, and the women's movement has given these issues top priority" (227). These problems have become front and centre during the pandemic. Now, we must collectively build a feminist economic coalition focused on social justice, diversity, equity, inclusion, labour, and love (caretaking).

We already know what works: Women's participation in the workforce increases, alongside profits, when male and female workers of all races, and those across income brackets, can access affordable childcare, paid leave, flextime, and telework arrangements. This is the economic reality, but the benefits exceed the economics. By integrating family-friendly benefits, we strengthen families by improving financial security, boosting employee morale and retention, reducing the needs for welfare, closing the gender wage gap, and reducing long-term health costs (Boushey). The problem is, as a nation, we have continued to devise economic policies based on rhetoric, ideals, and values that are divorced from reality. In the U.S., in particular, the political rhetoric of family values, dating from the 1970s, has not promoted politics or policies that truly value families—we have instead initiated policies based on an imaginary traditionally gendered, nuclear family ideal without recognizing the realities and costs of truly loving and caring for one another.

There are some promising signs that the rhetoric is starting to shift to reflect the reality of Americans' economic and care needs. U.S. President-elect Joe Biden released his "Plan for Mobilizing American Talent and Heart to Create a 21st Century Caregiving and Education Workforce" in September 2020. Biden's plan proposes the following: "If we truly want to reward work in this country, we have to ease the financial burden of care that families are carrying, and we have to elevate the compensation, benefits, training and education opportunities for certification, and dignity of caregiving workers and educators." The plan prioritizes the value of caregiving, economic contributions of careworkers, and the demands on families facing a caregiver crisis, both during the pandemic and in its aftermath. The plan would be revolutionary for the U.S., which has infamously ranked as one of only three of the world's richest countries to lack paid family leave policies (Livingston and Thomas). Significantly, the Biden plan recognizes that for families "caregiving decisions [come] with great financial, professional, physical, and emotional costs," that those providing outsourced care are disproportionally women of colour, and that those who are socioeconomically insecure "have been underpaid, unseen, and undervalued far too long."

Bolstering such a platform are a number of intersectional coalitions of activists working to address workplace justice and workplaces that work for families, including Paid Leave for All, the Center for Equitable Growth, and Family Values @ Work. Other organizations are forming the foundation for a united mothers' movement, including MomsRising, Mocha Moms, and Mothers and More. For example, Jocelyn Crowley highlights the work of the activist group MomsRising, which "started placing greater emphasis on issues that have wider appeal to racial minorities and those experiencing financial vulnerability … [including] paid family leave, paid sick days, family economic security, and ending hiring and wage discrimination against mothers of color" (187). The U.S. House of Representatives recently launched Democrats Organizing for Working Families, and the socialist-democratic movements, arising from Occupy Wall Street, as well as Bernie Sanders supporters have begun to address issues of workplace justice. At a broader level, political platforms, such as the Green New Deal, show momentum towards "involving the entire citizenry in the shared project of adapting to the 21st century" by materially improving the lives of the poor and working class through rebalancing "the economy and political system" and moving "away from a monomaniacal focus on private good, toward a more generous view of public goods and public purpose" (Roberts). Carework must be prioritized as a public good and considered and theorized as an essential part of our economic infrastructure.

Conclusion

Political theorist Kathi Weeks writes: "The problem with work is not just that it monopolizes so much time and energy, but that it also dominates the social and political imaginaries." Weeks then asks, "How might we conceive the content and parameters of our obligations to one another outside the currency of work?" (36). Such a question addresses both the politics of race and class while highlighting how the futures of women, work, and working families are embedded in social justice movements. The COVID-19 pandemic has highlighted problems across all spheres of life, affecting people in every class, race, and gender; it has strained the public health system and further impoverished both labour and love in the form of human-centred carework that sustains both communities and economies. Yet the costs and sacrifices of the pandemic, both human and economic, expose that the safety and protection of both are interwoven. Until we prioritize responsibilities to one another alongside the responsibilities of work and economic growth, we will continue to undermine our own survival.

Beginning with the Women's March in 2017, we have seen evidence of intersecting and intersectional coalitions of feminist activists working on a wide range of issues, including racial justic, equal pay, reproductive justice, sexual harassment and discrimination, climate change, and relief for working families. Glenn writes: "The possibilities of struggling together toward something more beautiful, more humane, fill me with hope" (206). She concludes that feminists and rhetoricians have a shared goal—"to articulate a vision of hope and expectation" (212). The feminist progress being made in the coalition of work-life activists, twenty-first-century mothers' movements, and social democrats fill me with feminist hope and the promise of a more just future for American workers, their families, and their wellbeing. The confluence of work-life issues as embedded in the COVID-19 crisis discloses that we cannot address solitary problems one at a time. Solidarity must inform a diverse and inclusive movement to collectively create a new feminist future focused on labour and love.

Works Cited

Borda, Jennifer. "Lean In or Leave Before You Leave? False Dichotomies of Choice and Blame in Public Debates about Working Motherhood." *The Mother-Blame Game*, edited by Vanessa Reimer and Sarah Sahagian, Demeter Press, 2015, pp. 219-34.

Boushey, Heather. *Finding Time: The Economics of Work-Life Conflict*. Harvard, 2016.

Cobble, Dorothy Sue. *The Other Women's Movement: Workplace Justice and Social Rights in Modern America*. Princeton University Press, 2004.

Collins, Patricia Hill. *Black Feminist Thought: Knowledge, Consciousness, and the Politics of Empowerment*. Second Edition. Routledge, 2014.

Crittenden, Ann. *The Price of Motherhood*. Holt, 2001.

Crowley, Jocelyn Elise. *Mothers Unite!: Organizing for Workplace Flexibility and the Transformation of Family Life*. Cornell University, 2013.

Davis, Dána-Ain. *Reproductive Injustice: Racism, Pregnancy, and Premature Birth*. New York University Press, 2019.

Ewing-Nelson, Claire. "Four Times More Women Than Men Dropped Out of the Labor Force in September." *National Women's Law Center Fact Sheet*, Oct. 2020, nwlc.org/wp-content/uploads/2020/10/september-jobs-fsl.pdf. Accessed 3 Jan. 2021.

Gerson, Kathleen. *The Unfinished Revolution: Coming of Age in a New Era of Gender, Work, and Family*. Oxford University, 2010.

Ginsburg, Ruth Bader. "Ruth Bader Ginsburg's Advice for Living." *New York Times*, 16 Oct. 2016, nyti.ms/2dtHcrW. Accessed 3 Jan. 2021.

Glenn, Cheryl. *Rhetorical Feminism and This Thing Called Hope*. Southern Illinois University Press, 2018.

Glynn, Sarah Jane. "Breadwinning Mothers Continue to Be the U.S. Norm," *Center for American Progress*, 10 May 2019, www.american progress.org/issues/women/reports/2019/05/10/469739/breadwinning -mothers-continue-u-s-norm/. Accessed 3 Jan 2021.

Grose, Jessica. "Mothers Are the 'Shock Absorbers' of Our Society." *New York Times*, 14 Oct. 2020, nyti.ms/2SZBrFb. Accessed 3 Jan. 2021.

Hallstein, Lynn O'Brien. "What Do Mothers Need?: Not To Give Up on Their Own Ambitions and Persistence in Securing Partner Participation in Family Life." *What Do Mothers Need? Motherhood Activists and Scholars Speak Out on Maternal Empowerment for the 21st Century*, edited by Andrea O'Reilly, Demeter, 2012, pp. 185-201.

Hays, Sharon. *The Cultural Contradictions of Motherhood*. Yale University, 1996.

Hesse-Biber, Sharlene Nagy, and Gregg Lee Carter. *Working Women in America: Split Dreams*. Oxford University, 2005.

Hirshman, Linda R. *Get to Work: A Manifesto for Women of the World*. Viking, 2006.

Hochschild, Arlie R. *The Time Bind: When Work Becomes Home and Home Becomes Work*. New York: Henry Holt, 1997.

Karageorge, Eleni X. "COVID-19 Recession Is Tougher on Women." *Monthly Labor Review, Bureau of Labor Statistics*, Sept. 2020, www.bls.gov/opub/mlr/2020/beyond-bls/pdf/covid-19-recession-is-tougher-on-women.pdf. Accessed 3 Jan. 2021.

Kasmir, Sharryn. "Precarity." *The Cambridge Encyclopedia of Anthropology*, edited by Felix Stein, Cambridge, 13 Mar, 2018, http://doi.org/10.29164/18precarity. Accessed 13 Jan. 2021.

Lewis, Helen. "The Coronavirus is a Disaster for Feminism." *The Atlantic*, 19 Mar 2020, www.theatlantic.com/international/archive/2020/03/feminism-womens-rights-coronavirus-covid19/608302/. Accessed 3 Jan. 2021.

Livingston, Gretchen and Deja Thomas, "Among 41 Countries, Only U.S. Lacks Paid Parental Leave," *Pew Research Center*, 16 Dec, 2019, pewrsr.ch/2dmpMug. Accessed 14 Jan. 2021.

Miller, Claire Cain. "'I'm Only One Human Being': Parents Brace for a Go-It-Alone School Year." *New York Times*, 8 Sept. 2020, nyti.ms/2Q42alV. Accessed 3 Jan. 2021.

Morgan, Danielle Fuentes. "Visible Black Motherhood is a Revolution." *Biography*, vol. 41, no. 4, 2018, pp. 856-75.

Nash, Jennifer. "The Political Life of Black Motherhood." *Feminist Studies*, vol. 44, no. 3, 2018, pp. 699-712.

"Plan for Mobilizing American Talent and Heart to Create a 21st Century Caregiving and Education Workforce." *Joe Biden for President Official Campaign Website*, 2020, joebiden.com. Accessed 3 Jan. 2021.

Ridgeway, Cecilia. *Framed By Gender: How Gender Inequality Persists in the Modern World*. Oxford University, 2011.

Roberts, David. "The Green New Deal, Explained." *Vox*, 20 Mar. 2019, www.vox.com/energy-and-environment/2018/12/21/18144138/green-new-deal-alexandria-ocasio-cortez. Accessed 3 Jan. 2021.

Rottenberg, Catherine. *The Rise of Neoliberal Feminism*. Oxford University Press, 2018.

Shah, Sonia. "It's Time to Tell a New Story About Coronavirus—Our Lives Depend on It." *The Nation*, 14 July 2020, www.thenation.com/article/society/pandemic-definition-covid/. Accessed 3 Jan. 2021.

Slaughter, Anne-Marie. *Unfinished Business: Women, Men, Work, Family*. Random House, 2013.

Swinth, Kirsten. *Feminism's Forgotten Fight: The Unfinished Struggle for Work and Family*. Harvard University, 2018.

Weeks, Kathi. *The Problem with Work: Feminism, Marxism, Antiwork Politics, and Postwork Imaginaries*. Duke University, 2011.

Williams, Joan. *Unbending Gender: Why Family and Work Conflict and What to Do About It*. Oxford University, 2000.

Williams, Joan. *Reshaping the Work-Family Debate: Why Men and Class Matter*. Harvard University Press, 2010.

Williams, Joan. "Jumpstarting the Stalled Gender Revolution: Justice Ginsburg and Reconstructive Feminism," *Hastings Law Journal* vol. 63, no. 1267, 2012, pp. 1267-1296.

Chapter Seven

Pink Tax: How COVID-19 Inadvertently Became a Field Experiment to Test Gender (In)justice in South Asia

Saba Karim Khan

I'm a doctor, a dog-lover, a mother, an aging tree buckling under the weight of the fruit it bears. An activist too. I embrace all those titles. But mostly, I'm an apologist, a "guilty feminist."

—Laila, intervieweel

It's close to midnight when I'm speaking to Laila over a metallic computer screen; she has a baby wreathed around her bosom, silhouetted against a distracting Zoom background detailing some far-off galaxy. Each of us is silently hoping the kids sleep through the interview, despite the audible confessions of two guilty feminists streaming through the corridor. Laila appears weary but dogged; her eyes haven't lost their sparkle. She's invested in our conversation, despite how COVID-19 has upended her life. We talk about nature and how it represents healing and mediates birth and death. We bring up nature most of all because the miracle of creating a life within a life, as a result of comingling, is borne by women.

The image of a woman—much like a tree, with her roots entrenched firmly in the soil—arches beneath the horizon as those around her carry on savoring the glorious summer afternoon. She is pathos ridden and powerful—an adjunct to male demands and desires. The scene of the woman and her surroundings could be biblical or perhaps a space odyssey. I'm hooked to Laila's metaphorical prowess.

When I think about the interview later, it isn't emblematic of defeat, yet it hardly signals triumph. COVID-19 has worked as a litmus test, a reminder that the woman, much like the tree, if careworn and compelled, will eventually wither and droop. It may continue to offer healing, but the process of annihilating itself would have begun.

Figure. 1. A Facebook post I uploaded on May 28, postlockdown in the United Arab Emirates (UAE), to share the physical and emotional fallout experienced by women the world over due to the pandemic.

As a working mother of South Asian origin, based in the Arabian Gulf, with two young daughters, the patriarchal burden of the pandemic hit me firsthand. My anecdotal experience inspired an empirical inquiry into this topic, extracting personal narratives which lie at the heart of this chapter. "Pink Tax" offers South Asian women a platform to tell their story in their own voices instead of being represented by someone else. Interviewees were recruited through snowball sampling, and conversations took place virtually due to the pandemic.

Drawing on qualitative interviews with mothers of South Asian origin currently residing in Pakistan, India, the United Kingdom, and the United Arab Emirates, I examine the following questions: (1) How is COVID-19 reproducing individual and structural barriers for working mothers? Are we witnessing a patriarchal pandemic?; (2) What coping mechanisms are South Asian mothers devising to mitigate this burden?; and (3) What might an inclusionary feminist movement in South Asia look like? My sample comprises cisgender, heterosexual, and able-bodied women. Some are married, and others are divorced, and some are employed, and others are stay-at-home mothers. All have children under the age of twelve.

My data indicate that although the COVID-19 pandemic has been a social leveler in some respects, it has also peeled back layers of gender inequality. In one stroke, it has infringed upon the baby steps that feminism in South Asia had witnessed, bringing the engine of gender justice to a sudden halt. The pandemic has placed unfavourable scope conditions upon South Asian women through three sites of contestation: (1) the albatross of expectations stacked against women; (2) the glorification of maternal martyrdom; and (3) the stigma associated by labelling women "troublemakers," aiming to punish them for deviating from conventional gender norms. Subsequently, I examine microsites of interaction, social media in particular, and how they are opening windows into imagined possibilities and alternative futures for South Asian women. I conclude by critiquing cookie-cutter feminism, illustrating why South Asia needs a movement that encapsulates a syntax and vocabulary that is locally comprehensible.

The Albatross of Expectation

If gender norms in South Asia were previously skewed, the pandemic has launched and solidified new expectations for women. As we celebrate the turning of the decade by hoarding sanitizers and toilet paper, mothers the world over are folding under pressure. Yet testimonies from South Asia—as Saman, a mother of twin girls in Karachi vividly depicts—tell an even graver story:

> Not only are women working from home, [but] they are now working from home in addition to cooking, cleaning, homeschooling, and babysitting. In South Asia, since most families include in-laws, they are also looking after them and, on average, are responsible for eight to ten people—All the while dealing with reduced shop hours ... limited if any domestic help, and increasing financial strain. None of the above accounts for the cabin fever and social isolation that she [the mother] is encountering along with her kids.... We went through Ramazan during lockdown, in which the average South Asian woman spends hours toiling in the kitchen at sehri and iftar[2] while she fasts ... Add to that the general doom and gloom of 2020, the stress of surviving COVID-19, and a recession, and, God forbid, if you or a family member actually gets sick, then it's game over.

Saman's public posting illuminates how the pandemic has exacerbated the gender roles South Asian women are expected to perform. These expectations stem from the revered label of "SuperMom," seen as a badge of honour, which women in South Asia are constantly striving to achieve. The ideal South Asian woman suffers from historically misplaced expectations; she can be a Fortune 500 CEO but must remain a mother and homemaker. The "SuperMom" phenomena—now a rage in South Asian circles—posits motherhood as a rat race to outdo other mothers and secure the most accolades. The toll such pressure takes on mothers is downsized but is often captured in sentiments shared over WhatsApp, such as this image sent by Alizeh, a mother of an eleven-year-old, living in the Gulf.

Figure 2. An image shared over WhatsApp by a working mother in the UAE as the lockdown kept getting extended.

Women, however, are not always passive recipients of "supermom" trophies; often, they buy into the brainwashing. Ghazal, an educationist and a mother of three living in Pakistan and tackling postpartum depression, describes the supermom expectations she has faced during the pandemic and has conceded to tacitly accepting these expectations. In a single excerpt, she refers to "expectations" nine times:

I'm expected to wake up in the morning; I'm expected to send my kids to school; I'm expected to make breakfast for the whole family then I'm expected to give my 100 per cent at work. After I get home, I'm expected to cook for my family, then I'm expected to help my kids with their homework [laughs]. I'm basically expected to do everything.... But I feel it's a social norm that it's the woman; it's the mother who has to take care of them [kids] no matter what ... it's also the expectations we [her family] have; he [my husband] doesn't contribute much in the kitchen's work, and I don't expect him to.

Women's complicity in propelling unrealistic expectations for mothers, wives, daughters, and professionals is complex; microsites of aggression and strife combine with structural barriers—gendered social roles, discriminatory laws as well as state norms, and workplace sexism—to reproduce patriarchal categories. As a result of individual and structural hurdles, unlearning normative messaging is a tall order, requiring both individual will and institutional reform.

Laila, a South Asian mother of a two-year-old, living in a joint family and working at a research organization for a government ministry, has also embodied traditional gender expectations. Although she describes how COVID-19 has thrown her daily routine into disarray—forcing her to invent ways of mushing food into her toddler's mouth, as she tries typing on her laptop with oily fingers—she only minimally resists this new normal: "I think it's the way we grew up. It's always on the mother; the burden is always on the mother. Like I wouldn't expect, or even ask him [her husband], to change the diaper. It's also in our culture because she [their baby] is a daughter ... so that sort of responsibility is obviously on a mother."

Despite the unprecedented shock of the pandemic, few South Asian women are questioning the burden of these expectations. Living in a society that has tried to subdue feminist voices, South Asian women face an existential crisis. They navigate supermom expectations—performing duties that their husbands neglect, whilst adjusting to changing spatial structures, the last stemming from a collapse between the first and second shifts (Hochschild)—that is, between paid and domestic labour shifts—due to the COVID-19 pandemic.

Figure 3. Spatial divisions between the first and second shifts of office and home have collapsed during COVID-19, whereas homeschooling continues. Toddlers often invade workstations and mothers rely on fast food to get by. This extra work has rapidly become the norm.

Glorifying Martyrdom

Mothers have martyred themselves in their children's names since the beginning of time. We have lived as if she who disappears the most, loves the most. We have been conditioned to prove our love by slowly ceasing to exist.... If we keep passing down the legacy of martyrdom to our daughters, with whom does it end? Which woman ever gets to live? And when does the death sentence begin? At the wedding altar? In the delivery room? ... When we call martyrdom love we teach our children that when love begins, life ends. This is why Jung suggested: There is no greater burden on a child than the unlived life of a parent.

—Glennon Doyle

In place of resistance, the COVID-19 pandemic has foregrounded a particular form of martyrdom for South Asia women—a gradual effacing of the self, spurred by the acquiescence of the martyr herself. Years of socialization block pathways that resist the glorification of maternal sacrifice. Hala, a lecturer in development studies with a toddler, emphasizes how she has to be reminded during the pandemic that motherhood is not a contest: "One of my daughter's consultants told me not to become a supermom because nobody is going to give you any sort of reward, so stop being worried all the time about your daughter." Yet the road to "saying no" remains hard for women, deterring the probability of having male members perform their share of domestic tasks during the pandemic. The key question becomes, where has such stigma against speaking up come from? The answer lies in the troublemaker syndrome.

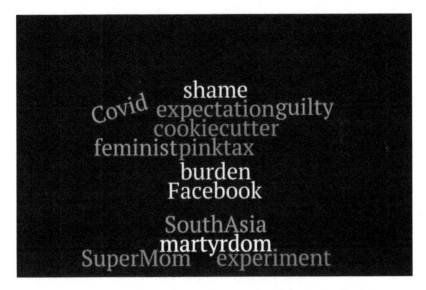

Figure 4. The word cloud above offers a linguistic snapshot of the burden on South Asian mothers during the pandemic through such labels as "supermom," which amplify the expectations, and resulting pressure, they face.

The Troublemaker Syndrome

Labels and messaging have reproduced and exalted motherhood martyrdom, which get amplified during times of crisis. In the event of a woman's deviance from this trend of sacrifice, a profound labelling of shame and blame gets attached to her. As Ghazal outlines below, any time a problem arises on the domestic front, a mother's professional ambitions are held responsible: "If I sit in a family gathering, the one thing I get to hear is 'since you're a working mother, your child is not getting the right attention,' or if I need to go out for a while, I'll hear 'since you're a working mother, you don't have the time to cook.' I hear this sentence a lot. A lot. If anything at all goes wrong, it is simply because I am a working mother."

Negative social sanctioning is not meted out to working mothers by men alone; interviewees describe how they receive criticism from other women for challenging expectations of martyrdom. Leah, an Indian mother of four, expresses frustration with female colleagues lambasting her for relying on nannies for childcare:

I returned to work after the lockdown was lifted and felt placed under a microscopic lens, awaiting judgment by three other women, the irony of it—[making me feel] guilt about leaving my children with house help. "I'd never dream of leaving my daughter alone with a maid," one of them said. "Who knows what they might do to the child. I don't believe in [spy] cameras; it's all rubbish." And then, "I know of someone whose maid spat in the child's food to take revenge from the mother. Shudder! COVID or no COVID, how can any mother be so heartless?"

Silencing South Asian women's dreams and desires has been a norm for decades. At its core, this socially constructed narrative propagates the belief that women must be without desire—sexual, professional, emotional—which reinforces the subject-object statuses associated with the sexes. The negative connotations accompanying ambitious women are real and are unfolding before us; the pandemic has illuminated these masked fault lines. Across multiple interviews, the women discussed how during the pandemic and its periods of isolation, their desires have been further clamped down upon. Disrupting this status quo induces guilt, producing the identity of the "guilty feminist." Hala reiterates how the guilt plagued her during lockdown, forcing her to perform voluminous labor under extraordinary circumstances:

Every day I used to tell myself that I have accepted this challenge, and this is a challenge for me. If I collapse, who will take care of my house and who will take care of my child? And the students, they should not suffer because of my health. They are my responsibility, and the university is paying me.... I was running around. I had no help. I had no driver, no cook, no babysitter with me. I was cleaning the house. I was washing the dishes. I was handling her [daughter] also, but I felt that she was getting ignored.... At the end of the day, I used to ask myself, "What did I actually do today? Did I achieve something? Did I do something productive? And the answer used to come back to me that, no, the day just slipped out of my hand, and I did not do anything productive.

Gatekeepers of religion and culture worsen the gender imbalance in South Asia. Women who challenge orthodoxy—for example, mothers negotiating gender roles with partners or allocating "me-time" during the crisis—quickly get labeled troublemakers. In turn, this deters women from demanding equal rights. The troublemaker badge is heavy to bear.

Other Windows, Other Worlds

Access to digital ecosystems, however, is helping women achieve their dreams and desires in South Asia. Force-fitted into claustrophobic lifestyles, South Asian women are, for the first time, gaining unobstructed access to cultures and alternative ways of being. Online platforms are providing coping mechanisms, enabling women to tap into social networks spanning across the world. The appetite for ambition is surging, as Nadia explains below:

> For most of the lockdown, I've been stuck in this tall, ancient apartment building with tiny windows. My husband hasn't allowed us to step out even for groceries. Sometimes, I would stare out of the kitchen window while preparing meals, curious to see what people might be up to outside. I realized that previously, school runs, extra tuition classes for kids, super-market trips took up so much of my time that ... even though everyone was at home, I was bored. I started spending a lot of time on Facebook after the kids went to bed. My friend invited me to join a women's group for new businesses; she assured me it was female only so I wouldn't get into trouble at home. My in-laws are very conservative. I started visiting the page daily. It was miraculous, thousands of followers on the group. So many women, so much talent: painting, sculpture, pottery, furniture. I'd been dreaming about a food business for years but couldn't muster up the courage to start. Also, my family wouldn't allow me to go out and work on it. This group, its supporters, seeing other women do it, made me finally experiment from home. I launched over the summer, and it's done wonders already.

Although widespread approval of women's aspirations remains a pipedream in South Asia, online portals offer a starting point for subverting female complicity and for instilling *imagined possibilities and alternative futures*. Through microsites of online interaction during the pandemic, South Asian mothers are expressing isolated agency, a way to counter socially constructed and hegemonic ways of "doing gender" (West and Zimmerman).

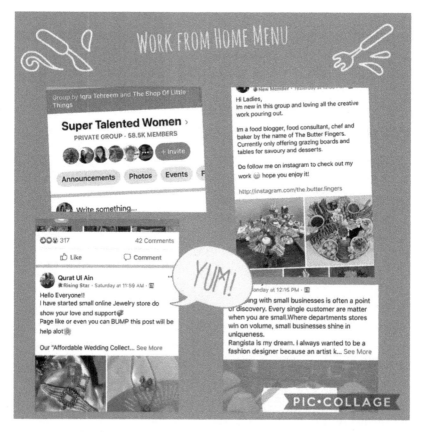

Figure 5. A Facebook group with 78,400 members that aims to support and connect women across the globe, especially female entrepreneurs.

Similar to Nadia's case, social media access during the lockdown has helped female digital entrepreneurs across a range of socioeconomic categories in South Asia. Facebook and Instagram pages for home-based enterprises are mushrooming in cities and villages, as is evident by groups such as Super Talented Women, shown in the image above, with 78.4K members. Not only do online communities such as this provide fraternal support, but they also offer avenues to forge professional identities, including revenue streams for women's financial independence while they work from home. These newfound opportunities may not represent complete parity, yet they provide a hopeful first step.

Why Cookie-Cutter Feminism is a Nonstarter

The issue of gender discrimination extends beyond the present pandemic; COVID-19 has simply exposed the glib foundations of feminism taking root in South Asia, as Zehra, a working mother of Pakistani origin, now living in London, illuminates: "It shows that the movement towards equality was based on a false foundation. The outsourcing of tasks like cleaning, cooking (think school dinners, takeaways), and childcare is what was really allowing the working mum to survive. When that infrastructure collapsed, the pressure went right back." A major obstacle for feminism in South Asia is that it gets viewed as an invasion—of male power, egos, and patriarchal tapestries. It is seen as a movement that excludes men instead of one that invites collaboration between sexes. Hala elaborates on this:

> No pandemic can bring positive change in a man. Positive changes in a man can happen through his upbringing, when his mother is inculcating social values in him as a child ... unless men realize gender equality, things will not change; the tables cannot turn. If they are willing to give liberty to their wives, if they're willing to give respect to their wives, only then will things change. If they respect the unpaid work which they do in the house, only then will things change but unfortunately, they are not willing to do so. The biggest clash in our society is that with time women have become financially independent.... They want their men to liberate them, but the men are not willing to do so. A woman who is earning but does not have a say in the decision making in the household is not empowered. I am simply going to give you my example. I am earning. I am financially independent, well off. But I don't have a say in the

decision making of my house. That means that no matter what
I do, I am not an empowered woman.

Accusations that feminism employs antimale rhetoric give the
impression that it celebrates the victory of women over men instead of
fighting for equality. Although interventions signal preliminary
progress, feminist movements erupting in South Asia often rely on
adopted models and exclusionary vocabulary—what I term "cookie-
cutter feminism." These are smoke screens, sparking ephemeral rage,
but without the efforts for real change to be sustained. It is hardly
surprising that in such a context, many in South Asia argue that only
women can be feminists (Khan).

The loss provoked by COVID-19 for mothers and mothering in
South Asia is real; the pandemic is characterized by everyday combat,
as multiple testimonies in this chapter evidence. COVID-19 has
revealed systemic failures and provoked important questions to be
asked. What was the starting gun for feminism in South Asia? Have
we already experienced its first or second wave? Are we delivering
feminist messaging in a democratic manner, reaching men and women
in remote neighbourhoods? Or are we alienating a segment of potential
allies? In our eagerness to jump on the seasonal bandwagon, have we
cloned a Western template, catapulted into an advanced stage of
feminism, one we are not prepared for and one in which we do not
necessarily offer solutions? Are we erroneously assuming people will
understand what we are saying and join our ranks?

It seems we are expecting a building to live within, without
implementing a strong foundation, which kills the spirit feminism
needs to survive. Undoubtedly, cookie-cutter feminism promises a
powerful photo-op, but it does not allow us to travel far from the
atavistic, exclusionary ideals that have defined and strengthened
patriarchy for long. Among the slate of life-lessons individuals are
learning because of the pandemic, for South Asian feminism, the move
towards fighting sexism has never been clearer. Igniting a movement
that takes aim at contexts beyond the West, which leverages the
momentum gathered elsewhere, yet does not appear blind to the
complexities and nuances lying at the heart of the South Asian
woman—that is a destination worth wandering to. Only then can we
hope for the pink tax, paid by South Asian mothers, to become a
historical artifact.

Acknowledgments

This publication was made possible by the generous support of the NYU Abu Dhabi Grants for Publication Program.

I thank NYU Abu Dhabi's Social Research and Public Policy Program Head, John O'Brien, for his support towards this grant and chapter. I also thank Museera Moghis, Gohar Khan, Saman Qureshi, Sanam Kohati, Sarah Siddiqi, Alizeh Zaidi, and Amina Ansari for their contributions towards this chapter.

Endnotes

1. Pseudonyms have been used for interviewees in places throughout the chapter to protect their anonymity
2. Sehri is the predawn meal consumed early in the morning by Muslims before fasting during the Islamic month of Ramadan, whereas Iftar is the meal eaten by Muslims after sunset during Ramadan.

Works Cited

Doyle, Glennon. *Untamed*. The Dial Press, 2020. Audiobook.

Hochschild, Arlie Russell. *The Managed Heart*. University of California Press, 2003.

Hochschild, Arlie Russell. *The Second Shift: Working Families and the Revolution at Home*. Penguin Books, 2012.

West, Candace, and Don H. Zimmerman. "Doing Gender." *Gender & Society*, vol. 1, no. 2, 1987, pp. 125-51.

Chapter Eight

When COVID-19 Hit, Our Worlds Turned Upside Down: A Feminist Antiracist Ethnographic Reflection on Postsecondary Accommodations and the Work of Disability and Carework

Elizabeth Brulé

My son, who is autistic, was attending his first year of college when the World Health Organization (WHO) announced on March 11, 2020, that the COVID-19 virus had resulted in a worldwide pandemic. As someone who is neurodiverse, attending a postsecondary educational institution where the pedagogy is oriented towards neurotypical people presented him with learning challenges. Regardless, he was doing fairly well—enjoying his classes, getting support with notetaking and assignments, and connecting with his teachers and classmates in ways he had never done before. But when COVID-19 hit, his world turned upside down.

Over the years, my son has educated me on the daily challenges he confronts as a neurodiverse person in a neurotypical world. As his mother, the carework involved in advocating for educational support—such as transcription technologies, notetaking, extended time for assignments and tests, and academic accommodations in general—has been extensive and not always forthcoming, even though the Ontario Human Rights Code mandates that postsecondary institutions provide equal and equitable access to students with disabilities. The lack of accommodations for those with physical, intellectual, mental, or sensory disabilities, especially from marginalized communities, often requires that caregivers step in. This work I call "motherwork" or "caregiver" work.[1] Although I am in a privileged position as a postsecondary educator and have had the ability to provide my son with extensive educational, emotional, and social support, as a single mother working full time, I was not prepared for the pandemic. When COVID-19 hit, my world turned upside down.

This dispatch is an ethnographic reflection from a feminist anti-racist perspective on how the work of disability and caregiver work has been socially organized around ableist and Eurocentric educational practices (Battiste; Davis and Craven; Smith). While seemingly a result of COVID-19, I argue that the remote learning practices that were put into place are indicative of an ableist, Eurocentric educational framework, which has long been entrenched in postsecondary educational institutions. Moreover, this framework has relied on the work of caregivers, primarily mothers and the 2SLGBTQ+ community—work that has been exacerbated by school closures due to COVID-19.[2] Drawing on my experience working with my son, my community, and my students, as well as students' public accounts on Reddit, I attend to the ways in which postsecondary institutional practices and policies have influenced the social organization and the social relations of this work.[3]

When COVID-19 Hit, Our Worlds Turned Upside Down

On Wednesday, March 11, 2020, my son and I attended the sold-out opening night and reception of the twenty-year-anniversary celebration of the Kingston Canadian Film Festival. That evening, the WHO declared the COVID-19 virus a global pandemic. The following day the film festival was cancelled, and the City of Kingston declared a state of emergency, as did the province of Ontario and the Canadian federal government. On Friday, March 15, 2020, Queen's University cancelled all its classes and advised all students living in residence to return home. St. Lawrence College followed suit. We were on lockdown. Two weeks later, postsecondary institutions throughout the provinces had pivoted to remote course delivery.

Reviewing my journal entries of events that followed seems somewhat surreal. Justifications for closing our educational institutions to reduce transmission between students, staff, and faculty made complete sense, and measures to ensure that all students were able to participate in a physically safe environment through remote learning also made sense. What did not make sense, however, were the educational practices of a remote delivery model that would be put into place for the fall term, 2020.

At Queen's University, the Centre of Teaching and Learning provided much needed support to help professors pivot to remote delivery. And the speed with which they were able to do so is commendable—tutorials on how to use online synchronous platforms, such as ZOOM, Teams, and our OnQ platform, provided my colleagues and me with an enormous amount of support and relief as many of us were unfamiliar with remote teaching. This said, future technological resources and training emphasized an asynchronous model of course delivery. Software, such as Rise and Camtasia, was introduced and mounted on our OnQ platform to help facilitate asynchronous delivery, and closed captioning, while not initially available, was provided. Resources for state-of-the-art video recording equipment along with funds for newly hired staff to train faculty were made readily available to all departments. Providing increased support and resources for students with learning disabilities—such as attention deficit hyperactivity disorder (ADHD), autism spectrum disorder (ASD), as well as physical disabilities, like blindness and deafness—seemed, however to be an afterthought, and, for the most part, support was not forthcoming.

Following the shutdown, I dedicated Sunday evenings and Monday mornings (and then Fridays) to helping my son decipher his upcoming week's assignments, tests, and scheduling of various online tasks—all of which required an enormous amount of time. Prior to COVID-19, staff in the accommodation office at his institution provided much of this support work. Extended time and a separate location for in-class tests, the transcription of lecture material and/or the use of notetakers, along with the explication of assignments were just some of the practical support provided. When his school shutdown, this support disappeared overnight. Fortunately, I was able to fill in this gap (to varying degrees), and over the next few weeks, I helped my son muddle through to finish the term.

Over the summer months, my email inbox was inundated with messages of upcoming workshops on the "how-tos" of remote teaching in preparation for the fall term: how to mount a quality asynchronous online course, how to mount online discussion boards, and how to incorporate online asynchronous quizzes, to name just a few. While asynchronous models of delivery may have met a utilitarian function, providing service to the large number of students who are arguably neurotypical, students with learning disabilities, such as ADHD and autism have struggled, as have students whose learning is relationally driven. The push for an asynchronous delivery model was justified in terms of allowing the largest number of students to participate due to varying time zones, family situations, and access to technology and the internet. And though the use of accessibility software, such as speech-to-text technology, made class material more accessible to some students with disabilities (Harris), the lack of external structures, external supports, and familial relations made access more difficult for others (Zender).

Online learning is challenging for most people, but it poses particular challenges for those with ADHD or autism. As Cady Stanton, who coaches people with ADHD and autism, states:

The problem is that we need structure and if we have ADHD or we have autism, we tend not to have as much of the internal structure—the internal regulation, which we typically call executive function—as someone might otherwise. So you really need those external structures, those external supports in place to help you be successful. If you're online...it's going to be way easier to procrastinate. It's going to be more difficult to stay focused and to stay on task. And it's also going to be more difficult to organize and plan your day. (qtd. in Zender 2)

As Stanton points out, everyone can experience executive function challenges, but those with ADHD or autism tend to have more challenges and need extra support. As she further points out, one of the challenges that online learning poses is that it is difficult to ask professors for support. The individualized nature of the present system for accommodations relies on those with disabilities to do the work of disability—that is, to contact educators to get the support and accommodations they need. Not only is reaching out challenging for someone with autism or ADHD, but it also relies on self-disclosure in a very ableist environment, which only serves to foster the stereotype that the disabled do not "fit in" and are "un-able" to follow the rules (Titchkosky). This previous fall term, I watched my son struggle to request extra time for assignments and tests from his professors, only to have such requests refused time and again—even with a letter of accommodation from the disability office. The frustration and emotional toll that the work of accommodation requires of disabled students is extensive and exhausting. As a mother, witnessing the impact of this work on my son is heartbreaking.

Since COVID-19, this situation has worsened (Langille and Kannen), requiring an increase in advocacy work by caregivers to insist that accommodations be provided. The advocacy work of caregivers, typically mothers and the 2SLGBTQ+ community, requires time and patience as well as knowledge about the institutional legal requirements to accommodate those with a disability. For caregivers and students from Black, Indigenous, and people of colour (BIPOC) communities, time and patience can wear thin with an institutional system that is at once racist, ableist, and Eurocentric (Henry et al.) The rate of disability for Indigenous peoples in Canada is twice that of the non-Indigenous population (Hahmann, Badets, and Huges). This, combined with limited resources, poverty, remote location, and lack of internet connectivity and transportation for those on reservations, only add to the challenges facing Indigenous peoples with disabilities.

Despite the adoption of a universal design for learning model (UDL)—which advocates for multiple means of representation, action, expression, and engagement to ensure the broadest access to learning for all students (Bradford, Brown, and Cocking)—postsecondary institutional recommendations in Ontario continue to advocate for an asynchronous model of remote learning. This model has posed serious problems not just for students with learning disabilities but the student population in general. Since classes resumed in September 2020, several of my students have reported increasing levels of loneliness, disaffection, and general malaise. Matthew Mellon, the commissioner of external affairs for the Alma Mater Society of Queen's University, released a recent brief on the Fall 2020 undergraduate academic experience. The brief outlines the following challenges that students experienced during the remote fall term:

- Students are overwhelmed by course instructors that assign several small assignments;
- Some course instructors have drastically increased the volume of work assigned;
- Engagement and interactivity are lacking due to asynchronous courses;
- Synchronous office hours can be inaccessible;
- Disparities between platforms being used can cause confusion for students;
- There are concerns around whether students are meeting their program's required learning outcomes;
- Feedback is a necessity ahead of the Winter Term. (Mellon 1-2)

Dr. Rina Gupta, director of counselling, Student Wellness Services at Queen's University, has echoed these concerns. She outlines how students are finding it exceedingly difficult to stay on task and organize their work. The loss of class structure through asynchronous remote teaching has also contributed to a lack of motivation and increased difficulty in completing assignments. For students with accommodations, the situation is dire. As Dr. Gupta states:

We are hearing that students who have LOAs [Letters of Accommodations] via QSAS [Queen's Student Accommodation Services] feel that the request for accommodation is poorly received by professors and they feel a sense of judgement. They are being told things like "COVID times are hard for all students, it's normal and your accommodations don't apply in these circumstances." (1)

Rather than take up this issue as a systemic problem that needs to be addressed with all faculty across all departments and the university community in general, Dr. Gupta makes the following suggestion: "If students are registered with QSAS, they can copy their QSAS advisor when they communicate with instructors so the advisor can take it up with the professor if there are questions" (2). While arguably sound advice, it is, nonetheless, an individualized solution, which requires that students approach each professor to request that their accommodations be respected and upheld. Students with mental health conditions are also in dire need of support. Dr. Gupta adds the following: "Students with pre-existing mental health conditions seem to be struggling more than their counterparts. Anxiety is worsening, depression is deepening, eating disorders and obsessive compulsive tendencies are resulting in more severe presentations. This all can affect one's ability to perform academically" (2). These reports highlight the individualized accommodation framework that students with disabilities engage with and its reliance on the work of the disabled and caregivers to meet their diverse pedagogical needs.

Student Comments on Reddit

Prior to COVID-19, demands for campus mental health services nationwide was at an all-time high, with mental illness reaching crisis proportions (Nichols and Lewington). As Naomi Nichols and Sarah Lewington report: "One in five Canadian post-secondary students are depressed, anxious or experiencing mental health difficulties, including thoughts of suicide" (2). With the onset of the COVID-19 pandemic, mental health and accommodation issues among students throughout the postsecondary sector continue to rise requiring increases in accommodation resources and services (Hawkins and Wright).[4] For those students with mental health challenges, getting accommodations can be even more difficult. Recently, while perusing students' online posts on Reddit. I came across a plethora of comments by Queen's University students on their online learning experience since the onset of COVID-19.[5] The following posts highlight the multitude of mental health and accommodation issues that students are presently contending with.

One post generated over thirty responses on the Reddit thread, "Does Queen's Just Not Give a Sh..t about Mental Health?" In response, one post reads:

> Accessibility services is awesome but they do not have control over other departments handling of accessibility issues. I am a student with a disability and I am absolutely disgusted with how little most departments know about accessibility policies, even the simplest one.... I know staff are busy, but I have been trying for close to two years to get answers. I thought universities were mandated to accommodate. (Fabulous Fab Friendship)

Another post under the same thread reads:

> Everything is harder now. Just getting up is difficult. Going to school, you get up and go to a class, you have a schedule. That helps you keep on top of things. But now, I have no schedule and there is no structure. When I attended classes, I was able to stay on top of things. Even if you were a disorganized person, you would fall into line. Would anyone purposely miss a test? No, but with COVID it is easy to do because there is no structure and if you have a learning disability or mental health issue it is even worse. (foxtail)

The worsening mental health crisis of postsecondary students is best reflected under the following thread: "Everything I Loved about University Is Gone and I Feel Like I'm Failing." This thread generated over seventeen comments by students, healthcare providers, and parents alike—illustrating how concerned everyone is for the wellbeing of our children, friends, and students. And while the institutional response has been empathetic, the resources needed to respond to the pedagogical, economic, social and mental health needs of our students are not forthcoming. The post reads:

> Sorry if this is a mess, I've spent the last half hour sobbing in bed. I don't even know where to start. My favourite libraries on campus are closed, and I miss lectures so, so much. I hate all my classes even though some of them are things I usually love. I took an online course last year and struggled so much that I

told myself I wouldn't waste money on another online course but here we are. Beginning of the semester I was so so excited to go back even with everything online, and then I ended up having to drop a course because I couldn't spend 10 hours reading through what was supposed to be 3 hours of lectures. I was ready to work hard because I started to be sure I wanted to study medicine and I really thought that I could do well enough in undergrad that I would get in but now I feel like a I can't and I don't know what else to do. (Rant/TLC needed).

Of the seventeen responses to this student's call for help, ten suggest that she go home (if possible) to spend time with her mother, dog, and best friend for care and support. Others provide antidotes to their care regime, sharing their stories on how to get institutional support and providing university resources and contact information for emergency counselling services. What these students' comments highlight is the ongoing struggle that the present framework of accommodation poses, especially during the COVID-19 crisis

This individualized framework of accommodation is further illustrated in the comments below, with students having to contend with their professors on a one-to-one basis. Students commented on the unreasonable workloads and professors' expectations when the fall term moved to remote instruction. They cited excessive hours of asynchronous and synchronous lectures, and which required excessive amounts of weekly readings, assignments, and blackboard discussion posts. Moreover, the lack of compassion and care exhibited by some professors is well depicted in the thread "Support for Struggling Students" and in the following post: "The professors this year, amidst a pandemic and amidst financial woes for many (something which the school has stayed majorly silent in addressing) have asserted a much tougher position this year. The amount of weekly activities we're given in this online setting is so far beyond what our normal class workload would be" (LOOTER). Another post in response to this thread reads:

As a senior student, the faculty should be absolutely ashamed of how they have handled the transition to online. I've studied here for multiple years and "earned my stripes" and I've never seen such callous disregard for the wellbeing of students as displayed during this academic year. Professors are, as Looter pointed out, ramping up the workload and associated grading components in a careless as well as arbitrary manner. (Boxer-micks)

As stated earlier, negotiating academic accommodations is an individualized process and requires an enormous amount of a student's time and effort, including the work involved in demonstrating their eligibility for accommodations. Add this to the unequal power relations between students and their professors and you have a very inequitable system.

All of these responses are indicators of the caregiving work that students engage in to help themselves and one another cope with their mental health and disabilities in an ableist Eurocentric educational system that is fraught with systemic racism (Bueckert; Henry et al.). Katherine Breward, an associate professor at the University of Winnipeg and a disability accommodation specialist, argues that universities must take responsibility to accommodate and address these students' needs beyond the pandemic, but as she states: "When there's a lot of high-priority problems, the historical reality is that the more marginalized the population, the lower priority their problems tend to be" (qtd. in Harris 10).

Conclusion

These comments are limited in terms of their capacity to illustrate the wider effects of COVID-19 on students' learning experiences. Nonetheless, they draw our attention to the structural inequalities that those with physical, intellectual, mental, or sensory disabilities contend with in order to simply participate in postsecondary education. Future research that addresses the intersectional aspects of disability with race, class, sexual orientation, and gender is needed. This said, a lot can be done in the short term. Reaching out to our students who are struggling, providing them with alternative options for online assignments and exams, and allowing them to participate in multiple formats both synchronously and asynchronously to ensure accessibility and, ultimately, student success is the least we can do. Though remote teaching during the COVID-19 pandemic is complicated, students with disabilities and mental health challenges must be provided with the broadest consideration for accommodations. As a mother, feminist and anti-racist educator, and social justice advocate, I believe it is time we move away from the individualized framework of accommodations and adopt one that provides alternatives for all learners to access, as well as participate and progress in, our educational institutions. Equally important is the need to move beyond the limited Eurocentric and racialized understandings of what constitutes knowledge acquisition and expand our pedagogical approaches to teaching and learning. The structural inequality of accommodation is a systemic problem that can be changed. COVID-19 is shining a light on the path forwards.

Endnotes

1. I use the term "caregiver" to disrupt the heteronormative cisgender assumptions of the work of caring and to acknowledge the work of the two-spirit, lesbian, gay, trans and queer plus (2S-LGBTQ+) community.

2. See Kate Power on the increased care burden of women and their families since the COVID-19 pandemic and Zamira Duraku and Mirjeta Nagavci on the impact of the COVID-19 pandemic on the education of children with disabilities.

3. Feminist institutional ethnographer, Dorothy E. Smith, uses the term "work" to examine both the formal and informal ways in which we engage in labour. "Work" in this sense is generous and includes anything that "people do that takes effort and time, that they mean to do, that relies on definite resources, and is organized to coordinate in some way with the work of others" (46).

4. See Thomas Hawkins and James Wright's overview of a survey they conducted of students' challenges with remote learning this past fall semester at Memorial University.

5. Several other students' posts referred in equal measure to their respective institutions, but because I work at Queen's, I thought I would highlight those that resonate with my own students' experiences. That said, examples can be found across the provinces in terms of student online commentary on their experiences since the onset of COVID-19.

Work Cited

Battiste, Marie, editor. *Reclaiming Indigenous Voice and Vision*. University of British Columbia Press, 2000.

Boxermick. "Does Queen's Just Not Give a Sh..t about Mental Health?" *Reddit*, 19 Nov. 2020, www.reddit.com/r/queensuniversity/comments/jtpwcu/does_queens_just_not_give_a_shit_about_mental/. Accessed 01 Dec. 2020.

Bradford, John D., Ann L. Brown, and Rodney R. Cocking. *How People Learn: Brain, Mind Experience, and School.* National Academy Press, 2000.

Bueckert, Kate. "Tuition, Online Learning and Mental Health Big Concerns for This Fall, Post-Secondary Students Say: Concerns of BIPOC Students Must Be Part of Any Plan to Help Universities and Colleges, MPP Says." *CBC Kitchener-Waterloo*, 24 Aug. 2020, www.cbc.ca/news/canada/kitchener-waterloo/university-college-education-covid-19-stress-finances-1.5697981. Accessed 01 Dec. 2020.

Davis, Dána-Ain, and Christa Craven. *Feminist Ethnography: Thinking through Methodologies, Challenges, and Possibilities.* Rowman and Littlefield Publishers, 2016.

Fabulous Fab Friendship. "Support for Struggling Students." *Reddit*, 19 Nov. 2020. www.reddit.com/r/queensuniversity/comments/jt16f0/support_for_struggling_students/.compact. Accessed 1 Dec. 2020.

Foxtail. "Does Queen's Just Not Give a Sh..t about Mental Health?" Reddit, 19 Nov. 2020, www.reddit.com/r/queensuniversity/comments/jtpwcu/does_queens_just_not_give_a_shit_about_mental/. Accessed 29 Nov. 2020.

Gupta, Rina. "Background Document, Director of Counselling, Student Wellness Services." Queen's University, 7 Oct. 2020. Internal Document.

Hamann, Tara, Nadine Badets, and Jeffrey Huges. "Aboriginal Peoples Survey: Indigenous People with Disabilities in Canada: First Nations People Living Off Reserve, Métis and Inuit Aged 15 Years and Older." *Statistics Canada*, 12 Dec. 2019, www.150.statcan.gc.ca/n1/en/catalogue/89-653-X2019005. Accessed 1 Dec. 2020.

Harris, Sherina. "It Took a Pandemic to Prove What Students with Disabilities Wanted for Years Is Possible: Schools' Responses to the COVID-19 Pandemic Shows Online Learning Is Possible—But Students with Disabilities Still Need Additional Support." *Huffington Post*, 24 Aug. 2020, www.huffingtonpost.ca/entry/covid-student-disability_ca_5f3ad4cfc5b670ab17ae9538. Accessed 11 Nov. 2020.

Hawkins, Thomas and James Wright. "More Activities Than Time: Students' Challenges with Remote Learning Fall 2020 Semester."

Centre for Innovation in Teaching and Learning (CITL), Memorial University. 23 Nov. 2020, citl.mun.ca/Student_experience_survey_report.pdf. Accessed 30 Nov. 2020.

Henry, Frances, et al. *The Equity Myth: Racialization and Indigeneity at Canadian Universities.* UBC Press, 2017.

Langille, Aaron, and Victoria Kannen. "Profs Teaching Online Need to Focus on Increasing Their Compassion toward Students: What the Rapid Shift to Remote Delivery Has Shown Us about the Value of Compassion." *University Affairs.* 16 Nov. 2020, www.universityaffairs.ca/career-advice/career-advice-article/profs-teaching-online-need-to-focus-on-increasing-their-compassion-toward-students/. Accessed 30 Nov. 2020

Looter. "Support for Struggling Students" *Reddit*, 19 Nov. 2020, www.reddit.com/r/queensuniversity/comments/jt16f0/support_for_struggling_students/.compact. Accessed 30 Nov. 2020

Mellon, Matthew. *Brief on Fall 2020 Undergraduate Academic Experience.* Queen's University Alma Matter Society Student Government, 2020. d3n8a8pro7vhmx.cloudfront.net/ousa/pages/2006/attachments/original/1605882851/Responding_to_COVID-19_Brief_2020_brief.pdf?1605882851. Accessed 02 Dec. 2020.

Nichols, Naomi, and Sarah Lewington. "The Work of Being Well on Campus: An Institutional Ethnography." *Journal of Youth Studies*, May 2020, pp. 1-19. https://doi.org/10.1080/13676261.2020.1757633

Power, Kate. "The COVID-19 Pandemic Has Increased the Care Burden of Women and Families." *Sustainability: Science, Practice and Policy*, vol. 16, no. 1, 2020, pp. 67-73.

Rant/TLC Needed. "Everything I Loved about University Is Gone and I Feel Like I'm Failing." *Reddit*, 19 Nov. 2020, www.reddit.com/r/queensuniversity/comments/jsgbdy/everything_i_loved_about_university_is_gone_and_i/. Accessed 30 Nov. 2020.

Smith, Dorothy E. *Institutional Ethnography: A Sociology for People.* AltaMira Press, 2005.

Titchkosky, Tanya. "The Bureaucratic Making of Disability." *New Formations*, vol. 101, no. 13, 2020, pp. 198-208.

Zender, Bree. "Covid-19 Online Learning Solutions Present Challenges for Students with Autism, ADHD." *KUNR Public Radio: Local News Feed*, 17 Mar. 2020, www.kunr.org/post/covid-19-online-learning-solutions-present-challenges-students-autism-adhd#stream/0. Accessed 14 Sept. 2020.

Chapter Nine

Mothers in the Legal Profession Doubling Up on the Double Shift during the COVID-19 Pandemic: Never Waste a Crisis

Rebecca Jaremko Bromwich

Introduction

As of 2020, it is statistically evident, and generally understood, that women do a disproportionate share of unpaid labour in Canada, as they do around the world (Mies). The COVID-19 pandemic has presented a double-edged scenario in respect to this "double shift" of paid and unpaid work, with childcare and school suddenly unavailable. When lockdowns came into place in March of 2020 across Canada and around the world, the double shift became double duty, expected not just to be done sequentially but done at the same time.

Although the COVID-19 pandemic has affected everyone, it has affected people differently. This chapter considers the ways in which the pandemic has compounded the impossibility of women's professional lives, particularly those of working mothers. Indeed, the pandemic has made working women's labour predicaments visible in new ways. The widespread move of white collar workers to "agile work" from home led to the simultaneous expectation that women would be doing their paid jobs while simultaneously caring for, and homeschooling, their children. That impossible expectation suddenly became more visible in the background of video conferences, with messy rooms and precocious children on full display. No digital Zoom background could effectively hide this reality. Women's unpaid work was no longer silent or invisible.

In the context in which I work, in a management role at a large international law firm, our staff and professionals were given the unmanageable task of trying to continue to work from home while caring for children and other dependents, including bearing primary responsibility for the care of elderly relatives. Largely, governments displayed a shocking lack of regard for this conundrum, although there were some important exceptions, including the Canadian government's September 2020 announcement that it would commit to national childcare and early learning support, yet officials have still not provided any details at the time of writing.

In this chapter, with reference to literature on women's unpaid work and about the gendered impacts of the pandemic, I discuss my personal experiences with trying to manage a large firm's response to the challenges, shifted visibilities, and new realities presented by the COVID-19 pandemic in a manner that fostered diversity and inclusion while caring for four children.

The Double Shift

The phrase "double shift" has been used to refer to women's combined paid and unpaid labour (Väänänen et al.), whereas the term "silent partner" has been used to refer to the unpaid work done by spouses, usually wives, to support the paid careers of their husbands and male coparents (Philipps). There is an abundance of research about women doing more unpaid labour than men statistically speaking in North America (Luxton; McMullen; Bains). The COVID-19 pandemic has presented a new challenge for women in general, and mothers specifically, because it has produced a context in which both the paid and unpaid labour done by women (De Paz et al.; MacDonald, Phipps, and Lethbridge) need to be done simultaneously—parents, disproportionately mothers, must homeschool their kids during lockdowns while working from home. One cannot simultaneously work in a paid job effectively while homeschooling children or caring for preschoolers and infants. Lockdowns demand the impossible, which led to mental health concerns for those, disproportionately women, faced with these simultaneous obligations. They also make visible existing conundrums and competing obligations that produce the impossibility of mothers' lives.

The Pandemic

The details of the COVID-19 pandemic are well known at time of writing, but I review them here in the sincere hope that, perhaps, you are reading this at a time when the events of 2020 have faded into history with a high survival rate. The COVID-19 pandemic, also known as the coronavirus pandemic, is a global outbreak of a coronavirus disease called COVID-19. The disease is itself caused by severe acute respiratory syndrome coronavirus 2 (SARS-CoV-2) (WHO). The disease was first identified in December 2019 in Wuhan, China. In March of 2020, it was declared a pandemic by the World Health Organization (WHO). As of 5 January, 2021, the time of writing, over 86 million cases of COVID-19 have been reported to the WHO. Reported cases span all known countries and territories, including Antarctica, and have resulted in more than 1,838,757 deaths. Although this is a large number of fatalities, in many cases, the disease is not fatal: more than 48.4 million people have been documented to have recovered from it (Johns Hopkins). To try to manage the impact of the pandemic, countries across the world have put their citizens into lockdown, have ordered them to shelter in place, and have implemented social/physical distancing guidelines. These measures meant that the majority of professionals would now be working from home, including legal ones.

The Legal Profession

The legal profession in North America and in the United Kingdom (UK) is notorious for requiring its professionals to work long hours and for being white, (ABA), male, conservative, inflexible, and adverse to technological advancements (Susskind; Blakely). There has been a professional culture of hostility towards alternative work arrangements, part-time work, and work from home (Wilder), which has made it a difficult space for mothers in particular, and women in general, to succeed (Stiller Rikleen). This culture of inhospitality to women, diversity, and change has resulted in a high attrition rate of women from the legal profession and especially from its most lucrative sector—private practice (Brown). Beyond its inflexible and gruelling culture, the legal profession is also infamous for the poor mental health of its members and for its alarmingly high suicide rate (Krieger). The trends of inflexibility and long working hours, as well as men dominating law firm leadership, unfortunately continue today with little change (Susskind).

My Experience

Having worked as a practicing lawyer for seventeen years, I left practice in 2019 and started work in a management role at a major international law firm. More specifically, I work as a national diversity and inclusion manager. We practice in a wide range of areas and have offices in nineteen countries. I am responsible for two of those countries: Canada and Russia. My colleagues who are based in the UK deal with diversity and inclusion in our other regions. The diversity and inclusion mandate is a big tent. We deal with inclusion and seek to eradicate bias and discrimination at systemic and individual levels within the firm regarding race, religion, sexuality, gender, gender identity, disability, socioeconomic status, age, and other aspects of human difference and embodiment.

In September 2020, after our entire workforce had been working from home since March due to COVID, our firm took the radical step of inviting the entire workforce, regardless of gender or role, to advise if they required accommodations with respect to caregiving work that would alter their schedule. I participated in online meetings from home, planning this initiative with my four teenaged children sometimes in the background. Although they were old enough to largely work independently on their schoolwork, there were certainly challenging moments, such as, notably, when one of my children dropped a drinking glass on the stairs, cutting himself, and I had to put a Zoom call on hold to clean up shards of glass and sprayed blood like a crime scene investigator. He was not badly harmed. We managed.

In addition to successfully transitioning to a remote workforce, our people were able to be accommodated with reduced or altered hours. The legal profession had, at least until 2020, seriously lagged behind other fields concerning the adoption of technological solutions, such as remote work and online meetings. Even before the pandemic, our firm had become a leader in allowing its employees to work from home on a flexible schedule, for both professionals and support staff. Once the lockdowns began, and it became evident we could conduct business remotely, we embraced flexible work on a large scale, allowing staff and professionals to work variable and flexible hours from home.

The pandemic has effected enormous changes to the legal profession by forcing the profession and the legal system to adopt ways of working that use technology to facilitate remote work. Remote hearings, online court scheduling, and even online trials—arrangements that had been technologically possible for at least a decade—were suddenly permitted in a work sector that had been hostile to technology and to change. The pandemic has also revolutionized the justice system across Canada, with the implementation of Zoom hearings for many matters and the widespread use of online platforms for mediations as well as for trials in certain circumstances.

The COVID-19 pandemic, and the inquiries and concerns raised in relation to it—anecdotally, in our firm's context—has made it clear that women still perform most caregiving duties. Researchers have long pointed out that even when both parents work full-time, women do the majority of the childcare and housework (Burkhi; Philipps). This situation was confirmed by the responses we received from our workers. I fielded many calls and emails about childcare being an issue in the context of remote work. Although there were, notably, some men who raised concerns about caregiving in the COVID-19 work-from-home context, the issue was overwhelmingly raised by women, and mothers specifically. Notably, COVID-19 and the resulting lockdowns also affected differently situated women differently; those in higher-paying positions were more privileged in terms of options and had more financial ability to hire a live-in caregiver, for example, which is one of the few viable childcare options available during lockdowns. With schools closed during the lockdowns and children as well as other family members at home and with access to childcare and babysitting circumscribed, it was abundantly clear that unpaid care and household work are necessarily implied by paid work, and that it remains disproportionately women—specifically mothers—who do that work (Burkhi). Before COVID-19, families often relied on paid third parties, also often women, to care formally or informally for their children or other dependents, clean their homes or cook meals, but such arrangements have been impossible to make during the pandemic. As a result, it became crucial that organizations like mine recognize that many workers, disproportionately women, had a full-time (unpaid) caregiving job outside of the office.

During the COVID-19 pandemic, our firm has faced many crises in many respects, including the ability of women, generally, and mothers, specifically, to remain within our workforce. Yet the pandemic has also provided evidence that the legal profession as constructed socially is far less flexible than it could be. Our firm, thus, decided to make changes to the norms of practice. A profession that had been notorious for its inflexibility suddenly became more flexible. It became normal for people to say they had to reschedule meetings to accommodate pick-up and drop-off times for their kids or to arrange their work schedules around their kids' naps. The performance of lawyers' identities suddenly became more authentic and less polished, with the presence of pets and kids in the background of online meetings becoming a recurring sight. We were both forced and empowered to talk about gender and motherwork differently, as the work of caring for children was impossible not to see.

Looking Ahead

Although Winston Churchill is often credited with saying "Never let a good crisis go to waste" during the bleak days of World War Two, as I have discussed in this chapter with reference to research about women, work, and the legal profession—and also in the context of my personal and professional experience as a lawyer and manager of diversity and inclusion with a large law firm—the COVID-19 pandemic has presented us with both challenges and opportunities. To improve the situation of women and mothers in professional roles within the legal profession, the imperative is to not waste the opportunities afforded by this crisis.

One opportunity presented by the COVID-19 pandemic is visibility, as it has brought the role of gender in society sharply into focus (Foster and Markham). It is important for employers to accommodate in real time the impacts the COVID-19 pandemic has had on women in terms of the intersection of gender and maternality. Significant research is being carried out about the pandemic and violence in the home, the pandemic's effects on caregiving, and what actually constitutes essential work. The pandemic presents a challenge to gender equality, yet it also provides new opportunities for us to confront the roles that gender plays in our personal and professional lives. Advocates and practitioners have been working to include substantive gender analysis in their studies for decades, but, still too often, such topics as foreign policy, crisis response, and international trade have been seen as gender blind or gender neutral (Foster and Markham). The pandemic's imperative for us to understand and respond to its effects on gender provides an unprecedented opportunity to implement enduring change to gender relations and to better include mothers in professional spaces, such as in the legal profession.

The COVID-19 pandemic is a global crisis and threatens to be a worldwide catastrophe. As John F. Kennedy famously said, a crisis is a combination of danger and opportunity (Foster and Markham). The COVID-19 lockdowns demonstrated how radically contingent the social status quo was; they showed that we can pause almost everything and that radical contingency plans, in turn, open up space to imagine different realities. This time of unprecedented possibility reveals that change can be made to all aspects of social life, including gender relations. In this chapter, I have argued that the COVID-19 pandemic presents opportunities for domestic and unpaid labour to be counted and for women's work to be valued. As Stephenie Foster and Susan Markham wrote of gender equity and the pandemic:

> We can use this as an opportunity to reimagine a different future, one that values gender equality, women's participation and women's leadership. Women must be part of COVID-19 response and recovery planning and decision making. We must value the unseen work done by women. We must use every tool possible to restructure caregiving systems and address the causes of domestic violence. We can do this, using everyone's

talent, skill and experience to inform our choices. (Foster and Markham)

Works Cited

American Bar Association. *Diversity and the Legal Profession: The Next Steps, ABA Presidential Initiative Commission on Diversity, 2009-2010.* American Bar Association, 2010.

Baines, D. "Seven Kinds of Work—Only One Paid: Raced, Gendered and Restructured Work in Social Services." *Atlantis,* vol. 28, no. 2, 2009, pp. 19-29.

Blakely, Susan Smith. *Best Friends at the Bar: What Women Need to Know About a Career in the Law.* Wolter Kluwer Law & Business/Aspen Publishers, 2009.

Brown, Anne Murphy. *Legally Mom: Real Women's Stories of Balancing Motherhood & Law Practice,* Chicago: American Bar Association, 2012.

Burkhi, Thala, "The Indirect Impact of COVID-19 on Women." *The Lancet,* vol. 20, no. 8, 2020, pp. 904-05.

Foster, Stephenie, and Susan Markham. "COVID-19 Demands We Rethink Gender Roles." *Diplomatic Courier,* 20 May 2020, www.diplomaticourier. com/posts/covid-19-demands-we-rethink-gender-roles. Accessed 5 Jan. 2021.

Johns Hopkins University. "COVID-19 Dashboard by the Center for Systems Science and Engineering (CSSE) at Johns Hopkins University (JHU)." ArcGIS, 2021, gisanddata.maps.arcgis.com/apps/opsdash board/index.html#/bda7594740fd40299423467b48e9ecf6. Accessed 5 Jan. 2021.

Krieger, Lawrence. *The Hidden Sources of Law School Stress: Avoiding the Mistakes that Create Unhappy and Unprofessional Lawyers.* Krieger, 2005.

Luxton, M. *More than a Labour of Love: Three Generations of Women's Work in the Home.*: Women's Educational Press, 1980.

MacDonald, M., S. Phipps, and L. Lethbridge. "Taking its Toll: The Influence of Paid and Unpaid Work on Women's Well-Being." *Feminist Economics,* vol. 11, no. 1, 2005, pp. 63-94.

McMullin, J. A. "Patterns of Paid and Unpaid Work: The Influence of Power, Social Context, and Family Background." *Canadian Journal on Aging/La Revue Canadienne Du Vieillissement,* vol. 24, no. 3, 2005, pp. 225-36.

Mies, M. *Patriarchy and Accumulation on a World Scale: Women in the International Division of Labour.* Zed Books, 1986.

Philipps, L. "Silent Partners: The Role of Unpaid Market Labor in Families." *Feminist Economics,* vol. 14, no. 2, 2008, pp. 37-57.

Stiller Rikleen, Laureen. *Ending the Gauntlet: Removing Barriers to Women's Success in the Law.* Thomson/Legalworks, 2006.

Susskind, Richard. *The End of Lawyers?* Oxford University Press, 2010.

Väänänen, Ari, et al. "The Double Burden of and Negative Spillover Between Paid and Domestic Work: Associations with Health Among Men and Women." *Women & Health,* vol. 40, no. 3, 2004, pp. 1-18.

Wilder, Gita. *Databook on Women in Law School and in the Legal Profession.* Law School Admission Council, 2003.

World Health Organization (WHO). "Naming the Coronavirus Disease (COVID-19) and the Virus That Causes It." *WHO,* 2020, www.who.int/emergencies/diseases/novel-coronavirus-2019/technical-guidance/naming-the-coronavirus-disease-(covid-2019)-and-the-virus-that-causes-it. Accessed 5 Jan. 2021.

Chapter Ten

Disappearing Act: Dance Artist Mothers in the Gig Economy of the Performing Arts in Canada

Susie Burpee

In the early weeks after the World Health Organization declared COVID-19 a global pandemic, I was doing what many mothers were doing at home—attempting to navigate my children's online learning portals, respond to their emotional needs and questions about our new reality, and carve out a corner of the busy household to hold Zoom meetings. I was also trying to figure out if there was a place in our house where I could do grand battements without kicking over a lamp or knocking the magnets off the fridge. I am a mother with two daughters, and I am also a self-employed contemporary dance artist, working professionally in the gig economy that is the performing arts in Canada. When lockdown measures were issued, I was in the middle of a teaching contract at Toronto Dance Theatre, a critically acclaimed dance company set to premiere a new work the following week. My teaching contract and their performances were cancelled. Theatre venues and rehearsal studios across the country closed indefinitely, and performing artists, most of whom work as independent contractors, were out of work—the future was uncertain. Like many artists with a partner, I am the lower earner in the household. My work stopped and his didn't. Like so many women during this time, I was left with the primary caregiving responsibilities of our six- and eight-year-old children.

Dance artists find themselves in a particularly precarious situation within the arts during these pandemic months. We have lost not only our work and source of income for the foreseeable future but our fundamental means to continue our physical practice in order to stay professionally relevant. We require studio spaces with special dance floors (now mostly closed) for daily training in order to keep up with the expectations of the field. Acknowledging both the loss of work and the loss of access to training, contemporary dance artist and mother Bee Pallomina asked the difficult question: "How am I going to get back to working if I'm completely disconnected from my practice for half a year?"

This disconnection from work is particularly dangerous for dance artist mothers. In a milieu where 86 per cent of dancers identify as women (Coles et al. 48), proportionally few women hold leadership roles in professional dance. Only 36 per cent of women in the performing arts in Canada hold positions of producers, directors, and choreographers (Hill, "Statistical Profile" 19). This has meant that the majority of women in dance in Canada have had to forge their own self-directed careers, administer their own companies, self-produce their shows, and hold multiple roles of performers, choreographers, and teachers. Working as a self-employed contractor in dance is financially precarious, particularly for racialized and Indigenous artists, who earn approximately one-third less than nonracialized and non-Indigenous artists (Hill, "Demographic Diversity" 1). For women and nonbinary dance artists to keep up with the demands of this gender-imbalanced field, it takes an enormous amount of time, energy, and a diverse skillset in constant need of upgrade.

A July 2020 study from the Royal Bank of Canada reports that the majority of childcare has been shouldered by women during the pandemic (Desjardins et al.). Because of this, mothers working in professional dance are negatively affected at this time, as they are unable to keep pace with their colleagues concerning grant deadlines, emergency community meetings, and networking—all necessary in order to continue to advance their careers. Kathleen Rea, artistic director and administrator of her dance company REAson d'etre, confessed: "I felt so depressed because I just didn't see the hope of recovery. I would sit in on Zoom meetings where people would lead with the statement, 'Now that we have time...' and I would think to myself, 'I can't breathe! I don't have any time!'" I felt similar to Rea. I was completely occupied with the wellbeing of my children, and I feared losing this career that I had invested in with my whole being for twenty-five years.

But I also felt motivated. If there was any time to reach out to other dance artist mothers, it was now. Conversations at the intersections of dance and mothering are rare; these are not public dialogues. Personally, I had always felt I needed to hide my mothering away from my professional dance life. Research towards this chapter has made it clear the reasons for this are systemic and complex. I spoke to thirty dance artist mothers from across the country, working in various professional dance forms including Kathak, African diasporic dance, Flamenco, and Indigenous contemporary dance, among others. Many women I interviewed run their own companies and studios, and all of them play multiple roles within the dance milieu. These artists shared feelings of invisibility; they felt they lacked support from the sector and had lost touch with their dance practice.

"In the early days of the pandemic, having been thrust into a 1950s housewife life, I lost a lot of my artistic drive. I cleared the floor of a room in our house for a studio, but I didn't have the energy to start working in it," said Jennifer Dallas, artistic director of Kemi Projects, and mother of a one-year-old. Sara Porter, mother of three teenaged boys, whose Toronto premiere was indefinitely postponed, recalled: "I know I fell into a sort of depression of my artist person—a sudden and complete disconnection from my art, and saturated with mothering work. My career was going very quickly in a positive direction, but I realized how fragile it all is. It could get taken away at any moment." Along with cancelled performances and touring, increased caregiving responsibilities for these dance artist mothers limited the hours of administration and networking that would normally happen from their home. Myriam Allard, a Montreal-based Flamenco artist with a busy touring career and her own studio, lost 80 per cent of these hours between March and July: "There was definitely an existential crisis. Should I continue? Should I stop? In my twenty-year career, I had never questioned it until now."

As women in dance, many of us have danced since we were very young. Not unlike mothering for some, it is an embodied practice, woven into the fascial identity of who we are. There is an emotional toll of this inability to exercise our life-long passion. Tracey Norman, a mother of two young children and a choreographer on the dance faculty at York University, said she hit some of her lowest points during the early pandemic months: "So much felt closed-off to me—I lost a sense of creative drive. I didn't even watch dance."

When Norman refers to "watching dance," she means watching it online. The performing arts scene in the last few months has, like everything else, been finding its way into the digital space. As artists pivot their careers in new directions, there is a widening of the gap between those who can and can't take on this new work. Pallomina stated: "This is a huge moment of professional development for some people. Without dependents, I know some artists that have been able to treat this COVID time as a giant residency." Toronto choreographer and performer Heidi Strauss commiserated about the following: "Other artists have time to vision and create a bigger picture of what the world might be. I feel like mine is getting smaller. There's not much time for anything other than my son's schooling and administration; there is very little space for artistic practice or creation."

In those early months, application deadlines popped up for new initiatives like the National Arts Centre's #Canada Performs, which offered artists one thousand dollars to livestream a work. I gave the application a scant glance between finding and then playing "Sweatin' to the Oldies" with Richard Simmons on YouTube (the kids love it!) and making multiplication flash cards. I had to disconnect from the aching feeling of falling behind professionally. Tara Cheyenne Friedenberg recalled being angry when she saw the National Arts Centre's posting: "I was locked inside with my child, barely able to do anything. I felt like I was climbing a greased pole."

But Friedenberg, artistic director of Vancouver-based Tara Cheyenne Performance, also spoke of a gratitude of being home with her son. "I had this initial feeling of 'Thank god I don't have to go back'. I had been running for my life, keeping many balls in the air, trying to survive, trying to stay relevant." Many dance artists I spoke to remarked upon this initial feeling of relief. Vancouver dance artist Lisa Gelley, at home with a three-year-old and a four-month-old, said: "I had spent the last three years juggling work and motherhood quite intensely. Now I didn't have to, in the immediate future, figure out how I was going to be a mother of two and a co-director of a company."

When I inquired as to what artists were feeling relief from, mothers spoke specifically to challenges in the field they had been facing for some time. The pandemic has exposed many systemic cracks and inequities, and the current concerns of mothers in dance in Canada are the canary in the coal mine for an exposition of a milieu that presents significant barriers to mothers. Mothers told stories of being asked in auditions how they were going to manage with children, of not getting their roles back after having children, of being asked by a teacher to "pull their uterus up," and of not disclosing a pregnancy to presenters (for fear of not closing the deal). But even more than sharing this evidence, mothers wanted to talk about systemic forces at work in the field. The dance artists I spoke to were keenly aware of the pervasive aesthetic and neoliberal values imposed by the cultural system in Canada that prevent not just mothers but women and other marginalized artists from advancing their careers. Said Dallas, "I believe dance is guilty of the push to produce—the dance community, its funders and patrons have bought into capitalism the same way that any industry has." Dance artist and advocate Shannon Litzenberger positioned the current climate as follows:

Canada's professionalized system of cultural production is shaped by aesthetics, values and economics rooted in its patriarchal, Western-European colonial history. Artists learn, through participation in this system, what kind of professional practice, artistic process, and creative output is rewarded and therefore deemed worthy or excellent. While progress has been made to create a more inclusive funding framework of a more diverse Canadian cultural expression, the conditioned tendencies of the system and its participants (particularly those individuals and institutions who hold significant power) are still, I would argue, deeply rooted in its founding ethos. It's also worth stating that there has never been a moment in the evolution of this system where women have been prioritized as an equity-seeking group.

Allard pointed out that this ethos has contributed to a product-driven approach to artistic practice, and she indicated that this can be in conflict with the maternal body and mothering: "The way we are taught in Flamenco—it's 'go, go, go'! You have to toughen up if you want to become a dancer. The characteristics of 'rounder' or 'slower' are not well received. Society wants productivity; these other ways of working are not allowed to exist."

Availability is a key attribute for dancers in this gig economy. We train our bodies to be available to carry out the multifarious physical demands of the work, and we must also be available to accommodate long rehearsal days, evenings and weekends in the theatre, touring schedules, and moving between gigs throughout the day. The role of "mother" does not fit this availability profile, as mothers have less time and less ability to travel, and their body is physically engaged with bearing or caring for children. Justine Chambers, mother of a five-year-old son, who has travelled globally with her work, said: "I'm burned out. I have a lot of questions around the nature of how we work, and I struggle with this idea of success. COVID made this all stop and gave us time to be with the angels and the demons. The demands of the dance milieu don't always meet my humanity."

Montreal-based professional teacher and dancer Jamie Wright echoed Chambers's interrogation of success, speaking of the extreme pressure of performance excellence. "I was the poster child of doing everything that was asked of me. I was so stimulated by what I was doing, but I made a lot of sacrifices. I would train on the weekends instead of being with my family. I travelled a lot—hard core touring on big stages. I missed my daughter's dance concert while on tour. She said to me, 'You're the only mom who travels.'"

Both Chambers and Wright referred to the challenge of having to work within imposed and demanding schedules. Chambers, specifically, said: "Historically, part of our training has been to infantilize us and remove our agency. The shift that needs to happen is a cultural undoing around ideas of 'how much and how high?'" Many mothers spoke of the need for flexible working hours, shorter rehearsal periods, and childcare subsidies, and some, including Chambers and Friedenberg, offered these options to artists who were in their employ. Lisa Gelley said: "I am experimenting with what can be made in smaller increments of time, on a flexible schedule, and shared in alternative ways. I want to trust that whatever it is that is created within these restrictions can and will be taken seriously, can be valued, and considered as valid as an hour-long work on a stage."

As well as shaping the working climate, the cultural underpinnings of the arts production system in Canada have cultivated a narrow view of the professional body. Aesthetically, the ideal body in dance is slim and lithe. Curvy bodies, 'natural' bodies, fat bodies, middle-age bodies, bodies changed by time and care—all of these body types are deemed as less than ideal or outside the professional standard. Single mother and dance and performance artist Allison Cummings said: "Mothering in dance is subjected to all the tropes. For example: 'Oh, she looks great for having a baby!' I think mother artists lose a bit of respect in dance—perceptions like 'they can't move the same way,' and so they're not as valuable."

I remember being in a professional dance class when my daughters were about three and five, and the teacher, a colleague of mine, stopped the class to give me a correction. As she placed her hands on my shoulders and rolled them back, she said in front of everyone, "Too many years of carrying your kids around." I was stunned. I felt completely devalued, and I stood there, unable to speak. Ali Robson, performer, teacher, and mother of three children, put this feeling into words:

> The parts of having children that were uniquely mine—how my body had changed and what I was now comfortable doing, acceptance that it was *one* part of my identity and not all of me, the thoughts, emotions, insights that I now had about the world and humanity that would feed my artistic practice as much as any other professional skill or attribute—these aspects of mothering are sometimes perceived as diminishing professionalism. And I think one could insert mental illness, fatness, skin colour, technical training, and gender expression in for mothering as diminishing professionalism.

Mothers and other marginalized groups can become disenfranchised within a system of cultural production that requires a particular profile of an artist to participate in its meritocracy. Natasha Torres-Garner, a Winnipeg-based dance artist beginning to explore her Latinx roots, had this to say: "I had been caught up in perfection, of ideas of what I 'should' be. The process of raising children cracked open a narrow idea of who I was as a dancer. Being a parent and allowing my body to change has opened up to different ways of how I could feel successful."

And Dallas ventured: "What if we respected that women who became mothers are taking on the biggest creative process of their lives and that they will likely, when they are ready, have some exquisite perspectives and artmaking to share?"

Many mothers spoke to the influence of mothering on their practice—a broadening of artistic choices, more access to deep emotional places, and greater ability to navigate problem solving and build relationships. But does the culture of professional dance in Canada place value on these attributes? Porter said, "I remember the rage I felt after I had birthed my first child; there seemed to be no place for the epic-ness of the knowledge I had gained." Chambers, too, has thought about the profound knowledge sources of mothers left untapped. For instance, she argued that distraction is not a deficit, but an incredible skill: "This radical focus, the ability to hold the past, present, and future—why are we not acknowledging this?" And she recalled a colleague telling her early on, "No one is going to defend your motherhood for you."

When I spoke to these women across the country, not only did they defend their value as mothers and artists, but they also offered concrete suggestions for new practices and working models within the changing field of dance. As well as rethinking notions of time and labour, they spoke of the need for more diverse representation on choreographic platforms and artist roundtables. Bharatanatyam and Odissi dancer Neena Jayarajan, related, "I am often invited around the table to represent artists of colour, but my perspective as a mother is rarely invited." Other desired changes included childcare as a budget line item on grants, representations of age on stage, prioritizing work with a relational world view, and community care. Penny Couchie, an Anishinaabe dancer, teacher, and community arts practitioner from Nipissing First Nation, talked about her first experience working with Jumblies Theatre in an intergenerational rehearsal process where grandmothers and babies were welcomed, and where there was food and childcare: "I remember thinking 'This is what I've been looking for'! Art-making in the everyday, with everyone." Couchie now runs a company and does just that. Many mothers questioned the role of professional dance education institutions and the ethics that were being transferred concerning the body. Couchie further said: "My daughter asked me to begin to train her, and I prioritized dancing with sovereignty and self-determination over pliés and tendus. I felt that a deep ability to listen to herself, to communicate through her body what she was thinking and feeling, would serve her better than being an obedient dancer."

Many artist mothers had already begun to engage in alternative practices, pre-COVID-19 era, as a pushback against an unsustainable capitalist model of artmaking, and as an extension of the dramaturgies of care they were already enacting within their own households. When the pandemic entered their lives, some mothers spoke of these practices as being useful when transferred back into caregiving within the home. "My artistic practice prepared me for COVID, a familiarity with working with the unknown, and a practice of constant letting go," said Torres-Garner. And Karla Etienne, administrative manager of Montreal's Compagnie Danse Nyata-Nyata, teacher, performer, and mother of Afro-descent, affirmed: "As artists we practice the unknown. You can transfer that knowledge, that search for meaning into the home. We don't always have the answers, but we can return to the practice and our humility. Moving forward, perhaps it is not about presenting what we know but presenting our questions. Does it always need to be about presenting a show?"

Etienne brought this idea of process over product into conversation with Cummings's statement that "with excellence as the driver behind what we do, you get this 'me first' kind of environment." Etienne offered a potent observation:

> As an artist, this notion of "my unique voice" [and] "my creativity" doesn't always acknowledge the ancestry that we carry; the idea that we aren't individual—that we are already part of a collective by way of lineage. For me, becoming a mother was never a question, and at Nyata-Nyata we hold this particular collective awareness. I think my kids, in this sense, were a part of the company's mission.

To understand the collective in this way that Etienne describes automatically includes the child and will never deny the mother.

The pandemic has made visible larger systemic questions around the invisibility of mothers in dance and with this comes an opportunity to renew a consciousness around the value of these roles. Litzenberger said, "Supporting mothers is a significant lever of systemic change that would advance the equality of women, not just in dance but in society." Throughout these pandemic months, because of increased caregiving responsibilities, I haven't been able to meet any grant application deadlines or build new professional relationships. This means that for the next couple of years, my choreographic work will not be present on the dance scene. If I were to open my email inbox today and see a call for a supported home residency, an online networking initiative, or a curatorial program on the theme of care (with a childcare stipend), then perhaps I may be able to vision how I, as a mother in professional dance, could continue to work in the field. We, the voices of dance artist mothers and our allies, are urgently calling for a paradigm shift. We are defending our essential motherhood with the hope that the sector will eventually do the same.

Works Cited

Allard, Myriam. Personal interview. 1 Sept. 2020.

Chambers, Justine. Personal interview. 16 Sept. 2020.

Coles, Amanda, et al. "The Status of Women in the Canadian Arts and Cultural Industries." *Ontario Arts Council*, Aug. 2018, www.arts.on.ca/oac/media/oac/Publications/Research%20Reports%20EN-FR/Arts%20Funding%20and%20Support/OAC-Women-the-Arts-Report_Final_EN_Oct5.pdf. Accessed 5 Jul. 2020.

Couchie, Penny. Personal interview. 27 Sept. 2020.

Cummings, Allison. Personal interview. 19 Sept. 2020.

Dallas, Jennifer. Letter to the author. 11 Sept. 2020.

Desjardins, Dawn, et al. "Pandemic Threatens Decades of Women's Labour Force Gains." *RBC Economics*, 16 Jul. 2020, thoughtleadership.rbc.com/pandemic-threatens-decades-of-womens-labour-force-gains/. Accessed 15 Sept. 2020.

Etienne, Karla. Personal Interview. 18 Sept. 2020.

Friedenberg, Tara Cheyenne. Personal Interview. 13 Sept. 2020.

Gelley, Lisa. Letter to the author. 9 Sept. 2020.

Hill, Kelly. "A Statistical Profile of Artists in Canada in 2016." *Hill Strategies Research, Inc.*, 27 Nov. 2019, www.hillstrategies.com/research/statistical-profile-of-artists-in-canada-in-2016/. Accessed 5 Jul. 2020.

Hill, Kelly. "Demographic Diversity of Artists in Canada in 2016." *Hill Strategies Research, Inc.*, 29 Jan. 2020, www. hillstrategies.com/resource/

demographic-diversity-of-artists-in-canada-in-2016/. Accessed 10 Jul. 2020.

Jayarajan, Neena. Personal interview. 3 Sept. 2020.

Litzenberger, Shannon. Letter to the author. 25 Sept. 2020.

Norman, Tracey. Personal interview. 17 Sept. 2020.

Pallomina, Bee. Personal interview. 11 Sept. 2020.

Porter, Sara. Personal interview. 14 Sept. 2020.

Rea, Kathleen. Personal interview. 29 Aug. 2020.

Robson, Ali. Personal interview. 31 Aug. 2020.

Strauss, Heidi. Personal interview. 27 Sept. 2020.

Torres-Garner, Natasha. Personal interview. 3 Sept. 2020.

Wright, Jamie. Personal interview. 1 Sept. 2020.

Chapter Eleven

Motherhood and Academia in Mexican Universities: Juggling Our Way through COVID-19

Lidia Ivonne Blásquez Martínez and Lucia Montes Ortíz
Translated by Laura Elliott

"Split," that would be the word. Even when what has to be done is done in different settings, it is always with the sensation of being fractured, divided."

—Part-time lecturer and mother of a seven- and a five-year-old

Introduction

This chapter presents the online exploratory research results on the situation of female Mexican academics, regarding the current distribution of paid and unpaid work during the COVID-19 confinement, along with their perception of their workload and some of the effects on their wellbeing. We argue that the gender divide has broadened during the pandemic because female faculty members are obliged to undertake the reproductive workload that state institutions have downloaded to women during the confinement period, such as homeschooling, mentoring, housework, and carework—which are traditionally viewed as female tasks. Yet despite this extra work, these female faculty members are still expected to maintain the same levels of productivity required by their job, thereby putting them in a precarious situation.

The survey was conducted via the internet between April 28 and May 30 in 2020. It obtained a sample of 329 survey respondents, of which 184 are mothers. This exploratory research addresses the reorganization of academic work and the consequences for women in the context of COVID-19 confinement in Mexico. We adopt the feminist approach developed by Silvia Federici that concerns housework and carework as the key features for the reproduction of labour power in society. At the centre of our discussion is the inequality facing Mexican faculty women to carry out their research work in a deeply rooted patriarchal society and in an academic environment guided by cognitive capitalism. We focus on the differentiated experiences of academic women and mothers from different generations.

In Mexico, the National Period of Healthy Distance (Jornada Nacional de Sana Distancia) began on March 16 and officially ended on May 30, 2020. It involved government directives to stay home, close educational institutions, and suspend work activities. Afterwards, the period called the "new normality" began, governed by an epidemiological traffic-light system that permits certain activities and movement of people based on the local infection rate. Until August 2020, the epidemiological curve continued to grow, so voluntary confinement was kept in place, in this point most of the Mexican territory remained in yellow light, which means a medium risk. Academic and educational activities were classified as nonpriority activities and would be carried out by digital resources until the traffic-light system changed to green.

For female Mexican faculty members, these measures have meant more work from home. Nursery schools and child daycares have remained closed. Remote education requires constant and dedicated guidance. Emergency remote teaching demands course material preparation in new digital formats. Regarding household work, cleaning services and paid caregiving continue to be intermittent. Mexican academic women, while they sometimes receive support from their partners, generally spend more time on household work and caregiving than men, both within and outside of their nuclear families. This means that female academics are forced to spend less time on research activities in order to fulfill the needs of their families. Moreover, Mexican faculty mothers must equally respond to the quantity and quality requirements for publications and research products, since the academic productivity criteria by which they are assessed will not change in the near future.

To address the reconfiguration of labour for Mexican academic mothers brought about by the COVID-19 pandemic, we first outline our research methods that explore differentiated experiences of reproductive work by Mexican faculty mothers. Next, we analyze the results of our online survey through the concepts of "reproductive labour" and "cognitive capitalism" that Silvia Federici points out, focusing on how the public decision making has reinforced patterns of gender inequality. We explain how gender inequalities are reproduced in Academe, as faculty mothers mainly undertake the reproductive workload, both in the household and in the university. Finally, we outline other findings that should be explored further: 1) the compensation that women's academic reproductive work represents to faculty functioning in the context of cognitive capitalism, where only marketable activities are funded; and 2) the appearance of a new kind of enclosure, as academic mothers' agency is substantially reduced by the isolation that prevents them from employing their support strategies and networks to achieve their research goals.

Research Methods

This exploratory research stems from a desire to understand the reorganization of academic work and the consequences for women in the context of COVID-19 confinement in Mexico. It is framed as an exercise in understanding the differentiated experiences of academic women and mothers. A questionnaire was designed to explore the differences among reproductive, care, and academic work. In view of the confinement, the decision was made to send a digital questionnaire entitled "Mujeres en la ciencia durante la COVID-19" (Women in Science during COVID-19" through the Google Forms application. The questionnaire ran from April 28 through May 30, 2020; it was distributed through snowball sampling done in social media groups frequented by academic women as well as through individual contacts.

A nonrepresentative sample of 329 survey participants and 176 testimonies was obtained. The answers were made anonymous with the aim of encouraging greater freedom of expression. Upon receiving the database automatically generated by Google Forms, the sample was reduced to 184 questionnaires from academic mothers once it was sorted to eliminate duplications of data or profiles that did not align with the survey's objective, such as undergraduate students who had yet to begin their academic careers. A descriptive quantitative analysis was done of the profiles of the female academics as well as their job categories and the hours invested in each one, both before and after COVID-19 confinement began. Likewise, the percentage of academic mothers who also cared for elderly or disabled family members was examined. In addition, using multiple-choice questions and testimonies, a qualitative analysis was done based on the self-perception of one's emotional state and health, considering the effects of the availability of space and resources for doing their academic work or the lack thereof. We present below the results obtained through the survey.

Reproductive Work during Confinement

Of the 184 academic mothers (39 per cent of the sample), ninety-nine are between thirty-six and forty-five (54 per cent); forty-six are between twenty and thirty-five (25 per cent), and seven are over fifty-seven (4 per cent); 103 have a child (56 per cent), sixty-nine have two children (37.5 per cent), and ten have three children (5.4 per cent). Most of the children are aged between four and seven (see Graph 1).

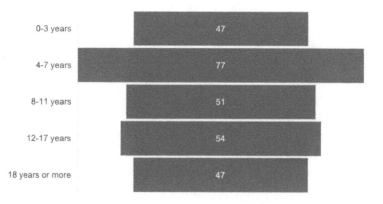

Graph 1. Children's Age Ranges

133 mothers live with their partner and children (72.2 per cent); twenty-one live with their children (11.4 per cent); nineteen live with relatives or friends (10.3 per cent); eight live with their partner (4.3 per cent), and three live alone (1.6%). 21.2 per cent are responsible for an elderly or disabled family member (see Graph 2).

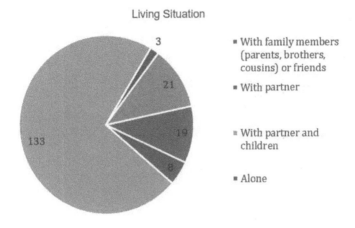

Graph 2. Forms of Cohabitation of Academic Mothers

Of the 184 academic mothers, 136 have PhDs (73.9 per cent), 38 have a master's degree, and ten have a bachelor's degree; in the latter two cases. The majority of the women are in the social sciences and humanities, followed by biological sciences and health sciences and then basic sciences, engineering as well as inter, trans or multi-disciplinary studies (see Graph 3).

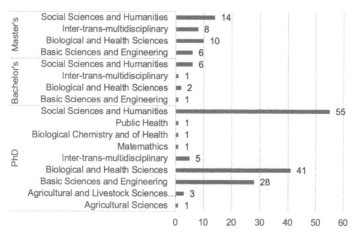

Graph 3. Education Level of Academic Mothers

Before confinement, 58 per cent of the academic mothers spent seven to nine hours a day on their professional activities, and 16.3 per cent spent ten to twelve hours a day on them. During confinement, 65.7 per cent only spent between four and six hours a day on their academic activities. It is worth noting that between a 5.9 and 7.6 per cent increase was observed in women who spent more than twelve hours a day on their professional activities (see Graph 4). That is, 46 per cent of the academic mothers had to reduce the amount of time they spent on their academic and professional activities by approximately three hours a day during confinement.

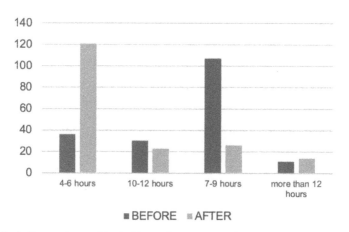

Graph 4. Comparison of Daily Hours Spent on Academic and Professional Activities

Remote work was one measure that universities and research centers imposed during confinement, and women have confronted some physical impediments as a result. For example, 56 per cent of the academic mothers stated that they did not have a space in their home dedicated exclusively to their professional activities that was equipped with a computer, internet, plus any other necessary component for doing their work. Consequently, they created an improvised space in a common area of their home and dealt with constant interruptions, among other inconveniences. Often, they shared the space with their children in order to supervise distance education and alternate the use of computer equipment.

Of those surveyed, 8 per cent had to put their academic activities on hold entirely because they need specialized equipment only available to them at their workplaces. Likewise, some were able to carry out their academic activities but were so overwhelmed with reproductive labour that they decided to wait for confinement to end before resuming those activities (see Graph 5).

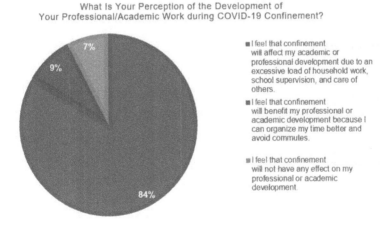

Graph 5. Perception of Academic Work

Regarding hours spent on reproductive labour—which includes cooking, cleaning, caregiving for family members, and other household work—63 per cent of the academic mothers mentioned that before confinement, they would invest less than one hour in planning and preparing meals each day. In contrast, during confinement, 53 per cent of the academic mothers spent three to four hours a day on these activities (see Graph 6).

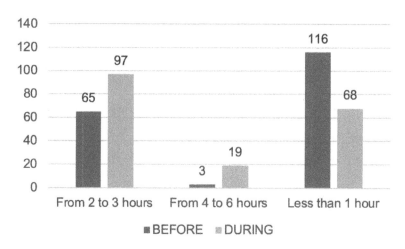

Graph 6. Comparison of Daily hours Spent on Meal Planning and Preparation

For 72 per cent of the academic mothers, the time invested in housecleaning was less than one hour a day before confinement, whereas after, 59 per cent spent three hours a day or more on these activities (see Graph 7).

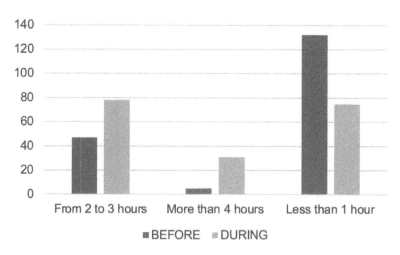

Graph 7. Comparison of Daily hours Spent on House Cleaning

Before confinement, the academic mothers were nearly divided in terms of their perception concerning the equal distribution of household chores. That is, 47 per cent answered that this work was fairly distributed among the members of their homes, whereas 49 per cent considered that it was not; 4 per cent did not answer. However, once confinement began, 56% of the interviewed mothers indicated that the distribution of household work among the nuclear family was not equal (see Graph 8).

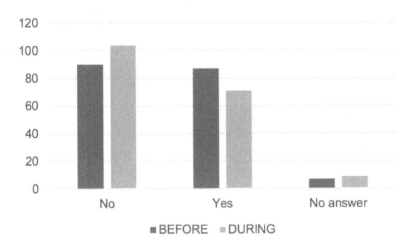

Graph 8. Balance of Household Workload

The category of providing care work for other family members is very broad; family members may include a partner, parents or grand-parents, children, as well as those who are dependent because of their age or due to an illness or disability. Before confinement, 52 per cent of the interviewees stated that they invested two to three hours a day in caring for others, including the time spent helping their children do homework (see Graph 9).

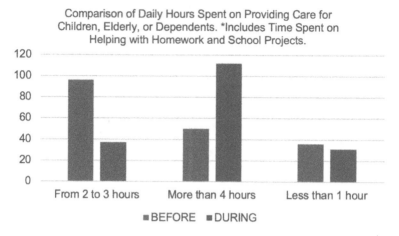

Graph 9. Daily Hours Spent on Carework

Emergency public policies imposed numerous tasks, particularly on mothers, in order to make the distance education model viable. The extent of this new workload can be observed in the responses from academic mothers, as 61 per cent of them indicated that since the beginning of confinement, they had invested more than four hours a day in caring for others.

The crisis created by the public health contingency plan has placed academic women in highly stressful conditions, defined by great psychological and emotional vulnerability. Our research clearly found that assuming extra responsibilities and merging spaces have led to difficulties for academic mothers struggling to manage the multiple household and academic roles.

COVID-19 Era: Motherhood, Academe, and the Triple Bind Oppression Crunch

Of those surveyed, 95 per cent stated that during confinement, they experienced a lack of energy, the sensation of being overworked, as well as feelings of anxiety, depression, or a mixture of these. Women responded to the demands of reproductive work at the cost of abandoning their emotional and physical self-care. A researcher and a mother of a teenager said the following:

I feel like I'm starting to go crazy. I can't finish anything. My postgrad students find it strange that now they are the ones having to contact me to review their progress. I'm sick of cleaning, washing, cooking, and then having to spend the rest of the day in front of a screen only to clean, cook, wash, etc. all over again. There are still people that tell me, "Take advantage to learn how to do something new, clean the studio, throw out clothes, exercise." (I want to kill them.)

Here, there are two elements of what Federici has defined as the "patriarchy of the wage." On the one hand, COVID-19 has revealed the centrality of "care work and reproductive work" for the accumulation of capital (28), as the unpaid work done by women contributes largely to the capitalist system; moreover, the patriarchal system justifies women's free labour as a selfless expression of love. On the other hand, there is the capitalist belief that technological and scientific development are the means to reduce work. The COVID-19 pandemic clearly shows that technology has not reduced women's reproductive workload. Currently, with the distance education system, mothers have been assigned a new role as a guide for their children's online learning process. Furthermore, female academics are the ones who have a greater workload of teaching and mentoring, as male researchers consider these activities to be unproductive or time consuming.

The Social Sciences Feminist Network Research Interest Group defines teaching, mentoring, and community service as invisible work (231) largely delegated to academic women. As Federici points out, carework and reproductive labour have the greatest breadth and demand because it does not begin or end at the doors of the factory, office, or university. At present, the reproductive workload has increased for women in academia, household, and care work (29). A full-time professor and mother of two children offered the following:

Working from home is not feasible, and the worst thing is that home schooling is not either. So, it is not an option for family-work conciliation. It is impossible to have the same productivity levels as men (my husband is a researcher) in these circumstances since, because of our nature as caregiving mothers, we spend more time with our children and take more interest in them than our partners do.

Furthermore, confinement has put women's strategies for managing reproductive and paid work to the test. Historically, women have endured triple exploitation by stacking work shifts at different sites with defined hours in combination with functioning support networks (Federici 29). Likewise, they have delegated part of the care and reproductive work to other women. During this contingency plan, they cannot apply these strategies, which overloads them, since men do not necessarily assume responsibility for part of the excess work. A graduate student and mother of a young child said, "I am trying to find time at night to make quicker progress. It is difficult to be a mom, student, teacher, wife, and woman in only one place."

Throughout their careers, generations of academic mothers have resorted to the strategy of using nights as a time for research and writing. Yet the separation of spaces and routines allowed them to organize their time. Currently, their reproductive labour responsibilities, along with the excess workloads resulting from the suspension of state functions, have deprived them of rest, leisure, and recreation time, which are fundamental for maintaining mental and physical health. A researcher and mother of two children had this to say:

> "My children demand too much attention, and I'm not able to concentrate. In order to work, I have to stay awake after everyone else has gone to sleep. I work until 3:00 or 4:00 a.m. and have to wake up at 7:00 a.m. so my children will be ready for online schooling. It is really tiresome."

Likewise, public health measures hindered these mothers' ability to delegate reproductive labour and carework to family members, to government childcare programs, or to paid third parties, which obligates women to invest more time in these activities. As an example, in Mexico, before the COVID-19 pandemic, on average, women spent a total of forty-three hours and forty-seven minutes a week on unpaid work compared to the average number of hours that men spent on the same work—nine hours and thirty-seven minutes (Pedrero 16). Our research shows that during confinement, women are working an addition twenty hours of unpaid work every week.

Academic and Household Reproductive Labour in the COVID-19 Era

At the start of the twentieth century, the nuclear family acted as the reproductive basis of capitalism, in which only the man received wages to cover his family's needs; women were confined to the domestic space and were exclusively assigned carework and reproductive labour. This was partly the result of epidemics, such as cholera (1817), the flu (1889 and 1918), and typhoid fever (1900), and capitalism reorganized around the nuclear family as a stabilizing strategy of labour power (Federici).

The second half of the twentieth century was characterized by the widespread incorporation of women in wage-earning jobs, which was motivated by a variety of reasons that ranged from the war to personal fulfillment to contributing to an insufficient family income. The COVID-19 pandemic has brought about another transformation of the working world by accelerating teleworking around the world. Nowadays, social distancing and conditions of confinement, which states have adopted as a containment policy for the accelerated spread of the disease, have transformed homes into schools, offices, and recreation areas, all at the same time. Because of COVID-19, the State has transferred again to women workloads that they have managed to partly distribute to private and public institutions, through labor rights movements during the last two centuries. Consequently, women have been the ones to cover for State activities, and, concurrently, face the new demands of adapting to remote work and using new digital technologies to meet the needs of their families in isolation.

Alessandra Minello has pointed out that the COVID-19 pandemic will have serious consequences on women's professional careers. Women faculty members have carried the burden of what Mary Ann Mason, Nicolas Wolfinger, and Marc Goulden call the "motherhood penalty" (29). In addition to this, the neoliberal shift of universities and research centres over the past four decades, which can be considered part of *cognitive capitalism*, entails the commodification of academic work (Federici 18)—that is, "the pursuit of profit by academic institutions through selling the expertise of their researchers and the results of their inquiries" (Radder 4). When these institutions become commodified, the measure of researchers' worth is through prod-uctivity: the number of published journal articles, the capacity to attract funding, and the commercialization of intellectual products. Commodification imposes meritocratic careers while deepening inequalities. For academic women, the COVID-19 pandemic has meant an increase of reproductive labour. Some editors of specialized journals have noted that since confinement began, the gender divide in article submissions to their journals has widened, with an increase of up to 25 per cent in male submissions; the percentage of female submissions is the same as it was in 2018 (Flaherty). Before the COVID-19 era, faculty women who received grant funding to lead research projects, on average, were required to be 2.5 times more productive than their male peers to be considered as having the same competency level (Malisch et al.).

Final Remarks

In conclusion, in its wish to bring about maximum autonomy of work through information technology, cognitive capitalism has intensified the accumulation of capital through women's reproductive labour. In the course of the COVID-19 pandemic, the State has transferred again to women a growing amount of reproductive work, which increases gender inequality. Moreover, it prevents academic mothers from reaching the levels of productivity that Academe demand for holding the best positions, receiving funding and leading the best research projects. The merging of certain spaces—the home, work, and school—has also reduced the agency of academic mothers. Finally, extensive studies should be pursued to explain if the expansion of teleworking could take the shape of a "new enclosure" (Federici 29), which is seen in the isolation hindering women from establishing collective strategies and support networks to achieve their professional goals.

Works Cited

Federici, Silvia and George Caffentzis. "Notes on the Edu-Factory and Cognitive Capitalism." *The Commoner* (Spring/Summer 2007): 63-70. https://thecommoner.org/wp-content/uploads/2020/06/Federici-Caffentzis-Notes-of-the-edu-factory-and-cognitive-capitalism.pdf.

Federici, Silvia. *El patriarcado del salario. Críticas feministas al marxismo.* Madrid: Traficantes de Sueños, 2018. digital creative commons.

Federici, Silvia. *Re-enchanting the World*. Oakland: Kairos/PM Press/BTL, 2019. Print.

Flaherty, Colleen. "No Room of One's Own." *Inside Higher ED*, 2020, www. insidehighered.com/news/2020/04/21/early-journal-submission-data-suggest-covid-19-tanking-womens-research-productivity. Accessed 6 Jan. 2021.

Malisch, Jessica, et al. "In the Wake of COVID-19, Academia Needs New Solutions to Ensure Gender Equity." *Proceedings of the National Academy of Sciences of United States of America*, 2020, www.pnas.org/content/ 117/27/15378. Accessed 6 Jan. 2021.

Mason, Mary Ann, Nicholas H. Wolfinger, and Marc Goulden. *Do Babies Matter? Gender and Family in the Ivory Tower*. Rutgers University Press, 2013.

Minello, Alessandra. "The Pandemic and the Female Academic." *Nature*, 2020, www.nature.com/articles/d41586-020-01135-9?fbclid=IwAR 0lbPbd-C6Q43TGukFa5rzdtI5YX41gL7BbMgjy7kACufs4PQP5UpYI2 Qs. Accessed 6 Jan. 21.

Pedrero, Mercedes. *El trabajo doméstico no remunerado en México . Una estimación de su valor económico a través de la Encuesta Nacional sobre Uso del Tiempo 2002*. INMUJERES, 2005, biblioteca.clacso.edu.ar/Mexico/ crim-unam/20100517095149/El_trabajo.pdf. Accessed 6 Jan. 2021.

Radder, Hans. "The Commodification of Academic Research." *The Commodification of Academic Research: Science and the Modern University*, edited by Hans Radder, University of Pittsburgh Press, 2010, pp. 1-23.

Social Sciences Feminist Network Research Interest Group. "The Burden of Invisible Work in Academia: Social Inequalities and Time Use in Five University Departments." *Humboldt Journal of Social Relations*, vol. 1, no. 39, 2017, pp. 228-45.

Chapter Twelve

An Ode to Academic Mothers: Finding Gratitude and Grace in the Midst of COVID-19

Sara Hayden and Lynn O'Brien Hallstein

By mid-March 2020, most United States (U.S.) universities and colleges sent students home and moved all teaching online due to the COVID-19 pandemic. By mid-April, reports began to surface that "early journal submission data suggest COVID-19 is tanking women's research productivity" (Flaherty). On May 20, 2020, *Nature* published an article revealing that "early analyses suggest that female academics are posting fewer preprints and starting fewer research projects than their male peers." (Viglione). Like other motherhood scholars (O'Reilly; Willey), we were not surprised by these reports. A large body of literature (Cohen Miller; Dickensen; McCutcheon and Morrison; O'Brien Hallstein and O'Reilly; Willey) has addressed the unique challenges faced by women professors who are mothers. Among heterosexual couples who are raising children, women continue to perform the bulk of childcare and homecare work (Lewis). For mothers in academia, this disparity has significant consequences. Research demonstrates that academic women publish less than academic men, and one reason posited for this difference is that academic women may take breaks to have children and they hold more responsibilities related to raising children (McCutcheon and Morrison 93; O'Brien Hallstein and O'Reilly). Correspondingly, academic mothers are more likely to hold lower-status positions, including instructors and lecturers, and they are less likely than men or childless women to reach the rank of full professor (Cohen Miller 183; Dickenson 76; McCutcheon and Morrison 92; Young ix). The *Nature* findings generated a firestorm of response both online (Twitter and Facebook) and in print and television news, which brought some of these issues into sharp relief outside motherhood studies. As Nicole Willey notes, "It is unfortunate that it has taken a global pandemic and changing working conditions for academics everywhere for *The Chronicle* and *Inside Higher Ed* to start taking seriously the plight of academic mothers" (21).

Because we do take the plight of academic mothers seriously, we wanted to learn more about how academic mothers were experiencing the pandemic. However, we wanted to know more than just the impact of COVID-19 on academic mothers' research. We wanted to know how COVID-19 affected all parts of women's academic mothering—their professional lives, their mothering, their relationships with their partners, and how those parts were working in relation to one another. To that end, we interviewed academic mothers living with minor children to learn about their experiences during COVID-19. We found much of what we expected. In line with recent studies, many of the academic mothers we interviewed struggled to cope with the stresses of their daily lives (Grose). We document some of those struggles in this chapter; what we want to highlight, however, is the gratitude and grace with which our interviewees often responded to them.

Methods

To recruit volunteers, we posted a call for participants on academic list serves and social media. Within thirty-six hours we were contacted by eighty-six people, pointing to the importance of these issues to academic mothers. Between May 21 and June 13, 2020, we conducted fifty-four interviews. This chapter is our first effort to reflect on those data; it is based on an analysis of twenty interviews.

Recognizing that countries approached COVID-19 differently, we chose to focus on academic mothers in the U.S.[1] Interviewees included graduate students, lecturers, professors at all levels, and administrators. They ranged in age from thirty-three to fifty-three and worked at institutions ranging from small liberal arts colleges to R1 universities. Their fields spanned the humanities, social sciences, natural sciences, business, and the arts. We did not ask our interviewees to identify their race; however, two of the mothers explicitly identified as Black. Six of our interviewees did not live with a partner; of those who did, forty-four of our interviewees' partners were men, three were women, and one was nonbinary. One of our interviewees identified as nonbinary; the remainder identified as women. Our interviewees had anywhere from one to seven children; on average, they had two children, with ages ranging from a few months to seventeen years.

Interviews were recorded and transcribed using Zoom; transcripts were edited to ensure accuracy. Before each interview, participants were asked to sign an institutional review board form and complete a short demographic survey. The interviews were semistructured, which provided for a level of consistency across the conversations while also allowing flexibility to explore issues of importance to the participants. Interviews lasted an average of twenty-five minutes. Themes were developed using grounded theory (Strauss and Corbin). Names were changed to protect interviewees' privacy.

Results and Interpretations

Anticipated Challenges

Our interviewees described facing challenges that previous research suggests are common to academic mothers; however, they indicated that many of these challenges were made more difficult due to COVID-19. Even though there were some differences in terms of whether our interviewee's states shut down fully or not, all of their universities and colleges went online by mid-March, as did their children's schools. This meant that all the academic mothers we spoke with were mothering and working from home. For most of the academic mothers, this meant that their workload as mothers increased, whereas the amount of time they had to do their academic work decreased.

Office, School, Sewing Dining Room Table

The increase in family work was exacerbated by the loss of any sense of clear boundaries between their professional work, their mothering, and their children's schools. Nancy revealed: "One of the challenges is that it just, it never ends, right? There's always work to do. And so ... the lines, the sort of boundaries [between] work [and parenting] are already often blurred, and bringing, you know, the kids at home and having to kind of juggle that without clear daycare lines or work hours in the same way, has blurred." Jessica reflected on how much harder it was to separate work and home during the COVID-19 pandemic:

> Like, looking back, I thought things were really hectic. But in some ways, you know, the days that I knew I had to walk out of the office at 4:45 so I can pick [my daughter] up from after-school care and come home, and I will be able to set work aside and, you know, talk with her and have dinner and clean up and then maybe go back on [the computer to work] later at night for a little bit [were easier].

The increase in work and lack of boundaries were made more challenging due to the difficulty of finding support. Eliza reported that her husband is a healthcare worker who works with COVID-19 patients, which made it impossible for them to bring babysitters into their home. Allison lamented: "I think the challenge is really in the jugg[ling], so not being able to have childcare, because everything was closed and because, you know, relatives are scared to come over and possibly expose us or us possibly expose them." Lara explained that while prior to the pandemic they paid someone to help clean the house, COVID-19 made this unsafe. As a result, the "last week [of May 2020] ... was only the second weekend since the pandemic that I didn't spend three or four hours cleaning, laundering, all of that."

It is hard to overstate how much the shift to online learning at home increased the academic mothers' workload during the early days of the pandemic. It is well known that mothers are involved in their children's schools both in terms of in-school activities, such as attending parent-teacher conferences and volunteering at school, and outside-school activities, such as reading to children and communicating and reinforcing schools' expectations in terms of behaviour, school work, and participation (Godnik; Hill and Tyson; Hong and Ho; Jeynes). What is unprecedented about COVID-19 is what schools asked of mothers when schools pivoted to online learning. After noting that managing homeschooling was entirely her responsibility, Ann explained:

> At first, it was a lot about helping [my two daughters] understand the technology, both of them. And dealing with teachers that weren't using the same platforms ... my oldest daughter just started middle school, so she has six different teachers. Some of them were using Google Classroom, some weren't. Some were asking us to ... take pictures of the kids' work and send it to them. It was so disorganized and crazy.

As the term wore on, the workload did not lessen. Callie, who has twins, described a typical day:

> One of the twelve-year-olds [Jesse] wakes up right around 7:00, 7:30, and comes down and we try to ... get breakfast and everything. And then [we] start with remote schooling with that child for about an hour and a half to two hours, which is pretty hands on. Even though [he is] twelve, there's been a lot of resistance to doing it solo. And so there's a lot of me ...

learning about algebra again in ways I didn't know were going to happen.... And Jesse and I usually try to do different joint projects where I see if I can get more grading or work done after his schoolwork is done [and] before his sister Ann wakes up.... Then Ann gets up, and it's another hour and a half to two hours of working with her on her schoolwork.... And then usually we're done with school work [at] about two

The increased motherwork our interviewees experienced negatively affected their professional lives. Many of our interviewees talked about having to "sneak" in work between parenting and other household responsibilities. Julia described one such scenario: "I've been on the phone with ... prospective students who want to know information, and I'm cooking the girls lunch. And one of them has a meltdown.... There's so many distractions." Some mothers tried to work late at night after their children were in bed, although they were often too tired to do so. As Barbara explained, "I could ... squeeze in a little more work at night, but usually by that point, I was just so physically and mentally exhausted and ... my spouse and I would just sort of collapse." Others noted that they worked early in the morning before their children woke up. Leslie described this strategy well:

So, then, to finish my book, I was getting up, like before ... [COVID-19] I would get up around like 5:00, which for, sadly for me, is early, to write. And [once COVID-19 required everyone to work from home] I just thought I couldn't get enough done. So, then I would get up at 4:30, and then I got up at 4:00. So usually I would get up at 4:00 and write for a few hours and then my kids would get up and [I would] sort of toss them the iPad or whatever [to] get them ... [watching] shows until 7:30. Then we kind of did breakfast and then I would teach.

Exacerbating the challenge of meeting their professional responsibilities, several of our interviewees talked about privileging their husband's need to work over their own, a pattern that is well documented in heterosexual marriages (Stone; Lovejoy and Stone; O'Brien Hallstein and O'Reilly). Leslie reported how this happened in her home after a disagreement with her husband. Because his job is classified as essential, he could work at his office outside of the house, leaving her at home to manage working and childcare on her own. She reported their conversation this way: "The other day he was [at his office], and he's like, 'Listen, here's the deal: If I'm here, I'm paying so-and-so at the office to be in, and they're not working if I'm not in.' And I'm like, 'Alright, oh my god, like, just go. Go!' So, it's really, you know." In fact, the interviewer didn't know how Leslie felt about this argument and wonders whether Leslie, too, is trying to work through the implications of what happened. Other academic mothers described less overt but still challenging examples of their partners' work being privileged over their own. Because many of our interviewees did some of their work at home prior to the pandemic, many of them had home offices. However, once everyone had to stay at home, some of the interviewees gave their home offices to their partners. Similar to Leslie's struggle to articulate how befuddling and uprooting the fallout from COVID has been, Maeve also seemed at a loss for words when she mentioned her decision to give up her study: "I know he's taken over my office and, you know, he has to, but, boy, it's really different."

Makeshift Desk

When they were able to work, most of our interviewees prioritized teaching. Every one of them talked about how much more their students needed from them after their schools went online. Many specifically described students as understandably needier due to the sudden shift to online learning coupled with how scary the pandemic was for everyone. After reporting that she has low-income, high-needs students, Leslie said: "I've done a lot more email, checking in, things that have definitely been much appreciated by them. Just looking for like, the CARES Act, stuff like that, disseminating information for them, how to get help in that way." Maeve reported: "I felt that we were all flung together in a kind of emotional intimacy, and I felt a real genuine concern for the students, you know, especially at the beginning when we didn't know what was happening." Many of our interviewees explicitly noted how much more emotional labour was required of them as teachers, something already expected of them as women-identified professors (Bartos and Ives; Bellas; El-Alayli, Hansen-Brown, and Ceynar). Emily summed this up well: "We also know that women bear that emotional labour more as faculty anyway. And, you know, ... I felt a weight of that, that I hadn't ... felt before."

Finally, in line with reports of women's submissions to academic journals going down, we, too, found that many of our interviewees saw a significant drop in their research productivity. As Maeve put it: "I'm not getting any of my [research] done. Nothing, nothing. I have four people in the house, usually five because my daughter and her boyfriend are usually here, too. So, it's been very chaotic. And I need quiet to do work." Near the end of her interview, Maeve fretted: "I hope I'm not judged harshly by the university for not turning out research and writing right now." Even if they were able to do their own research, most of these academic mothers still found it challenging. As Jessica put it: "In terms of keeping up [a] research agenda and, you know, just trying to find that normal academic balance, I would say it just feels like extraordinary times to be carrying on business as usual."

Met with Gratitude and Grace

Despite the challenges these mothers experienced as they attempted to work and parent during the pandemic, we were struck by the gratitude and grace our interviewees exhibited. To be sure, many of our interviewees expressed frustration and anxiety, but many also acknowledged their privilege, conveyed concern for those less fortunate, and found silver linings in their situations.

The majority of our interviewees noted the privileges they

experience because of the nature of their jobs. Married to a professor, Callie shared that they set up their household so that she is the primary parent; in turn, her life during the pandemic has been far more stressful than her partner's. While she expressed frustration about this, she also said: "When I compare myself as an academic parenting to other women parenting outside of academia, I feel like I got off really easy.... I keep ... just hurting for people. I don't know how you do it if you don't have a job that gives you that flexibility ... I know they're probably really big struggles and losses." Barbara similarly commented that the flexibility of academic life allowed her to keep working, even if doing so was difficult: "I feel very privileged that I have a job that I have been able to continue doing. And I feel very privileged to know that even if we couldn't do daycare at all ... that we would somehow be able to make it work."

In addition to appreciating the flexibility and security their academic careers afforded them, several of our interviewees noted that academia has given them skills that allow them to help their children with homeschooling. As Katherine put it: "Even though I'm not great at everything that my ten-year-old is learning about, I do know about learning, and so I think I'm able to help facilitate his schooling from home a little bit. Even if I don't know the answer to the math question, I can help him try to find it because I have some research skills available."

Not only did our interviewees appreciate having the skills to help their children with home schooling, many acknowledged the benefits they received from spending time with their children, even when those benefits were paired with hardships. Julia is one of several interviewees who clearly stated that she never wanted to be a stay-at-home mother. Although she claimed that parenting and working during the pandemic have been "extraordinarily challenging," she also experienced some personal growth: "I've learned . . . [my children's] learning styles more intimately than I even knew. I can talk more intelligently about the way that my daughters learn, and the different ways that they learn, to the point where we're ... kind of considering some changes." Katherine similarly commented: "I feel like I'm spending a lot more time with my children, and I'm enjoying that aspect of it, but everything feels completely unmanageable." Thus, even as they struggled and even as they faced circumstances they never imagined they would face, many of the mothers we interviewed found value in the midst of adversity.

Finally, for some of the mothers we interviewed, the pandemic brought about changes they hope to incorporate into their postpandemic lives. Amy now appreciated spending more time with her family outdoors: "At a family level I think we're doing new things as a family that we weren't doing before.... In the past, I would say, 'Would anyone want to go for a hike?' and nobody would want to come with me. Somehow, I've managed to ... get everybody on board, and it's just become a habit." Lara noted that she is more relaxed both as a mother and a teacher, which she attributes, in part, to having more time at home. She is now "sleeping longer and sleeping better." Indeed, the changes brought about by the pandemic have Lara reconsidering what "work-life balance" means to her and how she may strike that balance in the future, indicating that she will try to spend more time at home when the pandemic ends.

Final Thoughts

The pandemic has been hard on everyone; however, it has hit some communities harder than others. Communities of colour have been disproportionately affected (Centers for Disease Control) and front line workers regularly put their lives at risk to provide basic services, including groceries and healthcare. With no foreseeable end in sight, pandemic fatigue is real. For academic mothers, challenges related to the pandemic are exacerbated, as they continue to provide the bulk of care for their children, manage homeschooling, and meet their professional responsibilities. The academic mothers we spoke with were aware of both the challenges they faced as mothers and the privileges they experienced as academics. To be clear, we do not want to essentialize these academic mothers. They are not perfect people, and we should not expect them to be. Indeed, many of our interviewees freely admitted where and when they fell short by being impatient with their children or partners or not meeting the expectations that they and others had of them. Nonetheless, we offer this ode to academic mothers as a first step in a larger project that seeks to acknowledge the work academic mothers are doing during COVID-19 and to honour the grace with which they often meet the challenges they face.

Endnotes

1. Of course, states responded differently to the pandemic as well; as such, we asked our interviewees to explain what was happening in the states where they lived and worked and how state laws affected their daily lives.

Work Cited

Bartos Ann E., and Sarah Ives. "Learning the Rules of the Game: Emotional Labor and the Gendered Academic Subject in the United States." *Gender, Place and Culture*, vol. 26, no. 6, 2019, pp. 778-94.

Bellas, Marcia L. "Emotional Labor in Academia: The Case of Professors." *The Annals of the American Academy of Political and Social Sciences*, vol. 561, no. 1, 1999, pp. 96-110.

Centers for Disease Control and Prevention. "Health Equity Considerations and Racial and Ethnic Minority Groups. Coronavirus Disease 2019 (COVID-19)." July 24, 2020, www.cdc.gov/coronavirus/2019-ncov/community/health-equity/race-ethnicity.html?CDC_AA_refVal=https%3A%2F%2Fwww.cdc.gov%2Fcoronavirus%2F2019-ncov%2Fneed-extra-precautions%2Fracial-ethnic-minorities.html. Accessed 7 Jan. 2021.

Cohen Miller, A. S. "Artful Research Approaches in #amwritingwithbaby: Qualitative Analysis of Academic Mothers on Facebook." *Learning Landscapes*, vol. 9, no. 2, Spring 2016, pp. 181-195.

Dickenson, Martoma. "The Joys and Challenges of Academic Motherhood." *Women's Studies International Forum*, vol. 71, 2018, pp. 76-84.

El-Alayli, Amani, Ashley A. Hansen-Brown, and Michelle Ceynar. "Dancing Backwards in High Heels: Female Professors Experience More Work Demands and Special Favor Requests, Particularly from Academically Entitled Students." *Sex Roles* 79, no. 3-4, 2018, pp. 136-50.

Flaherty, Colleen. "No Room of One's Own: Early Journal Submission Data Suggest COVID-19 Is Tanking Women's Research Productivity." *Inside Higher Ed*, 21 Apr. 2020, www.insidehighered.com/news/2020/04/21/early-journal-submission-data-suggest-covid-19-tanking-womens-research-productivity. Accessed 7 Jan. 2021.

Godnik, Wendy. "Mothers' Motivation for Involvement in their Children's Schooling: Mechanisms and Outcomes." *Motive and Emotion*, vol. 39, 2015, pp. 63-73.

Hill, Nancy E. and Diana F. Tyson. "Parental Involvement in Middle School: A Meta-Analytic Assessment of the Strategies that Promote Achievement." *Developmental Psychology*, vol. 45, no. 3, 2009, pp. 740-63.

Hong, Sehee, and Hsiu-Zu Ho. "Direct and Indirect Longitudinal Effects of Parental Involvement on Student Achievement: Second Order Latent Growth Modeling across Ethnic Groups." *Journal of Educational Psychology*, vol. 97, no. 1, 2005, pp. 32-42.

Jeynes, William H. "A Meta-analysis of the Relation of Parental Involvement to Urban Elementary School Student Academic Achievement." *Urban Education*, vol. 40, no. 3, 2005, pp. 237-69.

Lewis, Helen. "The Coronavirus Is a Disaster for Feminism." *The Atlantic*, 19 Mar. 2020, www.theatlantic.com/international/archive/2020/03/feminism-womens-rights-coronavirus-covid19/608302/. Accessed 7 Jan. 2021.

Lovejoy, Meg, and Pamela Stone. "Opting Back In." *Gender, Work & Organization*, vol. 19, no. 6, 2012, pp. 631-53.

McCutcheon, Jessica M., and Melanie A. Morrison. "'Eight Days a Week': A National Snapshot of Academic Mothers' Realities in Canadian Psychology Departments." *Canadian Psychology*, vol. 57, no. 2, 2016, pp. 92-100.

O'Brien Hallstein, Lynn, and Andrea O'Reilly, editors. *Academic Motherhood in a Post-Second Wave Context: Challenges, Strategies, and Possibilities.* Demeter Press, 2012.

O'Reilly, Andrea. "I Should Have Married Another Man; I Couldn't Do What I Do Without Him: Intimate Heterosexual Partnerships and their Impact on Mothers' Success in Academe." *Academic Motherhood in a Post-Second Wave Context: Challenges, Strategies, and Possibilities*, edited by Lynn O'Brien Hallstein and Andrea O'Reilly, Demeter Press, 2012, pp. 197-213.

Stone, Pamela. *Opting Out? Why Women Really Quit Careers and Head Home.* University of California Press, 2007.

Strauss, Anselm, and Juliet Corbin. *Basics of Qualitative Research.* Sage, 1998.

Young, Anna M. "Introduction." *Teacher, Scholar, Mother: Re-Envisioning Motherhood in the Academy*, edited by Anna M. Young, Lexington Books, 2015, pp. vii-xii.

Viglione, Giuliana. "Are Women Publishing Less During the Pandemic? Here's what the Data Say." *Nature*, vol. 581, 2020, pp. 365-66.

Willey, Nicole L. "Parenting Policies and Culture in Academia and Beyond: Making It While Mothering (and Fathering) in the Academy, and What COVID-19 Has to Do with It." *Journal of the Motherhood Initiative*, vol. 11, no. 1, 2020, pp. 201-17.I

Section II

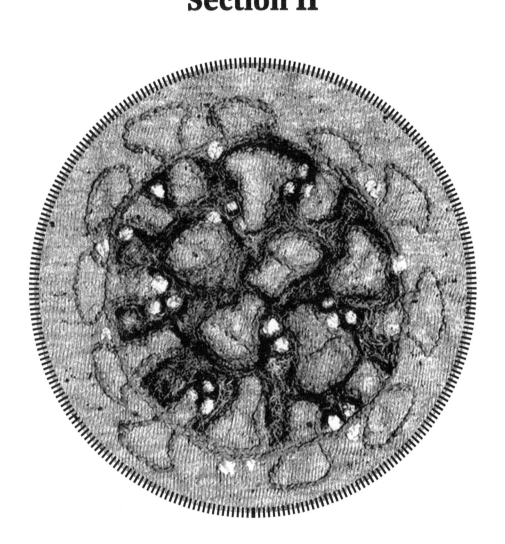

Mothers and Carework

Chapter Thirteen

20/20 Vision

Maya E. Bhave

Memory lingers like droplets
Invisible—permeating, settling
in the crevices of our skin—
under our fingernails
on cardboard box corners, and porous granite countertops
around steel-plated door handles, and on old silver picture frames
Embedded history

We don physical masks now
Some plain blue, others purloined N95s, but mostly homemade ones
They are to shield us
From strangers, our neighbours, even our own family
The certain and the uncharted—married anew
Yet how do we protect you through this?
Will you even remember all this?

Communities are locked down, people cloistered—as
it might be settled on the yellow linoleum school cafeteria floor
Mingled with tater-tot remnants on long rectangle tables
Stuck on the ATM screen at the barren, shuttered banks
Or in the desolate grocery store aisle
masked behind the last can of Heinz baked beans
adhered to the vacant, lonely store shelf where flour and yeast once
mingled

The virus waits like a forlorn furloughed college student
Watching classmates in square zoom boxes
Teachers commenting on childhood wall mementos
as homelives are revealed for the very first time
We are people today that we weren't yesterday
So, how do I parent this adult?
How do we "do" college or high school at home?

Time paradoxically stands still
Brimming with emptiness and secrecy
Our circumspect personalities battle with her dour plodding hours
The world doesn't feel safe anymore
We can't dictate schedules in the muted minutes
The mundane has vanished
As tumult screams from our expectant lungs

They tell us to sing happy birthday as we wash—twice
But you don't remember the words or the rules
You forget the common phrases now—quarantine, masks,
and lockdown
The hallways and activity rooms in your building now idle,
as you roam
craving companionship, chatter, and noise
Anything to break the hush
Even as you can't decipher the severity of these dampened days

How will you remember this?
You probably won't hold the details
Maybe this is the only blessing during the pandemic
You won't remember the exact number of dead
The daily count of ICU cases
The state-by-state percentages
Or the ever-changing international curves

I yearn for what was, unsure of what will come
I know this will pass, and my kids will soon move on
My tears left here
filling their groomed, sterilized rooms
But what of you, my dear mom
What will become of you?

I can't protect you through this
Not through the glass window of your facility
Not through my packages mailed with gloved hands
But my memory of all you've done for me permeates—deeply
And I hear you soldiering on
Always positive, seeing the beauty in the bleak
And never complaining

Your constant knowledge that the boundaries of motherhood
don't disperse easily; won't shift in unexpected, rapid ways,
and can't be tidied, or disinfected with Clorox wipes or hand
sanitizer
That in fact our journey is one of grief coupled with gratefulness
Discordant families always tied messily together
Like the ever-growing laundry piles,
strewn, twisted athletic sweatshirts and food-crammed refrigerator

These roles were never full of lucidity
Never lustrous and polished
The words don't always come for you, but the centrality of your role
remains
And so you stay
Covering my skin, close to my bones, in my scars and wrinkles
Your history so ingrained—not to be dusted away
Your words and inspiration will remain far long after the virus is
gone

Chapter Fourteen

Breathe. Exhale. Repeat: A Reflection on Love, Caretaking, and COVID-19

Haile Eshe Cole

2:00 a.m.

If there were an invisible elephant in the room, I am sure that it must have been sitting on my chest, all five hundred pounds suffocating me under its colossal weight. Lying on my back, I focused intently on my laboured breathing—each intake deep and intentional.

Deep breath in. Hold for five, four, three, two, one, and then exhale slowly until each lung is as empty as possible. Repeat.

I glanced over at my five-year-old son, who was sleeping soundly next to me in my queen-sized bed with his one tiny foot seemingly glued to my side and mirroring every movement of my body. Unlike him, I was wide awake in my small apartment in a northern suburb of Chicago. My mind was racing with unrelenting thoughts. What were those symptoms again? I reached for my phone but hesitated. No. Everything's fine. I restlessly searched for unfamiliar or telltale sensations in my body—headache, fever, sore throat. Why did it feel like my heart was racing when I was lying completely still, and why could I hear my heartbeat pulsing in my temple and breaking the silence of a not so silent city night?

Breathe in. Was that a tickle in my throat?

It was highly unlikely that I was sick, right? I had barely left my house in months, outside of playing in the driveway with my two children and taking my mother to her dialysis treatments three times a week. Social distancing, wearing masks, ordering groceries—was it all in my head? I had recently read an article, or rather, a number of articles in the news while obsessively scrolling through the news feed on my phone. "COVID Is Crushing Black Communities" one said (Ollove and Vestal). Another inquired "Why Are More Black Americans Dying of COVID-19?" (Seervai). Yet another stated that "Nearly Three Times as Many Black Americans are Dying from COVID Compared with White People" (McCarthy). Little did I know that a particularly glaring article would be released months later by the Centers for Disease Control that would assert that "Almost All of the US Kids and Teens Who've Died from COVID-19 Were Hispanic or Black" (Brueck). Why was I not surprised? I considered the very visible toll that the pandemic was taking on essential workers, first responders, and poor and working-class people of colour—not to mention the role that Black and Brown women and mothers historically played and continue to play in the service industries. As the pandemic ravaged various parts of the world, Black and Brown communities were suffering from not only heightened exposure but ultimately significant losses of life in the United States (U.S.). Given my academic and community work on maternal health, the familiarity of this incessant pattern was not lost on me. Similar to other indicators, COVID-19 had proven to be little different, as racialized health disparities remained constant.

Exhale. A small rattle in my chest?

I was the caretaker for my elderly mother and two young children. As a Black mother in the United States, I was all too familiar with fear and risk. Bearing the weight of COVID-19 while cities across the country also burned in protest, it felt that I was surrounded by—no, drowning in it. The stakes were always high, and one thing was for certain: I could not afford to get sick.

Breathe in. Cough.

I glanced at the clock. 4:00 a.m. My eyes had started to feel heavy. My breathing had relaxed. My mind had slowed from a rapid drumroll to a steady, stabilizing pulse. I finally felt myself melting into sleep.

6:00 a.m.

I heard the slight creak of the floorboards. My eyes popped open even though I was well aware of the presence occupying my room. Standing over me was my daughter, hesitantly watching to see if I was awake. Despite the fact that my eyes were still blurry from sleep and my glasses were resting on the black bookshelf next to my bed, glancing up, I could still see the grateful smile as it spread across her face. "Good morning, Mommy," she said in that sweet way that I had grown accustomed to hearing every morning for eleven years. I repositioned my body to make as much room as possible on the edge of the bed without shifting my son too much or waking him. My daughter snuggled in next to me, and I gave her a kiss on the cheek. Her curly and disheveled black locks of hair were strewn all over my pillow and touching my face. The scent of her hair, smelling of oranges and sweet cream, wafted past me.

Slow, deep breath in. Exhale.

Despite the chaotic shift to our lives the last few months and the respective isolation of a global health pandemic, I appreciated the slower pace—the lack of hustle and bustle or the daily grind. It was not only a welcome respite but also a privilege afforded to me given the flexibility of my job—one that given the current circumstances, I would be thoughtless to take for granted. Wedged between two small bodies and with barely any sleep under my belt, I still made sure to relish these small moments. Behind me, I felt the movement of small limbs underneath the cozy flower-patterned comforter. I turned to see my son's large, curious, and sparkling almond eyes staring back at me from the middle of his chubby hazelnut face. "Good morning Mommy. I'm hungry."

9:00 a.m.

School had been transitioned to remote learning, and my son's preschool had closed. My mornings now consisted of ABCs, 123s, math, and art—only on the good days. We even built a small parachute to drop from the patio of the third-level flat to see if it would float and salvage the egg from breaking. Science. I had become the teacher. "Did you complete your assignments for today? Did you login for your check in with the teacher? Where is your iPad?" There was no time to wait for an answer today. Although I had made breakfast, I hadn't eaten myself. I grabbed myself a cup of hot, herbal tea. I was already late for my morning Zoom meeting.

11:00 a.m.

My mother was a fighter.

A single mother, raised by a single mother in a little Texas town, she had taught me to love hard and to put family first. A creative free spirit, writer, teacher, and natural nurturer, I learned much of what I know about taking care of others from her.

I could hear her coughing in the next room over. She clenched to her chest the red, heart-shaped pillow, covered in the whimsical scribbles and doodles of doting grandchildren. It had only been a few months since she had been released from the hospital. A heart attack months prior had resulted in a triple bypass, open heart surgery—multiple surgeries—a few major complications, infections, and residence at three short-term rehabilitation facilities. After months of therapy to help her regain her strength and ability to walk, she was allowed to return home. Lucky for us, she had been released home only a month before the uptick in COVID-19 cases, the subsequent shut down, and the large spread of COVID-19 in nursing homes and rehabilitation facilities around the country. Unlucky for us, my family and I were relatively new to the Chicago area and far from our community and support system back home in Texas.

In the kitchen, I prepared a small lunch. It was time to visit the clinic for one of my mother's four-hour long treatments. The sessions drained her strength and energy, so it was important that she had something to eat beforehand. In addition to the roles of cook, maid, and caretaker, I had also been promoted to nurse. Twice a day, I needed to clean and dress the wound from my mother's surgical site. With strict instructions from the doctor, the small table in her bathroom had become a makeshift nurse's station.

Before leaving the house, I bandaged my mother's knee and helped to secure her leg brace that provided additional support as she climbed up and down the stairs. Although a welcome change from hauling a heavy wheelchair in the back of my small SUV for months, walking was a spectacular feat for her. A few months ago, she could not stand unassisted. I was so proud and in awe of mother's desire to recover, to grow, to live. Yet the fear of an impending fall and its potentially damaging physical impacts weighed heavily on all of us. What if the support failed? Would it buckle under the weight or give out over time? If she lost her balance, could I catch her? Would my arms and legs have the strength to bear the weight of her body and mine? Was I strong enough?

5:00 p.m.

Breathe.

I was tired. The toll of restless nights was catching up with me, and I was running on fumes. Being cooped up in the house for days on end with a five- and eleven-year-old was good for no one. My afternoon had been filled with soccer in the yard, elaborate chalk paintings on the concrete, board games, and walks around the neighborhood— not to mention the sprinkle of a few more virtual meetings interspersed here and there. We had just returned home from picking up my mother, and I scanned the freezer to see what I would prepare for dinner. Maybe, we would order out tonight. Yes, delivery and a movie on the couch sounded about right.

8:00 p.m.

Inhale. Hold for five, four, three, two, one.

I stared at the white lights and garland strung over the fireplace that still hung from Christmas. With only the slight glow from the streetlights beaming through the large bay windows, the room was calm and serene. It was my favourite place to be in the house and had become a tranquil space for me during the pandemic. I could hear my children chatting and playing while I sat alone in the middle of the living room with my legs crossed and eyes closed, taking deep breaths in and out and trying to relax and clear my mind.

Sometimes, I imagined being by the water—the salty foam and waves from the Gulf of Mexico splashing about with my breathing and body matching the rhythmic rock of the blue-green water. Sometimes, I imagined the sparkling white lights as stars, encircling me with their brilliance and lifting me up and away to less complicated days.

Exhale slowly until each lung is as empty as possible.

Laughter. This time it was my mother accompanied by the rambunctious high-pitched giggles. It was rowdy and interrupted my brief meditation, yet I smiled, despite it all. Breaking the silence further was the rumble of running feet coming closer and closer and … "Mommy."

Breathe.

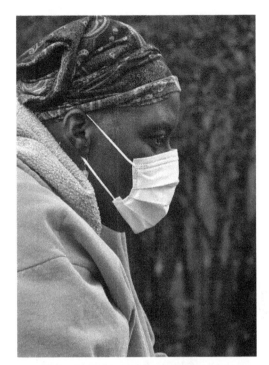

Works Cited

Brueck, Hilary. "CDC: Almost All of the US Kids and Teens Who've Died from COVID-19 Were Hispanic or Black." *Business Insider*, 15 Sept. 2020, www.businessinsider.com/cdc-black-and-brown-children-dying-from-the-coronavirus-2020-9. Accessed 7 Jan. 2021.

McCarthy, Niall. "Nearly Three Times As Many Black Americans Are Dying From Covid-19 Compared With White People As Pandemic Death Toll Surpasses 150,000 [Infographic]." *Forbes*, 30 July 2020, www.forbes.com/sites/niallmccarthy/2020/07/30/nearly-three-times-as-many-black-americans-are-dying-from-covid-19-compared-with-white-people-as-pandemic-death-toll-surpasses-150000-infographic/. Accessed 7 Jan. 2021.

Ollove, Michael, and Christine Vestal. "COVID-19 Is Crushing Black Communities. Some States Are Paying Attention." *The Pew Charitable Trusts*, 27 May 2020, www.pewtrusts.org/en/research-and-analysis/blogs/stateline/2020/05/27/covid-19-is-crushing-black-communities-some-states-are-paying-attention. Accessed 7 Jan. 2021.

Seervai, Shanoor. "Why Are More Black Americans Dying of COVID-19?" *Commonwealth Fund*, 26 June 2020, www.commonwealthfund.org/publications/podcast/2020/jun/why-are-more-black-americans-dying-covid-19. Accessed 7 Jan. 2021.

Chapter Fifteen

Caesura

Jennifer Long

Caesura developed from my observations of the struggle my daughters grapple with as they find a balance between their dependence on me and their growing independence—a situation that has intensified with the COVID-19 pandemic. By photographing domestic still lives, our interactions, and the spaces in between, I am capturing the texture of this time and our experiences within it. These images are ordinary and fleeting scenes, reflecting on intergenerational experience and familial understanding.

1. Observations from isolation, Day 60: Mirroring

2.

3.

4.

Observations from isolation
2. Day 38: Eggshells and Ice Cubes
3. Day 45: Rolled Leaf
4. Day 191: Binoculars

5.

6.

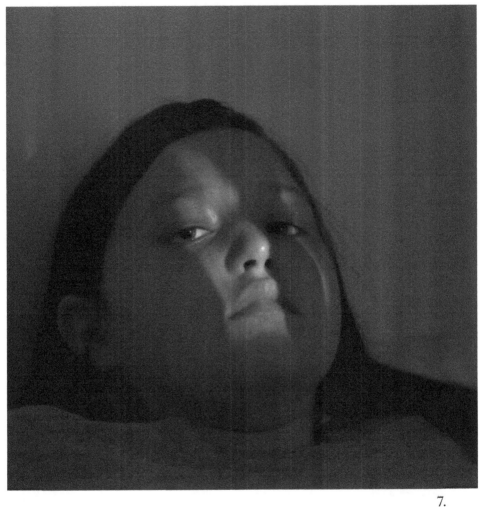

7.

Observations from isolation
5. Day 5: Staring into Seas of Blue
6. Day 117: Cottage Towels
7. Day 11: Boredom

9.

8.

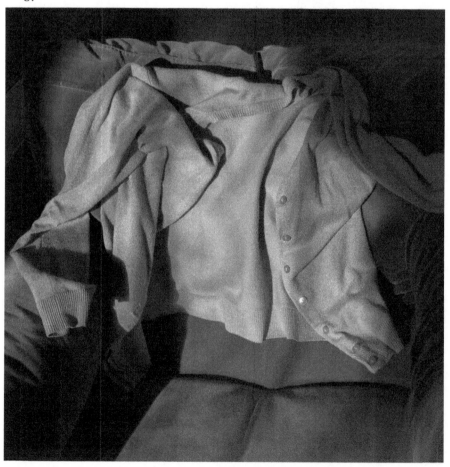

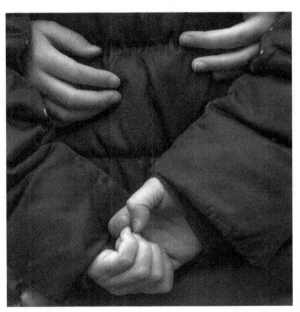

10.

Observations from isolation
8. Day 37: Vanishing Act
9. Day 100: Three Leaves
10. Day 5: Embrace

11.

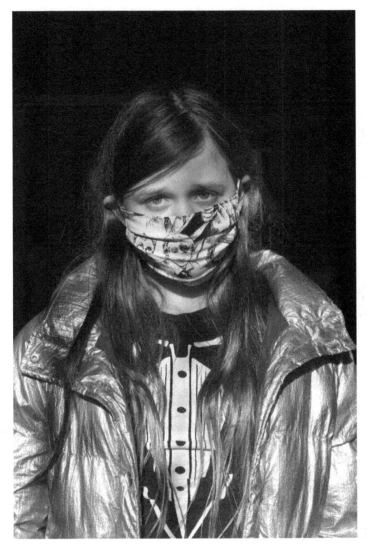

12.

Observations from isolation
11. Day 168: Ranunculus and Milk Tags
12. Day 26: Rielynd in Her Harry Potter Mask

Jennifer Long, from the *Caesura* series, 2020, (Original images in colour).
Caesura is created with support from Canada Council for the Arts, Ontario Arts
Council, and Toronto Arts Council with funding from the City of Toronto.

Chapter Sixteen

Knock Down Series

Barbara Philipp

1. Dear Josefine

There were two inhuman sides of the political decisions to prevent the spread of the virus, which influence our most personal "habitat": to prohibit staying close to a dying one, somebody who cared for you so much but now must leave alone; and to mandate a mother give birth without the partner or a close friend to help the mother in labour and to welcome the child into life.

Taking care of others gets outside of the system. It must be controlled. But people who are getting paid for care are not protected well enough. A system of paradoxes. Awful conditions. "Off" the advice.

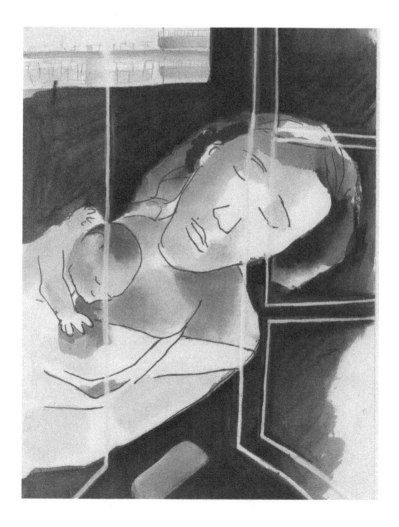

2. Shut Up!

I am not allowed to say anything. Stay home. Be silent. I got a muzzle. I am not comfortable behind my muzzle. My mask. I bark. They are afraid that I bite. Mom is biting. What happens if I do not perform? To see friends is a risk. And not accepted in public or in private places. Meeting in secret. Against the law and the public opinion. Heavy restrictions are made, and to question their usefulness puts me immediately in the conspiracy corner of deniers. "I am too tired to be (a mother)."

3. Vital Line

Injections of life. Bloodletting. Boom barriers. New carers are closed up in quarantine. Rich countries are waiting for these carers.

Who needs the money to sustain their families? Exploitation. The avarice to have cheaper offers and cheap workers brings the risk of a collapse in care.

The price will be paid by...

4. Caring

This caregiver has a family at home. She has to decide. Taking care of the elderly people in a strange country or getting home, crossing the borders, which will be closed just behind her. Or they are already closed. So she cannot go back in her home country. She mothers an old man. She is his nurse, his carer. She is in his home while her family and children are behind the borders. The family of the old man is not allowed to see his children. They are blocked in front of the house.

5. Net Is Working

I am caught in the net. I have the net behind me. It is my backyard, my sky, my universe. The net. I lost my first skin, which I just pick up from the ground. The loss of my motherly body. Me naked again. Skinned. Without glitter. Looking at the spectator who has an open view of me.

Chapter Seventeen

The Balancing Act Is Magnified: U.S. Mothers' Struggles amidst a Pandemic

Molly Wiant Cummins and Grace Ellen Brannon

S uccesses are often noticed in reflection after an event; struggles are felt in the moment. When COVID-19 was recognized as a public health emergency in the United States (U.S.), many mothers felt their struggles more acutely. Much of 2020 feels like a pressure cooker for mothers, where the steam valve does not fully relieve the mounting pressure they felt because of COVID-19. Most families are experiencing additional stress due to COVID-19, but in heterosexual couples, that work disproportionately falls to women, as they are spending, on average, fifteen hours more per week on education and household tasks (Cohen and Hsu). This additional work reflects the normative discourse of intensive motherhood, which society uses to judge mothers as good or bad. Coined by Sharon Hays, intensive motherhood is *"child-centered, expert-guided, emotionally absorbing, labor-intensive, and financially expensive"* (8). Jean-Anne Sutherland notes that intensive motherhood requires mothers always give of themselves "physically, emotionally, psychologically and intellectually" (313). In this chapter, we argue the COVID-19 pandemic has amplified the demands of intensive motherhood on mothers. From suddenly becoming at-home educators to the difficulties of managing a family in quarantine, mothers during the pandemic are experiencing added stressors, affecting every aspect of their lives.

In this chapter, we provide mothers' perceptions of their struggles during the early weeks of the COVID-19 pandemic, which were collected via telephone interviews in May and early June 2020. All eighteen mothers live in the U.S., are over age eighteen, and are cisgender women married to men. The participants' reflections on their struggles before and during the pandemic highlight how mothers experience the increased demands of intensive motherhood through the lens of COVID-19. We first discuss intensive motherhood and how participants relate it to their struggles. Then, we turn to the participants' answers and self-reflections. Lastly, we draw some implications about the effects of COVID-19 on intensive motherhood.

Intensive Motherhood

Intensive motherhood as a normative discourse requires mothers to spend time, energy, and money on their children as informed by expert advice. Susan Douglas and Meredith Michaels extended Hays's definition to include the media's role in perpetuating intensive motherhood discourse in an easily consumable format. Harmony Newman and Angela Henderson call it the "modern mystique"—a "seemingly ubiquitous ideology of motherhood as the ideal despite a general sense of dissatisfaction with it" (474). Intensive motherhood also narrows the category of who can be considered a good mother: typically married, white, middle-class, cisgender, heterosexual, and able-bodied women (O'Brien Hallstein). Those who fall outside of this ideal cannot reach good mother status because they are deemed inappropriate by intensive motherhood, reinforcing the dominance of the discourse (O'Brien Hallstein). Yet there is an allure to good mother status, as the label offers security, self-worth, and belonging (Ennis).

Andrea O'Reilly explores "ideological assumptions" of what she terms "patriarchal motherhood" (14). Among these assumptions are idealization, which "sets unattainable expectations of and for mothers," and individualization, which requires "mothering to be the work and responsibility of one person" (14). Through individualization, mothering experiences are thought to be unique to the individual, not elements of a collective experience. So, although mothers certainly experience similarities in their childraising (e.g., a child taking their first steps or losing their first tooth), individualization causes mothers to feel alone in the experience. The feeling of being alone also falls under the assumption of privatization, which "locates motherwork solely in the reproductive realm of the home" (14). As a result, mothers are physically separated from others in similar situations.

That mothers feel alone in their motherhood is not an accidental function of intensive motherhood. O'Reilly explains that normative motherhood discourses "are rewritten in response to, and as a result of, significant cultural and economic change" (44). She sees intensive motherhood as a response to the rise of neoliberalism, an ideology predicated upon individualism and the removal of government interference in both the market and in life more generally. A neoliberal normative motherhood discourse, thus, compels mothers to see their experience and responsibility as only their own. As Fiona Green posits, intensive motherhood "serves the interests of neo-liberal, white supremacist, capitalist patriarchy" (199). In this way, intensive mother-hood charges mothers as the primary caretakers of their children—an individualizing experience keeping mothers so focused on private concerns that they have no time or energy to spend in collective reimagining. These societal and simultaneously internalized pressures can further exacerbate the day-to-day issues mothers face by increasing the stress on them.

Additionally, intensive motherhood establishes expectations that are almost impossible to meet, assuring mothers feel guilt and shame in their failure. However, O'Reilly believes guilt and shame are "neither accidental nor inconsequential" but are "deliberately manufactured and monitored" to psychologically regulate mothers (58). Sutherland underscores this mother guilt: "The notion of maternal guilt is so pervasive in our culture as to be considered a 'natural' component of motherhood" (310). Moreover, the demands of modern consumerism complicate mothers' experiences with their children, causing them not to question the standards to which they aspire but instead to perceive themselves as failures (Sutherland). In other words, mothers internalize intensive motherhood predicated upon neoliberalism to find themselves constantly failing; then, they assume it is a personal, individual issue rather than a problem with society at large.

In this project, we ask participants about their struggles both before and during the pandemic. Admittedly, we are asking mothers to focus on the ways they perceive themselves not living up to the so-called good mother expectations they have, which are informed by intensive motherhood. Yet in listening to their individual perceptions, we can better understand their lived experiences. Their answers demonstrate, subsequently, the increased demands intensive motherhood has placed on mothers as a result of the pandemic through such challenges as social distancing and quarantine.

Interviews and Participants

After obtaining approval from the institutional review board, we recruited participants from fellow members of private Facebook groups specifically aimed at mothers, allowing us easy access to eighteen mothers over the age of eighteen. We interviewed participants from around the U.S. via recorded phone calls, which lasted between twenty-two and fifty-four minutes. All participants were cisgender women married to men, and all had between one and four children. Although the children's ages ranged from seven weeks old to adults (in their thirties), most of the children were five years old or younger, meaning the struggles the mothers experienced might have been tied to the higher dependency of young children on parents for their everyday needs. Notably, our snowball sampling allowed us to interview two grandmothers as well. Some of the participants were moms of multiples (i.e., twins), and some had children with various diagnoses, ranging from time spent in the NICU after birth to ADHD. Most of the participants were in their thirties or forties, and most were working mothers. A few participants were highly educated, holding at least a master's degree. Most participants were white and at least middle class. With these demographics, the participants fulfill the ideal of intensive motherhood—that is, society likely sees them as good mothers, even though most of them challenge intensive motherhood by not being stay-at-home parents. Instead, most participants work both outside and inside the home, managing both a job and their household simultaneously. All participant names reported are pseudonyms chosen by the women.

From the Mothers

In this section, we analyze the mothers' words in their descriptions of their struggles, which while varying widely, still bear some common themes. For the purposes of analysis, we will separate the mothers' perceived struggles pre-COVID-19 and during COVID-19 to feature how the struggles shifted due to the pandemic. As we discussed above, when mothers inevitably fall short of the intensive motherhood ideal, they feel guilty. It should come as no surprise that two of the most common words the women used to describe their struggles were "guilt" and "enough." Mothers felt guilty when they did not live up to their own expectations, such as Mandy, a white mother to a three-year-old son and three-month-old twin boys, who often felt guilty when she was short-tempered with her children. Similarly, mothers frequently asked themselves whether they were doing enough. Carol, a mother to three daughters, aged between three and eight, asked: "Am I balancing their meals enough? Am I giving them enough opportunities to do whatever? Am I spending enough time with them?" These common patterns are important to keep in mind as we turn to the struggles participants experienced as mothers.

Struggles Pre-COVID-19

Given that most participants were working mothers, the number one issue they struggled with before the pandemic was time. This included balancing life between work and home and being present with children when at home. As Leslie, a white lawyer and mother to an eight-year-old daughter and a four-year-old son, remarked, "It just seems like there's never time to do everything well, and I feel guilty." Leslie's comment encapsulates what many working mothers said and felt. Another common struggle experienced by participants was discipline, whether how to adequately discipline children or how to strike a balance between being too strict and too permissive. Sparrow—a white, stay-at-home mom with a master's degree and three daughters five and under (the youngest having been born during the pandemic, which in itself presents a unique set of parenting circumstances)—explained discipline can be frustrating and overwhelming when trying to figure out various styles without relapsing into the way her parents parented (e.g., spanking), which she does not necessarily want to emulate. Many mothers also struggled with yelling or displaying a lack of patience with their children, thereby increasing their feelings of guilt. For example, Kate, a white mother with a four-year-old son and a two-month-old son, who also holds a PhD, said she struggles with yelling "too quickly." Participants' struggles before the pandemic centered on the balancing act these mothers engage to try to do everything well.

Some mothers struggled with the isolation of not having friends or family nearby to help, which, again, can increase the chance of losing patience with children. This is best summarized by Tasha, a white military spouse with two children under four, who felt isolated because she did not have other adults to relate to around her. She said this isolation made it difficult for her to remember that other mothers were struggling as well; she felt alone in the experience as a military spouse unfamiliar with others in her community. Furthermore, she described that she was "just waiting for this period of life to be over," but she also sadly acknowledged that it was not leaving anytime soon. Thus, most of the issues mothers in our study struggled with before COVID-19 revolved around a lack of balance—an imbalance between working and making time for children, an imbalance regarding the right amount or type of discipline, and/or an imbalance concerning the time spent with their children and the time spent away from them.

Struggles during COVID-19

We conducted interviews in May and June 2020, amidst the chaos of quarantine, the end of an unusual school year, and with little hope on the horizon of when normalcy might return. As a result, asking mothers to explain their struggles during the COVID-19 pandemic was perhaps the easiest question for many of them to answer. As Tasha said, the pandemic "has just amplified the stressors and the struggles of motherhood and parenthood a lot." Indeed, many participants identified something similar in their answers by explaining that they thought their struggles were like those of other parents in the pandemic. In contrast to the way that time was a struggle for many mothers prepandemic, it is a different burden during COVID-19. This is perhaps best explained by Gail, a white working mother of two sons under the age of nine, who observed that it feels bizarre to say there is not enough time when, if anything, there seems to be more time. In other words, now that families were isolating at home, they technically had more time together, yet the pressures of a full-time job did not dissipate, and the duties of managing a home increased due to the number of people occupying the same space consistently for greater time periods. Like Gail, many participants reiterated the feeling of not having enough time to accomplish everything, even though mothers were around their families for more of the day. Some mothers indicated that they were struggling with the reality that everyone being together all day meant they themselves had no alone time, increasing their own frustration with the situation. Mothers also struggled with creating or establishing structure during the pandemic, especially with keeping children occupied. Martina, a white part-time nurse and mother to a nine-year-old son and four-year-old twin boys, said she did not feel like she was "resourceful enough" to keep her children entertained at home, triggering guilt when they ultimately watched more television than she would have allowed prepandemic.

Another major struggle for mothers was remote education. For example, Gail said parents were now expected to work full-time as well as teach and parent full-time, which she declared an unsustainable endeavour. Patricia Cohen and Tiffany Hsu posit that in heterosexual married couples who work full-time, mothers "provide close to 70 percent of childcare during standard working hours"—a "burden" that was "supersized" in the face of quarantine. Intensive motherhood prescribes women pick up the slack of excess parenting in order to be good mothers free of guilt. During the pandemic, mothers obliged to stay home were pushed further into intensive motherhood; they had to do excess parenting without the additional support of other adults, such as teachers, grandparents, or childcare providers. Thus, the demands of intensive motherhood have amplified the struggles mothers have faced during the COVID-19 pandemic.

Implications

The struggles mothers faced before the pandemic centred around balance, trying to juggle multiple responsibilities without dropping everything. Recognition of COVID-19 as a public health emergency in the U.S. only increased their number of responsibilities, as mothers now had fewer support systems upon which to rely—a decidedly neoliberal move that requires mothers do more work with fewer resources (O'Reilly). Like Kate noted, "I'm totally down with a village" of people to help raise children as "there are people that are just wired better for the patience and letting them [children] explore." Yet in the pandemic, these support structures have been virtually nonexistent. Similarly, Suzanna, a white mother with two daughters under ten, prioritized a "stellar job performance" in order to avoid the possibility that she could be laid off. These mothers struggled to balance their multiple roles as mother, employee, educator, advocate, and partner. Some mothers, like GH, a white teacher and mother to a five-year-old daughter and a seven-month-old daughter, explained women just figure it out. A friend of GH's told her she could be a "great teacher and a good mom or a great mom and a good teacher;" GH chose to be a great mom and is just figuring out how to best fulfill that role.

Much of this balancing act is because, as Solveig Brown argues, the U.S. has "relied on intensive mothering norms to bridge the gaps between cultural change and its effect on childrearing" (40) rather than putting in place policies that effectively support parents. The reliance on mothers has only increased during the pandemic, as mothers have become at-home educators, housekeepers, and/or personal assistants for their families in addition to whatever other responsibilities they may hold (e.g., their job or service or community activities, such as being a local board member). Even as participants referred to the fact that others were similarly struggling, the mothers still experienced the pandemic as an isolating experience, as they did not have access to support systems that they might have had prepandemic. The combination of isolation and increased demands on a mother's time escalated the pressures of intensive motherhood so that when mothers inevitably dropped one of the responsibilities they juggled, they felt guilt. Unfortunately, the pandemic is one more instance in which the U.S. will continue to rely on mothers shouldering the slack created by a society unprepared to adequately handle such a crisis.

Yet if normative motherhood discourses are affected by "significant cultural and economic change" (O'Reilly 44), then certainly COVID-19 marks a place of possibility for the normative discourse of intensive motherhood to be shifted. One participant, Anne, noted how mothers and parents need to cultivate themselves "as parents in communities." Anne explained that no one teaches mothers how to parent except their children, to some degree, so figuring out how to parent well should be a societal issue rather than an individual one. Instead of creating societal parameters of success or failure, as intensive motherhood does, Anne suggested we find ourselves communities of others who validate and support our way of parenting, not without challenging us to be better parents, but where we can stop worrying whether we are good enough as parents. Amidst an isolating pandemic, the Facebook groups from which we recruited participants may serve as that kind of community, allowing mothers to be honest about their struggles in a place where others listen and understand rather than judge. Other participants, too, echoed that support from likeminded people helped them manage the stressors of pandemic life.

Conclusion

In this study, we interviewed eighteen mothers who primarily fit the intensive motherhood ideal about their struggles both before COVID-19 and during the pandemic. Since most participants were working mothers, their major struggle was balancing home life and work life. Intensive motherhood claims that a good mother would not need to find balance; she would already be at home with the children. As a result, many participants struggled with guilt over some of the choices they made as mothers and wondered whether they were doing enough for their children. The pandemic only amplified mothers' struggles. The demands of intensive motherhood became more intense. Again, mothers struggled to find balance. Although there was seemingly more time, mothers still felt there was less time to do everything well. Unfortunately, the excess parenting that the pandemic created, especially around remote learning and childcare, fell to mothers. COVID-19 has made parenting a harder experience in myriad ways, some of which we have not yet even discovered.

Works Cited

Brown, Solveig. "Intensive Mothering as an Adaptive Response to Our Cultural Environment." *Intensive Mothering: The Cultural Contradictions of Modern Motherhood*, edited by Linda Rose Ennis, Demeter Press, 2014, pp. 27-46.

Cohen, Patricia, and Tiffany Hsu. "Pandemic Could Scar a Generation of Working Mothers." *The New York Times*. 3 Jun. 2020, www.nytimes.com/2020/06/03/business/economy/coronavirus-working-women.html. Accessed 7 Jan. 2021.

Douglas, Susan J., and Meredith W. Michaels. *The Mommy Myth: The Idealization of Motherhood and How It Has Undermined All Women*. Free Press, 2004.

Ennis, Linda Rose. "Intensive Mothering: Revisiting the Issue Today." *Intensive Mothering: The Cultural Contradictions of Modern Motherhood*, edited by Linda Rose Ennis, Demeter Press, 2014, pp. 1-23.

Green, Fiona Joy. "Re-conceptualising Motherhood: Reaching Back to Move Forward." *Journal of Family Studies*, vol. 21, no. 3, 2015, pp. 196-207.

Hays, Sharon. *The Cultural Contradictions of Motherhood*. Yale University Press, 1996.

Newman, Harmony D., and Angela C. Henderson. "The Modern Mystique: Institutional Mediation of Hegemonic Motherhood." *Sociological Inquiry*, vol. 84, no. 3, 2014, pp. 472-91.

O'Brien Hallstein, D. Lynn. "Introduction to Mothering Rhetorics." *Women's Studies in Communication*, vol. 40, no. 1, 2017, pp. 1-10.

O'Reilly, Andrea. *Matricentric Feminism: Theory, Activism, and Practice*. Demeter Press, 2016.

Sutherland, Jean-Anne. "Mothering, Guilt and Shame." *Sociology Compass*, vol. 4, no. 5, 2010, pp. 310-21.

Chapter Eighteen

Mothering Beyond Monogamy: Navigating Nontraditional Relationships of Care in the Society of Individuals during COVID-19

Stevie Lang Howson

Perhaps we can say, we are all vulnerable to those environmental and social structures that make our lives possible, and that when they falter, so do we. To be dependent implies vulnerability: one is vulnerable to the social structure upon which one depends, so if the structure fails, one is exposed to a precarious condition
—Butler, *The Force of Nonviolence* 46

Introduction

As I write this chapter, I am still processing what happened in 2020—the ways it affected my life and those around me and the ways in which mothering, relationships, and care were integrally bound up in how those effects patterned themselves across my life. In many ways, my contribution to this collection on mothering and COVID-19 is a way of handling these experiences within myself, of deploying one of the most stable elements of my life—my love of research and theory—to make sense of the turbulence of the past seven months. As such, this is a profoundly personal chapter.

As we entered March 2020, and COVID-19, or coronavirus, as we were calling it then, went from a vague, international concern to a turbulent force restructuring all areas of my everyday life, I was precariously employed teaching sociology at a university in Australia, working on my PhD. I made just enough money to rent a small apartment for myself and my four-year-old child. I was also part of a network of people across Sydney who engaged in a practice known as ethical non-monogamy—that is to say, we structured relationships that involved love, sexuality, care, and support in ways that are outside of the organizing principles of the monogamous couple and the nuclear family. In addition, many, if not most of us, were also queer, trans, disabled, and neurodivergent. As we entered the COVID-19 pandemic, I had several deeply supportive relationships, which helped in mothering my child. Not all these relationships were partnerships in any way that would be recognized within prevalent social norms, but all of them were profoundly important to the structure of my life. In addition to this, at the start of the pandemic, there were between two and four people whom I might have called partners in some sense, including Rob and Kira, whose experiences feature in this chapter.

Throughout this chapter, I share and try to make sense of my personal experiences mothering as a nonmonogamous person during the COVID-19 pandemic. In so doing, I make the argument, following Judith Butler's analysis of the social contract, that neoliberal society is foundationally structured as a society of individuals—that is, under neoliberalism, society is imagined as something that emerges after, and by the agreement of already-existing individuals and, therefore, can be suspended if necessary, as it was argued was the case during the pandemic. I also draw on critiques of neoliberalism from scholars of care, who argue that the vulnerability of each person and our needs for care cannot be reconciled with neoliberal notions of subjectivity. I argue that the nuclear family and, by extension, the monogamous dyad are a core strategy within neoliberalism to structure and contain relationships of care within gendered dynamics, which are reliant on unpaid labour of women and marginalized people. Under neoliberalism,

I argue that the nuclear family and the mononormative couple become the only socially sanctioned means of accessing care and support outside the market. I suggest, therefore, that nonmonogamous ways of structuring dependency, care, and affection can be disruptive to the logics by which care is managed under neoliberalism. Finally, through an exploration of the complex process of reading public health orders and COVID-19 restrictions as a person whose care and support structures fell so far outside the nuclear family, I argue that these restrictions were made on the basis of the foundational assumption that individuals precede society, that society can be suspended as needed, and that care outside of the monogamous dyad or the nuclear family is inherently optional. I go on to suggest that on a fundamental level, the structuring of legal restrictions around these premises represents an erasure of the collective work of care that mothering demands, and in addition operated in ignorance of and erasure of alternative ways of structuring care, dependency and love.

1. Day One, March 2020

I was lying in bed beside my partner, Rob. Despite being next to someone who loved and cared about me, I felt panicked and alone. I was on my phone, reading the news and flicking through messages from friends. One was taking their children out of school, pre-emptively—the schools would close any day, they said. Another was leaving Sydney for their parent's home in a regional centre. Others had lost their work. The international news was reporting that they were setting up field hospitals in parks in New York City.

It seemed imminent that there would be a lockdown of some sort. This felt important, necessary. I was worried about people who would die from this disease and about the immunocompromised and higher-risk people who were already having to isolate themselves. I felt frustrated we weren't already taking more serious action. I wanted to do everything I could to reduce the risk that I would contribute to the spread of the disease.

My kid was with my mother. It was a Sunday morning. I'm a sole parent.

The idea of possibly being stuck alone in my home with my small, disabled child panicked me. I didn't mother alone. I never have. I don't know that I can. I depend on my mother for one night of uninterrupted sleep every two weeks. I depend on childcare professionals to be able to work. I depend on being able to work my hours, in my precarious casual job without leave or allowances and on being able to pay for the housing and food my child and I need.

It seemed in that moment that the fragility of the structures that made my life liveable was revealed. I felt like I had grasped hold of a string in the fabric that clothed me and the whole thing had unravelled, leaving me naked, exposed to whatever was to come, and alone.

I tried to explain these feelings to Rob. "I'll come and stay with you," he replied.

And I tried to explain how part of my income came from a government welfare payment for single parents. The government agency responsible for administering these payments do not define what makes someone single or not; it is a discretionary decision that is vaguely based around financial ties as well as whether you live with someone, whether you have a sexual relationship with them, and whether you are seen as a couple socially. The fact that Rob and I had a sexual relationship meant that his living with me might jeopardize my access to my payment and, worse, expose me to criminal offences should I fail to properly disclose such an arrangement to the authorities. I was afraid of being utterly alone facing whatever was to come, but also afraid of losing the financial resources that would ensure my survival.

In that moment, it felt that whatever remained of my grasp on a neoliberal, individualist selfhood failed. I faced, in that moment, the enormity of my dependence. The non-traditional, post-nuclear-family network of care I had set up around myself did not make me less dependent. It was a novel solution to, and at times an obfuscation of, the radical dependence I had on the others who facilitated my life and my mothering. Although coming to terms with vulnerability has been a feature of my research for years, as well as a hallmark of the personal work I have done since becoming a mother, what Butler means when they say that "the relational understanding of vulnerability shows us that we are not altogether separable from the conditions that make our lives possible or impossible" (46). Put simply, I could not survive alone.

2. The Neoliberal Subject and the Society of Individuals

We order and understand our lives, and the crises within them, through the framework of neoliberalism. Neoliberalism is more than a set of principles or an ideology about economics. It is, at root, a set of connected statements about what it is to be human (Foucault; Read). The neoliberal subject is envisaged as radically individual, agentic, and, above all, responsible for furthering their own goals and pursuing his own happiness (Hoppania and Vaittinen). Under neoliberalism, suffering is understood to be the consequence of poor choices, a failure to properly exercise the responsibility for making oneself happy (Baker). The failure to create a happy life for oneself, through rational choice, jeopardizes one's subject position entirely. Thus, subjectivity is increasingly provisional under neoliberalism; it must be earned (Butler, *Precarious Life*; Hoppania and Vaittinen), and there are no means for asserting an alternate framework of subjectivity (Rustin). The individualist neoliberal framework of subjectivity represents the only viable means for recognition as a subject. As Hanna-Kaisa Hoppania and Tiina Vaittinen argue, "In the neoliberal order, the subjects who are incapable of filling the subject position of homo economicus are denied a subject position altogether" (83).

The neoliberal mode of subjectification finds itself uncontested, precisely because avowal of the rational individual has been a core project of Western philosophy since the Enlightenment. Butler identifies the collective phantasy of the 'state of nature' at the core of the key Enlightenment, liberal doctrines, which continue to underpin our understanding of society (*The Force of Nonviolence* 30). The state of nature is understood as a state in which individuals existed without the organizing principle of society in a state of conflict, greed, and violence (Butler, *The Force of Nonviolence* 30). Society is, according to this phantasy, an agreement made between people (i.e., men) who are already individuated, who are already adult, and whose care needs are invisible, in order to avoid the violence inherent in the state of nature (Butler, *The Force of Nonviolence*, 30). Foundationally then, the society that emerges out of the state of nature is a society of individuals—of persons who were always-already individuals and whose needs for connectedness and care are invisible and unnoticed.

3. A Few Days Later, March 2020

I was reading the text of public health orders with my partner, Kira.

Kira also lived in a separate household to me, but they had a train set and toys for my kid there. My kid was attached to them. I depended on them as someone who was able to help me at the last minute, pick up my kid from childcare, or help me when I realized I was missing some essential item from the shop after my kid was asleep.

Kira was central to my network of care and probably would have been my first choice for someone to come and stay with me. The mostly nonsexual nature of our relationship seemed easier to reconcile with the restrictions on my welfare payments. However, they were deeply involved in caring for their other partner, who was, at the time, in the early stages of recovering from gender affirming vaginoplasty, a procedure that involves a substantial physical recovery process as well as a complex care and maintenance regimen in the months following.

We were trying to decide if it would still be possible under the compassionate grounds provided for in the public health orders for them to continue visiting to help me out with my kid or for my kid to visit their home.

Later that day, the public health order was clarified by the New South Wales commissioner of police, who gave a public statement saying that, of course, people were permitted to visit their partners who they didn't live with. The police commissioner made reassuring statements and cited the mental health of all concerned. They didn't want to be inhumane. But there was no clarity about what constituted a partner, although it seemed clear that the police commissioner and most of the media who reported his remarks knew exactly what they were talking about.

I couldn't shake the question that if this was about mental health, why couldn't my kid continue to spend weekends with my mother. That would still only mean seeing one person. Surely, I thought, my mental health matters too?

4. Maternal Silence, Dependency Work

The liberal phantasy of the state of nature—with its always already independent individual—occurs on the site of "an annihilation" (Butler, *The Force of Nonviolence* 38). This annihilation is the erasure of the maternal origin and with it the silencing of the reality that human beings are profoundly interdependent and unlike the needless and solitary individuals of the 'state of nature,' we emerge from the body of another person, unable to care for ourselves and dependent on the affection, attention, and nurturance of (m)others in order to survive. Feminist theorizations of mothering (Beauvoir; Rozmarin; Oliver) point to the silencing of the maternal origin as the key symbolic act that facilitates the emergence of the individuated subject, whom we meet again in Butler's account of the phantasy of the state of nature (*The Force of Nonviolence*). The erasure of the maternal origin is, thus, key to the phantasy that underpins the society of individuals, and the reality of mothering is, therefore, profoundly disruptive to its prevailing logic. The erasure of the maternal origin and the disavowal of dependency to create the society of individuals produces a society that is profoundly ambivalent about care (Read; Rustin). This discomfort with care—and with those who are seen as needing care and those who do the work of caring—does not merely take the form of an awkwardness; rather, the management of vulnerability is one of the core preoccupations of neoliberal policy as well as a core project of the neoliberal subject.

Mothering under neoliberalism is, thus, underpinned by tension. Neoliberalism presents a reality in which women and mothers are no longer exempt from the project of individual pursuit of happiness, they too are responsibilized towards their own happiness (Baker). Yet, feminist scholars have pointed out (Büskens, Hochschild) the work of care inherent in mothering, and which remains preponderously the task of women, does not avail itself to the demands of the modern world or even to any mother's pursuit of happiness (Büskens). The care of others operates against the core logics of neoliberalism. As Butler writes, "Care is not always consensual, and it does not always take the form of a contract: it can be a way of getting wrecked, time and again, by the demands of a wailing and hungry creature" (*The Force of Nonviolence* 50). Furthermore, this work of care generates dependency on the part of mothers (and caregivers more broadly). Eve Kittay describes a *secondary dependency* that attaches itself to those whose capabilities and efforts are tied up in the work of caring for another and, in turn, renders them reliant on others for their own care (42). That mothering produces dependency—under the conditions of an economic system and mode subject formation that excludes from the category of people who are dependent—creates a gendered experience of structural and personal distress as one tries to fit the essentially preindustrial demands of mothering into the demands of producing and asserting a neoliberal, rational subjectivity (see Büskens; Hochschild). To fully admit to the extent of one's dependency as a mother is to remove oneself from the society of individuals and to jeopardize the ongoing and provisional project of achieving subjectivity.

5. June 2020

At the beginning of 2020, I went to a queer conference and presented on non-monogamy. We talked about things like "couple's privilege" and the "relationship escalator"—the idea that society offers benefits to specific types of relationship which follow a socially dictated norm, involving romance, exclusivity, enmeshment of social lives and finances, legal commitments like marriage, cohabitation, and raising children. We knew on some intellectual level that these relationships enjoyed a social seamlessness and legitimacy that ours did not. Yet the way we did relationships also produced unique benefits.

Having the support of a range of different adults in my kid's life meant that the village it takes to raise a child was, for me at least, not quite metaphorical. I felt that my child's understanding of the world was enriched by the perspective of the different people in his life. I had never realized the stakes were so high. I had never imagined a situation in which the government would mandate whom I see and whom I don't see, and I could not imagine a situation in which I would be broadly supportive of efforts to drastically reduce the number of people I was in contact with.

But although my support of avoiding risk and minimizing infection remained intact, and as we watched in horror what happened in the United States and other countries where the virus spread unchecked, it seemed increasingly clear that throughout the public health orders ran a logic that pandemic or no pandemic, there were certain aspects of life and certain relationships of care that were assumed to be immune to disturbance and others that were always deemed to be optional.

6. The Nuclear Family, Mononormativity, and the Regulation of Care

As discussed, the individual of the 'state of nature' emerges adult and unencumbered, ready to enter into an agreement with other individuals to create society (Butler 2020, 30) with their needs for care and companionship invisible. This invisibility is not illusory. It is achieved and sustained through the unpaid labour that takes place within the home, which primarily remains the work of women and through an ever-encroaching "commodity frontier" of paid services (Hochschild) that allows people with economic privilege to meet their care needs within the anonymity and the empowerment of the market.

Even as neoliberalism has seen an increasing number of aspects of care that used to be undertaken within families and communities outsourced to the market (Hoppania and Vaittinen), the rise of neoliberal ideology has been accompanied by a drastic increase in attention to the family and indeed a valorization or reification of family values, particularly, the figure of the wife/mother (Hochschild). However, this valorization is a that of the happy, financially supported mother. Neoliberalism has also overseen the devastation of welfare provisions that support mothers, particularly single mothers (Hall). At its core, the neoliberal family too must be entirely independent; whatever dependency it represents must be contained within its borders. To admit to the need for financial support is to bring oneself, one's family, and one's children under punitive regimes of welfare provision that undermine and degrade the humanity of those within them (Wacquant).

Thus, the neoliberal family is foundationally and compulsorily monogamous. It is monogamous in a sense that extends beyond romantic and sexual monogamy on the part of the conjugal couple. It is monogamous in its expectation that the individuals within it derive all their real and significant care needs within its confines, excepting those for which they have the personal resources to outsource to the market. The nuclear family and the unpaid, gendered labour it represents, is one of the key strategies for the regulation of vulnerability within neoliberalism. This strategy is supported and enforced through mononormativity, that is the "institutionalised legitimization, naturalization and privileging of monogamous couple relationships"

(Lamont). Mononormativity is precisely why the New South Wales police commissioner did not feel the need to clarify what he meant by a "partner" when he stated that seeing one's partner was so essential for mental health that it could justify an unstated exception in the public health order.

Non-monogamy in this context—and by "non-monogamy," I mean romantic, sexual, and interpersonal relationships that by agreement and intention deviate from the monogamous nuclear family—can represent an intervention in the neoliberal strategy for the management of vulnerability and allow for contemporary collective experiences of interdependence and care. The challenge of non-monogamy operates on both a personal and political level. Personally, it provides an alternate framework for understanding the ways in which we are already interdependent on one another. Politically, it challenges the neoliberal siloing of care needs into the gendered arrangements of the nuclear family and allows for networks of dependence and care to emerge based on intentionality and arrangement (Gusmano).

Nonmonogamous arrangements of care, love, intimacy, and affection undermine the compulsory nature of monogamy and demonstrate alternatives to the enforced independence of the nuclear family (Gusmano; Heckert). As such, they have the capacity to not only point towards the radical equality that operates outside the phantasy of the society of individuals but also to direct us towards the recognition of the manifold ways in which we are always-already caught within networks of dependence and care that exceed us, even if we do not choose to acknowledge them.

The lockdown restrictions that took effect in New South Wales in March and April 2021 and that exposed me and those around me to such profound precarity were fundamentally an attempt to balance the need to minimize social contact and prevent the transmission of a socially transmitted virus. Ultimately, these measures were largely successful in containing the spread of coronavirus in Australia, and as I write this in October 2020, life feels eerily normal. However, the experience of living through the assertion of government policy assessments of what constitutes necessary and unnecessary social contact and witnessing the extent to which they took as their basis the society of individuals and the subject without needs has still left me rattled. These restrictions presumed the ability to take society apart, to rewrite the social contract, to return us to our original state of individuality, and to put society on hold, except for those exceptional and pitiable persons who really need care.

Butler writes: "We can assert in a general way that social interdependency characterises life, and then proceed to account for violence as an attack on that interdependency, an attack on persons, yes; but perhaps most fundamentally it is an attack on 'bonds'" (*The Force of Nonviolence* 16). The idea that we can undo society and revert to individuality, that dependence is optional, and that we can retreat into our homes and not account for the damage that will be wrought upon our bodies and our capacity to cope is itself a violence. It's a violence precisely because the society of individuals is not a fact; it is a phantasy, one that was never intended to be representative of all or even most people. The independent individual of the state of nature, who we meet again as the subject of neoliberalism, was never a mother. He is a man, supported by his wife who finds her happiness in serving him, and attended and supported by the labour of other men who are racially and economically marginalized. He is the classical philosopher, the Enlightenment slave-owner, the 2020 millennial guy who was carried through the lockdown by Netflix, brown men with bags of food on delivery bikes and regular visits from his girlfriend for sex. His life was never thrown into precarity, his needs, his care was always already 'essential.' More than that, it was never even seen as care.

The excessive needs of mothers have never featured within our vision of society; the mother must be erased from the state of nature before the society of individuals can be erected over it. And, thus, the needs of mothers never featured in the plans that were made to suspend society in a time of crisis, precisely because mothering is a relation of dependency that cannot be wholly managed or wholly erased. To account for mothering and to acknowledge the needs and humanity of those who mother, we need an entirely different framework for understanding society—a framework based on the radical equality that emerges from our shared interdependency and looks to a promiscuous proliferation of the love, care, and dependency we are capable of sharing with one another.

Conclusion

Throughout this chapter, I argued that the foundational phantasy of liberalism—the social contract—presupposes that society is created by the agreement of individuals for their convenience and that, therefore, society itself can be disestablished when it is no longer convenient. Following Butler, I argue that the phantasy of the pre-existing, adult individuals who form the social contract meet upon the site of a profound erasure—an erasure of the ontological vulnerability and interdependency of every person and our need for care. As such, care, and specifically mothering, is excessive to neoliberalism, which works to manage and contain it within specifically sanctioned contexts, namely the mononormative dyad and the heteronormative nuclear family. Structures of care that fall outside of the nuclear family and the monogamous dyad are both in resistance to neoliberalism as well as actively undermined by it, particularly during the COVID-19 pandemic, when mononormative conceptualizations of the family and care were enforced with the coercive power of the state. Mothering beyond monogamy—and the broader collective structures of care, affection, and support that it represents—exists in a state of profound tension with neoliberal systems in which care is regulated.

Works Cited

Baker, Joanne. "Neoliberalism and the Depoliticising of Motherhood: Reflections on the Australian Experience." *Mothering in the Age of Neoliberalism*, edited by Melinda Vandenbeld Giles, Demeter Press, 2014, pp. 169-83.

Beauvoir, Simone de. *The Second Sex*. Vintage Books, 2010.

Büskens, Petra. "The Impossibility of 'Natural Parenting' for Modern Mothers: On Social Structure and the Formation of Habit." *Journal of the Motherhood Initiative for Research and Community Involvement*, vol. 3, no. 1, 2001, pp. 75-86.

Butler, Judith. *Precarious Life: The Powers of Mourning and Violence*. Verso Books, 2004.

Butler, Judith. *The Force of Nonviolence: The Ethical in the Political*. Verso Books, 2020.

Foucault, Michel. *The Birth of Biopolitics: Lectures at the Collège de France, 1978–1979*. Edited by Michael Senellard. Translated by Graham Burchell. Palgrave Macmillan, 2004.

Gusmano, Beatrice. "The Kintsugi Art of Care: Unraveling Consent in Ethical Non-Monogamies." *Sociological Research Online*, vol. 24, no. 4, 2019, pp. 661-79.

Hall, Stuart. "The Neo-Liberal Revolution." *Cultural Studies*, vol. 25, no. 6, 2011, pp. 705-28.

Heckert, Jamie. "Love without Borders? Intimacy, Identity and the State of Compulsory Monogamy." *Understanding Non-monogamies*, edited by Meg Barker and Darren Langridge, Routledge, 2010, pp. 255-66.

Hochschild, Arlie Russell. *The Commercialization of Intimate life: Notes from Home and Work*. University of California Press, 2003.

Hoppania, Hanna-Kaisa, and Tiina Vaittinen. "A Household Full of Bodies: Neoliberalism, Care and 'the Political.'" *Global Society*, vol. 29, no. 1, 2015, pp. 70-88.

Kittay, Eva Feder. *Love's Labor: Essays on Women, Equality and Dependency*. Routledge, 2019.

Lamont, Ellen. "*Beyond Monogamy: Polyamory and the Future of Polyqueer Sexualities* by Mimi Schippers." *Social Forces*, vol. 96, no. 1, 2003, pp. 1-3.

Oliver, Kelly. *Subjectivity without Subjects: From Abject Fathers to Desiring Mothers*. Rowman & Littlefield, 1998.

Rozmarin, Miri. "Maternal Silence." *Studies in Gender and Sexuality*, vol. 13, no. 1, 2012, pp. 4-14.

Read, Jason. "A Genealogy of Homo-Economicus: Neoliberalism and the Production of Subjectivity." *Foucault Studies*, no. 6, 2009, pp. 25-36.

Rustin, Michael. "Belonging to Oneself Alone: The Spirit of Neoliberalism." *Psychoanalysis, Culture & Society*, vol. 19, no. 2, 2014, pp. 145-60.

Wacquant, Loïc. "Three Steps to a Historical Anthropology of Actually Existing Neoliberalism." *Social Anthropology*, vol. 20, no. 1, 2012, pp. 66-79.

Chapter Nineteen

A Single-Parent Multigenerational Family Testimony: Living under COVID-19 and Other Orders in Silicon Valley

Perlita R. Dicochea

E very time I drive away from home with my two toddlers in tow, ages four and five, I wonder how many of the few cars sharing the road with me are single parents driving their children to meet with their children's other parent? How many, like me, have children who spend time in two multigenerational households? I recall a diagram I saw in mid-March of 2020, which appeared in my transnational Twitter feed, showing a nuclear family with a line drawn around them. It was a PSA urging folks to "stay in your bubble." Surely, that bubble does not know multigenerational families—never mind families whose lives are shaped by court orders.

In this chapter, part testimony and part research, I reflect on the challenges and support I encounter as a single working Chicana mother of two small children living in a multigenerational household in the heart of Silicon Valley, where the United States' (U.S.) first-reported COVID-19 deaths occurred (DeBolt and Crowley) and where the Latinx population is contracting the virus at disproportionate rates (Webeck, "Coronavirus"). My experience of mothering during the COVID-19 pandemic is situated within the greater context of multigenerational Latinx households and the many Latinx children living with one parent. I contend that in Santa Clara County, a look at the presence of single mothers and families living in multigenerational households, particularly those who are Latinx, may help us understand patterns of experiences among Latinx children and, thus, determine the kind of support these children and households need. To be sure, my own stresses working from home with a kindergartener and preschooler have required a more flexible bubble—one that accommodates social and emotional support and a court-ordered visitation agreement.

Alternative (Nonnuclear) Traditional Families

Despite the dominant narrative of the American nuclear family, which is reinforced in popular culture and is many a Chicana's life goal, California has the second-to-highest percentage of multigenerational households in the U.S. at 5.77 per cent, or 754,667 total households (Madison 25). Of all Hispanic/Latino children in Santa Clara County, where I live, 19.9 per cent reside in multigenerational households. Similar numbers appear for African American and Asian American children. By contrast, only 6.5 per cent of all white children's living arrangements are multigenerational (Population Reference Bureau).

Living Arrangements of Children/Youth (ages 0-17) in Santa Clara County Households, 2014-2018 Percent of children by living arrangement				
	(Mother-Only)	(Father-Only)	Single-parent (mother-only or father-only)	Multi-generation
African American/Black*	S	10.8%	S	18.7%
American Indian/Alaska Native*	S	S	1.2%	S
Asian American*	7.5%	2.9%	10.5%	14.9%
Hispanic/Latino	28.0%	8.8%	36.8%	19.9%
Multiracial*	14.4%	4.7%	19.1%	12.8%
Native Hawaiian/Pacific Islander*	S	S	S	S
White*	10.5%	5.8%	16.3%	6.5%
*Not Hispanic/Latino				
Notes	Data exclude children living in group quarters. Racial/ethnic categories are mutually-exclusive. Multi-generational households include households with at least one co-resident grandparent. The notation S means data are suppressed because the margin of error was greater than +/-5 percentage points or there were fewer than 3 records in that group.			
Source	Analysis by Population Reference Bureau (PRB) of data from U.S. Census Bureau, American Community Survey, Public Use Microdata 2014-2018.			
Citation	Kidsdata.org, estimates tabulated by Population Reference Bureau from the American Community Survey (April 2020).			
This work was completed by the Population Reference Bureau through a contract with the Lucile Packard Foundation for Children's Health Kidsdata Program.				
Chart by Ortiz Design 2020				

Figure 1. Living Arrangements by Race and Gender in Santa Clara County, 2014-2018

A recent story brought to light the adjustments multigenerational families have made post-#StayHome to keep everyone, particularly grandparents, safe (Anthony 5). Some describe carving out private spaces within the home. For instance, one grandmother has her own room in which to isolate herself; another family maintain social distance within the home; and in another still, the grandparents had not left the home in four weeks at the time of their story's publication. In my household, the children stopped using the living room as one of their play spaces so as to give their grandparents a separate leisure space in the home. We also have meals at different tables—my parents sit at the dining room table, and my children and I sit at the kitchen table. Efforts to maintain separate spaces within the home are particularly important, as my children continue on the same visit schedule with their father as before the pandemic, potentially exposing two sets of grandparents. It is a great burden to bear.

As we try to enforce new rules and habits, we have found social distancing within the home a challenge. I remind my toddlers to keep a distance from their grandparents, and we have changed how we do things in the home accordingly. But my parents oscillate between maintaining distance and choosing not to stay away from them. Admittedly, so do my children. My toddlers understand why Mommy works at home. They understand why we have not been able to go to their favourite playgrounds or to school for the past eleven months. To increase understanding and decrease fear, the county sent each of my children booklets about a coronavirus donning thick glasses and a few lashes. (My daughter has since been referring to the virus as "she."). It is hard for my children to grasp how something so small can cause so much havoc. As a result, at times, my children confuse the coronavirus with the great battle we were engaged in just as the virus landed in our county—with head lice. Meanwhile, my children are aware that people we know and care about continue to leave their homes nearly every day to go to work.

Figure 2. Coronavirus Children's Book

COVID-19 Contexts and Data Gathering

My family is, to oversimplify, Catholic Mexican/Mexican American. I am a single Chicana mom of two children and one socialized Chihuahua living with my eighty-seven-year-old mother of four (and her own Chihuahua) who immigrated to San José, CA, in the mid-1960s after spending several years as a college professor in Navojoa, Sonora, Mexico. My seventy-six-year-old father was born to Mexican immigrant parents in Brawley, CA, and raised in Los Baños, CA. He attended the University of California, Berkeley, as an undergraduate just before the social movements of the 1960s. Thus, my family was raised in a middle-class life, as we moved from a diverse, mixed-income neighbourhood in North San José to a decidedly middle-to-upper class and predominantly white area of West San José. This move was a result of my entrepreneurial parents and their tax business success in the 1980s. Our family has experienced the benefits and challenges of living in the high-tech bubbles of Silicon Valley. Although I achieved the highest level of education in my family, professional trials and personal tribulations led me back to my parents' home with my small children. Over the last two years, our focus has been on helping my folks keep their home. While working on this article, my oldest brother who lives in the Netherlands tested positive for COVID-19 and was going on week four in an ICU. He spent much of that time in a medically induced coma. In Santa Clara County, Latinos account for almost 60 per cent of all COVID-19 cases, but make up only 25 per cent of the population (Webeck, "Santa Clara"). The death rates among the Latinx community are greatest in the East Side zip codes (Castañeda; Kelliher). My heart goes out to the hundreds of thousands suffering from COVID-19 in so many different ways (Wamsley; Webeck, "Coronavirus").

As I began my research on how families similar to mine are coping with COVID-19 and shelter-in-place orders, I discovered that the data on single parents by race and gender in Santa Clara County were not accessible. This discovery furthered my sense that families like mine are living in the shadows, left to fend for ourselves. U.S. Census data show that 35 per cent of all children in the country live in single-parent households. Of those, 53 per cent are American Indian; 15 per cent are Asian and Pacific Islander; 65 per cent are Black or African American; 41 per cent are Hispanic or Latino; 24 per cent are non-Hispanic white; and 40 per cent are two or more races (Annie E. Casey Foundation). The breakdown by race in the state begins to tell a distinct story. The available 2018 data for California drawn from the Current Population Survey show that of all Hispanic/Latino children, 30.6 per cent do not live with two parents present, and of those, 22 per cent live with their mother present only. Comparatively, 21.4 per cent of all white children live with only one or no parents present, and for Asian Pacific Islander children, the figure is 14.8 per cent. (Lucile Packard Foundation). Across the board in the state and across the country, the large majority of children who do not live with both parents live with their mothers present only (Medina and Lerer).

United States	Percent			
Race/Ethnicity	Two Parents Present	Mother Present Only	Father Present Only	No Parents Present
African American/Black	39.6%	48.2%	5.0%	7.3%
Asian/Pacific Islander	86.1%	9.0%	2.1%	2.9%
Hispanic/Latino	67.0%	24.9%	4.0%	4.2%
White	77.2%	14.7%	4.7%	3.4%
Other	59.9%	28.3%	5.0%	6.7%

California	Percent			
Race/Ethnicity	Two Parents Present	Mother Present Only	Father Present Only	No Parents Present
African American/Black	S	S	6.9%	8.0%
Asian/Pacific Islander	85.2%	8.3%	1.9%	4.6%
Hispanic/Latino	69.4%	22.0%	4.6%	4.0%
White	78.5%	15.2%	4.4%	1.8%
Other	S	S	4.4%	6.1%

Figure 3. Living Arrangements by Race in US and CA

Santa Clara County	Percent
Two Parents Present	73.7%
Mother Present Only	16.6%
Father Present Only	6.2%
No Parents Present; Other Relatives Present	2.8%
No Parents or Other Relatives Present	0.7%

Figure 4. Living Arrangements, All Children in Santa Clara County, 2018

This is where my research hit a dead end—I could not find the figures by race and gender for children's living arrangements in Santa Clara County. I reached out to Lori Turk-Bicakci, director of the Kidsdata Program of the Lucile Packard Foundation for Children's Health. She explained the suppression rates are often too high, meaning there are not enough respondents to represent the data I sought in a meaningful way at the county level. Given the large population in Santa Clara County (1.9 million), Turk-Bicakci thought we might have some luck.

After revisiting the data, aggregating the numbers from 2014 through 2018, what the nonprofit found is striking: Almost 37 per cent of all Santa Clara County Hispanic/Latino children live with one parent present only and 28 per cent of those live with their mother present only. Comparatively, 10.5 per cent of all Asian American children and 16.3 per cent of all white children live with a single parent. The total for all children who live with a single parent in the county is 22.8 per cent. For some perspective, Hispanic/Latinos make up 25 per cent of the county's population, non-Hispanic whites make up 31 per cent, and Asians make up 38 per cent. Children represent 449,000 of the county. Nearly 144,260 of those are between the ages of zero and five.

The data tell us what I had suspected all along—there are many single Latinx mothers in Silicon Valley, and there are many more children living in single-parent households. Furthermore, the available data clearly show that Hispanic/Latino children living with one parent, predominantly their mothers, represent a significant percentage in Santa Clara County and disproportionately so compared to other racial groups and to the total number of single-parent households in the county and state. Knowing what we do about race and gender income inequality, communities must consider the support structures needed for the health and wellbeing of these families, particularly during this global public health calamity. Moreover, now that Santa Clara County data on single parents by both race and gender are available, governmental and nongovernmental agencies will be in a better position to speak to the health and wellness of the high number of Hispanic/Latino children living with a single parent and in multigenerational homes in this prolonged moment of crisis. We can also gather that a significant percentage of the families represented by the above data abide by legal or informal visitation agreements.

Families under Orders

Families with custody and visitation orders face unique challenges in the path of COVID-19. As Turk-Bicakci asserts, "Clarity about custodial arrangements in the midst of stay-at-home orders could ease the strain on families and protect children's emotional health." How do we factor in the emotional and overall health of all those living under more than one roof during this pandemic, particularly those with custody and visitation orders? Several stories have emerged of families negotiating children's timeshare, some with more success than others. One report addresses coparents' increased billable hours with divorce attorneys, the personal wounds that resurface during this stressful time, and the added anxiety due to a shutdown family court system (Villano). In another reported California case, a single-mother's ex-husband would not release their two children at the scheduled pickup time. The father of the children stated to police that he was worried the mother, an emergency room doctor, was exposing their children to the coronavirus (White). In what is framed as an amicable positive scenario, a separate pair of coparents agreed their daughter would remain with the mother full-time instead of the usual three days a week she usually spends at her father's home (Villano).

Unless amicable agreements are made, the primary legal recourse parents have in California to change a current visitation schedule is by way of a temporary emergency order, which may be granted if one's child is immune compromised or otherwise high risk. One lawyer states a parent must show "persuasive evidence that parenting time would create risk of transmission" (Peterson). Of course, by April of 2020, we had learned that asymptomatic people can also spread the virus (Courage). In any case, most courts throughout the country did not appear to be prioritizing nonemergency visitation changes at this time (Villano). As an aside, in the immediate aftermath of shelter-in-place orders, domestic violence cases have skyrocketed, both globally (Neuman) and in the U.S. (Simon 18). Only toward the end of March did Santa Clara County Superior Court issue a clear public statement that courts remain open for emergency orders, including those related to domestic violence, child custody and visitation, and gun violence, among others (Superior Court of California).

One California-based attorney, Michael C. Peterson, CFLS, confirms that as COVID-19 shelter-in-place orders were implemented, there has been a great lack of clarity offered for coparents across the country. According to Peterson, Texas is the only state that made a clear declaration in late March 2020 that child custody and visitation orders are to remain in place, regardless of stay-at-home decrees. Peterson elaborates: "Anecdotally, any elementary school teacher knows that little kids are basically germ and virus incubators, and many children do not adhere to the prevention methods for spreading viruses.... Having children in the home in proximity to grandparents is much like being quarantined on the 'Disaster Princess' [i.e., the Diamond Princess]".

Similar to other attorneys, Peterson recommends children (who, by the way, are small humans, not "virus incubators") remain in one home for the time being and engage in virtual communication with the noncustodial parent, making-up for the noncustodial parent's lost time after the shelter-in-place orders are lifted. This advice assumes that coparents communicate effectively and are able to come to agreements. These suggestions also do not consider the waves of COVID-19 infection surges many counties have seen, including Santa Clara County, and the resultant loosening and then tightening of lockdown measures—which may subsequently affect children's need for structure and stability, particularly if their coparents change visitations agreements in kind. What is truly the best for the children and the grandparents? What other guidance may help coparents determine this?

Keeping It Together

Since we are discussing bubbles and single parenthood, I have determined that my support (and sanity) have taken on a shape similar to those my children create with their giant bubble wands. These clusters reflect the changing colors of dusk and provide at minimum an hour of joy for the entire household. It is a precarious, fragile joy. Similarly, and in an odd way that does not make any sense, my COVID-19 support network has brought both relief and angst because of a crucial person in my support circle, my significant other. I have battled with anxiety for several years, but once stay-at-home orders began my bouts with panic became too frequent for me to manage without him. I have leaned on my boyfriend for friendship, comfort, and survival as well as for help in keeping my children out of the room during virtual work events. He has brought food when I did not have time to prepare meals. He has taken my children out to the park when I had to stay indoors to join a virtual meeting. He has set up a peaceful workspace that fits in the only available corner of the bedroom I share with my toddlers. (I am somewhat of an attachment mom.) In the context of COVID-19, my boyfriend's support makes daily life manageable and lighter, even with the lurking questions. What are my other options? Am I supposed to keep my significant other out of my bubble and succumb to work-life imbalance? Is not he a part of my family? How does one weigh the clashing layers of risk and tradeoffs that leave little space for love?

As I continued to work on this chapter, my oldest brother slowly began to show signs of recovery and is no longer in a medically induced coma. His lungs are no longer infected. His wife was overjoyed with his responses to her during hospital visits. With the assistance of the ICU nurses, we began scheduling family video chats with him and experienced some of those early brief responses as well. His slight movements filled us with enormous hope. As weeks passed, my brother made miraculous progress—he began to breathe entirely on his own, talk, and eat solid food. Just before Christmas, he was moved to a rehabilitation center where he practices walking, sitting up and many daily activities the rest of us often take for granted. Meanwhile, there are little things my small ones and I do as best we can to try and control everything that we cannot. These include washing our hands before greeting the grandparents, before and after any transition, and not touching our faces, or, at least, not touching each other's faces (they are four and five—it's very difficult). We pick up meals for the household from the school down the street to minimize shopping trips and try to maintain everyone's health. I order food delivery once or twice a week when juggling work and my children make cooking impossible. We are much more conscious of our use of space in the home to minimize my parents' exposure to us. And we have leaned on more lengthy evening family prayer time.

In another effort to minimize exposure and channel connection, my dear friend from graduate school—turned hermana (sister) to me and comadre (comother, or godmother) to my daughter—drove by our home with her husband and twin daughters for a no-contact gift exchange. We had not seen each other in person since last winter. We have discussed the possibility of a grand party when all of this is behind us—if we have not already both lost our minds.

I can imagine what other Latinx multigenerational families in Santa Clara County with court-ordered visitation schedules are going through, and now we know they/we exist. Recall, the numbers for my county were not so apparent when I started working on this story in mid-March, 2020. As a result, I must state the not so obvious—single parents with court-ordered visitation schedules living in multigenerational households are legitimate families. Many coparents must also feel they are alone, haunted by the possibility of putting their loved ones in danger through the movement of their own children. And many single working parents have to seek the help they need to manage working from home and raising school-aged children at their own risk.

At the same time, those parents able to work from home like me, single or not, are experiencing the joys of being more involved in their children's daily lives and schooling. Like other adults living with their folks, I can share everyday moments, silly and sweet, that toddlers are so good at creating as we support each other during this frightening pandemic moment (Todd). What's more, I have greatly benefited from learning a few of my mother's recipes and, as a result, I make a mean sopita de fideo (Mexican angel hair tomato-based soup). As another silver lining in chaotic times, when my children catch me in a bout with stress, they stop what they are doing to remind me to take deep breaths. The breathing breaks often conclude with piles of toddler kisses. These are just a few of the reasons I cannot imagine any parent missing their work commutes too much—I, for one, do not. And it has been refreshing to see colleagues of mine holding their children during virtual meetings and hear dogs barking in the background—we are human, after all.

Even so, I cannot help wonder how a resource-rich region like Silicon Valley could implement better outreach, particularly to the significant percentage of single Latinx mothers and the many more Latinx children living in supportive home environments that may also be fraught with more worry than any one adult or child should expect to manage alone. To conclude, it is my hope that with more accessible and thorough county level children's data broken down by both race and gender, local COVID-19 policy, public service announcements, social services, and other agencies may be moved to consider the fullness of family experiences that shape and are shaped by children whose lives reflect something other than a nuclear family bubble. In the meantime, as working single parents make the tough choices to get through each hour of each day, may we all keep it together, together.

Works Cited

Annie E. Casey Foundation Kids Count Data Center. "Children in Single-Parent Families by Race in the United States." *Kids Count*, Jan. 2020, datacenter.kidscount.org/data/tables/107-children-in-single-parent-families-by-race#detailed/1/any/false/1729,37,871,870,573,869,36,868, 867,133/10,11,9,12,1,185,13/432,431. Accessed 8 Jan. 2021.

Anthony, Cara. "How Multigenerational Families Manage 'Social Distancing' Under One Roof." *National Public Radio,* 5 Apr. 2020, www.npr.org/sections/health-shots/2020/04/05/826485036/how-multigenerational-families-manage-social-distancing-under-one-roof. Accessed 8 Jan. 2021.

Courage, Katherine Harmon. "How People Are Spreading Covid-19 without Symptoms." *Vox.* 22 Apr. 2020, www.vox.com/2020/4/22/21230301/coronavirus-symptom-asymptomatic-carrier-spread. Accessed 8 Jan. 2021.

DeBolt, David, and Kerry Crowley. "Santa Clara County Had Nation's First COVID-19 Deaths, Weeks Earlier than Thought." *The Mercury News,* 21 Apr. 2020, www.mercurynews.com/2020/04/21/coronavirus-earliest-covid-19-deaths-in-bay-area-occurred-in-february-not-march/. Accessed 8 Jan. 2021.

Castañeda, Leonardo. "Death Reports Show Coronavirus Hit San Jose's Poor, Latino Neighborhoods Hardest." *The Mercury News,* 10 May 2020, www.mercurynews.com/2020/05/10/coronavirus-deaths-east-san-jose-poor/. Accessed 8 Jan. 2021.

Hoff, Madison. "Social Distancing May Be Harder for Families Who Live with Elderly Relatives. Here Are the 15 States with the Largest Share of Multigenerational Households." *Business Insider,* 25 Apr. 2020, www.businessinsider.com.au/the-states-with-the-most-multigenerational-households-2020-4. Accessed 8 Jan. 2021.

Kelliher, Fiona. "As Coronavirus Rips through East San Jose, Leaders form Racial Equity Task Force." *The Mercury News,* 28 May 2020, www.mercurynews.com/2020/05/28/as-coronavirus-rips-through-east-san-jose-leaders-form-racial-equity-task-force/. Accessed 8 Jan. 2021.

Lucile Packard Foundation for Children's Health Kids Data Program. "Living Arrangement for Children, by Presence of Parents and Race/Ethnicity (California & U.S. Only)." *Kids Data,* Nov. 2018, www.kidsdata.org/topic/539/families-with-children-type-race10/Pie#fmt=723&loc=2&tf=108&ch=7,1428,1427,1426,1431&pdist=194. Accessed 8 Jan. 2021.

Medina, Jennifer, and Lisa Lerer. "When Mom's Zoom Meeting Is the One That Has to Wait." *New York Times,* 22 Apr. 2020, www.nytimes.com/2020/04/22/us/politics/women-coronavirus-2020.html. Accessed 8 Jan. 2021.

Neuman, Scott. "Global Lockdowns Resulting in 'Horrifying Surge' In Domestic Violence, U.N. Warns." *National Public Radio,* 6 April 2020, www.npr.org/sections/coronavirus-live-updates/2020/04/06/827908402/global-lockdowns-resulting-in-horrifying-surge-in-domestic-violence-u-n-warns. Accessed 8 Jan. 2021.

Peterson, Michael C. "Child Custody Disputes, Child Exchanges, COVID-19, and Shelter in Place Orders: Some Pointers." Thurman Arnold, 31 Mar. 2020, www.thurmanarnold.com/family-law-blog/2020/march/child-custody-exchanges-covid-19-and-shelter-in-/. Accessed 8 Jan. 2021.

Population Reference Bureau and Lucile Packard Foundation for Children's Health Kidsdata Program. "Living Arrangements of Children/Youth (Ages 0-17) in Santa Clara County Households, 2014–2018." *Kid Data,* April 2020, www.kidsdata.org/region/59/santa-clara-county/summary#6/demographics. Accessed 8 Jan. 2021.

Simon, Scott. "Reports of Domestic Violence Rise in Recent Weeks amid Coronavirus Lockdowns." *National Public Radio,.* 18 April 2020, www.npr.org/2020/04/18/837855166/reports-of-domestic-violence-rise-in-recent-weeks-amid-coronavirus-lockdowns. Accessed 8 Jan. 2021.

Superior Court of California, County of Santa Clara. "Public Access to Court for Emergency Motions." *Superior Court of California,* 27 Mar. 2020, cases.primeclerk.com › McDermott › Home-DownloadPDF. Accessed 8 Jan. 2021.

Todd, Sarah. "Moving Back In with Your Parents May Be Your Worst Fear—and your best idea yet." *Quartz,* 19 Aug. 2020, qz.com/1894046/the-economic-and-social-benefits-of-living-with-your-parents-as-an-adult/. Accessed 8 Jan. 2021.

Villano, Matt. "Navigating Child Custody in the Time of Coronavirus." *CNN,* 9 Apr. 2020, www.cnn.com/2020/04/01/health/child-custody-wellness-coronavirus/index.html. Accessed 8 Jan. 2021.

Wamsley, Laurel. "As U.S. Reaches 250,000 Deaths From COVID-19, A Long Winter Is Coming." *National Public Radio,* 18 Nov. 2020, www.npr.org/sections/coronavirus-live-updates/2020/11/18/935930352/as-u-s-reaches-250-000-deaths-from-covid-19-a-long-winter-is-coming. Accessed 8 Jan. 2021.Webeck, Evan. "Coronavirus: California's Latinos

Shoulder Weight of Virus, Poll Finds." *The Mercury News*, 28 July 2020, www.mercurynews.com/2020/07/28/coronavirus-californias-latinos-shoulder-weight-of-virus-poll-finds/. Accessed 8 Jan. 2021. Webeck, Evan. "Santa Clara County Health Officer 'Extraordinarily Distressed' by Rising Rates of COVID-19." *The Mercury News*, www.mercurynews.com/2020/11/17/coronavirus-santa-clara-county-health-officer-extraordinarily-distressed-by-rising-rates-of-covid-19/. Accessed 8 Jan. 2021.

White, Dawson. "Social Distancing and Child Custody: How the Coronavirus Is Complicating Co-Parenting." *Miami Herald*, 25 Mar. 2020, www.miamiherald.com/news/coronavirus/article241492011.html. Accessed 8 Jan. 2021.

Chapter Twenty

Walking the Talk: (Counter) Narratives for Pandemic Parenting Young Black Children

Brooke Harris Garad

A deficit perspective characterizes dominant narratives about Black people in the United States (U.S.)—and the race-related stories surrounding COVID-19 have been no different. The disproportionate impact of COVID-19 on the Black community has been erroneously linked to everything from poor hygiene to genetic predisposition (Horowitz Menasce; Siemaszko), yet racism and socioeconomic inequities are more accurate explanations (Graylee). As a middle-class mother of Black children, I experienced class privilege while sheltering in and managing remote learning. The divide between my family's experience and the experiences of Black folks as depicted in the media required me to find age-appropriate ways to talk with my young children about economic and educational inequities, to contradict problematic narratives about COVID-19 and Blackness, and to clarify our place at the intersection of these sociological dynamics.

When the pandemic arrived in my part of the world in March 2020, our district closed schools indefinitely, and my spouse and I joined the ranks of parents working and educating children at home. While sifting through a cacophony of misinformation and trying to keep our family healthy and grounded, we established new routines of online meetings, grocery pickups, and virtual playdates. Despite the arguable chaos occurring in my home, I began to observe a peacefulness in my children. I began to wonder: How can I use this time to invest in my family and parent purposefully?

In this chapter, I will draw from research on Black motherhood, educating Black girls, and children's literature to reflect on my experience of mothering during the COVID-19 pandemic. I will also discuss how Black women's ways of knowing and being enabled me to parent with the purpose of imparting cultural values, a sense of community, and self-love in my daughters. In solidarity with mothers from all spheres, it is important to note that I write from a place of stable employment and workplace flexibility. I also write from the perspective of a Black scholar and mother whose story adds nuance to existing narratives about the Black experience in the U.S. Despite the innumerable challenges of mothering during the COVID-19 pandemic, this chapter offers a unique perspective on parenting Black children that will enrich our understanding of the impact of this historic moment.

Remote Learning, "the Sickness," and Black Lives Matter

Black parents have dealt with two crises during the COVID-19 pandemic: a health crisis (which my young children have consistently referred to as "the sickness") and the ever-present crisis of racism. With Black Lives Matter signs adorning our neighbourhoods and school closures upending the daily lives of my preschooler and kindergartener, I answered more questions than usual about illnesses and Blackness. I sought to give my children information in age-appropriate and accessible ways, but one of the hardest questions to answer—to the extent that it exemplifies how racism and the impact of COVID-19 converge—was this: "Why haven't I seen some of my classmates online?"

The response requires context. My children attend a public magnet school in a predominantly Black, lower-income, and urban school district. Until a couple of years ago, when the district placed a new principal with a new mission into the building, our school was an underperforming neighbourhood school. Nowadays, the school offers a highly sought after program with seats for students distributed via lottery. Although the lottery is arguably equitable in giving families across the district a chance to attend, certain factors—such as living close to the school, having sibling priority, and/or having a parent working within the district or at the partnering university—lend weight to an application. After visiting the short-list of higher performing public schools in our district, our current school became my family's first choice, and we gained admission via lottery.

Through the school search and application process, I wrestled with the kinds of questions many parents consider when seeking solid educational experiences for their children: Is the school high quality, close to our home, affordable, and aligned with our values? As a mother of Black children, I also wrestled with culturally rooted ideas about school quality. For me, an all-white school would be a bad fit for my children, despite competitive test scores or a good reputation; a good-fit school would offer racial diversity and an expressed commitment to equity.

As an educational researcher with experience working in urban schools internationally, I know that school communities all over the world offer caring teachers, loving parents, and brilliant children, despite deficit-oriented narratives that suggest otherwise. I also know that ongoing de facto segregation and the link between taxation and school funding mean parents face the reality of separate and unequal schools. There exist exceptions to this trend, but it rings true in my school search experience. In our case, barring admission to our current school via lottery, we could have attended our "neighbourhood" school—a school (not located in our neighbourhood) that is operating under probationary accreditation, a failing grade according to Indiana state standards, and a recent history of principal turnover. The racial makeup of this school is 79 per cent Black, 5 per cent white, 9 per cent Hispanic, 6 per cent multiracial, and less than 1 per cent Asian (Indiana Department of Education).

Dani McClain addresses race, equity, and school choice in her book, *We Live for the We: The Political Power of Black Motherhood*, describing the conundrum many Black parents face as we seek academically rigorous and culturally rich educational experiences for our children. Describing the challenge of navigating segregated and unequal schools, a mother named Monifa Bandele quoted in McClain's book said: "We have no options as black mothers. Either you put your kids in a racially hostile environment, or you put your kids in a quote-unquote bad school... Where all the kids are black, there's trauma. Where all the kids are white, there's trauma. There's not a lot of in-between" (224). I continue to wonder if our school is in between.

Recent statistics from the state department of education show our school demographics as 37 per cent Black, 40 per cent white, 12 per cent Hispanic, and 9 per cent multiracial, with Asian and Native American students rounding out the student population (Indiana Department of Education). The test scores and state grade depict a higher-performing institution, and the school leadership operates within a district-wide racial equity initiative. Despite these factors, and the small role I play as a parent to contribute to equity at the school, I wonder about sustainability. As the lottery for seats becomes increasingly competitive, incoming classes are comprised of more white students.

COVID-19 shed light on some of the educational inequities that exist at the intersection of class and race in schools all over the country. So, when my daughter asked, "Why haven't I seen some of my classmates online?" I wanted to tell her that it is about "the sickness" and the impact of longstanding racist policies and practices that mean a disproportionate number of Black folks face unemployment, work frontline jobs, and have limited access to the internet (Gould and Wilson).

I applaud our school district for approaching remote learning with equity in mind. Given the demographics in our district, remote learning was not mandatory between March and May 2020. Instead, the district prioritized implementing a system for distributing free food as well as paper learning packets and for broadcasting lessons via television. My daughter's teacher also offered live meetings for students during the day and evening to try to accommodate different families' needs. Still, my daughter and I noticed the absence of our Black peers in both the student- and parent-support sessions.

Aside from knowing that one student's parent is an essential worker in the medical field and that another spends her days with her grandmother, I do not know the specific reasons for the absences. Collecting their stories could be the focus of another chapter, but their absence alone—whether by choice or circumstance—is telling. I told my daughter, "no matter where the classmates are, they are learning." Together, we imagined their stories, adding nuance to unidimensional discussions of COVID-19-related learning loss. Bolstered by research on culturally affirming literacy practices (Scott and Purdum-Cassidy) and the children's literature I will subsequently reference, I showed my daughter that Black people have a long history of excellence and resilience.

Using the context of our school and school search process enabled me to provide details about how the impact of COVID-19, the movement for Black lives, and my family's experience with remote learning are interconnected aspects of deeply rooted inequities in our society. In as much as the movement for Black lives is about the material consequences of police brutality in the Black community—and one iteration of this issue exists in schools with the criminalization of young Black students and prevalence of the school-to-prison pipeline—the movement for Black lives is also about our humanity and dignity. Including Black voices in the documentation of this historic moment is one way to show that our lives, stories, perspectives, and experiences matter.

Walking, Wellness, and Black Motherhood

I show my children that Black lives matter by taking care of my health. Three months before the pandemic arrived, I left a routine physical with a doctor's recommendation for more physical activity, but doctor's orders did little to change my behaviour. Rather, the orders added guilt to my lack of motivation. As an academic and mother of two young children, I was accustomed to both a sedentary work life and prioritizing the needs of my children. Months into the pandemic, with my doctor's orders compounded by doctors' warnings about the links between underlying health conditions and the harshest effects of COVID-19, I remained inactive. I, like many others, battled fear of the unknown and mounting responsibilities at the intersection of motherhood and my career. Then, I found GirlTrek.

GirlTrek is a nonprofit organization geared towards improving the physical activity, health, and life expectancy of Black women and girls in the United States and globally. I found the organization through social media, but their *TED* Talk is what inspired me to join their movement of walking for community and social change. In their talk, "The Trauma of Systematic Racism Is Killing Black Women. A First Step toward Change...", the cofounders of the organization, T. Morgan Dixon and Vanessa Garrison, offer an answer to the following question: Why are Black women dying of preventable diseases? They describe a generational trauma characterized by the long-lasting pain and suffering of injustice. Behind the statistics are actual mothers losing children to gun violence, actual families separated by incarceration, and actual dreams deferred by educational inequities and discriminatory housing practices. Dixon and Garrison acknowledge the physical and mental toll of injustice, thus framing the health and wellness of Black women as a social justice issue.

The idea that injustice and oppression are more than abstract concepts when we look at their impact on real lives is a perspective shared by Sonya Renee Taylor, author of *The Body Is Not an Apology*. Taylor writes: "When we speak of the ills of the world—violence, poverty, injustice—we are not speaking conceptually; we are talking about things that happen to bodies. *Injustice* is an opaque word until we are willing to discuss its material reality" (4). Following this quote, the author goes on to describe the suicide of Kalief Browder, a teenager who endured years of beatings and solitary confinement in Riker's Island prison—and the fatal heart attack that took his mother—as evidentiary of the material implications of injustice.

As Taylor, Dixon, and Garrison exemplify, identifying injustice is only part of the work. Taylor offers radical self-love, whereas Dixon and Garrison offer radical self-care as a means to heal ourselves, improve our communities, and disrupt the impact of systems of oppression. Although radical self-love and radical self-care are distinct ideas worthy of further explanation, both of these approaches require the unapologetically self-centred (in a good way) and community-oriented pursuit of social change. To explain how walking can mobilize women to collaborate for self-care and social change, GirlTrek evokes the power of historical and contemporary figures ("foremothers," civil rights leaders, artists, activists, and everyday people) who exemplify Black resistance and the quest for Black liberation.

A scan of GirlTrek's social media presence portrays a value system rooted in Black women's ways of knowing and being. Quotes like "Nobody's free until everybody's free"—attributed to freedom fighter Fannie Lou Hamer—emphasize the importance of civic engagement, collective action, sisterhood, and service to our communities. GirlTrek's Instagram feed shows images of Black women and girls of every skin shade and age dancing, jumping rope, playing music, celebrating one another, celebrating Black men and boys, flexing muscles, meditating, praying, and prioritizing their mental and physical health by walking. The lens is inclusive, global, rooted in reverence for elders, and oriented towards freedom and justice.

Mothering during the COVID-19 pandemic left little time for reading print books, but reading GirlTrek's online resources, and listening to their podcast while walking, gave me a sense of productivity and purpose. Participating in GirlTrek's Black History Bootcamp allowed me to practice self-care, walk for my health, engage with a likeminded community, and learn more about the history and values I wish to teach to my children. GirlTrek's bootcamp curriculum, coupled with research on Black motherhood, provides me a framework for helping my children develop a strong connection to their racial identity and articulate why it is important.

Showing Black children the value of authoring our own narratives is an important part of helping them connect to their racial identities. Authoring our own stories increases the likelihood of nuanced and multidimensional portrayals that prove there are many ways to be Black. Similar to the divide between my family's COVID-19 experience and the depiction of its impact in the Black community, I do not see myself reflected in every GirlTrek post. Yet I want to teach my children that the differences within our community are not justification for demeaning others or disconnecting from our people. Dawn Marie Dow expands on this perspective in *Mothering While Black: Boundaries and Burdens of Middle-Class Parenthood* when she describes the desire among parents to prepare their children to be both confident in themselves and comfortable around all kinds of people. Using the term "border crossers" to describe the ability to adjust to any setting (including a diverse school or predominantly Black neighbourhood), the author writes:

> On the one hand, border crossers wanted to help their children develop certain middle-class skills. On the other hand, they also chose activities with an eye toward fostering a specific version of African American identity—a border-crossing

identity—that tied them to their family and community and gave them skills to safely negotiate spaces that were not marked by privilege. (73)

Border crossing is important while Black children explore their identity because there is often a difference between how they see themselves and the way the world sees them. Instead of using class differences or middle-class privilege to distance oneself from other Black people, this parenting philosophy promotes a Black identity rooted in solidarity with and love for oneself and one's community. This approach lays the groundwork to demonstrate that all Black lives—independent of socioeconomic status, skin shade, gender or sexual identity, nationality, creed, or otherwise—matter.

Another important aspect of cultivating a strong cultural identity is rooted in the idea of shared goals. Trina Greene Brown, author of *Parenting for Liberation: A Guide for Raising Black Children*, challenges parents to "raise Black children without fear and instead parent for liberation" (12). The author emphasizes cultivating connections to ourselves, our communities, and our children as a roadmap through healing to liberation.

While the concepts of "border crossing" and "parenting for liberation" are different, they highlight how multiple perspectives can coexist and complement one another with shared values and goals in mind. Just as middle-class status does not preclude many Black people from police brutality, COVID-19 statistics suggest a shorter degree of separation from the disease within the Black community. These problems require collective action. Thus, much like the movement for Black lives should involve solidarity across differences, parenting in the Black community should involve working together to protect our children from real threats.

Educating Black Girls: Counternarratives and Children's Literature

"Black girls are the only group of girls to be over-represented across the entire continuum of school discipline: expulsions, suspensions, arrests, corporal punishment, referrals to law enforcement, re-straints" (*Pushout*). As a Black woman, critical educator, and mother of Black girls, I know this data highlight a serious flaw in the educational system, not an inherent problem with Black girls. Instead of operating from the false assumption that Black girls and "bad" behaviour are responsible for disrupting their education, the film *Pushout: The Criminalization of Black Girls in Schools* and the associated research of Monique Morris show how punitive discipline, rooted in the adultification of Black girls, disrupts their educational attainment.

Based on a survey of more than three hundred adults conducted by researchers at the Georgetown Law Center on Poverty and Inequality, Morris draws a connection between the adultification of Black girls and the harsher punishments they receive in schools. The survey results suggest the misconception that Black girls—often perceived as older than their age—need less nurturing and protection than their white girl peers (Morris). This data make me wonder what lessons my daughters have already learned—at four and six years old—about their ability to express themselves fully and exist freely at school.

The data, coupled with research about the institutionalized devaluation of nonwhite cultures and students in school (McClain), begin to explain what fellow mother and scholar Monisha Bajaj describes as a sentiment among parents of colour who view schooling at home as an act of resistance. After acknowledging the widespread suffering associated with COVID-19 among many families, the author points towards another trend: "For parents of color, [the coronavirus pandemic] means a chance to educate our children as we see fit. We have an opportunity to offer counter-stories that focus on people who look like us, as opposed to having our children forced to learn from narratives written from a European or white perspective."

Schooling at home as an act of resistance is a perspective with which I relate even though I like and respect my children's teachers. Schooling at home as an act of resistance and prioritizing perspectives that are not exclusively rooted in white cultural values are approaches with which I relate even though I really like our school and the racial and socioeconomic diversity it offers. My feelings about our school and my knowledge of educational inequities are not mutually exclusive, and, together, they have informed my approach to mothering during the pandemic. Thus, I return to the aforementioned question: If this pandemic has provided a once-in-a-lifetime opportunity to maintain employment and spend my days with my children, how can I use this time to invest in my family and parent purposefully to impart cultural values and cultivate community and self-love in my daughters?

Drawing from children's literature and GirlTrek's podcasts and social media posts, I taught my daughters that Black women and girls can be environmentalists, like Wangari Mathaii, and ecoentrepreneurs, like Mikaila Ulmer. Black women and girls can overcome challenging circumstances to succeed, like Misty Copeland and Wilma Rudolph. Black women and girls can be political change makers, like Shirley Chisholm and Kamala Harris. Black women and girls are scientific and mathematical minded high achievers, like Mae Jemison and Katherine Johnson. Black women and girls are beautiful, like the characters in the book *Princess Hair* (Miller), and Black women and girls—like my daughters—are what Nina Simone called "young, gifted, and Black."

After reading about Katherine Johnson, my oldest daughter—who already has a passion for STEM subjects—told me that she wants to become a mathematician. Since she did not say the same thing about becoming a ballerina after reading Misty Copeland's biography, I used the information to inform my parental and pedagogical approach with her. Now, when doing math work, I encourage her to overcome adversity, like Katherine Johnson, by choosing challenging numbers, trying multiple math strategies, and practicing the strategies she has yet to master. If she were in school, I might have missed the opportunity to encourage this academic and culturally rooted interest.

As Greene Brown suggests in *Parenting for Liberation*, "we must educate [our children] on inequities that they may face" (80), but we also must envision and parent in pursuit of a world full of Black joy, healing, and freedom. When deficit-oriented narratives abound, I want to shield my children's ears. When statistics about school discipline and Black girls surface, I want to keep my children home indefinitely. However, the Black experience in the U.S. is not only a story of pain and suffering; it is a testament to the resilience needed to endure both racism and the coronavirus pandemic.

Conclusion

As I write the conclusion of this chapter, our school district is preparing to return to in-person instruction. Our schools will finally join the well-funded and over-resourced neighbouring private schools that have been conducting in-person instruction for months. As for my family, despite my impression that virtual instruction is far from ideal, we will continue with remote learning for the remainder of 2020. We will continue using this special time to explore our history and cultural values, practice radical self-love and self-care, and pursue liberation for our community and ourselves.

When I return to the doctor for my next routine physical, I hope that my health will have noticeably improved, but I have already proven that I have the means and motivation to sustain myself and care for my family during a global pandemic. Although I am less optimistic about a foreseeable end to the pandemic of racism, I am consciously working towards raising culturally rooted, self-confident, and border-crossing Black daughters, who will sustain the legacy of their equity- and justice-seeking predecessors. I am hopeful.

Works Cited

Bajaj, Monisha. "For Parents of Color, Schooling at Home Can Be an Act of Resistance." *Citizen Ed.* Brightbeam, 14 May 2020, citizen.education/2020/05/14/for-parents-of-color-schooling-at-home-can-be-an-act-of-resistance/. Accessed 8 Jan. 2021.

Brown, Trina Greene. *Parenting for Liberation: A Guide for Raising Black Children.* First Feminist Press, 2020.

Dixon, T. Morgan, and Vanessa Garrison. "The Trauma of Systematic Racism Is Killing Black Women. A First Step toward Change..." *TED: Ideas Worth Spreading,* Apr. 2017, www.ted.com/talks/t_morgan_dixon_and_vanessa_garrison_the_trauma_of_systematic_racism_is_killing_black_women_a_first_step_toward_change/reading-list. Accessed 8 Jan. 2021.

Dow, Dawn Marie. *Mothering While Black: Boundaries and Burdens of Middle-Class Parenthood.* University of California Press, 2019.

GirlTrek. *GirlTrek.* 2020, www.girltrek.org. Accessed 8 Jan. 2021.

Gould, Elise, and Valerie Wilson. "Black Workers Face Two of the Most Lethal Preexisting Conditions for Coronavirus—Racism and Economic Inequality." *Economic Policy Institute,* 1 June 2020, www.epi.org/publication/black-workers-covid/. Accessed 8 Jan. 2021.

Gravlee, Clarence. "Racism, Not Genetics, Explains Why Black Americans Are Dying of COVID-19." *Scientific American,* 7 June 2020, blogs.

scientificamerican.com/voices/racism-not-genetics-explains-why-black-americans-are-dying-of-covid-19/. Accessed 8 Jan. 2021.

Horowitz Menasce, Juliana. "Views on Why Black Americans Face Higher COVID-19 Hospitalization Rates Vary by Party, race and ethnicity." *Pew Research Center*, 26 June 2020, www.pewresearch.org/fact-tank/2020/06/26/views-on-why-black-americans-face-higher-covid-19-hospitalization-rates-vary-by-party-race-and-ethnicity/. Accessed 8 Jan. 2021.

"Annual School Performance Reports." *Indiana Department of Education*, 13 July 2020, www.doe.in.gov/accountability/annual-school-performance-reports. Accessed 8 Jan. 2021.

McClain, Dani. *We Live for the We: The Political Power of Black Motherhood.* Bold Type Books, 2019.

Miller, Sharee. *Princess Hair.* Little, Brown and Company, 2014.

Morris, Monique. *Sing a Rhythm, Dance a Blues: Education for the Liberation of Black and Brown Girls.* The New Press, 2019.

Pushout: The Criminalization of Black Girls in Schools. Directed by Jacoba Atlas, performances by Monique W. Morris, 2019.

Scott, Lakia M. and Barbara Purdum-Cassidy, editors. *Culturally Affirming Literacy Practices for Urban Elementary Students.* Rowman and Littlefield, 2016.

Siemaszko, Corky. "Ohio Politician Fired as ER Doctor after Asking Whether 'Colored Population' More Likely to Get COVID-19 Because They Don't 'Wash Their Hands as Well.'" *NBC News Digital,* 11 June 2020, www.nbcnews.com/news/us-news/ohio-politician-fired-er-doctor-after-asking-whether-colored-population-n1230096. Accessed 8 Jan. 2021.

Taylor, Sonya Renee. *The Body Is Not an Apology: The Power of Radical Self-Love.* Berrett-Koehler, 2018.

Chapter Twenty One

Planet COVID-19: Single Mothering and Disability

Euphemia Bonnitcha

The beginning of quarantine was a welcome break as an autistic mother with an autistic daughter. My daughter and I are both socially awkward and prefer to spend time alone surrounded by our pets, hobbies, and our own thoughts. Quarantining in our own home is far less stressful than bright lights, loud noises, and intrusive questions from strangers or the social pressure of having to perform small talk.

This feeling lasted for several weeks while the world dramatically shifted, as if now suddenly designed to meet the needs of autistic people. I did not have to put on my neurotypical mask in the office or race home and attempt to force my daughter into the car to attend the psychologist, paediatrician, or occupational therapist. Our service providers magically appeared online, and my daughter could sit on her bed with the dog and chat without the stress these appointments had previously caused.

Fast forward four months, and the paediatrician is trying to admit my twelve-year-old daughter to a psychiatric ward. Her anxiety and depression have escalated, her medication has increased, and her weight has dropped. She has not left her bedroom for anything other than the toilet in twenty weeks. School resumed in person without her, and a second more restricted lockdown has sent our lives into crisis.

This chapter will explore pandemic mothering from the perspective of a feminist, lesbian, autistic, single, white, Australian, and middle-class mother working full-time and the steady increase in panic I felt as my autistic daughter fell into a chasm. It will deal with the failures of my workplace, which has not been responsive to me as a single mother, followed by a description of how being an older neurodivergent (ND) mother has increased my own distress. The chapter then outlines my daughter's complex needs to identify the terrain I have had to traverse as her mother in the context of the pandemic. It will conclude by outlining the concern I have for the toll this next phase of transition to the new COVID-19 normal will have on my daughter and me as well as for the long-term effects this pandemic-induced trauma will have on us.

Being a Working Single Mother during the COVID-19 Pandemic

Prior to the pandemic, I worked full-time researching violence against women in an open-plan office space. I had a hard won "working from home" day once a week—a day that acknowledges that for research, it is essential to have a quiet, nondistracting space to do some deep analytical work away from meetings and the chatter of colleagues. Eighteen months before this, I was an independent consultant working from home full-time. This was a productive way for me to work, allowing both flexibility with my primary-school-aged daughter and my need for a quiet space to work.

When COVID-19 first granted us the ability to work from home, I was delighted because I anticipated an increase in productivity. The reality has been in stark contrast to this initial feeling. As Neil Webb insightfully stated in the early days of the pandemic: "You are not working from home. You are at your home in a time of crisis trying to work." Dr. Fiona Jenkins from the Australian National University says something similar: "Suppose we say that what we have actually just done by closing down workplaces and substituting 'working from home'; is in effect a requisition of people's homes as their place of work... acting as if home is a costless resource that is free for appropriation in an emergency." This co-option of our private space has completely blurred the lines of paid work and private life, with the economic benefits going to the employer.

My paid work in combatting violence against women has

skyrocketed during this pandemic. We have introduced various new initiatives to address the increasing levels of domestic violence under COVID-19 conditions. My own experience of adolescent family violence has also increased. This is an under-reported and under-researched form of violence from children, especially autistic teenagers.[1] Ironically, instead of being offered family violence leave or a decreased workload, I have been expected to increase my output in response to the need to address violence "out there," whereas my own family violence remains invisible. I am working harder with longer hours as a single mother of a child with disabilities in my home, which has become a workplace as well as a site for the very problems we seek to address.

In terms of housework and carework, as a single mother, these have also increased dramatically. I do not have to deal with sharing an unequal burden of feminized labour with a partner, as I shoulder this full burden. However, I had contracted out the cleaning and gardening tasks to self-employed women (one also being a single mother of a child with autism), both of whom lost work through this pandemic. Adding these additional household tasks to my already impossible load has been physically exhausting. When I needed support before the pandemic, I would call my mother or sister, who both live in another state in Australia. I would either fly to them with my daughter or fly them down to be with us. The pandemic, however, has stopped all travel in Australia; thus, this critical source of support has vanished.

Being a Mother with Autism at Fifty-Four during the COVID-19 Pandemic

I was diagnosed with autism spectrum disorder (ASD) two years ago at the age of fifty-two, two weeks before my now twelve-year-old daughter's diagnosis. We both had prior diagnoses of attention deficit disorder (ADHD), and we both live with depression and anxiety. In addition, my daughter also has dyslexia, pathological demand avoidance (PDA), and sensory processing disorder (see next section).

My own family also criticizes my mothering. Autistic women and girls mask a great deal more than males with autism. Mimicking the behavior of neurotypical peers to fit in takes a great deal of focus, and after my daughter either returns from school or a visit to my family, she melts down. Autistic meltdowns are more commonly done in the presence of mothers, as we are their safe space. In an article about the difficulties of homeschooling autistic children face, one mother states, "Because they're at home, they're not masking so that means I get their raw, full emotion because this is their safe environment" (qtd. in Hermant, Campanella, and Kent).

Due to the masking, my family see my daughter's behaviour as that of a neurotypical child and chastise me for pandering to her needs and mollycoddling her. They blame my mothering. They claim I am too soft and do not reinforce boundaries. They say I create the problem. Once when my sister visited us, she put my daughter on a strict routine (which PDA children find extremely difficult). My daughter behaved perfectly and did everything she was asked. When my sister departed, my daughter broke down. My sister's response was a five-page letter on how to be a better mother. In a similar vein, when I disclosed my own diagnosis to my family, I was told that everyone is a little bit on the spectrum—a comment those of us with autism often receive. Not only does such a perspective completely misinterpret what the spectrum of autism is,[2] but it also negates my issues, identity and struggles. I continue to just be viewed by them as eccentric and obsessive, terms they have used for me throughout my life.

Even when my daughter's father lived in the same country and we shared custody, my daughter hid her ND behavior in front of her father. My ex-husband, who is very strict, reinforced the idea that all my daughter's problems were my doing and blamed me for escalating her distress. Autistic mothers are significantly more likely than neurotypical mothers to experience motherhood as an isolating experience and less rewarding; they are also more likely to feel judged, to have difficulty coping, and to be unable to ask for support (Pohl et al. 7-8).

Living with autism brings social anxiety, and I left the house rarely prior to the pandemic. Some studies on people with autism during the pandemic have argued that since autistic people are "natural quarantiners" (Kapp qtd. in Cassidy et al. 110), they would do better under lockdown. However, Jac den Houting points out that choosing to self-isolate is very different than being mandated to self-isolate. She also identifies that the self-isolation of autistic people is often not due to preference but to self-perseveration because of exclusion, bullying, harassment and abuse, as well as a lack of services and supports (104). In fact, she points to how this process of social isolation is linked to loneliness and can increase mental illness (103).

The new flexible structures and strategies to access specialist services online during lockdown, including telehealth, have been a huge benefit for me personally, as it has enabled me to finally be able to access counselling for myself. As a single working mother, accessing counselling had been difficult in the past, since I prioritized my leave at work to take my daughter to her multiple medical specialists. An added benefit to the online experience is that I did not have to sit opposite the therapist in her office, squirming and fidgeting while I discussed issues that heightened my anxiety. I am now able to access online support while I craft, or if I am talking with the counsellor on the phone, I garden at the same time, which calms me and assists my ADHD focus.

Many people with autism and ADHD also live with depression and anxiety. Marcia Gardner et al. cite that 80 per cent of people with Asperger syndrome (now categorised under ASD) report psychiatric disorders, such as comorbidities, most commonly ADHD, depression, and anxiety (30). In the context of COVID-19, research from the University of Melbourne shows that mental distress has doubled since the pandemic for parents of primary-school students, with those who are also employed being four times more likely to experience high mental distress (Ziwica).

The problem is that our mind never rests. We are constantly worrying about the consequences of our actions and are deeply and empathically linked to the concerns of others. These traits have led many of us to become chronic smokers. The panic I feel in relation to COVID-19 has exacerbated my stress, which has increased my smoking, which, in turn, increases my health risks regarding COVID-19 due to my lung capacity. The way my brain is wired leads me to the conclusion that I am at increased risk of death if I contract the virus. As a result, my own behaviour becomes extreme, such as wearing plastic gloves whenever I leave the house. I was wearing a mask from the outset of COVID-19, four months before it was mandated. At the height of the crisis, I would have palpitations at the thought of having to leave the house and go to the supermarket. Ultimately, it was not so much the fear of death for myself but for my daughter, as I am the critical support for everything in her life. This may sound dramatic, but an article in *Ms.* on single mothers and COVID-19 indicates I am not alone. A Seattle mother posted the following to the Facebook group Empowering Solo Moms Everywhere: "Hello fellow single moms. Does anyone have a GOOD plan for if you were to get VERY sick? Who will take care of your child(ren) if you need to quarantine solo?" (qtd. in Lindholm). The responses were filled with fear but no concrete solutions.

A forty-nine-year-old woman with ADHD and dyspraxia explains what it is like living with those conditions: "We have to work so hard to adapt to a world that is straight and linear, when our brains are made up of squiggly lines and we have four conversations with invisible people going on at once." Concerning the lockdown, she adds: "[It] adds another layer of pressure. People with ADHD tend to be high achievers—we hyper focus on the things we are most passionate about. We set high standards for ourselves. I've been scared to waste this opportunity—I've felt the pressure to use this time wisely, and do all the things I have been putting off" (qtd. in Kavanagh-Hall).

I have also felt this need to overachieve and overproduce during the lockdown. Although I have been able to access an online counsellor during this time, she is not a specialist in my needs. I need a psychologist or trauma therapist that has a background in autistic women, ideally autistic motherhood. Since my diagnosis, I have been searching for resources on how to be an autistic mother. Motherhood has always been difficult for me, which began with severe postnatal depression. Even though my daughter is now entering her teenage years, my anxiety regarding being a good mother has never subsided. I constantly see other mothers enjoying their role, breezing through events and decisions that I find debilitating, even simple tasks.

Since my diagnosis, I have begun to unpack why I have found so many daily activities so difficult. It is a relief to finally have a reason for my problems, and I have stopped trying to fit myself into situations that cause me discomfort. This avoidance may calm me, but, at times, it becomes an excuse for never leaving the house, never attending parties, and avoiding connections that could lead to greater fulfillment. I have been seeking positive strategies to assist being a competent and content neurodivergent woman in a neurotypical world, but more than that, I crave resources on how to mother effectively with autism.

Autism has traditionally focused on male traits and manifestations leading to higher diagnosis in boys, as girls more traditionally mask or camouflage their autistic traits. One study shows that girls are underdiagnosed and talk of being misunderstood, as their behavior is often labelled as "laziness or willful defiance" (Bargiela, Steward, and Mandy 3291). The recent focus on girls with autism is welcome, but none of this literature looks at the critical role of being a mother with autism. My online searches have revealed an expansive choice of books and journal articles providing tips and case studies of being a mother to autistic children, and even specifically for autistic girls, but very rarely do these works include reflections on being an autistic mother (although a book titled *Spectrum Women: Autism and Parenting* has been released).

One of my autistic obsessions is research, and being a researcher helps satiate my need for evidence and information. Consequently, I decided to write this chapter to give me a deadline and to help focus my ADHD mind. My self-care is appalling (linked to depression), and I can go days without showering or making meals for myself. Writing this chapter became a form of self-care, providing me an opportunity to put a framework around my racing thoughts of living under the pandemic. This process has been exceptionally helpful, as there have been several studies indicating the mental crisis for adults and children with ASD. I have discovered that it is not just me or my daughter who have suffered. Around the world, the pandemic has created acute anxiety and despair for people like us with ASD. And few services exist to address our needs.

Mothering a Child with Disabilities during the COVID-19 Pandemic

As stated at the outset of this chapter, the beginning of lockdown appeared to suit me and my daughter. My daughter's sensory processing disorder creates an extreme aversion to loud noises, crowds, and bright lights; she also feels extreme anxiety with people she does not know. Even before the pandemic, we could not visit cafes, restaurants, festivals, school parties, sporting events, or even dog parks. Visiting other people's houses is stressful for her, so our social life had focused on people visiting us. With this one outlet for social interaction forbidden under COVID-19 restrictions, we have barely seen anyone else in six months.

Online telehealth with her occupational therapist worked well at the beginning, but now my daughter will not open the laptop or speak with the therapist on the phone. She has shut herself in her bedroom and spiralled into a deep depression. She has refused homeschooling and has not even contacted her friends on the phone or electronic media. She has gone six weeks at a time without a shower and has refused to brush her teeth sometimes for up to a week. This crisis has led me on a constant search for professional support to assist her. I often spend three hours a day online with providers. Sourcing this expertise has been debilitating, as I have had to tell our story repeatedly to new people. This is emotionally draining for me and usually leads to my own shut down and need to sleep.

My daughter's school has been excellent, in that it has given attention to our needs. Her teacher has called every morning and the welfare officer every afternoon. We had a virtual meeting to structure a program to return to school, but none of the strategies worked. In Australia, school welfare officers are not trained; they are regular teachers who take on the role and are often far less aware of the educational needs and strategies to deal with children with complex needs than parents who have done extensive research. Over time, my daughter has refused to take phone calls from her teacher and welfare officer. I often spend at least an hour a day discussing possible work tasks or activities to engage her, which have not been fruitful.

Fiona Sharky, CEO of the Amaze organization, which assists people with autism, in Victoria, Australia, has raised the issue of families of children with disabilities having to develop their own solutions to homeschooling during lockdown: "There's just been no special information on how parents can seek support. It's very much [that] the burden is on parents and on individual schools.... The silence is really deafening from the [education] department" (qtd. in Herment, Campanella, and Kent).

The conflicting specialist advice has also been extremely debilitating. In the past few months, my daughter has begun repeating the phrase "I am dead," which may be in response to me asking how she is, or it may be simply something she mutters to herself when she wanders from her bedroom to the toilet. I asked her if she wanted to be dead, and she replied that it would be easier not to be living. I asked if she would ever do anything about it, and she responded that she hates pain too much to do anything. I spent a great deal of time talking to her after this and immediately contacted our general practitioner as well as an autism psychologist. Interestingly, the autism psychologist claimed it was a serious concern, as it represented suicidal ideation, although she assessed her as too depressed to act on it. Our general practitioner stated it was not suicidal ideation and that it could simply be teenage existential angst.[3]

The paediatrician (a leading autism paediatrician in my home city) has stated that my daughter is too complex for a paediatrician and she needs a child psychiatrist to address her medications. My daughter has had severe reactions to most medications, including insomnia for seventy-two hours, dizziness, nausea, and increased anxiety. The current mental health crisis, however, has meant that child psychiatrists with any background in autism are fully booked and have closed their waiting lists at least until next year. In the absence of this support, the paediatrician has recommended I admit my daughter to a psychiatric clinic; I called the clinic repeatedly, but each time it gave me contradictory advice on whether she is eligible.

Most recently, the paediatrician told me take my daughter to emergency and demand admission. This advice sent me into crisis. How could I get my daughter to an emergency ward when she refused to leave the house and when her only sense of safety was her bedroom and her dog? The mere mention of the word "hospital" sent her into an uncontrollable rage. Even if I could force her (as I do not have the physical strength to do so), I would violate her trust in me, her only safe person, and she would experience (further) trauma. She would bear witness to me explaining the ghastly context of her current behaviour to a medical clinician, who, I am sure, would say it is not their specialization. We would then be passed onto several other people, and in all likelihood, we would be sent home. Even if we were admitted, she would be without her dog as well as her specialist foods; she would be in bright lighting surrounded by strangers encroaching upon her private space.

Our general practitioner fully concurred with my assessment; however, the response from the paediatrician to our general practitioner was to question whether my daughter was at risk in my care. The anger

I felt at this accusation, as well as the fear that my child could be taken from me, compounded my personal crisis. A.L. Pohl et al. have noted that autistic mothers are more likely to be scrutinized by medical professionals and social service providers and are more likely to have their children taken from them (9). Dr. Baron-Cohen, director of the Autism Research Center at the University of Cambridge, has noted that autistic mothers have been falsely accused of Munchausen syndrome by proxy, with the assumption that they were making up the autism of their children (qtd. in Malia). Lana Grant, author of *From Here to Maternity: Pregnancy and Motherhood on the Autism Spectrum*, adds that mothers often do a great deal of research to assist their children; as a result, they are often seen as too knowledgeable and hysterical and are assumed to be telling professionals how to do their job (qtd. in Malia).

I have researched my daughter's needs on my own, using journal articles, books, and online seminars, yet I have been assessed as possibly the problem by the paediatrician I currently deal with. This accusation makes me feel like a failure as a mother—a belief that already exists in mind because of the comments made by my family and my ex-husband.

Having researched the impact of COVID-19 on adults and children with autism, I believe my situation as well as my daughter's is not dissimilar to many thousands of other autistic women and girls. Studies in Australia, Canada, Italy, Serbia, Turkey, the United Kingdom (U.K.), and the United States (U.S.) have all illustrated that the COVID-19 pandemic has caused a mental health crisis for autistic people. A U.K. study in the United Kingdom of parents of with neurodevelopmental disorders conducted since the COVID-19 outbreak has found that the neurodivergent children had a higher prevalence of emotional symptoms than neurotypical children (42 per cent vs. 15 per cent), conduct problems (28 per cent vs. 9 per cent), and fewer prosocial behaviours (54 per cent vs. 22 per cent). Girls with ASD also had considerably more higher emotional symptoms than boys (Nonweiler et al. 2).

An Italian study of 527 parents and guardians of ASD children found that behavioural problems since COVID-19 had become more intense (35 per cent) and more frequent (41.5 per cent) (Colizzi et al. 5). Additionally, families with ASD children were more likely to report greater stress than those with children with other forms of disability (Colizzi et al. 12).

An Australian study on autistic people and their families under lockdown (Pellicano et al. 7) found that parents had noted increased panic attacks, self-harming and/or talking about suicide among their ASD children. This included (in a minority of cases) participants or their family members hospitalized for acute psychiatric care for attempted suicide or severe mental health distress. In direct contrast to this dire situation, this Australian study and U.S. surveys of parents of autistic children and adults had a high number of participants expressing positive experiences under lockdown; the participants spoke about the extra time they had for their families and hobbies and their ability to access health professionals online. Stephanie Ameis et al. note it is likely these U.S. respondents had access to better resources and are not representative of the wider autistic population.

A final piece of research that I found useful was a rapid synthesis review addressing the impact of COVID-19 on the mental wellbeing of caregivers and families of autistic people; it highlights ASD children's increased frustration, aggression, and violence towards self and others (Lee et al. 24). The peer-reviewed literature includes a Serbian study, which shows 59 per cent of parents of ASD children reported feelings of helplessness, and a Canadian survey, which identifies 67 per cent of parents felt COVID-19 had negatively affected their ASD child's emotional and mental health. In the Canadian study, the parents' own wellbeing was characterized by experiencing feelings of worry (85 per cent), anxiousness (86 per cent), stress (86.1 per cent), depression (58 per cent), and isolation (77 per cent) (Lee et al. 24).

This research has helped me to quell my own anxiety about whether my own mothering is to blame for the traumatic context that my daughter and I find ourselves in. However, as a feminist mother, a gender specialist, and an intersectional researcher, I am surprised that none of the papers cited above—in looking at the impact of COVID-19 on ASD children and their parents—identify the specific burden on women as mothers. The studies have not visibly disaggregated data for the sex of the parents who have been survey respondents. The assessment of parental stress levels does not highlight gender differences, even though it is clear that women are experiencing higher levels of stress and anxiety.

Through scanning Facebook groups of parents of neurodiverse children over the past two years, I have found that 95 per cent of comments are from mothers. As other articles in this volume will attest, COVID-19 is a gendered pandemic, as is the impact of parenting ASD children within this crisis. Surprisingly, we have seen a variety of global studies looking at the impact of COVID-19 on mental health, yet the gendered nature of the unpaid and highly stressful work of addressing the multiple needs of children has been largely absent from these studies. In my context, this also includes being a single mother, autistic, and working full-time. I feel invisible in policy discussions, and my needs are ignored in mainstream services responding to the pandemic; in fact, my needs are so specific that mainstream services are not useful.

Transitioning Out of Level Four Lockdown

My life as an autistic single mother working fulltime and caring for an autistic daughter with ASD and PDA and who suffers from severe depression is not a fairy tale, and there is no happy ending. The focus is now on school reopening. All the specialists concur that the likelihood of my daughter returning is slim, yet I have a plethora of meetings to develop another return-to-school plan. Since the second and more restricted lockdown, my daughter's situation has significantly worsened. My greatest fear is that she will not return to school for the remainder of the year, in which case, her last year of primary school will not have a closure and will not be accompanied by the celebrations that all children have at this milestone in their life. Missing those celebrations will make her transition to secondary school all the more difficult.

These issues occupy my thoughts at night, and I fear the result of our situation will create long term trauma for both of us. Before COVID-19, my daughter was attending school almost every day, and I had a steady job with daily interaction with people in my workplace. This pandemic has changed our lives significantly on all levels; my daughter has been clinically identified as in crisis, which has led to personal crisis for me as her mother. This is unsustainable. I have no answers, only constant racing thoughts that I am failing as a mother.

One issue that most of the research on COVID-19 and autism has highlighted is that the road out of lockdown and a return to what is now termed a "COVID-19 normal" will be another stressful transition for those with ASD. We never fitted into the old normal, and being expected to adjust back into old systems when we are still in crisis will require a great deal more understanding from every section of society.

Endnotes

1. Although it is noted that they can be violent towards themselves (Lee et al.), I was unable to locate any studies on the violence of autistic children, especially teenagers, towards others, especially siblings and mothers. Violence by autistic children and adolescents is illustrated daily in Facebook groups of parents of children with autism. The most common images and comments from parents on adolescent violence come from mothers. From anecdotal involvement in these groups over the past two years, I have noted teenage boys are more likely to cause damage to homes (often punching walls or throwing items), whereas girls tend to hit, kick, and bite their mothers.

2. For an excellent illustration of the autism spectrum, see Crosman.

3. Her medication has subsequently been increased, and various other specialists have confirmed that she is not a risk of harming herself at present.

Works Cited

Ameis, Stephanie H. et al. "Coping, Fostering Resilience, and Driving Care Innovation for Autistic People and Their Families during the COVID-19 Pandemic and Beyond." *Molecular Autism*, vol. 11, no. 61 2020, pp. 1-9.

Bargiela, Sarah, Robyn Steward, and William Mandy. "The Experiences of Late Diagnosed Women with Autism Spectrum Conditions: An Investigation of the Female Autism Phenotype." *Journal of Autism and Developmental Disorders* vol. 46, no. 10, 2016, pp. 3,281-3,294.

Colizzi Marco, et al. "Psychosocial and Behavioral Impact of COVID-19 in Autism Spectrum Disorder: An Online Parent Survey." *Brain Sci*, vol. 10, no. 6, pp. 1-14.

Crosman, Cassandra. "The Autism Spectrum Is Not Binary." *In the Loop*, 6 Mar. 2019, intheloopaboutneurodiversity.wordpress.com/2019/03/06/the-autism-spectrum-is-not-binary/. Accessed 9 Jan. 2021.

Gardner, Marcia, et al. "Exploratory Study of Childbearing Experiences of Asperger Syndrome." *Nursing for Women's Health*, vol. 20, no. 1, 2016, pp. 29-37.

Herment, Norman, Nas Campanella, and Lucy Kent. "Parents of Children with Disabilities Are Struggling to Teach Their Children during COVID-19." *ABC News Australia* 6 May 2020, www.abc.net.au/news/2020-05-06/coronavirus-parents-need-help-teaching-students-disabilities/12211664. Accessed 9 Jan. 2021.

Houting, Jac den. "Stepping Out of Isolation: Autistic People and COVID-19." *Autism in Adulthood*, vol. 2, no. 2, 2020, pp. 103-5.

Jenkins, Fiona. "Did Our Employers Just Requisition Our Homes?" *The Canberra Times*, 4 Apr. 2020, genderinstitute.anu.edu.au/news/did-our-employers-just-requisition-our-homes. Accessed 9 Jan 2021.

Kavanagh-Hall, Erin. "A Different Headspace: Six People on Being Neurodivergent during Lockdown." *The Spinoff*, 24 Apr. 2020, thespinoff.co.nz/ society/26-04-2020/a-different-headspace-being-neurodivergent-during-covid-19/. Accessed 9 Jan. 2021.

Lee, V., et al. "Impact of COVID-19 on the Mental Health and Wellbeing of Caregivers and Families of Autistic People: A Rapid Synthesis Review." *Canadian Institutes of Health Research*, 2020, cihr-irsc.gc.ca/e/52048.html. Accessed 9 Jan. 2021.

Lindholm, Marika. "Single Moms and COVID-19: Lessons in Desperation and Strength." *Ms.*, 4 Apr. 2020, msmagazine.com/2020/04/08/single-moms-and-covid-19-lessons-in-desperation-and-strength/. Accessed 9 Jan. 2021.

Malia, Jen. "My Daughter and I Were Diagnosed with Autism on the Same Day." *New York Times*, 15 Apr. 2020, www.nytimes.com/2020/04/15/parenting/autism-mom.html. Accessed 9 Jan. 2021.

Nonweiler, Jacqueline, et al. "Prevalence and Associated Factors of Emotional and Behavioural Difficulties during COVID-19 Pandemic in Children with Neurodevelopmental Disorders." *Children*, vol. 7, no. 9, 2000, p. 128.

Pellicano, E., et al. "'I Want to See My Friends': The Everyday Experiences of Autistic People and Their Families during COVID-19." *University of Sydney*, 2020, www.sydney.edu.au/dam/corporate/documents/sydney-policy-lab/everyday-experiences-of-autistic-people-during-covid-19---report---july-2020.pdf. Accessed 9 Jan. 2021.

Pohl, A. L., et al. "A Comparative Study of Autistic and Non-Autistic Women's Experience of Motherhood." *Molecular Autism*, vol. 11, no. 3, 2020, pp. 1-12.

Webb, Neil. "You Are Not Working from Home." *Twitter*, 31 Mar. 2020, twitter.com/neilmwebb/status/1245012958415073282?lang=en. Accessed 9 Jan. 2021.

Ziwica, Kristine. "Yes Pandemic Parental Burnout Is a Thing and You're Not Alone." *Women's Agenda*, 10. Sept. 2020, womensagenda.com.au/life/jugglehood/yes-pandemic-parental-burnout-is-a-thing-and-youre-not-alone/. Accessed 9 Jan. 2021.

Chapter Twenty Two

"Your 'Only' Is My Everything": Mothering Children with Disabilities through COVID-19

Kinga Pozniak and Olaf Kraus de Camargo

Introduction

In the first few weeks of the COVID-19 pandemic, in the spring of 2020, a meme circulated on Facebook groups for parents of children with disabilities, with the slogan "Your 'only' is my everything" superimposed on a child's picture. The meme's intended message was to protest the popular rhetoric prevalent at the time that only the already-vulnerable were at risk of COVID-19—a belief that parents of children with disabilities felt denied their children's value and dismissed them as disposable and expendable.

This chapter examines the experiences of mothers of children with disabilities during the first six months of the COVID-19 pandemic. Although it is increasingly well documented that the COVID-19 pandemic is taking a disproportionate toll on the lives of mothers everywhere, mothers who have children with disabilities face particular challenges. However, many of the COVID-19-related phenomena that the majority of people experience as a profound disruption of their normal lives are, in fact, nothing new to these mothers. Paradoxically, they also benefit in unexpected ways from some of the new mechanisms of access and connection that have been widely adopted as a result of COVID-19. The mothers' accounts point to the need to rethink many aspects of our social organization, central among them being the role that carework plays in the functioning of society.

Background

There is mounting evidence that shows women are uniquely affected by the COVID-19 pandemic, due, in part, to the persistence of traditional gender roles, which render them more likely to assume the bulk of unpaid caregiving responsibilities for their family members and/or to be employed in frontline caregiving professions, such as in healthcare, childcare, or education (O'Reilly; Power; Thomason and Macias-Alonso; Johnston, Mohammed, and Linden). Furthermore, gender intersects with other "drivers of vulnerability and marginalisation" (Ryan and El-Ayadi 1405), including age, ethnicity (and racism), indigeneity, socioeconomic status, geography, sexuality, religion, migration/refugee status, disability, and other structural conditions (for example, political and environmental stressors, such as war) (Ryan and El-Ayadi).

Of particular relevance to our focus in this chapter is the intersection between gender and disability in the lives of mothers. Many children with disabilities have underlying medical conditions that place them at a higher risk of COVID-19-related complications (WHO). Moreover, parents of children with disabilities also face a host of additional challenges as a result of COVID-19-related measures. Many of their children require medical procedures, therapies, home-based nurses/ personal support workers (PSWs), or school-based supports—many of which were cancelled during the COVID-19 lockdowns and school closures (Lee; Phoenix). The heightened health risks, coupled with loss of supports, created additional logistical and emotional challenges for parents/caregivers (Phoenix; Arim, Findlay, and Kohen; Klass; Reid).

Methods

This article is based on interviews with nine Canadian mothers who have children with disabilities. The interviews were part of a larger study about the needs and supports of people with disabilities and parents/caregivers of people with disabilities during the pandemic, which was led by Olaf Kraus de Camargo—developmental paediatrician at McMaster University and a researcher with the university's CanChild Centre for Childhood Disability Research. The interviews were conducted over the phone or videoconferencing software by Kinga Pozniak, a postdoctoral researcher at CanChild, whose research focuses on the experiences of parents who have children with disabilities. The mothers were recruited through the Centre's parent networks, including its newsletter and Facebook group for parent affiliates. Although the data we present here are drawn from the interviews, the interviews are informed and contextualized by Pozniak's ongoing interactions with parents in a number of different research studies and her regular participation in CanChild's Facebook group for parents. All of the names used in the chapter are pseudonyms.

Although we did not collect demographic information on the mothers, we sketch out some trends relevant to the discussion that will follow. Five of the mothers were residing in Ontario, whereas two lived in Alberta and two lived in Saskatchewan. All spoke English with nativelike proficiency, although one mother was born outside of Canada (in the United States), and English was not her first language. We did not ask the mothers about their ethnic backgrounds or about whether they identified as members of any visible minority groups, and none of the mothers made any reference to this. The mothers' ages ranged from early forties to early sixties, and their children ranged in ages from four to thirty-two. All of the mothers had at least one child (sometimes more) with a medical diagnosis, and the diagnoses included cerebral palsy, autism spectrum disorder, and rare conditions. All of the mothers were primary caregivers to their children before COVID-19, which they combined with a variety of work and volunteering arrangements. Giselle was a nurse pursuing her PhD and teaching at the university level. Janelle had her own part-time housekeeping business. Maria was a business analyst for a government health agency. Valerie taught English as a second language online to international students. Cathleen had a home daycare. Diana was a public speaker, writer, and activist. Jackie worked part-time for a national disability advocacy organization and volunteered as president of her local branch. Kate had quit her job a few years ago when her son graduated high school, and Tammy was home full-time looking after her four children, all with different diagnoses and needs. All the mothers continued to be the primary caregivers to their children during the COVID-19 lockdown period, the only exception being Maria, who had maintained her job due to her need of its healthcare benefits while her freelance contractor husband looked after their three children. Although we did not probe into the mothers' family composition or relationship status beyond what they themselves volunteered in the interviews, all of the mothers alluded in some way to having a spouse or partner, eight of whom were male, and one was female. In all, the mothers occupied relatively secure socioeconomic locations; they were all able to provide an adequate standard of living for their children, and many were involved in various advocacy or research activities related to their children's diagnoses.

Results and Discussion

In what follows, we present the complex, and sometimes unexpected, ways that mothers of children with disabilities were affected by the COVID-19 pandemic. While they, their children, and their families were particularly affected by COVID-19-related public health measures, their experiences also show pre-existing vulnerabilities resulting from structural cracks in the system that have always marginalized them. The silver lining of COVID-19 may be that it forced the mainstream society to create certain accommodations from which these families are poised to benefit.

Disability Exacerbates the Toll of COVID-19, and COVID-19 Exacerbates the Challenges Posed by Disability

As exemplified by the "Your 'only' is my everything" slogan, people with disabilities face an increased risk of adverse health outcomes related to COVID-19. Furthermore, in addition to being more medically vulnerable, children with disabilities and their families are affected in multiple other ways by COVID-19-related restrictions.

These children often require frequent medical or therapy appointments, the majority of which were cancelled or postponed during the lockdown. For example, at the beginning of the lockdown, Tammy was worried about the cancellation of her teenage daughter's scheduled corrective surgery, which needed to be done before her daughter's growth-plates closed. She told Pozniak that delaying the surgery by even a few months could affect her daughter's future ability to walk.

Parents with adult-age children who reside in care homes were often shut out of their children's care, resulting not only in potential isolation and trauma to both parents and children, but also in potential medical complications. Diana, a mother of an adult son with cerebral palsy who was living in a residential care home, told Pozniak that because of COVID-19, all of her son's standing appointments at a pain clinic were cancelled, and as a result, his implanted pain pump did not get refilled. Since she was not allowed inside the care home to visit her son, she was not aware of the cancelled appointment, nor did she realize that the care home did not reschedule it. Her son went into life-threatening withdrawal and ended up in the emergency room, where she was also not allowed to be present. Summing up her story, Diana said the following: "COVID made it very difficult to look after somebody in long-term care.... Normally we would have a clear role as an advocate, as a backstop for medical error, and for making sure that everything is fine. We simply aren't there, and we don't know what's going on day to day."

Another issue that frequently surfaced in mothers' accounts was schooling. Although many parents struggled with supporting their children's learning during school closures, mothers of children with disabilities faced additional issues. Many of these children lost their school-based supports, such as therapies as well as the help of support workers and learning aides. Furthermore, for children with sensory or emotional difficulties, school offers routine and structure. For these children, virtual learning is often a mixed experience. Some of the mothers reported that their children, in fact, did quite well learning from home; for other children, virtual learning did not work at all, since they were unable to regulate themselves, concentrate, and follow a virtual interaction. Even when the virtual format worked for the children, mothers reported spending significant time and energy on supporting their children's learning by adapting the material, troubleshooting technology glitches, and liaising with teachers. Although some mothers found this process altogether manageable, others described it as a "shit show" and as a "nightmare."

COVID-19-related restrictions also meant the loss of essential supports to parents whose children need constant care and who rely on the help of nurses, PSWs, or respite workers. Because these workers usually rotate between multiple homes in any given day, many parents cancelled their services due to risk of transmission. However, this left them without respite, leading to burnout and stress. Giselle, a mother of a teenage boy with a rare condition who required 24/7 supervision, decided to keep her nanny during the COVID-19 lockdown to help care for her son, as she herself was working and pursuing a PhD. However, the nanny got COVID-19 and eventually infected her son. Fortunately, her son was able to recover at home, but Giselle lost her son's entire support team, which consisted of a nanny, a behavioural aide, respite workers, a physiotherapist, an occupational therapist, and a speech therapist. She reflected on her experience in these terms:

> Society expects mothers to be superheroes when you have a child with disabilities, and I think it's because no one knows how to help you or no one knows what to do. No one really wants to burden themselves. There's not enough money. There's not enough help. And so, if you want your child to live with you and to have a certain quality of life; then, you have to sacrifice yourself. And there's no empathy about that.... It's just you're supposed to do it.... So, I think COVID would just magnify that a whole lot more. Because, again, parents are in their home trying to homeschool, trying to find medical care, behavioural care, trying to provide therapy, with no supports to help them.

Giselle's quote illustrates that although COVID-19 has presented some unique challenges, the underlying structures of marginalization were present in mothers' lives long before the pandemic—a theme to which we now turn.

"Nothing New": COVID-19 Exposes and Magnifies Existing Cracks in the System

For the majority of society, COVID-19-imposed restrictions represented a profound disruption of normal life. However, many mothers of children with disabilities never had the luxury of living a normal life. Many were already feeling isolated, overwhelmed, and marginalized. Many of them had children who regularly missed school for prolonged periods of time due to sickness. Although the disastrous impact of COVID-19 on mothers' paid employment is making headlines (Ruppanner, Collins; and Scarborough; Linden), many mothers of children with disabilities were forced to leave the paid workforce long before the pandemic because they have never been able to secure adequate supports and funding to allow them to combine caregiving with paid employment. Kate—a mother of an adult son who quit her job four years ago because her son aged out of school and she was not able to secure adequate care for him—told Pozniak that "nothing has changed":

> Things aren't very different; he and I are at home. We're not really missing out on anything that we would have had before.... This is where we were at anyway. And I'm hearing that from a lot of parents and a lot of families, saying, "Well, we were already isolated. We already were stuck at home with no way to get out or [with] no meaningful activities for us".... So, for a lot of families, nothing has changed in a way.

A theme that came up in a number of conversations is that for these mothers, COVID-19 is, indeed, nothing new. Although there are undeniably at least some unprecedented things about the pandemic, this statement is meant to draw attention to the fact that missing out on important life experiences (such as school, social connections, or recreational opportunities) is only seen as a problem when it affects the able-bodied population. The fact that for mothers of children with disabilities the isolation is nothing new exposes the cracks in the system that people with disabilities and their parents/caregivers have always fallen through.

The Silver Lining: New Ways of Access and Connection

The pandemic forced mainstream society to rethink existing ways of living, leading to new ways of accessing schools, healthcare, and workplaces as well as new ways of making social and community connections. Paradoxically, for families of children with disabilities, these coping measures constitute the silver lining of COVID-19, since they create new possibilities that were hitherto not available when it was only the disabled population who needed to be accommodated. For example, a few of the mothers noted that their children, in fact, did well with virtual learning, since they were able to proceed on their own terms and pace. Many mothers also positively commented on the possibility to access at least some of their medical appointments virtually instead of in person. This was especially the case for mothers whose children see a multitude of specialists, some of whom may be based at hospitals located hours away. As Tammy put it: "Some stuff you need to see the doctor for. You can't get Botox injections [to relieve muscle spasticity in people with cerebral palsy] over the Internet. For some of the other stuff, where you're just checking in, you don't need my kid's body."

Lastly, mothers also remarked on the availability of other online supports that were previously not open to people with disabilities and their caregivers. Kate, who quit her job when her son aged out of the school system, told Pozniak that even prior to COVID-19, she had difficulty finding programs for her son and support networks for herself. However, the pandemic-imposed lockdowns resulted in many programs switching to virtual delivery formats. Mothers commented on the availability of online recreation (e.g., free yoga videos), mental health supports (e.g., mindfulness apps and virtual therapy), and opportunities for networking and connecting (e.g., virtual caregiver group meetings, music therapy for children, and church services). Importantly, they noted that these only became possible when the mainstream, able-bodied population began to need them. As Kate put it: "Many people with disabilities, any kind of disability at all, adult or child, whether it's intellectual or physical, they're all saying 'We've been asking for this for decades. Why can't we have had this online stuff before.' And everybody kept telling us we couldn't. And then, boom. Once all the able[-bodied people] ... needed this, suddenly they can do it."

As Kate underscores, new accommodations became possible only when they were needed by the able-bodied population. However, this silver lining of COVID-19 can serve as an impetus for the mainstream society to reconsider some of the values we live by and their accompanying social arrangements.

Towards a New Normal: Rethinking the Value of Caregiving

The COVID-19 pandemic created a renewed impetus to recognize the essential nature of the care economy to the functioning of society as well as the interrelated networks of carework that compose it. Mothers of children with disabilities are particularly attuned to this interrelated nature of carework, since they often have more complex and longer-lasting caregiving responsibilities than the average mother. Furthermore, their children also require a more extensive network of careworkers, often including nurses, PSWs, and respite workers.

All of the mothers in our study were primary caregivers to their children before COVID-19, and most of them continued in this role throughout the pandemic-related closures of schools, day programs, therapy, and respite support. The case of Diana, the mother who was shut out of her adult son's care—with near-disastrous consequences—poignantly illustrates the essential role of caregivers and what happens when suddenly their presence disappears.

The mothers' stories expose the intertwined systemic inequities that characterize the lives of mothers and other careworkers, making them particularly vulnerable at times of crisis, such as COVID-19. All of the mothers in our study reported a lack of adequate support with their caregiving responsibilities. Insufficient funding was a common theme running through the mothers' stories. Even when funding was available and supports existed in theory, they were described as inadequate, bogged down by red tape, and not flexible enough to meet each family's unique circumstances. Kate, for instance, noted that while she was very fortunate to have funding for caregivers, the high turnover rate in the profession meant that she was unable to keep any respite worker for longer than a few months, in effect rendering her unable to hold down a job.

Furthermore, people who perform carework for wages are often poorly compensated, making both themselves and those for whom they care more vulnerable. This is why Tammy, Maria, and Kate decided to cancel their respite workers due to the heightened risk to their children. Giselle was the only mother in the study who decided to keep her nanny (because she was still working full-time). She paid dearly for this decision when her nanny—an immigrant woman who lived in shared accommodations with several other people who worked in long-term care homes—got COVID-19 and infected her son. In telling her story, Giselle explicitly underscored the interconnected nature of carework and the need for systemic change:

> So, it becomes that those that are vulnerable become more vulnerable because they expose other people…. I was like "of course she got COVID because she's living with people who work in long term care." And so, it's just like this pattern, this algorithm you can expect is going happen because we're all drawing from the same pool of people who are low-income service workers who are taking the jobs that other people don't want. So … again, these systemic inequities … are leading to problems for seniors [and] problems for children with disabilities.

Taken together, these stories point to the need to fundamentally reorganize social arrangements to recognize the true value of carework. In a recent policy brief about carework, Kate Power outlines a "5-R" framework for revaluing the care economy. This framework recommends that unpaid carework be recognized, reduced (through public investment in infrastructure), and redistributed (among different institutions), whereas caregivers need to be represented in decision making and appropriately rewarded for their labour (Waring; Bjornholt and McKay).

The mothers' stories contained a number of suggestions for bringing this about. These start with the explicit recognition of the essential role played by mothers in their children's education, healthcare, and day-to-day life, whether these children are young or grown up, and regardless of whether they live at home or in residential care. Institutions, such as hospitals or care homes, need to implement concrete mechanisms for incorporating caregivers (Thomson). The mothers' stories also highlight the need for varied and flexible financial and other supports that meet each family's unique situation. For example, both Tammy and Maria positively commented on the expansion of certain disability funding schemes to support the purchase of at-home recreation and therapy equipment, such as sensory toys or an above-ground pool. Other strategies that alleviated the caregiving burden include the possibility of virtual healthcare appointments for children as well as virtual mental health supports for parents. Finally, mothers recognized the fact that all carework is intertwined. While outlining their own needs for support, they underscored the fact that those employed in caregiving occupations (e.g., health workers, PSWs, and respite workers) also need to be properly compensated.

Conclusion

Mothers' accounts reveal the compounded challenges of mothering a child with a medical condition during the COVID-19 pandemic, which has highlighted and exacerbated the struggles that have always characterized their lives. The fact that the new challenges imposed by COVID-19 are seen by some mothers as nothing new reveals the profound failure of the system to meet the needs of these families in the first place. Paradoxically, COVID-19 has also forced society to adopt measures that benefit these families, such as virtual services, supports, and community-building opportunities. The silver lining of COVID-19 may be that it presents an opportunity to rethink existing social arrangements and rebuild a more equitable post-pandemic society.

Works Cited

Arim, Rubab, Leanne Findlay and Dafna Kohen. "The Impact of the COVID-19 Pandemic on Canadian Families of Children with Disabilities." *Statistics Canada*, 27 Aug. 2020, www150.statcan.gc.ca/n1/pub/45-28-0001/2020001/article/00066-eng.htm. Accessed 10 Jan. 2020.

Bjornholt, Margunn, and Ailsa McKay. *Counting on Marilyn Waring. New Advances in Feminist Economics.* 2nd ed. Demeter Press, 2014.

Johnston, R., A. Mohammed, and C. van der Linden "Evidence of Exacerbated Gender Inequality in Child Care Obligations in Canada and Australia During the COVID-19 Pandemic." *Politics & Gender*, vol. 16, no. 4, 2020, pp. 1131-41.

Klass, Perri. "The Pandemic's Toll on Children With Special Needs and Their Parents." *New York Times* 27 July 2020, www.nytimes.com/2020/07/27/well/family/children-special-needs-pandemic.html. Accessed 10 Jan. 2021.

Lee, Joyce. "Mental Health Effects of School Closures during COVID-19." *The Lancet*, vol. 4, no. 6, 2020, p. 421.

Nessa E. Ryan, and Alison M. El Ayadi. "A Call for a Gender-Responsive, Intersectional Approach to Address COVID-19." *Global Public Health*, vol. 15, no. 9, 2020, pp. 1404-12.

O'Reilly, Andrea. "'Trying to Function in the Unfunctionable': Mothers and COVID-19." *Journal of the Motherhood Initiative*, vol. 11, no. 1, 2020, pp. 7-24.

Phoenix, Michelle. "Children with Disabilities Face Health Risks, Disruption and Marginalization under Coronavirus." *The Conversation*, 11 May 2020, theconversation.com/children-with-disabilities-face-health-risks-disruption-and-marginalization-under-coronavirus-137115. Accessed 10 Jan. 2021.

Power, Kate. "The COVID-19 Pandemic Has Increased the Care Burden of Women and Families." *Sustainability: Science, Practice and Policy*, vol. 16, no. 1, 2020, pp. 67-73.

Ruppanner, Leah, Kaitlyn Collins, and William Scarborough. "COVID-19 Is a Disaster for Mothers' Employment. And no, Working from Home Is Not the Solution." *The Conversation*, 20 July 2020, theconversation.com/covid-19-is-a-disaster-for-mothers-employment-and-no-working-from-home-is-not-the-solution-142650. Accessed 10 Jan. 2021.

Reid, T. "Canadians with Disabilities Left with Few Alternatives amid COVID-19 Shutdowns." *CBC News*, 19 Apr. 2020, www.cbc.ca/news/health/covid-19-impact-on-canadians-with-disabilities-1.5525332. Accessed 10 Jan. 2021.

Thomason, B, and I. Macias-Alonso. "COVID-19 and Raising the Value of Care." *Gender Work Organisation* 27, 2020, pp. 705–8.

Thomson, Donna. "Now Is the Time for More, Not Less, Caregiver Partnership." *National News Watch*, 12 May 2020, www.nationalnewswatch.com/2020/05/12/now-is-the-time-for-more-not-less-caregiver-partnership/#.X_sXNtg3nIU. Accessed 10 Jan. 2021.

Linden, Clinton van der. "The Moms Are Not Alright: How Coronavirus Pandemic Policies Penalize Mothers." *McMaster University*, 3 Sept. 2020. brighterworld.mcmaster.ca/articles/the-moms-are-not-alright-how-coronavirus-pandemic-policies-penalize-mothers/. Accessed 10 Jan. 2021.

Waring, Marilyn. *If Women Counted: A New Feminist Economics.* HarperCollins, 1988.

World Health Organization. "Disability Considerations during the COVID-19 Outbreak." WHO, 26 Mar., www.who.int/publications/i/item/WHO-2019-nCoV-Disability-2020-1. Accessed 10 Jan. 2021.

Chapter Twenty Three

Digitally Mediated Motherhood during the COVID-19 Pandemic

Kate Orton-Johnson

Introduction

The lockdown and self-isolation measures put in place in response to COVID-19 have pushed us further into digital spaces in order to connect. Social media platforms and apps have become communicative lifelines as the temporal rhythms of daily life are disrupted in unprecedented ways. For mothers in the Global North, online networks have long been important cultural domains for exchanging information, seeking support and confiding fears. The current absence of face-to-face support has meant that digital communities have become arenas in which new dynamics and stresses of motherhood are being articulated and played out. They afford mothers spaces of solace and solidarity, enabling them to share anxieties over home-schooling, finances and the burden of care in the face of the pandemic. However, multiple platforms and channels of communication have also created new demands and expectations and have thrown up stark inequalities.

This chapter will argue that social media, as well as being an invaluable source of social support, has become a fourth shift for mothers during the pandemic. The concept of a fourth shift is grounded in Arlie Hochschild's work on the dual burden of paid employment alongside unpaid domestic labour, household tasks and childcare—what she has described as a "second shift" that is disproportionately shouldered by women. It also builds on Andrea O'Reilly's notion of the "third shift of mothering", which encompasses the emotional and intellectual labour of organising and planning the minutiae of family life. As the second and third shifts of motherhood were intensified by the physical and emotional demands of managing the lockdown family, I argue that online networks occupied an uneasy space as a fourth shift of pandemic motherhood. The solidarity they provided was tempered by new kinds of hyperconnectivity, contradictory discourses and competing realities. The chapter will outline the impact of ubiquitous digital devices during the pandemic, emphasising the emotional intensity with which they were experienced and framing them as a form of digital labour.

This chapter draws on data from online interactions with ten mothers of school-aged children in the United Kingdom (U.K.). At the start of lockdown, I contacted mothers who had participated in a previous research project on digital technology and motherhood. Ten mothers, of the original sample of thirty-two, agreed to stay in contact with me over the lockdown period. During this time, I conducted at least one interview with each respondent and exchanged emails and social media messages with them from March to August. In addition to these one-on-one interactions, we established a group chat on WhatsApp, where we discussed experiences of home-schooling and family life during the pandemic. Although the sample represents a rather homogeneous and narrow demographic in terms of ethnicity, class, age and sexuality (white, middle-class, middle-aged, and heterosexual women), it presents a snapshot of data that heeds Andrea O'Reilly's call to make visible the labour of motherhood in the pandemic.[1]

The Shifts of Motherhood

Hochschild's work on the reality of dual career households introduced the concept of "the second shift" of domestic labour. On returning to their home from working in the labour force, women perform the majority of unpaid domestic work, childcare and housework as well as experiencing more pressure and emotional exhaustion (Milkie,

Raley, and Bianchi). This second shift is compounded by what has been defined as a "third shift" of motherhood—the mental labour of planning, scheduling, negotiating and problem solving for the family (O'Reilly).

Coupled with the demands of these multiple shifts are experiences of motherhood framed by cultural scripts and neoliberal discourses, which portray the maternal role as an intensive and individual enterprise (Güney-Frahm). Mothers are seen as the primary caregivers and successful motherhood requires relinquishing autonomy to a child-centered and idealised view of women and children, which bears little relation to the realities of most mothers' everyday lives (Douglas and Michaels).

The pandemic lockdown created a perfect storm for these neoliberal discourses to combine with the multiple shifts of paid and domestic labour, leaving mothers feeling responsible for, and overwhelmed by, a large burden of care. Research has shown that the pandemic disproportionally affected women (Office for National Statistics); compared with fathers, mothers spent less time on paid work and spent more time on household responsibilities. Even in families where mothers were the higher earner before the crisis, and both partners were still working, they did more childcare and the same amount of housework as their partner (Andrew et al.; Collins et al.). Mothers were largely responsible for homeschooling and working mothers at home managed to do only one hour of uninterrupted paid work for every three hours of their male partner (Collins et al.).

The boundaries between work and family life collapsed during the lockdown and exposed the challenges of simultaneously managing paid labour, domestic labour and homeschooling. As women's unpaid care-related duties increased, the already precarious balance between work and domestic life intensified, reinscribing and exacerbating domestic divisions of labour. In this space, social media became a tool and a source of connectivity that provided support for mothers. Yet it also further blurred public and private boundaries and forced mothers to take on a fourth shift of digital labour as part of the experience of lockdown motherhood.

Digital Ubiquity and Intensity

Digital technologies enabled us to stay connected while we were apart in lockdown. Technologies that were widely used prior to the pandemic became further entrenched in our lives as lockdown forced digitisation upon us (Volodenkov and Pastarmadzhieva). We were "digital by default" (Livingston), as social media became a lifeline to stay in touch with family and friends, socialise, celebrate virtual birthdays, participate in virtual quiz nights, connect with community groups, organise help and support and maintain some kind of work normality. Digital devices played a positive social role while we stayed home, enabling us to be connected while physically distanced. For the mothers in my sample, presence and interaction in social media platforms provided a sense of reassurance and community. This not only took the form of digitally mediated communication between existing friendships, but also as part of groups that were formed across a range of social media platforms in response to lockdown.

When schools closed for the majority of children in the U.K. on Mar. 20, 2020, families faced the prospect of home-schooling their children during a time of anxiety and uncertainty while, for many, juggling the demands of paid employment. All of my respondents found support from groups that formed around their children's schools as mothers created, joined, and invited others to school class-specific WhatsApp, Facebook, and messenger groups. Although many of these groups had existed in some prior form, they had been primarily used to post announcements about parent council meetings and lost property or to ask questions about school events or requirements. Before lockdown, they were instrumental tools for the exchange of practical information rather than spaces of friendship and conversation. As home-schooling began, these previously quiet digital spaces became animated with mothers expressing their fears and concerns about balancing children at home with paid work and with questions about how others were managing. For many, these exchanges were a source of comfort, as home-schooling failures and stories of tantrums and conflict were shared. Mothers found reassurance in sharing their own experiences and from hearing from others whose children were at the same age and stage as their own. As one respondent suggested, "It's the feeling that we are all in the same awful boat that makes me feel better." The mothers I talked to spoke of forming quick and close bonds with one another, which often came from sharing jokes and exchanging memes about the reality of homeschooling and parenting fails. This online interaction provided welcome relief and a means through which the emotional burden of dealing with lockdown was diffused. The connections made were felt to be necessary and important at a time of great anxiety and stress and the lifelines that social media provided were highly valued. As one participant put it: "It has felt like coming together at a time of crisis and huddling in to give each other support, even though we're not really friends outside of this; the fact that our kids are in the same class seems to be enough to make me feel bound to them for sanity and support." These previously loose networks, now digitally bound together, played an important social role and felt like an indispensable source of connectivity in lockdown isolation, as one respondent described: "Having this [class WhatsApp group] has literally been a saviour. I don't know how I would have got through the first few weeks of home-schooling without knowing I had them to turn to. It's honestly been what has kept me going at times." Despite these benefits, the value of these connections was tempered by their accompanying demands.

Emotional Intensity and Digital Labour

Although the groups were a source of emotional support, they were also described as frustrating and exhausting. The mothers I spoke to felt committed to these new networks but also found their intensity overwhelming. Particularly at the start of lockdown, the levels of interaction in the groups felt unrelenting and being bombarded by a never-ending feed of notifications became a lockdown norm (Holland). The multiple layers of communication, facilitated by different digital platforms dramatically increased levels of digital communication and for many mothers this was a markedly different way of being. On top of all of the lockdown-related changes to domestic life, many mothers felt that digital interaction was another thing to manage: "It's like I need a PA to get me through the day. I woke up to eighty-five WhatsApp messages and twenty-seven messenger notifications. Don't get me wrong. I get how lucky I am, but it is also another thing I have to do. I'm thinking about having to reply and make sure I'm part of the chat. Thank god for long supermarket queues so I can catch up on it all while I'm waiting".

This added stress was especially the case for mothers with more than one child, who found themselves members of multiple online groups: "I've got two kids, and there is a class WhatsApp for each of them, plus the class Facebook page, which is a slightly different set of mums. So, before I've even got to my usual friends, I've got four different sets of 'pings' going off constantly." The issue of constant connectivity is a feature of our embodied digital technologies. Our mobile phones have altered the way in which we conduct our everyday lives (Plant); they are constantly with us and connecting us with others. This ambient intimacy makes us feel close to one another through digitally mediated interaction (Hjorth and Hinton), but our ever-present mobile devices mean that the boundaries that separate us from our social networks are blurred and diaphanous (and never more so than during the pandemic). The value of this hyperconnectivity among the mothers was evident in the support they gave and received, but the price was the feeling of always being at their devices' beck and call. As one mother explained: "I'd be lost without the chat, but it also makes my phone feel like a ball and chain. I can't bear the constant beeping [of notifications], and I find just keeping up with what's going on obviously a pleasure but also quite full on and quite draining." This feeling was especially problematic at a time when tensions over acceptable screen time were at their most acute. Although children's use of screens provided a much-needed respite for many harried parents and provided a primary means for children to communicate with their friends, mothers also felt the pressure and guilt of balancing screen time with family health and wellbeing. They were aware that they were not modelling healthy screen use and were conscious that their children were noticing their divided attentions. Another mother said: "My phone is constantly going. I feel like I'm glued to a device between all the chat and my work. At the same time, I'm trying to tell them to get off their screens [and] they, quite rightly, just point that I'm on them all the time." The collapse of the boundaries between the home and the socially distanced outside world was keenly felt, and my respondents acknowledged, with a sense of guilt, the impact that their increased reliance on their mobile devices had on their parenting during lockdown.

In addition to the digital intensity of constant notifications and attention to devices, another trade-off of access to these support networks was the emotional demands that they placed on mothers. As friends brought together by the shared circumstance of their children's school, there was a level of reciprocity and expectation that was different from other more anonymous online spaces that the mothers engaged in. As one mother explained: "I don't feel like I cannot reply or just disappear from a chat because these are people in my life that I'm going to keep seeing. It's not like being on Mumsnet or Twitter or something, where if you don't want to be involved anymore, you can just log off. I feel morally obliged to respond." This moral obligation brought support and reassurance that felt meaningful, as it was coming from people within their local networks rather than online strangers, but it also was experienced as draining at a time when emotional reserves were low: "There are days when I am just so fed up with it all and need someone to talk to, and I know that they [WhatsApp school group] know exactly what I am going through, and we are there for each other. But at times, it makes me feel like I am being spread so thin, giving time and energy that I just don't have. It feels relentless."

The sense of community and solidarity formed in these online spaces provided value for these mothers, but they also created a sense of emotional commitment and burden that at times felt overwhelming. But anxieties also came from interactions that resulted in comparisons between members of the groups. The mothers I spoke with were torn between wanting and needing to share their experiences and concerns with other mothers and fearing the feelings of guilt, stress and worry that arose when online discussions were not reassuring. The constant connectivity and high levels of interaction regularly highlighted different experiences, expectations and feelings about lockdown. The mothers in the sample felt that they were invariably comparing themselves to standards of mothering that in the context of the pandemic were unrealistic. The description of one mother was particularly representative: "There have been some days when it has been one big shit storm from beginning to end. We have argued over school work. I've missed things at work. The house is a tip and the kids have sat in front of the TV eating crap. And on those days, logging on to see pictures of homework-related home crafting, kids baking cakes, and wholesome outdoor play is about enough to finish me off." The idea of online spaces as sites of comparison is not a new phenomenon. In their work on mothers' interactions online, Sarah Pederson and

Deborah Lupton found that mothers consistently drew comparisons between what was perceived as the behaviour of a good mother and their own feelings and behaviours. Good mothers are assiduously devoted to their children's needs and desires; they prioritise their children's growth and health as well as their development and emotional wellbeing. Mothers not meeting these standards are culturally judged. Discussions about the internalisation of these standards, and the resulting shame and guilt about failing to meet them, have been a feature of the support mothers find in online spaces. In the context of the pandemic, part of the value of online interactions was trying to find reassurance that the anxieties and frustrations of lockdown motherhood were universal and normal. Yet the pervasive feeling of not attaining a standard of motherhood was a constant source of anxiety in my respondents' discussions of their experiences. As one mother noted: "I know that we're all going to have good and bad days. But there is still that sense that everyone is doing better than you and managing better and that people in the chat are just trying to make you feel better by saying 'me too.' So, on one hand, I love the sharing [of the WhatsApp group], [but] on the other it also makes the mum guilt even stronger." This combination of long-standing cultural standards and judgments about motherhood, as well as constantly shifting understandings of what normal looks like in lockdown, meant that finding reassurance and support was complicated by comparisons and exacerbated by feelings of guilt and envy. The experience of lockdown motherhood was characterised by the juggling of multiple, often contradictory roles. As Burk, Mausolf, and Oakleaf argue, "Mothers are caught, tethered among a myriad of roles, constantly wondering if they are spending 'enough' time 'being' any of [them]."

Conclusions

The concept of a second shift of motherhood focuses our attention on how social structures and changes to the wider economy affect family dynamics and domestic roles. The third shift of emotional labour reveals the additional and unequal burden taken on by mothers. In this chapter, I argue that the concept of a fourth shift can be applied to women's digitally mediated interactions during the pandemic. This fourth shift combines the practical tasks of second shift motherhood—in the form of home-schooling and the domestic labour demanded by having children at home during lockdown—with the emotional labour of the third shift. It placed considerable emotional and temporal demands on mothers as they used digital technologies to connect and find support. In an age where ubiquitous social networking and mediated connectivity are increasingly the norm, the fourth shift highlights the additional ways in which family dynamics are unequally experienced.

The mothers I spoke with used their digital networks to find support, solace and connectivity in a time of social distance and isolation. However, these benefits also placed considerable emotional and temporal demands on mothers. The challenges of the first, second and third shifts of motherhood have been well documented in the literature around the domestic division of paid and emotional labour. Adding the concept of a digital fourth shift to these debates contributes to our understanding of the gendered effects of the pandemic by highlighting the ways in which these shifts have exacerbated and reinscribed gender roles. Mothers experienced the pandemic in ways that were profoundly shaped by socioeconomic inequalities, ethnicity, family structure, and job security. The small sample of relatively privileged mothers that I draw on here provides one contribution to this collection, which helps to make visible the labour of motherhood in the pandemic. This chapter also opens up debates about the legacy the inequalities and domestic divisions of labour during lockdown will have on mothers.

Endnote

1. I was acutely aware of the irony of asking mothers, exhausted by digital technologies in the context of COVID-19 to further engage with these technologies, and with me, and to add to the demands and the labour that they faced in lockdown. I thank them for their generosity in continuing to engage with my research.

Works Cited

Andrew, Alison, et al. "How Are Mothers and Fathers Balancing Work and Family under Lockdown?" *Institute for Fiscal Studies*, 2020, www.ifs.org. uk/publications/14860. Accessed 10 Jan. 2021.

Burk, Brooke, Anna Pechenik Mausolf, and Linda Oakleaf. *Pandemic Motherhood and the Academy: A Critical Examination of the Leisure-Work Dichotomy.* Leisure Sciences 2020.

Collins, Caitlyn, et al. "COVID-19 and the Gender Gap in Work Hours." *Gender, Work & Organization* 2020, onlinelibrary.wiley.com/doi/full/10.1111/gwao.12506. Accessed 10 Jan. 2021.

Douglas, Susan, and Meredith Michaels. *The Mommy Myth: The Idealization of Motherhood and How It Has Undermined All Women.* Simon and Schuster, 2005.

Güney-Frahm, Irem. "Neoliberal Motherhood during the Pandemic: Some Reflections." *Gender, Work & Organization*, vol. 27, no. 5, 2020, pp. 847-56.

Hjorth, Larissa, and Sam Hinton. *Understanding Social Media.* SAGE Publications Limited, 2019.

Hochschild, Arlie. *The Second Shift: Working Families and the Revolution at Home.* Avon Books, 1989.

Holland, Mary. "How to Take a Digital Detox during the Covid-19 pandemic." *BBC* 17 May 2020, www.bbc.com/worklife/article/20200513-how-to-take-a-digital-detox-during-the-covid-19-pandemic. Accessed 10 Jan. 2021.

Livingston, Sonia. "Digital by Default: The New Normal of Family Life under COVID-19." *LSE Blogs* 21 May 2020, blogs.lse.ac.uk/medialse/2020/05/21/digital-by-default-the-new-normal-of-family-life-under-covid-19/. Accessed 10 Jan. 2021.

Milkie, Melissa A., Sara B. Raley, and Suzanne M. Bianchi. "Taking on the Second Shift: Time Allocations and Time Pressures of US Parents with Preschoolers." *Social Forces*, vol. 88, no. 2, 2009, pp. 487-517.

O'Reilly, Andrea. "'Trying to Function in the Unfunctionable': Mothers and COVID-19." *Journal of the Motherhood Initiative for Research and Community Involvement*, vol. 11, no. 1, 2020, pp. 7-24.

Office for National Statistics. "Coronavirus and the social impacts on Great Britain: 25 September 2020." *ONS*, 2020, www.ons.gov.uk/releases/coronavirusandthesocialimpactsongreatbritain25september2020. Accessed 10 Jan. 2021.

Pedersen, Sarah, and Deborah Lupton. "'What Are You Feeling Right now?' Communities of Maternal Feeling on Mumsnet." *Emotion, Space and Society*, vol. 26, 2018, pp. 57-63.

Plant, Sadie. *On the Mobile: The Effects of Mobile Telephones on Social and Individual Life.* Motorola, 2001.

Volodenkov, Sergey, and Daniela Pastarmadzhieva. "Digital Society in the Context of the COVID-19 Pandemic: First Results and Prospects." *Journal of Political Research*, vol. 4, pp. 80-89.

Chapter Twenty Four

Mothering and Family Language Policy During a Pandemic: An Analysis of Korean Immigrant Mothers' Narratives

Hakyoon Lee

Introduction

This empirical study investigates how immigrant mothers who live in a southeastern city of the United States (U.S.) construct their identities through stories about their lives in a pandemic. Two Korean immigrant mothers participated in this study, and their interview data (4 hours and 20 min.) were transcribed and examined through narrative analysis. Notably, the study explores how COVID-19 affects the mothers' roles in their children's education at home as well as their perception of COVID-19's impact on the immigrant families' home language development and maintenance. Using feminist and post-structuralist perspectives on identity, this chapter examines how the mothers construct their identities as caregivers, women, and breadwinners in response to COVID-19 and their shifted roles at home. In particular, it explores how Korean transnational mothers reshape their sense of bilingualism and language education in the midst of the pandemic and to what extent the mothers' experiences during the pandemic affect their identity construction. In this study, I argue it is crucial for researchers to use more dynamic perspectives to better understand language, heritage, education, and mothering of immigrant families in the context of COVID-19.

Immigrants and gendered identities have been widely discussed in previous studies (Cameron 482-502; Gordon 437-57; Hirsh 369-389; Hondagneu-Sotelo 1-19; Menard-Warwick 48-75; Norton 20-57). This study contributes to this body of work by adding another dimension to the relationship between gender and the mother's role; specifically, it demonstrates how women construct gendered identities during the pandemic. Drawing on socio-cultural and post-structural perspectives on language, identity, and power (Duff 309-319), I follow Julia Menard-Warwick's (27) use of the term "gendered identity" instead of "gender identity" because this choice reveals the emphasis on gender in relation to other identities—identities are influenced by gender rather than gender being defined solely by gender itself. By investigating how the mothers enact their gendered identities in the process of telling stories, this study offers detailed descriptions of what constitutes a good mother through local constructions. This chapter addresses how mothers are (un)able to access language resources to (re)construct their gendered identities in an immigrant context during the pandemic, with a focus on gender in migration contexts and immigrant families' literacy practices (e.g., Volk and de Acosta 8-48).

Mothering during the Pandemic

A dictionary definition of mothering is "nurturing or protective behavior reminiscent of that performed by a literal mother" ("Mothering"). The traditional gender role expectation of motherhood entails nurturing children as caregivers and comforters, whereas fathers' role expectations are that of protectors and providers. However, the roles of mothers and fathers have overlapped in many aspects in recent years, as many women are also in the workforce. Now, women are employees by day at their workplaces and mothers by night at home. Nevertheless, mothers are still responsible for their children's welfare and education.

During the COVID-19 pandemic, researchers have noted that the mothers' roles and responsibilities have increased to a greater extent than those of the fathers' ("The Impact of Covid-19"). A new Center for American Progress analysis of the Household Pulse Survey finds that during the COVID-19 pandemic, millennial mothers are nearly three times more likely than millennial fathers to report being unable to work due to a school or childcare closure. In addition, the data indicate that women are often responsible for a much greater share of childcare and household labour, particularly in the case of education (Malik and Morrissey). In this chapter, I closely look into the mothers' increasing responsibilities and roles in their children's education at home, the challenges they face, and the conflicts these different social roles may generate within the context of the COVID-19 pandemic.

Mothers' Involvement in Education

Many studies have claimed that parental involvement positively influences a wide range of children's learning outcomes, such as academic achievement as well as behavioral and emotional development through all ages, to greater or lesser degrees (Aspiazu et al. 1-20; Durand 255-78; Gonzalez-DeHass et al. 99-123; Topor et al. 183-97). The mother's role is especially critical. Tina Durand explored six Latina mothers' beliefs and practices about their children's education and their roles as caregivers, finding that the mothers played a key role in supporting their development and learning. David Topor, et al. also suggested that parental involvement is meaningfully related to children's academic performance, their perceived cognitive competence, and the quality of the student-teacher relationship. Alyssa Gonzalez-DeHass et al. also found that parental involvement positively affects children's intrinsic and extrinsic motivation and school engagement.

Although it is clear that parental involvement is positively associated with children's educational outcomes, parental involvement has different implications in diverse cultural, ethnic, and social contexts. For instance, among Pacific Islanders, the traditional education system involves both the home and community, and involvement in community activities has higher value than parental involvement in their children's school system (Koki and Lee 1-5). This study argues for the importance of considering the cultural conditions and for connecting home, school, and communities in planning parental involvement in their children's school. Sociohistorical contexts, people's traditional beliefs and practices, and different educational backgrounds also need to be considered to better understand parental involvement in children's education.

In Korean society, the family is the centre of all practices and decisions (Cho 148-71); it is viewed as the link between individuals and society, with particular emphasis placed on education. Education facilitates social mobility and self-realization as well as the family's success and glory. This emphasis on education has contributed to the distinctive gender roles found in the child-centered Korean family. Raising a child well is the most important priority of the family. In this context, the mother's role as a caregiver is considered critical.

Family Language Policy during the Pandemic

This study is grounded in the idea that the home is the key place where languages are learned, managed, and negotiated. Family language policy (FLP) is defined not only as explicit and overt but also as implicit and covert; it involves planning in relation to language use and literacy practices within the home and among family members (King and Fogle 1-13; King et al. 907-22; Curdt-Christiansen 277-95). FLP explores the interactions between caregiver and child, language ideologies and attitudes, and a child's language learning and use (King and Fogle 1-13). In FLP research, the home has been recognized as a critical setting, which allows family members to form linguistic spaces for their children (Schwartz 171-92). For multicultural and multilingual families who try to maintain and follow languages and cultures different from mainstream society, the home has served as an even more critical domain, in which parents, children, and other family members become key participants, influencing language choices and beliefs (Spolsky 3-11). During the pandemic, family members often share linguistic and cultural resources at home, given the limited access to outside resources. In this situation, the parents, especially the mother, serve as a catalyst for their children's language education, and this practice has made the mothers reconsider their roles and identities during quarantine life.

This Study

This study is part of a larger research project that explores various types of at-home language practices among Korean transnational families; more specifically, it examines how language ideologies and sociocultural backgrounds affect the family's language policy at home. In this study, I focus on the case of two Korean-English bilingual immigrant families in the U.S. during the pandemic, and I analyze how they make sense of their efforts to manage their children's education and create a (bilingual) education environment.

Data Collection and Participants

This research was conducted from January to August in 2020. The primary sources of data in this study come from semistructured interviews with the participants as well as background information surveys. Two sets of semistructured interviews (about seventy minutes each) were conducted, and the interviews were recorded. The data were transcribed and translated for the analysis. Based on the commonly occurring themes that emerged from the participants' stories, I coded the collected narrative data. I adopt a narrative analysis to examine the salience of identity at certain points in their stories. Two Korean mothers who live in a major southeastern city of the U.S., which is among the top ten largest Korean immigrant communities in the country (Pew Research Center), participated in this study. MJ and SK are the two participants who shared their stories for this project. Although MJ and SK migrated to the U.S. at different times, they share similarities, including their child's age as well as the fact that both come from the Korean middle class.

Myungjin (MJ) and Sookyung (SK)

MJ is thirty-nine years old, and she worked at a public enterprise in Korea before moving to the U.S. Her family came to the U.S. in 2019 because of her husband's graduate studies. After coming to the U.S., she became a housewife and now supports her family. She has a ten-year-old daughter. During quarantine, the family members mostly work and study from home so as to limit their contact with other people. The second participant, SK, came to the U.S. after she married her husband, a 1.5 generation Korean-American (SK's husband was born in Korea and came to the U.S. when he was eleven years old). SK is first generation, and unlike MJ, she has lived in the U.S. for more than fifteen years. SK has one daughter, who is the same age as MJ's daughter. Her husband runs his own business, and she is a housewife. The dominant language of both families is Korean. The interviewees selected the language for the interviews, and both participants chose to use Korean. I later transcribed the recorded interview materials and then translated them into English to present in this study.

Narratives as a Space for Constructing Identities

A narrative is "an account of what one thinks one did in what settings in what ways for what felt reasons" (Bruner 119), so "subjective reality" (Pavlenko, "Autobiographic Narratives" 165) requires greater depth of understanding from the researchers. Narrative research is not an objective manner of reporting historical truth about the self. Following this understanding of narrative, I perceive interviews as a process of making sense of participants' experiences and as spaces through which to shape and share their perceptions with the researcher. In particular, identity transformation becomes apparent through the mothers' shifting standpoints and self-positionings as reflected in their storytelling (Lee 250-64). Narratives in this study serve as discursive sites that show degrees of identity shifts, ideology changes, and negotiation processes by recounting and reflecting upon the participants' lives.

Following previous studies that elicit people's narratives of their linguistic and cultural borders (Pavlenko, "Negotiation of Identities" 317-44; Pavlenko and Lantolf 155-77; Kinginger 219-42; Coffey and Street 452-64), the narratives in this study serve as a context in which the mothers' identity development occurs and is observed. In my interviews, the narratives often turn into a more relaxed conversation, in which the interviewer and interviewee co-construct meaning (Holstein and Gubrium 267-281). I shared the participants' experiences of raising a child in an immigrant context, of living and working abroad, and of having similar family relationships. The participants and I constructed repertories based on shared knowledge, such as Korean culture, educational systems, and local contexts. In this sense, I view the interviews as a process of co-constructing meanings, and the participating Korean mothers' narratives are the products of this process.

Findings

The findings indicate that COVID-19 has changed the education context, which has caused an increase in family interactions and contributed to detachment from the community. It has also brought challenges to the mothers who are first-generation immigrants and are unfamiliar with the dominant language, culture, and the education system. The mothers, however, overcame these limitations by intensifying their family language policy and promoting bilingual resources. This effort ultimately offers opportunities for heritage language maintenance.

Mothers' Shifted Roles and Increased Burden in Education

During the pandemic, home became a learning community of practice among family members, where they collaboratively construct knowledge and share experiences. In this situation, the mother's role becomes more significant in creating and managing the home as a sustainable learning environment. First-generation immigrant mothers in particular often share their concerns about their inability to be fully involved in guiding their children's learning because of their lack of experience with the U.S. educational system. KS told me: "I need to follow the American style. There are not many things I can do, and I am not familiar with the educational system here." The pandemic made KS felt helpless, which prevented her from taking an active role in facilitating her children's education and helping with the child's online classes. In the following excerpt, KS demonstrated the increasing responsibilities and challenges that she experienced during the pandemic as an educational manager at home. As KS indicated:

> In the past, she [her daughter] learned the important/main parts at school, and I just needed to help her with reviewing the things she learned at school and doing her homework. However, the situation has changed a lot, and even though she takes online classes with teachers, as she is studying from home, I feel more responsible for her education. Also, I feel like her results strongly depend on me.

In this study, the mothers feel an intense responsibility to manage their children's education. For example, a child's poor performance on assessments is interpreted as a failure of their parenting. Before the pandemic, language acquisition used to be accomplished at school. However, during the pandemic, the immigrant mothers in this study have language barriers, experience cultural differences, and have lack of educational experience in their host society, which made it difficult for them to perform the teacher role. As MJ said: "I feel like I need to do a mother's job and at the same time to be a teacher or manager of my daughter with my clumsy English during this time." In particular, MJ is concerned about her daughter's language development, since they recently arrived in the U.S. and the family has become isolated at home before the child's English proficiency has fully developed. MJ thinks COVID-19 could result in losing their opportunities to learn English:

> I'm worried about her English the most. She needs to speak in English a lot to improve her speaking skill, but she doesn't have much chance to meet American people these days.... It does not matter whom she talks with, but I just want her to have more opportunities to talk in English. I can teach her grammar and simple things, but both my husband and I can't speak English fluently, so I wish she could have a better environment to improve her speaking and writing skills.

MJ is frustrated that she is unable to create an English-speaking environment at home. Despite the strong feeling of responsibility, she feels that she cannot help her daughter's language development, particularly by providing her with bilingual literacy practice at home. Instead of providing knowledge as an English expert, MJ has become the model of learning for her child (as she took an ESL course by herself) by adopting a learning together strategy. Both MJ and SK learn and search for information online with their children. These two excerpts illustrate how the mothers' new responsibilities and roles are constructed and articulated at home. For newly arrived immigrant families, who wish to improve in speaking the host country's language and to adjust to society, the pandemic situation is even more challenging, since they do not have sufficient opportunities outside the home to learn the language and culture.

Loss of Community and Feelings of Isolation

Besides their increased responsibility in their child's education, the mothers have also experienced a loss of contact with the community in which they naturally received support and shared concerns before the pandemic. Before COVID-19 struck, both MJ and SK were deeply involved in their church communities. They communicated with other Korean immigrant mothers, and their children built strong social relations with their church friends, with whom they shared cultural and linguistic experiences as second-generation immigrants. After the pandemic began, however, almost all connections and relationships were disrupted, and the mothers expressed that they felt isolated. Various studies have shown that access to language resources within refugee, immigrant, and imagined communities can accelerate shifts in identities (e.g., Gordon 437-57). However, during the pandemic, access to community resources has been limited for MJ and SK. In the case of immigrant families, most of the family members and friends are in their home country, and this may increase dependency on the local immigrant families and communities. In my conversation with MJ, she shared that no one would contact her family after several refusals of playdate requests: "I am totally a loner these days. Some people are meeting each other outside, but I still feel uncomfortable and not as brave as to do so." MJ is concerned that her daughter has lost the chance to develop socially. MJ's only contact with someone outside of her family is through the occasional phone calls she makes to a friend in another state. MJ shares her conversation with her friend in the following excerpt.

> MJ: I was talking with my friend, and we thought "blue" sounds too optimistic. I know
>
> "feeling blue" means the depressed or sad feeling, but we were talking like "It's not the
>
> corona blues; blue is too positive" [laughter].
>
> Researcher: Yes, you are right.
>
> MJ: She said, "There is not much laughter these days, so I feel like my mind became gloomy. 'Blue' sounds too hopeful, so 'grey' is more suitable!"

MJ uses colour metaphors to express her emotion during the pandemic. When people refer to the gloomy situation as "corona blues," MJ and her friend jokingly said, "Blue is too optimistic to fully express the depression they go through." "Blue" in certain cultures, like Korean culture, represents optimism and hope. MJ and her friend position themselves lower on a scale of brightness, which highlights their feelings of frustration and depression. Although told in a joking way, this excerpt shows the emotional depression and loneliness MJ has experienced during the pandemic. Due to the lack of social activities, MJ feels secluded.

SK has also felt mentally insecure during the COVID-19 pandemic. Being with family members all the time and taking care of them without a break has put her under a great deal of stress:

> SK: I feel the corona blues these days. Also, I feel like I am in the endless tunnel. I think COVID-19 and the tunnel are similar in that we don't know when it will end. There is no feeling like "Oh, I can reach the end if I walk three more steps." It's more like we should just walk and wait until this long tunnel ends without knowing when that would be.

> Researcher: Yes, the situation is very tense. It's not easy to describe my feelings, but I feel like I am driving the train, and we can't stop the train. This train never stops.

The mothers in this study are experiencing excessive stress, feelings of loneliness, and depression due in part to their increased responsibilities. The metaphors that the mothers both use—an endless tunnel and a train that never stops—represent their emotional status. COVID-19 has exacerbated their feelings of disconnection from their ethnic or religious communities, which are indispensable assets for immigrants. Their limited access to the Korean community also means the closure of social networks. This lack of support and limited access to the community may not only affect immigrant mothers. However, I argue the pandemic more severely affects immigrant families and communities, especially concerning linguistic and cultural socialization, which may be related to a lack of networking. Their foreigner status—which is often associated with temporary situations, unstable legal status, and untransferable social capital in their host country—

has been significantly affected by the pandemic. As an example, both mothers have concerns regarding health insurance, and thinking about what they would do if they became sick gives them a great deal of anxiety.

The mothers also feel isolated at home. MJ feels alienated even at home because her husband and daughter devalue her roles and struggles during the pandemic. She states that her daughter thinks her father is a nice person who plays video games with her, whereas her mother is always serious and angry. MJ discursively constructs "othering" by assigning distance between herself and her other family members. SK also talks about her loneliness and fear concerning the uncertainty surrounding both the present and future: "I feel like we passed a certain phase at a very fast pace without any gradual stages. I don't know. I worry whether I can eventually return to the normal and put down roots permanently here [in the U.S.] for once in my life. Sometimes I ask myself, 'Where is my life as a person, a woman,' you know? Not just someone's mom or wife." This excerpt shows that the uncertainty of the present moment also extends into the future, which complicates SK's sense of belonging and identity in the context of migration. The pandemic evokes changes in how the mother sees herself and performs her duties. The quarantine has made her reflect on her life as an immigrant, woman, mother, and a wife. It truly has shaken her life to its roots.

The mothers' stories highlight their increased responsibilities, their separation from accessible linguistic resources and their communities, as well as their feelings of emptiness, loss, and loneliness. Dominant cultural ideologies as well as social changes interplay with their stories. The mothers' concern about the limited access to their communities has remained somewhat unsolved during the pandemic. However, despite the challenges, they want to maximize the resources and opportunities that they have at home. I argue this endeavour is a way for them to maintain ownership of their educational practices and construct the identity of a good, responsible, and devoted mother. Through fulfilling these practices, they are empowered in these perplexing times.

Discussion

I investigate how two Korean immigrant mothers in the U.S. reconsider their identities while they engage in dynamic practices at home during the pandemic. In this study, I view gender, language, and mothering through a social lens. In particular, I discuss how the new normal caused by COVID-19 affects the mothers' roles, responsibilities, and expectations in an immigrant context. This study conceptualizes the impacts of the pandemic on language learning and maintenance at home and argues that more dynamic perspectives are needed to better understand language, heritage, and mothering in immigrant families in the COVID-19 pandemic setting. Their stories reveal how the pandemic not only has shifted many aspects of these mothers' social lives but has also altered how they view themselves and others.

My findings also indicate that narratives create a space for these mothers to reflect on their changed lives, and through telling stories, they (re)construct their identities. In telling stories and sharing their struggles, these immigrant mothers redefine their motherhood and gender expectations, which helps them to cope with their emotional drain in transnational contexts. Furthermore, the collapse of community deeply affects immigrant families during the pandemic. The sudden closure of these vital lifelines reveals their fundamental necessity in the lives of immigrant families at many levels. This study also sheds light on how the insecurity caused by the pandemic becomes embodied through the Korean immigrant mothers' lives, which has yet to be fully acknowledged in the literature. The COVID-19 pandemic has forced these mothers to cross different terrains of gender and social status. Therefore, this study adds more dimension and complexity to understanding the experiences of mothers who are responsible for their children's education during this pandemic while making us rethink gender in transnational contexts.

Acknowledgment

This research was supported by Korean Studies Grant from the Academy of Korean Studies, South Korea (AKS-2017-R- 22 (17R22)).

Works Cited

Aspiazu, Gary G., et al. "Improving the Academic Performance of Hispanic Youth: A Community Education Model." *Bilingual Research Journal*, vol. 22, no. 2-4, 1998, pp. 1-20.

Bruner, Jerome. *Acts of Meaning*. Harvard University Press, 1990.

Cameron, Deborah. "Language, Gender, and Sexuality: Current Issues and New Direction." *Applied Linguistics*, vol. 26, no. 4, 2005, pp. 482-502.

Cho, Uhn. "Segyehwaui chumdane seon hangoogui gajok: singeulobeol mojanyeo gajok sarye yeongu" (Korean Families on the Forefront of Globalization: A Case Study on the Neoglobal Mother–Children Families). *Gyeongjewa Sahoe (Economy and Society)*, vol. 64, 2004, pp. 148–71.

Coffey, Simon, and Brian Street. "Narrative and Identity in the 'Language Learning Project.'" *The Modern Language Journal*, vol. 92, no. 3, 2008, pp. 452-64.

Curdt-Christiansen, Xiao Lan. "Negotiating Family Language Policy: Doing Homework." *Successful Family Language Policy: Parents, Children and Educators in Interaction*, edited by Mila Schwartz and Anna Verschik, Springer, 2013, pp. 277-95.

Duff, Patricia. "Second Language Socialization as Sociocultural Theory: Insights and Issues." *Language Teaching*, vol. 40, 2007, pp. 309-319.

Durand, Tina. M. "Latina Mothers' Cultural Beliefs About Their Children, Parental Roles, and Education: Implications for Effective and Empowering Home-School Partnerships." *The Urban Review*, vol. 43, 2011, pp. 255-78.

Gonzalez-DeHass, Alyssa R., et al. "Examining the Relationship Between Parental Involvement and Student Motivation." *Educational Psychology Review*, vol. 17, no. 2, 2005, pp. 99-123.

Gordon, Daryl. "'I'm Tired. You Clean and Cook.' Shifting Gender Identities and Second Language Socialization." *TESOL Quarterly*, vol. 38, no. 3, 2004, pp. 437-57.

Hirsh, Jennifer S. "En el Norte la Mujer Manda: Gender, Generation, and Geography in a Mexican Transnational Community." *Immigration Research for a New Century: Multidisciplinary Perspectives*, edited by Nancy Foner, Rubén G. Rumbaut, and Steven J. Gold, Russell Sage Foundation, 2000, pp. 369-389.

Holstein, James A., and Jaber F. Gubrium. "Context: Working It Up, Down and Across." *Qualitative Research Practice*, edited by Clive Seale, et al., Sage, 2004, pp. 267-281.

Hondagneu-Sotelo, Pierrette. "Gender and Immigration: A Retrospective and Introduction." *Gender and US immigration: Contemporary Trends,* edited by Pierrette Hondagneu-Sotelo, University of California Press, 2003, pp. 1-19.

King, Kendall A., and Lyn Wright Fogle. "Family Language Policy." *Language Policy and Political Issues in Education. Encyclopedia of Language and Education.* 3rd ed., edited by Teresa McCarty and Stephen May, Springer, 2017, pp. 1-13.

King, Kendall. A., et al. "Family Language Policy." *Language & Linguistics Compass,* vol. 2, no. 5, 2008, pp. 907-22.

Kinginger, Celeste. "Alice Doesn't Live Here Anymore: Foreign Language Learning and Identity Reconstruction." *Negotiation of Identities in Multilingual Contexts,* edited by Aneta Pavlenko and Adrian Blackledge, Multilingual Matters, 2004, pp. 219-42.

Koki, Stan, and Harvey Lee. "Parental Involvement in Education: What Works in the Pacific? Promising Practices in the Pacific Region." *Eric Digest: ED426835,* 1998, pp. 1-5, eric.ed.gov/?id=ED426835. Accessed 11 Jan. 2021.

Lee, Hakyoon. "'I Am a *Kirogi* Mother': Education Exodus and Life Transformation among Korean Transnational Women." *Journal of Language, Identity & Education,* vol. 9, no. 4, 2010, pp. 250-64.

Menard-Warwick, Julia. *Gendered Identities and Immigrant Language Learning.* Multilingual Matters, 2009.

Malik, Rasheed and Taryn Morrissey. "The COVID-19 Pandemic Is Forcing Millennial Mothers Out of the Workforce." *Center for American Progress,* 12 Aug. 2020, www.americanprogress.org/issues/early-childhood/news/2020/08/12/489178/covid-19-pandemic-forcing-millennial-mothers-workforce/. Accessed 11 Jan. 2021.

"Mothering." *Wiktionary,* 3 Dec. 2019, en.wiktionary.org/wiki/mothering. Accessed 11 Jan. 2021.

Norton, Bonny. *Identity and Language Learning: Gender, Ethnicity and Educational Change.* Longman, 2000.

Pavlenko, Aneta. "Autobiographic Narratives as Data in Applied Linguistics." *Applied Linguistics,* vol. 28, no. 2, 2007, pp. 163-88.

Pavlenko, Aneta "'In the World of the Tradition, I Was Unimagined': Negotiation of Identities in Cross-Cultural Autobiographies." *International Journal of Bilingualism,* vol. 5, no. 3, Sept. 2001, pp. 317-44.

Pavlenko, Aneta, and James Lantolf. "Second Language Learning as Participation and the (re) Construction of Selves." *Sociocultural Theory and Second Language Learning,* edited by James P. Lantolf, Oxford University Press, 2000, pp. 155-77.

Pew Research Center. "Top 10 Metro Areas by Korean American Population." *Pew Research Center's Social & Demographic Trends Project,* 8 Sept. 2017, www.pewsocialtrends.org/chart/top-10-u-s-metropolitan-areas-by-korean-population. Accessed 11 Jan. 2021.

Schwartz, Mila. "Family Language Policy: Core Issues of an Emerging Field." *Applied Linguistics Review,* vol. 1, 2010, pp. 171-92.

Spolsky, Bernard. "Family Language Policy—The Critical Domain." *Journal of Multilingual and Multicultural Development,* vol. 33, no. 1, 2012, pp. 3-11.

"The Impact of Covid-19 on Working Parents." *Catalyst,* 29 Sept. 2020, www.catalyst.org/research/impact-covid-working-parents/.

Topor, David. R., et al. "Parent Involvement and Student Academic Performance: A Multiple Mediational Analysis." *Journal of Prevention & Intervention in the Community,* vol. 38, no. 3, 2010, pp. 183-197.

Volk, Dinah, and Martha Acosta, de. "Reinventing Texts and Contexts: Syncretic Literacy Events in Young Puerto Rican Children's Homes." *Research in the Teaching of English,* vol. 38, no. 1, 2003, pp. 8-48.

Chapter Twenty Five

"I Am Always Caring at Home": Spanish Mothers and the Challenges of COVID-19 Lockdowns in Childrearing

Ana Lucía Hernández Cordero, Paula González Granados,
and Mar Dieste Campo

Introduction

The worldwide COVID-19 pandemic has led to the lockdown of millions of people, causing considerable negative effects. In this chapter, we focus on the lived experiences of mothers with young children who have had to work from home during this time. These months of lockdown have revealed the contradictions between productive and reproductive work. Being a mother not only requires being available to meet the needs of young children but also demands the planning and organizing of household chores. Mothers assume care in a greater proportion than fathers do, and during the COVID-19 pandemic, this has meant more stress for them.

This chapter explores the difficulties of working mothers living in Zaragoza, Spain (with children under the age of ten), who have worked from home during the COVID-19 pandemic. Through interviews, we see that this situation is not sustainable, and that another method of care is necessary. In this chapter, we develop three themes concerning motherhood during lockdown: 1) the work-life balance between childrearing and teleworking, 2) children's homework, and 3) the distribution and mental burden of domestic work.

In this current health crisis, we ask the following questions. How is childcare being performed within these families? How are people managing work-life balance problems during lockdown? What changes have taken place inside people's homes? Who is more affected by these new dynamics?

As anthropologists and social workers (two of us are also mothers), we decided that it would be interesting for us to examine what working mothers were doing in the city of Zaragoza, Spain, as well as the changes families were experiencing regarding the organization of domestic work and childrearing during lockdown. We designed qualitative interview questions that aimed to illustrate what life was like before and after COVID-19, and we looked for mothers who were interested in participating. During March, April, and May, we completed interviews via Google Meet, Zoom, Facebook, WhatsApp, and Skype with fifteen middle-class Spanish mothers between the ages of thirty and fifty from single- or two-parent households with one or two children between three months and twelve years old.

We asked about their caregiving dynamics, how they organized this care, and whether they had paid work during lockdown. Their narratives reveal how care of children is defined by gender inequality. However, at the same time, their experiences demonstrate that this period of lockdown has proved to be a useful moment to rethink how caregiving roles are distributed.

COVID-19 Arrived: Stay at Home. Everything Will Be Okay. Mom Will Take Care of Everything

A state of alarm was declared in Spain at the outbreak of COVID-19 that confined the majority of the population to their homes for almost three months, from March 16 to June 21. People were allowed to go out to buy food and medicine. The children were unable to leave their homes at all until April 26, when they were allowed to leave home for two hours a day and always with sanitary control measures. Schools and daycare centres were closed until September 2020, and not knowing the health measures that government would eventually have to implement. Lockdown meant that some people lost their jobs, whereas for those that kept their job, it meant working from home while trying to maintain a normal work day, which was nearly impossible to achieve. For parents working from home with children, they had to modify their family care dynamics and adjust their work demands to this new situation.

The current health crisis surrounding COVID-19 has highlighted the flaws that exist in the relationship between the productive and reproductive spheres of our society. One of these areas is the current model used to organize care in our society, which has proven to be deficient from the beginning of this pandemic. The administration's response to childcare has been insufficient, and private childcare services are costly because the reality is that care has always been thought of as a woman's role. One of the bases for this inequality is a maternity model that, as Sharon Hays has stated, is incompatible with the dynamics of a capitalist labour market. Under this model, caregiving is seen as woman's role, and, consequently, finding a balance between work and family life is an issue for working mothers. This imbalance is exacerbated when such factors as social class, position within the labour market, family type, access to social services, and nationality are considered.

Mothers: Care First and Everything Else Comes Second

Caring for another includes activities that regenerate the physical and emotional wellbeing of people on a daily basis (Finch). The assumption that women are natural caregivers makes them the primary person responsible for organizing the care of dependents. In addition to mothering being a purely physical event (gestation, pregnancy, and birth) for many mothers, it is also a social act, as society believes that being a mother implies assuring the care and wellbeing of their children. Having children is, therefore, socially symbolic (Takševa).

For this reason, no one questions that working mothers should also take care of the child-rearing or that grandmothers continue to care for their grandchildren or even great-grandchildren. Nor is it strange for people to hire a woman outside the family unit to take care of this domestic work. In all of these cases, the principal argument is that women have an almost natural disposition to take care of others

(Badinter). Feminized and naturalized concepts of caregiving are based on this most conventional notion of motherhood.

In 1996, Sharon Hays coined the term "intensive mothering" to describe the social demands placed on women to undertake and be responsible for all areas of care. Mothers are responsible for the socialization of their children, as not only should they know what is best for their children's wellbeing at all times, but they should also enjoy this role profusely. As a result, mothers are expected to dedicate a large amount of personal time and energy to children and leave behind all other aspects of their life, including their professional, personal, and social development, which are considered less important. These social expectations are still felt by many mothers (O'Brien; Bodendorfer).

According to this model, a woman is a mother above everything else. All women must fulfill the ideal of motherhood; she must self-sacrificing, selfless, and loving (O'Brien). This model is both unrealistic and incompatible with any other activity that the mother may want to carry out. In addition, as Catrina Brown has argued, women have been conditioned not to discuss their feelings of hostility, worry, and anxiety surrounding this crisis of care. This denial of allowing mothers to express their true feelings is based specifically on the assumption that all mothers naturally know how to care.

Finding a work-life balance is important for families. However, society accepts and promotes this as the mother's problem to solve on her own. Although there are social programs that exist in Spain, these are insignificant due to their limited scope and their inability to reach most of society (Pazos). For this reason, families, and specifically mothers, are faced with significant dilemmas. The mandatory lockdown has broken domestic arrangements that were meticulously organized to assist mothers' and families' functions in the labour market (Pazos). The pandemic has forced Spanish society back to a highly traditional domestic arrangement, in which the mother becomes, once again, the main person responsible for all caregiving duties.

Caregiving Requires Time and So Does Paid Labour: What Do We Do during COVID-19?

The closing of schools, daycares, as well as establishments dedicated to caring for the elderly and disabled has confirmed that work schedules are not compatible with caregiving now that this need for care has increased so dramatically. Because of COVID-19, caregiving help from outside the immediate family such as from grandparents, daycares, schools, as well as paid caregivers disappeared. Lockdown forced families to combine paid work with home care. From one moment to the next, and due to lockdown, parents, mainly mothers, have had to take care of everything. Children demand physical and emotional attention, especially since COVID-19 has caused many disruptions to their daily lives. Much of their contact with the outside world has ended, resulting in their needing more attention from people at home. Since this responsibility typically falls on the shoulders of mothers, they have less time for their having work time and for their personal care. One mother of two young children, but in a two-parent household, described this frustration in the following way: "There are days when you can take half an hour and have a shower, and there are other days when you have done nothing more than be with them, playing with them, cooking them food. You have taken the dog out and the day is over.... It's not that I had a long time before COVID-19, but now we even have less time."

In two-parent homes, mothers continue to be in charge of the child-rearing (in addition to doing her own work), but fathers have begun participating in housework, including doing the laundry, playing with the kids, and shopping for groceries. Although these represent some adjustments in work and domestic responsibilities, inequality still abounds. For example, fathers, in addition to doing their work, usually do the shopping. In the context of lockdown, leaving the home to buy food and medicine is a privilege that in many cases, only the fathers enjoyed. While mothers were the ones who always stayed home. As one mother of two young children said, "Before I did the bulk of the housework and taking care of the children. But now in the quarantine that has changed; the one who goes out to buy [groceries] for example is him [her husband].... Tasks that only I did, now he also does them."

In single-parent homes, the situation is even more unsustainable. For these families, the role of grandparents and social networks was indispensable to their daily life. During lockdown, these supports completely disappeared, and work-life balance proved impossible. One mother of a four-year-old has this to say:

"Now I can't take him to my parents and everything has been horrible. I can't do anything, or I work very little while he's awake. And when night comes I'm so tired that all I have left is to fall asleep after cleaning the house a little. Then I get up at four in the morning to work."

Many families, but single mothers in particular, have had to turn to working mainly at night while children are sleeping or watching screens (television, tablets, smartphones, etc.), which also increases stress because some studies insist too much screen time can be harmful for children. However, it seems that, for some households, it is the only solution. As one single mother insists,

When I have to connect for work meetings, the only thing I can do is put a movie or some program on television.... I don't like to do that, but if I don't, I know that I will have the child on top of me all the time." Another mother in a two-parent household said: "It is very difficult to work and take care of a three-year-old child. He asks us for a lot of attention all the time. We put on videos or movies and that way, we get to work a little."

Work related to caregiving during lockdown has entailed the immobilization of a large part of the society but not of its production. Some sectors of the labour market were determined to maintain their same prelockdown level of productivity, regardless of the effect of COVID-19 on family care dynamics. The women we interviewed have had major difficulties finding a work-life balance during this time. Being a mother, working from home, while attending to all of their children's needs, has overwhelmed them. If working mothers are at home, they must accomplish their paid work in front of a computer at the same time they are helping their children with their homework, which means, in most cases, that these constant work interruptions lead to longer working days. The work they previously completed in eight hours now takes them between ten and twelve. A mother of a four-month-old in a two-parent household elaborated: "The first weeks of confinement were a lot of work. In the morning, I would start with the work, teleworking, and the phone would ring throughout the day.

And then I would attend to my parent's and children's affairs."

Some men, though, have realized the amount of work caregiving requires and have been able to reflect on their role in perpetuating this inequality at home; they have started to understand each partner must work equally to achieve a well-functioning home. As one mother of young children said, "I had told him many times, but he did not understand it. Now, though, when he sees that making the shopping list takes almost as much time as going to buy the groceries, he sees all the work required in completing these tasks."

Kids' Homework: An Added Pressure

Homework is another aspect that has created stress for mothers. The closure of schools has not meant an end to school activities. Following the same logic as the working world, schools have continued with virtual classes and the job of keeping up with schoolwork has become the responsibility of the people in each child's home. Helping children with their homework has become yet another arduous task added to an already long list, and, again, responsibility for it usually falls to mothers.

In pre-COVID-19 times, the schoolwork was already considered too much for families, but with the pandemic, the situation has become unsustainable. Therefore, a mother's workday fluctuates between attending to the needs of her children, including their homework, and completing her work, both paid and unpaid.

Concerning homework, additional difficulties arise if a family only has one computer or one place to work. To complete telework as well as homework, family members have to manage their time even more carefully and be creative in order to for each member to complete their tasks. Stress as well as feelings of being overwhelmed, not to mention conflicts, which are usually resolved by the mothers. One mother of two children spoke about the difficulties in sharing one computer: "She [her daughter] had to do her homework with the computer ... but she didn't know how to handle e-mail well, so of course she was asking all the time, and, in the meantime, I had to do my work. In the end, I didn't have time to do nothing ... it was horrible."

Families acknowledge the efforts that education centres have made to continue teaching and, in some cases, these centres have offered computers so that every student could follow the classes. However, this was not always possible. The interviewees indicated that in order to face the next school year in September, schools, teachers, and families must coordinate to coordinate better, and teachers must improve their planning.

The Emotional Burden

Child-rearing also includes the activities that go beyond the direct care of the child, choosing their clothes, managing doctor appointments, knowing which lotions and medicines to use as well as their correct dosage, and planning and cooking meals for each day. The work that goes into this planning and organizing is referred to as an emotional burden (Brown). This invisible labour is also unequally distributed at home, as women are the ones who spend a large amount of time thinking about it (Ennis).

During lockdown, responsibilities have been modified, and there has been a significant increase in men's participation pertaining to housework as well as childcare. However, the imbalance between men and women persists because the emotional burden continues to fall on women, and, consequently, they spend more time than men in taking care of the home (Badinter). Women are the ones in charge of planning activities that take place during the week. They make sure everything goes as planned and react when setbacks do occur.

Conclusions

Staying home has blurred the line between caregiving and work responsibilities. Now, people are at home more often and need to dedicate more time for its upkeep. In addition, during the quarantine, it is more difficult to take care of the children. Eating, playing, and sleeping schedules have been greatly modified, yet children have had difficulty following these schedules during weeks of lockdown. Their moods change every minute and with an overwhelming ease. They, too, worry about the immediate future, which is uncertain and confusing. As one mother said, "The little girl gets tired very quickly; she gets frustrated quickly ... and I also yell at her, and then I feel bad."

Finding balance during the pandemic is complicated and

challenging. Mothers negotiate labour demands, parental obligations, and their desire to spend more time with their children stress free. Yet workloads have doubled, and mothers spend the whole day child-rearing, housekeeping, and teleworking. They postpone until the evening everything that can wait or requires a minimum amount of concentration and reflection.

In these conditions, work-life balance does not exist. Our patriarchal model for child-rearing and finding work-life balance is simply wrong and must be changed. But it is important to rethink both not just as a concern for families with children but as a more social and collective matter that concerns us all (Ennis).

We need social policies that take a range of different types of families into consideration. We need the labour market to become more family friendly, but we also need to understand that childrearing is everyone's responsibility so that it does not fall exclusively on mothers and grandmothers. Such a collectivization of care would be a sustainable and viable alternative to the present patriarchal model.

Works Cited

Badinter, Elisabeth. *The Woman and the Mother. A Controversial Book on Motherhood as a New Form of Slavery.* La esfera de los libros, 2011.

Bodendorfer, Catherine. "The Myth of Choice in Intensive Mothering." *Studies in the Maternal*, vol. 7, no. 1, 2015, pp. 1-4.

Brown, Catrina. "Speaking of Women's Depression and the Politics of Emotion." *Affilia: Journal of Women and Social Work*, vol. 34, no. 2, 2019, pp. 151-69.

Ennis, Linda. *Intensive Mothering: The Cultural Contradictions of Modern Motherhood.* Demeter Press, 2014.

Finch, Jane. *Family obligations and social change.* Polity Press, 1989.

Hays, Sharon. *The Cultural Contradictions of Motherhood.* Yale University Press, 1996.

O'Brien, Lynn. «Conceiving Intensive Mothering." *Journal of the Association for Research on Mothering*, vol. 8, no. 1-2, 2006, pp. 96-108.

Pazos, María. "Apuntes para una economía política feminista" (Notes for a Feminist Political Economy). *Ekonomiaz*, vol. 91, 2017, pp. 360-84.

Takševa, T. "Motherhood Studies and Feminist Theory: Elisions and Intersections." *Journal of the Motherhood Initiative*, vol. 9, no. 1, 2018, pp. 177-94.

Chapter Twenty Six

And Then We Went Outside: A Black Mothering Lens on Quarantine, Health Disparities, and State Violence

Zaje A. T. Harrell

Introduction

In early 2020, the novel coronavirus (COVID-19) began to spread throughout various American states. What had originally been a Chinese, then a pan-Asian, and eventually a European problem was now in New York and Seattle. On March 11, 2020, COVID-19 was declared a pandemic by the World Health Organization ("Rolling Updates"). Shortly thereafter, the United States (U.S.) was in a federal state of emergency, and many state governments soon followed. In my own state of Maryland, my children's school closed to in-person instruction on March 12 and quickly pivoted to online learning. At that time, there was an idea of a short-term, perhaps two or three weeks, quarantine period as a necessary step to "flatten the curve"—an epidemiological phrase characterizing attempts to mitigate the virus's spread, such that the capacity of the healthcare system would not be overloaded. We expected that we would return to normal on March 24, and then April 2. In reality, my three children, like most around the U.S., would not return to school again for the remainder of the academic year.

Psychoanalytic mothering theorist Nancy Chodorow reminds us that "Women as mothers are pivotal actors in the sphere of social reproduction" (11). It took a virus to restructure American mothers' roles, as the work of paid and family labour were required to take place under state-imposed, public-health lockdowns. The responsibility of work, health safety precautions, nurturing, and education fell disproportionately on mothers. The private sphere of home life was being transformed under varied and uneven state leadership and while national leadership flailed.

The management of COVID-19 in the U.S. fell behind that of comparably rich and not-so-rich nations around the globe (Shesgreen). The American slapdash approach to the handling of the virus led to inadequate distribution of supplies, confusing public health messaging, limited planning for vulnerable communities, and prioritization of economic concerns over that of health and wellbeing. Furthermore, outcomes for those infected have demonstrated disparities by race and class that fall along the fault lines of America's racial caste system (Yong). Eventually, by late June, 2020, when the curve of novel coronavirus infections should have flattened and dropped off, it took a sharp detour skywards (Leonhardt).

In the context of this social and policy failure, the publicly recorded killing of a Black man, George Floyd, at the hands of Minneapolis police officers played out to captive audiences around the world. The impact of disparities in health combined with such public state-sanctioned racialized violence created a conflict around preventive personal safety and responsible public action.

This chapter explores these tensions through the lens of personal experience framed through a multidisciplinary Black feminist lens on mothering. Feminist movements have addressed the fraught territory of women's lived experiences and sociopolitical realities. The African American experience provides us with a point of departure for understanding health disparities, the domestic and productive mandate of the pandemic, as well as the role of state repression. The timeframe for this exploration is March through June of 2020. At the time of this writing in the fall of 2020, the pandemic continues to unfold: There are 200,000 lost lives, and the U.S. nears a national election.

On Premature Death: Disparities and Despair

Premature death is a feature of oppression. Hussein Abdilahi Bulhan's analysis of the psychology of oppression highlights the following: "Every social order of course dispenses rights and privileges unequally. An oppressive social order deepens this inequality in how it dispenses life and death to its citizens" (176). As if to presage the striking racial disparities in the future pandemic of 2020, there was a public focus, beginning as early as 2018, on the disparities in the conditions around birth for Black mothers and babies in the U.S. Black mothers are two to three times more likely to die of pregnancy-related complications than their white counterparts ("Racial and Ethnic Disparities"). Black babies have higher mortality, higher birth complications and prematurity, as well as lower birth weight, which is predictive of other poor outcomes. They are also less likely to be breastfed, which is protective and preventive in infant health. The national attention around these poor outcomes was shared in features in *The New York Times* (Villarosa) and *The Washington Post* (Velarde). The crisis in Black maternal health is indicative of systemic racism.

In the U.S., social systems have historically limited African Americans' access to healthcare, quality food, and free-for-use public spaces for physical activity. The effect of resource deprivation and segregation overdetermines poor health outcomes among African Americans (Kochhar and Cillufo). Furthermore, these policies have for centuries limited opportunities for economic security, thus, effectively suppressing Black wealth ("Nine Charts on Wealth Inequality"). The idea of caste has been asserted as a way to characterize the racialized experience of African Americans (Wilkerson), as it helps to illuminate the multiple factors that disproportionately lead to poor outcomes among this group. As a result, the impact of COVID-19 has most brutally affected the lives of those already so disadvantaged by their social position.

The Politics of COVID-19 Domesticity

Once the virus had reached the point of community spread in the U.S., there were more unknowns to consider. Unlike the Asian and European countries that were simultaneously managing this crisis in the early months, the U.S. was a racially diverse, highly unequal country with a comparatively weak social safety net and no universal health care. The U.S. was also in the process of becoming a country in which two and half branches of its government were run by the Republican Party. The exploitation of inequality was arguably one of the party's most identifiably consistent policy goals.

However, it is important to remember that for a brief time, there was a different face of the virus, one that everyone had a stake in stopping. In March, elderly people who had taken exclusive cruises were returning with symptoms, and people who had travelled internationally were concerned about their health (Campbell). Although it was certain that those with fewer resources would suffer more, COVID-19 also posed a risk to the privileged. It was this fact that made the initial lockdowns more palatable as a measure of public safety.

The shuttering of schools, though, ripped a resource away from families. In the early days of the pandemic, an ethic of care and nurturing was emerging as dominant, presenting a maternal lens for the crisis. It was primarily mothers who were expected to make the pivot to creating a safe home amid the danger while also losing the resources of childcare and in-person education. Soon after the lockdown, my second-born daughter's second-grade parent chat group was flooded with pictures of the new workspaces that had been designated for distance learning. There were desks with laptops, tablets, and art supplies, which were pristinely arranged for the challenge ahead. In the middle of a plague, we were self-assured as decorators.

The writer Charlotte Perkins Gilman (1860–1935) warned of the constraints of domestic life as existential threats to human potential: "She is feminine, more than enough, as man is masculine, more than enough; but she is not human, as he is human. The house-life does not bring out our humanness, for all the distinctive lines of human progress lie outside (217)." Gilman did not live in the time of the internet and Zoom as well as housework However, her words echo a warning concerning the trap of a domestic life for women. "Safer at home" emerged as a public health message. The immediate mandate that the home be turned into both workplace and school carried with it a gendered implication. The risk in this scenario was that the domestic life would soon overtake other pursuits. And domestic hobbies like baking did become a hobby of the pandemic. There was lots of bread being baked and recipes being shared, from sourdough to banana.

Renowned scholar and activist Angela Davis provides a useful analysis of understanding the evolution of the bourgeois lifestyle as it evolved around housework and compulsory motherhood as specifically feminized modes of production. Black women provided domestic labour in their homes as well as in the homes of others. Privileged white women created conditions for their children to thrive with the assistance of other women (Davis 198). The lens of domestic perfection was idealized from a top-down perspective, though requiring a lot of invisible labour from women. Where domestic bliss is constructed, so is another narrative of motherhood for the women who fall short of idealized motherhood.

Historian Paula Giddings has argued that the Victorian cult of true womanhood was racialized in order to highlight the purity and virtue of white womanhood (43). This framing of womanhood was denied to Black women. During enslavement, Black women were property, forced to labour and breed. The construction of Black womanhood in the white supremist imagination portrayed them as lascivious and beasts of burden. Giddings's analysis helps clarify how Black social hygiene and respectability movements emerged. Black women's domesticity was a way of cultivating a type of nurturing that reclaimed Black family life. Historically, the making of a safe and beautiful home for others was the labour of Black women, often at the expense of their own family life. The autonomy to produce this for ourselves, for our own children, is in this way revolutionary. It is Michelle Obama—a double Ivy League educated lawyer—declaring herself "mom-in-chief," with a strong defense from Black feminists (Cooper 50). As a public Black mother, the First Lady disrupted the privilege of white idealized motherhood.

The quarantine moved from days to weeks, disrupting my sense of time; the days melted together. I considered that this history made my (Black woman) banana bread dialectically superior to that of white women. My bread resists the white supremist capitalist patriarchy; yours feeds it. My bread nourishes a community; yours is small and scarce. There is only enough for you.

Truthfully, I did not feel superior about banana bread or lovingly curated homework spaces. I felt utilitarian both in my ability to use every scrap of food and maximize every space. I was trapped in a sphere that was closing in around women who endeavour to be more than the concerns of nurturing. The clock was running out on us as we lost time and focus for our work. Instead, we focused on navigating apps and calming children while worrying about the threat and instability. The pandemic is patriarchal, and the patriarchy is maddening and not at all safe.

Big Mama and Jerome

Soon, a predictable trend began to emerge: The virus ravaged densely populated urban areas, with their rainbow populations, yet spared the more rural areas. As weeks of quarantine, distance learning, and lost employment began to take their toll, a new narrative began to take hold. The virus was selective, and the risk was uneven—the bodies were old and nonwhite. They were the "coloured people" who did not understand the importance of hygiene (Chiu). They were reckless with their lives as a matter of course.

Then Surgeon General Jerome Adams decided to speak. Under the Trump Administration, Adams was one of the few Black appointees. He was a former official when Mike Pence was governor of Indiana. That state administration was famous for another public health crisis—an HIV outbreak in rural Indiana because of a failure to use harm-reduction strategies, including needle exchanges. Now Pence, the vice president, was in charge of managing the pandemic response.

Dr. Anthony Fauci, the director of the National Institute of Allergy and Infectious Diseases, had spent decades in the public eye as a spokesperson to the American public about every pandemic and viral threat; he has advised six different presidents. He was expectedly defter at getting out this message, and his popularity grew, much to the chagrin of the administration. Adams, a health professional, was effectively neutered and relegated to the task overseeing the homemade mask-making project—masks that he had a few weeks earlier told the

American public they did not need. The failure to robustly correct this type of confusing health messaging was a major public health misstep. Adams did, however, feel the need to speak on the emerging "Negro Problem." In a press conference, he requested that Blacks address COVID-19 transmission by practicing social distancing and observing the lockdown requirements. He mentioned that the avoidance of alcohol and drugs was also important and that these actions should be done for the safety of all: "And speaking of mothers, we need you to do this, if not for yourself, then for your abuela. Do it for your granddaddy. Do it for your Big Mama. Do it for your Pop-Pop. We need you to understand—especially in communities of color. We need you to step up and help stop the spread so that we can protect those who are most vulnerable" (Aleem).

Adams's statement lacked context and smacked of victim blaming. While admonishing Black and Brown communities, Adams did not speak so earnestly about the need to increase the supply of personal protective equipment (PPE) so that he could stop having to run a craft segment on how to protect yourself with homemade materials. Almost comically, I was reminded of this verse: "You singing too, but your grandma ain't my grandma" (Bennett and Segal).

Instead of indicting the social contexts that produce health disparities, another vision was offered: a vision of dysfunctional Black family life as the cause of its own demise. It was as familiar as Moynihan's report on "Negro family life" that bemoaned single-female-headed households in Black communities. Moreover, Adams's use of the term "Big Mama" represents the entry of a Black female mammy archetype into the pandemic discourse. Big Mama in this scenario is vulnerable but not because of any oppressive social structures that have contributed to her ill health and limited resources. Rather, Big Mama is the victim of children, grandchildren, nieces, and nephews, who are so selfish that they have infected her with the virus. This Black mother is a mother, but, in fact, she is not a very good one, as the fruits of her labour demonstrate. Her family members are ungrateful and unruly. They are drinking and smoking and spreading disease. Big Mama was likely to get sick and die. She had the deck stacked against her, especially with her hypertension, obesity, and diabetes. Big Mama was a mother who had failed. How much were good Americans supposed to sacrifice for her? As the data emerged showing who the virus was affecting, a spate of reopen-now protests, fuelled by Republican operatives, began to occur (Gearan and Wagner). These were encouraged by President Trump. There was no vaccine, no federal reopening plan, and no mass testing, just a sense in some places that the threats this virus posed—and which had killed 100,000 in four months—were unreal or exaggerated.

My Son, George

The journalist Ida B. Wells-Barnett was born to people who had experienced bondage and was fearless in what Black feminist scholar Beverly Guy-Sheftall calls her "militant journalism." Wells-Barnett wrote the following:

> Our Country's national crime is lynching. It is not the creature of an hour, the sudden outburst of uncontrolled fury, or the unspeakable brutality of an insane mob. It represents the cool calculation and deliberation of intelligent people who openly avow that there is an "unwritten law" that justifies them in putting human beings to death without complaint under oath, without trial by jury, without opportunity to make defense, and without right of appeal. (70)

On May 25, 2020, George Floyd went into a corner store in Minneapolis. The clerk believed that he was using counterfeit bills. Floyd did not make a purchase and exited the store, yet law enforcement had still been called. Floyd was taken into custody, as a police officer named Derek Chauvin placed his knee on the handcuffed man's neck for eight minutes and forty-six seconds until he was dead (Taylor). Other officers looked on while community members and Floyd himself pleaded for his life. The murderer kept his hands in his pocket, nonchalant, like a hired torturer on the clock. This brutal act was but a slight deviation from the day's plans.

A few years ago, I took a selfie with my then four-year-old son. He was holding on to me. My dress was covered in red roses, and my son wore a shirt and tie and a wheat-coloured fedora; We both stared directly at the lens.

As his life was pressed out of his body, George Floyd called on his dead mother. In the days after his death, a picture of Floyd as a young boy in his mother's lap, sleeping, while her beautiful sepia face smiled at the camera, was circulated on social media. While I had avoided watching his killing, my numbness broke when I saw this photo. The pose, the cradled boy child, was all too familiar. George was my contemporary. He was my brother. He was my son. My insides ached for him, even though he was now beyond this life. I wept. A grown man calling for his mother while on the precipice of death is primal. The witness of his call saturated an already-stressed, captive population. There was a shared horror and a need for reckoning.

My children were restless. They had been inside for over two months. They were seeing their friends via screens. It seemed to me that they were simultaneously more tightly wound and unravelling.

Uprisings are to be expected, and this one was almost a requirement, because in addition to watching our leaders kill us slowly, I would now have to tell my children that cities were burning because a man had been murdered in the street. Not just one man. And not just a man—sometimes a woman and sometimes a child.

The agents of the state and their surrogates shoot with impunity and leave child witnesses. Rachel Jeantel was talking to her friend Trayvon while he was being stalked prior to his murder. Philando Castile was killed in front of his fiancé and stepdaughter; the child was left to comfort her hysterical mother while Castile bled out. Atatiana Jefferson was killed in front of her eight-year-old nephew. Her father would die a few months later, of a broken heart. Eric Garner was choked to death; his daughter, Erica, would protest by having "die-ins." A mother of two, she would soon be dead, at twenty-seven, of a broken heart. The violence of the state and of vigilantes, like George Zimmerman, is powerful enough to destroy a family and to end a childhood with just one bullet.

Keeping my children safe at home was a heavy burden. They were afraid of the virus, but we were learning to scoot around the risk with masks, social distancing and walls. My mind went to unfurled banners: *"A man was lynched yesterday"* I told them, "We will be going to a protest for someone who had been killed in Minneapolis, Minnesota." They had questions. "Is it safe? What about the coronavirus?" A virus had shut down their world, and now a murder would force them back into it. None of these seemed like the stuff of a happy childhood.

Death is all around us. The physical threat to our existence posed by the state was ever present. Parents often tell fanciful stories of the tooth fairy and Santa Claus. Nightmares are kept at bay with beloved stories of talking animals. These things grew quaint as the death toll rose and the unrest grew. Mothering required that I make a further demand of them. We cannot stay "safer at home"; we cannot stay inside. So, with our masks and hand sanitizer and homemade signs from cardboard delivery boxes—which was how we now got provisions safely from the outside world—we drove into the city. They had not been this far on a car ride for months. The children were afraid, but I assured them that their surgical masks protected them. They were back in the community; the streets were crowded, and they could see some classmates, with similarly obscured faces.

I was not sure if this was the right decision, but it was necessary. Black people were dying in hospitals and on city streets. At a time when we were supposed to fear the closeness of each other, I sensed our survival relied on our proximity. We gathered. We kept silence and put our bodies to the pavement for nearly nine minutes, kneeling in remembrance—a ritual with our covered faces and raised fists.

This chapter is dedicated to all of those who have fallen during this dark season.

Works Cited

Aleem, Zeeshan. "The Problem with the Surgeon General's Controversial Coronavirus Advice to Americans of Color." *Vox*, 11 Apr. 2020, www.vox.com/2020/4/11/21217428/surgeon-general-jerome-adams-big-mama-coronavirus. Accessed 12 Jan. 2021.

Bennett, Chancelor, and Nico Segal. "Sunday Candy." performed by Donnie Trumpet and the Social Experiment featuring Jamila Woods, 2015.

Bulhan, Hussein Abdilahi. *Frantz Fanon and the Psychology of Oppression.* Plenum Publishing Corporation, 1985.

Campbell, Colin. "Coronavirus Patients in Maryland Were on Cruise 'Not Affiliated with Baltimore,' Montgomery County Health Chief Says." *The Baltimore Sun.* 6 Mar. 2020, www.baltimoresun.com/coronavirus/bs-hs-coronavirus-friday-20200306-tzmaqfm7bvbpvox6qdvdwha5te-story.html. Accessed 12 Jan. 2021.

Chiu, Allyson. "Ohio GOP lawmaker Fired from ER Job over Remarks about 'Colored Population' and Covid-19" *The Washington Post*, 11 June

2020, www.washingtonpost.com/nation/2020/06/11/black-coronavirus-ohio-gop/. Accessed 12 Jan. 2021.

Chodorow, Nancy J. *The Reproduction of Mothering*. Berkeley: U of California Press, 1999.

Cooper, Brittney. "'Ain't I a Lady': Race, Women, Michelle Obama and the Ever-Expanding Democratic Imagination." *Melus*, vol. 35, no. 4, 2010, pp. 39-57.

Davis, Angela Y. "The Approaching Obsolescence of Housework: A Working-Class Perspective." *The Angela Y. Davis Reader*, edited by Joy James, Blackwell Publishing, 1998, 193-209.

Gearan, Anne, and John Wagner. "Trump Expresses Support for Angry Anti-Shutdown Protesters as More States Lift Coronavirus Lockdowns." *The Washington Post*, 1 May 2020, www.washingtonpost.com/politics/trump-expresses-support-for-angry-anti-shutdown-protesters-as-more-states-lift-coronavirus-lockdowns/2020/05/01/25570dbe-8b9f-11ea-8ac1-bfb250876b7a_story.html. Accessed 12 Jan. 2021.

Giddings, Paula J. *When and Where I Enter: The Impact of Black Women on Race and Sex in America*. Bantam Books, 1984.

Gilman, Charlotte Perkins. *The Home: Its Work and Influences*. University of Illinois Press, 1972.

Kochhar, Rakesh, and Anthony Cillufo. "Key Findings on the Rise in Income Inequality within America's Racial and Ethnic Groups." *Pew Research Center*, 12 July 2018, www.pewresearch.org/fact-tank/2018/07/12/key-findings-on-the-rise-in-income-inequality-within-americas-racial-and-ethnic-groups/. Accessed 12 Jan. 2021.

Leonhardt, David. "American Exceptionalism on the Virus." *The New York Times*, 29 June 2020, www.nytimes.com/2020/06/29/briefing/coronavirus-mississippi-new-england-patriots-your-monday-briefing.html. Accessed 12 Jan. 2021.

Moynihan, Daniel Patrick. *The Negro Family: The Case for National Action*. *U.S. Department of Labour*, 1965, www.dol.gov/general/aboutdol/history/webid-moynihan. Accessed 12 Jan. 2021.

"Nine Charts on Wealth Inequality." *Urban Institute*, 5 Oct. 2017, apps.urban.org/features/wealth-inequality-charts/. Accessed 12 Jan. 2021.

"Racial and Ethnic Disparities Continue in Pregnancy-Related Deaths." *Centers for Disease Control and Prevention (CDC)*, 5 Sept. 2019, www.cdc.gov/media/releases/2019/p0905-racial-ethnic-disparities-pregnancy-deaths.html. Accessed 12 Jan. 2021.

"Rolling Updates on Coronavirus Disease (COVID-19)." *World Health Organization (WHO)*, 31 July 2020, who.int/emergencies/diseases/novel-coronavirus-2019/events-as-they-happen. Accessed 12 Jan. 2021.

Shesgreen, Deirdre. "Senegal's Quiet COVID Success: Test Results in 24 Hours, Temperature Checks at Every Store, No Fights Over Masks." *USA Today*, 6 Sept. 2020, www.usatoday.com/story/news/world/2020/09/06/covid-19-why-senegal-outpacing-us-tackling-pandemic/5659696002/. Accessed 12 Jan. 2021.

Taylor, Derek Bryson. "George Floyd Protests: A Timeline." *The New York Times*, 10 July 2020, www.nytimes.com/article/george-floyd-protests-timeline.html. Accessed 12 Jan. 2021.

Velarde, Luis. "The Crisis in America's Maternity Wards." *The Washington Post*, 11 Feb. 2019, www.washingtonpost.com/health/2019/02/11/crisis-americas-maternity-wards/. Accessed 12 Jan. 2021.

Villarosa, Linda. "Why America's Black Mothers and Babies Are in a Life-or-Death Crisis." *The New York Times*, 18 Apr. 2020, www.nytimes.com/2018/04/11/magazine/black-mothers-babies-death-maternal-mortality.html. Accessed 12 Jan. 2021.

Wells-Barnett, Ida B. "Lynch Law in America." *In Words of Fire: An Anthology of African American Feminist Thought*, edited by Beverly Guy-Sheftall, The New Press, 1995, pp. 69-78.

Wilkerson, Isabel. *Caste: The Origins of Our Discontents*. Random House. 2020.

Yong, Ed. "How the Pandemic Defeated America." *The Atlantic*, Sept. 2020, www.theatlantic.com/magazine/archive/2020/09/coronavirus-american-failure/614191/. Accessed 12 Jan. 2021.

Section III

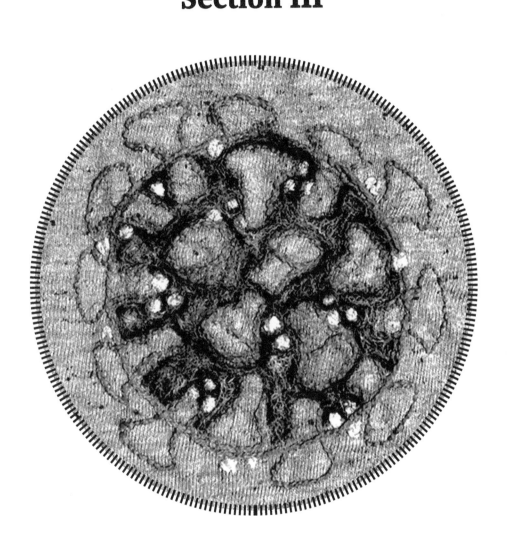

Maternal Health and Wellbeing

Chapter Twenty Seven

Taming the Virus, Midsummer Shaman, and Invisible Invaders

Catherine Moeller

While we all found ourselves confined at home during the early months of the Covid-19 pandemic, I was also very sick in bed for a very long time. I took up slow stitching, which I had done only once since my grandmother had taught me as a young child. The ability to represent the virus with embroidery threads and to hold it in my hands as something tangible helped me to quell my anxieties about it. During that time of uncertainty, I was drawn to stitch a protective shaman and goddess who could keep the virus under control and away from my family.

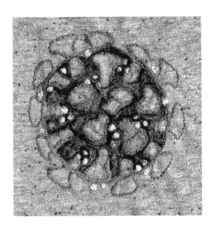

Taming the Virus

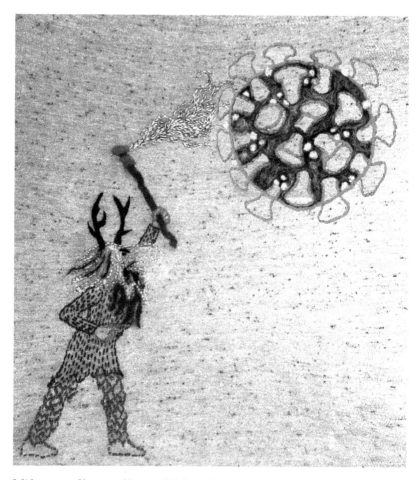

Midsummer Shaman, Yarn and Felt on Cotton

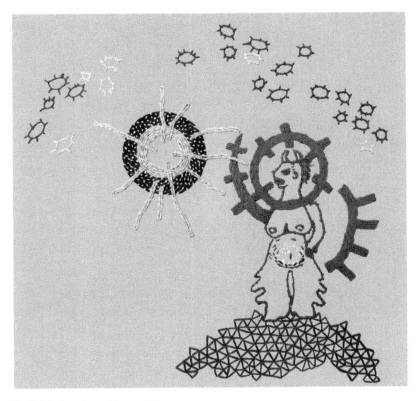

Invisible Invaders, Yarn on Cotton

Chapter Twenty Eight

Misericordia (1460–1462) Digital Drawing, Variable Dimensions

Helen Sargeant

I have drawn over the *Virgin of Mercy* to include a face mask, the virus, and the words "Prayers Can't Kill COVID-19." It was created out of a sense of helplessness and anxiety that I felt at being unable to protect or visit my elderly mother during the COVID-19 lockdown.

Image:
Prayers Can't Kill COVID-19 (after Piero della Francesca, Madonna della Misericordia, 1460-1462), Digital Drawing, Variable Dimensions, April 2020

Chapter Twenty Nine

The First Successful COVID-19 Birth in the World: Feminist Reflections on the Medical Model of Birth in a Pandemic

Holly Zwalf

I was one of the earliest cases of COVID-19 in Australia. I contracted the virus while on a flight home from the United Kingdom, a trip I had made to attend my wickedly wild grandmother's funeral. Two days before the funeral, however, my partner in Australia—a trans man who has cystic fibrosis and who was nearly nine months pregnant with his second child—had a minor car accident. Usually so calm and level-headed, he Facetimed me, concerned that the shock was bringing on early labour. I was terrified that I'd miss the birth so in a panic I decided to forgo the funeral and bought a flight back home that same day. His contractions didn't come to anything in the end, but two days after returning, I came down with a high fever. A week later, we had both tested positive to COVID-19. The law in Australia at the time required all positive cases to quarantine in hospital, so we were placed into mandatory isolation in two separate infection control negative pressure rooms, where we remained for the following nine days. My partner and his four-year-old were placed in one room, and I and my-four-year old were placed in another, and although we shared a wall, we were not allowed to visit each other. During this time my partner birthed his baby, making medical history as the first COVID-19-positive person to give birth outside of China and the first documented noncaesarean birth to a COVID-19-positive parent in the world.

This chapter combines feminist reflections on the medical model of birth with autoethnographic accounts of my experiences and observations surrounding my partner's birth to interrogate the success of the world's first unassisted birth to COVID-19-positive parents. I first describe our time in hospital quarantine leading up to and directly following the birth and then address the importance of mental health support during delivery by comparing a medical-centred versus a patient-centred model of birth. I then apply these models to the risks of birthing in a pandemic and finish by making a case for a middle-ground approach to delivery, which emphasizes that both the safety and autonomy of the patients must be respected by birthing professionals. I would like to note here that most of the references used in this chapter regarding feminist perspectives on birth use gendered language that is exclusionary to trans and nonbinary birthing people and is, therefore, not applicable to my family. Academic writing on pregnancy and birth still largely fails to move beyond essentialist gendered language that assumes that all people who get pregnant and birth are women or female identified, and this is a gap that I hope future writers will address.

Pregnancy, Birth, and Mental Health Support

In the hallways of our hospital, my partner's birth was heralded as a success. Up until this point, the only documented births to COVID-19-positive parents had been in China, and all these births had occurred via caesarean to avoid possible transmission to the child. All babies had been removed from their parents at birth and were only returned after the parent/s had finally been declared negative. The babies had all been bottle fed, and there had been no skin-to-skin contact. In many cases, partners had not been allowed to be present at the birth. In contrast to this, my partner's birth was, indeed, a success. I was permitted to be present; the baby was born without any intervention; the baby was not removed from their birthing parent or denied their parent's milk; and in all of this contact, no transference of the virus occurred. However, as M. C. Inhorn notes, "Women's health, as a discursive field, is usually defined by others" (348), of which my partner's birth was an example. The success of a birth needs to be measured by taking into account not only medical matters (in our case factors such as mortality and viral transmission) but also the patient's bodily autonomy and mental health as well as the preservation of the family unit. In these areas, our needs were badly neglected.

For the first five days in the hospital, our family was kept apart, and my partner and I were not allowed to visit each other, even though our rooms shared a wall. In my partner's room, his four-year-old child—who has special needs and who was scared and confused about being confined and repeatedly examined—started climbing the furniture, self-harming, and threatening to kill the doctors. My partner was unable to relax or sleep, and at nine-months pregnant was exhausted and emotionally distressed from trying to support his child. Through the wall we shared, I could hear him crying and his child screaming. My mental health also quickly deteriorated. In my room, which I was sharing with my four-year-old, there was a window that had no curtains, so the staff could watch us whenever they wanted. I took to crying in the shower because it was the only place where I was able to fall apart unobserved. After five days, my partner's child was finally released into the care of a friend. That same night midwives tried to bully my partner into an induction. They were worried that the virus would soon get into his lungs, and as a cystic fibrosis patient, they were concerned that he would soon become too sick to labour. This was a violation of the birth plan we had all agreed to less than twenty-four hours earlier, and he refused. He told them he was too mentally unwell to birth that day and pleaded with them to give him an extra night or two to get into a better headspace and get some sleep. Eventually, they agreed. On the day of the induction, several things happened to again breach our trust. Staff members were supposed to come and get me as soon as active labour began, but the message was not passed on, and by the time I was escorted to the birthing room, he had been labouring alone for over four hours. Staff members had agreed that my partner could use gas for pain relief, but by mid-labour, they had changed their minds, deciding this would pose a health risk. These deviations from our plans were distressing, but despite this, the baby was born healthy and without intervention. While the midwives cleaned up and completed the paperwork, we spent a couple of beautiful hours together as the baby had its first feed. Then it was time for my partner and the baby to be moved to a private room. We had assumed I would go with them, but we were told that this was not possible, and I was escorted back to my own room in a different part of the hospital and then was denied permission to visit them again for over twenty-four hours. My partner spent the first day following the birth caring for his newborn on his own, in isolation, with no support or visitors.

The medical response to our COVID-19 diagnoses consistently emphasized physical over mental health, an oversight that had a massive effect on our family's health. For the entire time we were in hospital, despite being examined every four hours around the clock, not once did anyone do a mental health assessment on any of us. My partner's child is ADHD and autistic, and I had recently experienced a period of post-traumatic stress, but both facts went completely ignored during our stay. We had to fight to get the hospital to recognize our family as human beings and not just as a virus, and we had to argue continually for our rights. By the time we were discharged to my house, nine days after first being admitted, our family was falling apart. Our children were deeply traumatized, and this resulted in violent and aggressive behaviour—behaviour my partner and I were ill-equipped to manage, being mentally unwell ourselves. My partner and I ordinarily live in separate houses one and a half hours drive from each other, and after a week, we made the difficult decision for my partner to complete the final two weeks of quarantine at his own house. Once again, the family was separated, and my partner was left to care for his distressed child and his newborn baby alone, with no support. As Edwin van Teijlingen notes, the "rationalising (i.e. nonemotional) rhetoric of many biomedical experts" does not take into account the importance of emotional bonding with a newborn (sec. 12.2)— something that Queensland Public Health was definitely not taking into account when they decided that due to quarantine laws, I wasn't legally allowed to visit them during those two weeks. Consequently, I missed out on crucial bonding time with the baby. It would be difficult for any medical assessment that considers mental as well as physical health to identify what the newborn was taken home to as a healthy environment.

Medical- versus Patient-Centred Birth

Several weeks after the birth, we were approached by an infectious disease specialist from the hospital, seeking permission to publish a medical journal article about our situation. We knew our story would help pave the way for other pregnant COVID-positive people to birth in a similar way if desired, so we agreed. The journal article was brief and focused on the medical details of our case, describing the birth as having "favourable" or "good clinical outcomes" (Walczak et al.). In feminist dialogues regarding birth, there is a strong differentiation between a medical model of care, which is focused on risk assessment (the risk of birth causing the death of either the infant or the birthing parent), and patient-centred care, which values these medical concerns as well as the birthing parent's autonomy, emotional needs, and mental health (Hill 60-61, 202-4). According to Deborah Davis and Kim Walker, although the safety of the birthing person and the baby is, of course, aspired to, in a patient-centred birth, the definition of a successful birth "is a birth with which the woman feels satisfied; it is her experience that is central" (605).

The experiences of the birthing person are important. From a medical model perspective, the positive analysis of our birth as being favourable was accurate: Both child and birthing parent came out of the birth alive and physically healthy. However, the medical model of care overlooks mental health, parent-infant bonding, and the importance of family involvement in a birth. And when viewed from a patient-centred model of care perspective, the birth was arguably less than favourable. I want to give Andrew Walczak credit here—the person who wrote the article about our experience—because when we gave our permission to write up our experience he verbally acknowledged that it would focus on the medical outcomes of the birth and wouldn't address the emotional hardships suffered. This chapter is not a critique of Walczak's article but rather a critique of a healthcare system that privileges a physically healthy baby above all else. The outcomes of a birth that focuses on the physical health, and not the mental health, of the birthing parent alone are not always positive, as our case attests.

The well-trodden adage in birthing dialogues that "all that matters is a healthy baby" is a pertinent issue for feminist scholars, and our story is proof that this is an inadequate yardstick to measure the success of a birth by. Milli Hill's popular new book, *Birth Like a Feminist*, reiterates what feminist birth activists have been saying for decades—that maternity care exists within and is, therefore, strongly affected by a patriarchal system that prioritizes the outcome of a live, healthy baby, sometimes at the expense of the birthing person's autonomy or mental health. As Hill argues, however, health does not "begin and end with simply having a pulse" (23). A healthy baby needs a healthy parent, and trauma, guilt, grief, and disempowerment can affect not only the birthing parent but also their relationship with their child: "A good outcome is most often measured not in terms of the woman, her feelings, her experience, and her postnatal mental health, but on the idea of the 'healthy baby'—indeed, women are frequently told that this is all that matters" (Hill 23). Hill then goes on to discuss how the subtext here is that the birthing person doesn't matter and that any negative experiences during the birth should be forgotten.

In more philosophical terms, maternal theorist Iris Marion Young describes the issue as follows: "Pregnancy does not belong to the woman herself" (45) but is instead claimed by those health professionals presiding over the pregnant body. Drawing on historical philosophies of medicine, she describes earlier approaches to health as being far more holistic than the current medical model and as strongly valuing physical as well as mental wellbeing in assessments of an individual's health (59). The Australian health system has gone through several overhauls in recent years, and it now professes to be similarly holistic, encompassing physical as well as mental health. But when push comes to shove, this inadequacy of the system is glaringly obvious. As Young goes on to argue: "Medicine must shed its self-definition as primarily concerned with curing. Given that nearly all aspects of human bodily life and change have come within the domain of medical institutions and practices, such a definition is no longer appropriate" (59).

Birthing in a Pandemic: Risk and Safety

In the case of birthing during a pandemic, it is apparent that the primary concern of medical professionals is to avoid death or transmission of the virus. In Walczak's article about the birth, he and his colleagues state: "This case demonstrates that patients with cystic fibrosis and pregnancy can have favourable outcomes in the setting of COVID-19. These patients should be managed by a multidisciplinary team to ensure optimal care, including infection control to prevent transmission, and consideration of parental wishes with regards to delivery and care of the neonate following birth." Optimal care is here first defined as "including infection control to prevent transmission," which is reasonable in itself, and, second, as the "consideration of parental wishes with regards to delivery and care of the neonate following birth." It is true that our wishes were considered regarding how the baby was birthed, who would be there, and that the baby would not be removed from my partner afterwards. However, regarding our wishes to be kept together as a family, or at least to be able to visit each other, transmission risks trumped our emotional needs, which were largely overlooked.

Hill talks repeatedly about the tendency of medical research to overlook the birthing person's experience, particularly when analyzing the risks and benefits of certain procedures (202). Diana Parry concurs: "Within medicalized contexts women's lived experiences with pregnancy are pushed to the periphery, ensuring women's perspectives and insights are rarely told, heard, or given any authority" (786).

It is glaringly obvious that Walczak's article makes no mention of the birthing parent or partner's health. We were also never asked how the experience had been for us. Had we been asked, our version would have been told differently. As Hill notes: "Leading bodies such as the World Health Organisation have expressed concern that the medicalisation of childbirth, with its focus on how to monitor, measure and control birth, has left the question of how women actually *feel* about their births completely off the agenda, potentially robbing them of a life-enhancing experience" (11). Hill later goes on to attribute "the justification for the over-medicalisation of birth or even for treatment lacking in empathy or compassion" (61) to risk and risk aversion, which refers to birth activist Sheila Kitzinger's studies of birth as illuminating "just how much of the humanity and spirituality of the event have been swallowed up in the medical quest for safety" (142). As Hill argues in relation to inductions, discussions regarding risk always focus on the risk of death for the baby if not induced, yet they rarely, if ever, discuss the risks inductions themselves pose or the effects an induction can have on the birthing person's mental health (202-4).

The decisions made regarding our family, as well as my partner's birth, privileged COVID-19-related risks above all else. It is interesting to note that there were no considerations for the risks posed to holding two young children in small rooms in quarantine for an extended amount of time, with no toys, games, or even access to internet provided by the hospital. This issue is, of course, not limited to our family—plenty of research is currently being conducted on the effect of COVID-19 and local lockdowns, home quarantine, and school closures on children across the world (Golberstein, Wen, and Miller; Liu et al.; Jones et al.). In relation to the attempts to bully my partner into an early induction, the dialogue regarding our choices always remained completely focused on the safety of the baby and on the virus. As with most births, we wanted what was best for the baby, so this wasn't something we were particularly cognisant of at the time, but when retrospectively reviewed through a feminist lens, it's impossible not to acknowledge this emphasis. Rarely are birthing people in the hospital system reminded that it is their body and their choices, and even more rarely is it made clear that it is always the birthing person's right to refuse treatment, even if it endangers them or their unborn child (Hill 36). An extreme example of this is a case Hill refers to in which a Brazilian court ordered Adelir—a person who was nine months pregnant at the time—to have a caesarean due to concerns that the baby would be at risk during an unassisted birth. Hill describes this as the long arm of the patriarchy, using risk assessments as a form of control over birthing bodies. Hill quotes Elizabeth Prochaska about the dangers inherent in risk discourse:

> Risk might sound appealingly scientific and rational, but it is not. When it is used to compel women to receive medical interventions, it is an expression of violent patriarchy, pure and simple. Would a Brazilian court order a man to undergo an invasive kidney transplant to save his dying child? No. Only women's bodies are treated as public objects subject to the whims of the medical profession backed by the coercive power of the state. (35)

The fact that in our case we would have made whatever decisions were deemed necessary to keep the baby safe is beside the point. Nobody considered that we might have wanted to do something other than what was medically recommended, and, consequently, certain choices were never presented to us.

A Middle Ground?

The solution Hill suggests to bridge the divide between a medical or a patient-focused perspective is to find a middle road that supports both safety concerns and the birthing person's autonomy. Hill quotes Professor Soo Downe in her efforts to shift birthing dialogue from an "either-or" attitude to a more encompassing "both-and" approach: "All those who want to improve maternity care, and outcomes for mother and baby, need to move to a 'both-and' message. This is about both safety and positive experience; both mother and baby; both clinical and psychosocial outcomes; both short and longer-term benefits" (143-44). For our family, respectful care would have meant valuing the importance of physical contact as a family as well as arranging for us to visit each other at a crucial family time. This would have meant assessing mental as well as physical health when caring for my partner and me and, more importantly, for our children. And this would have meant looking beyond the virus and treating us not only as COVID-19 patients but as human beings with emotional and social needs. As Hill notes, "When those situations that truly do require medical help arise, respectful care means continuing to keep women and their feelings at the heart of every action" (277). Ours was not a situation that required an either/or approach.

While writing this chapter, I have been tempted numerous times to temper my anger with such statements as "I don't want to sound ungrateful" or to make it clear that having a healthy baby was paramount and that in light of this, the traumas experienced by my family were relatively insignificant. However, I am aware that this perspective stems from my own socialized relationship with health services, which is always to be grateful as opposed to engaged. There were many individuals in the hospital who were kind and generous and compassionate to us all. But individuals alone do not comprise a system; rather, it is a series of underpinning philosophies, patriarchal histories, and insurance risk assessments. As Hill notes, "Listening to women, caring for them as individuals, and respecting them as the key decision maker in the birth room should cease to be seen as a shining beacon in the darkness and start to be viewed as the baseline norm" (11). Birthing people have the right to respectful birth experiences, regardless of the risks involved and regardless of whether or not they are birthing during a pandemic. Regardless of the risks, it is the birthing person who should make the final decisions regarding their own body as well as that of their unborn child. Feminists have fought long and hard for this right, but when faced with the current position of the Australian medical profession, it is easy to see that this dialogue still has a long way to go. But our story speaks to more than just the issues regarding patriarchal approaches to birth.

My family's situation is emblematic of the current response to COVID-19 in Australia, where physical health is being privileged above, and to the detriment of, mental health. Politicians and medical professionals are navigating extremely difficult circumstances in trying to protect our population, but if mental health continues to be overlooked to the extent that it currently is being neglected, the impact of COVID-19 will be far surpassed by a mental health epidemic that will affect both our health and our economy for many decades to come.

Works Cited

Davis, Deborah L., and Kim Walker. "Case-Loading Midwifery in New Zealand: Making Space for Childbirth." *Midwifery* vol. 26, no. 6, 2010, pp. 603-08.

Golberstein, Ezra, Hefei Wen, and Benjamin F. Miller. "Coronavirus Disease 2019 (COVID-19) and Mental Health for Children and Adolescents." *Jama Pediatrics*, vol. 174, no. 9, 2020, pp. 819-20.

Hill, Milli. *Give Birth Like a Feminist*. Harper Collins, 2019.

Inhorn, M. C. "Defining Women's Health: A Dozen Messages from More Than 150 Ethnographies." *Medical Anthropology Quarterly*, vol. 20, no. 3, 2006, pp. 345-78.

Jones, Benjamin, et al. "COVID-19 Pandemic: The Impact on Vulnerable Children and Young People in Australia." *Journal of Paediatrics and Child Health*, vol. 56, no. 12, 2020, 1851-55.

Liu, Jia Jia, et al. "Mental Health Considerations for Children Quarantined because of COVID-19." *Lancet*, vol. 4, no. 5, 2020, pp. 347-49.

Parry, Diana C. "'We Wanted a Birth Experience, not a Medical Experience': Exploring Canadian Women's Use of Midwifery." *Health Care for Women International*, vol. 29, no. 8 2008, pp. 784-806.

Teijlingen, Edwin van. "A Critical Analysis of the Medical Model as used in the Study of Pregnancy and Childbirth." *Sociological Research Online*, vol. 10, no. 2, 2005, doi.org/10.5153/sro.1034. Accessed 13 Jan. 2021.

Walczak, Andrew et al. "COVID-19 in a Complex Obstetric Patient with Cystic Fibrosis." *Infection, Disease & Health*, vol. 25, no. 4, 2020, pp. 239-41.

Young, Iris Marion. "Pregnant Embodiment: Subjectivity and Alienation". *The Journal of Medicine and Philosophy*, vol. 9, no. 1, 1984, pp. 45-62.

Chapter Thirty

"Knowing That I Had a Choice Empowered Me": Preparing for and Experiencing Birth during a Pandemic

Alys Einion-Waller and Maeve Regan

Childbirth is the physical birth of the relationship between the
mother and her baby; the father or other parent and the baby, and a
new family. It is a critical time for the formation of secure
attachments, the bond of love that will tie the family together and
help lay a firm foundation in life.

—Lesley Page, xiv

The global impact of the COVID-19 pandemic is changing
people's lives at a basic level. Nowhere is that more tangible
than in the experience of pregnancy and birth. Women and
pregnant people[1] are experiencing radical changes to the provision of
care, higher levels of stress (Barišić; Abdoli et al.), and a lack of choice
concerning important birthing decisions, such as place of birth and
companionship (Walton). Little evidence supports current policies,
and these restrictions will likely have long-term negative effects on
the physical and psychological health of women and families

(Topalidou, Thomson, and Downe). The restriction of healthcare and education within maternity services reflects overmedicalized, patriarchal models of care, which are a direct threat to women and birthing people's human rights.

COVID-19 has affected people's perception of birth and their decision making and has increased their loneliness and isolation. There seems to be a degree of consensus among service providers that COVID-19 has negatively affected people's birthing experiences, but there has been little response from healthcare providers. Yet maternity care should be about providing what women and childbearing parents want and need, which includes the best level of safety possible as well as a positive psychosocial birthing experience (Downe, Finlayson, and Oladapo).

This chapter explores the experience of expectant parents who accessed Centred Birth hypnobirthing online classes during the COVID-19 pandemic between March and August 2020. We explore what centred-birth classes are and discuss the culture of midwifery as well as the context and content of the classes. Following three months of online classes, with a total of 109 attendees, a short, mixed-methods survey was sent to participants to explore their experience of giving birth during the pandemic. The study was subject to ethical scrutiny and approval by the Swansea University College of Human and Health Sciences Research Ethics Committee. There were twenty-five respondents; twenty-three had not yet had their babies, and two responded after their births. All were mothers. The questionnaire contained basic quantitative questions on aspects of the classes and birth preparation as well as a series of qualitative (open-ended) questions relating to fears around childbirth and the impact of COVID-19 on pregnancy and preparation for motherhood.

We discuss select findings from the qualitative research that reveal important issues in relation to fear, empowerment, information seeking, support, and the lived experience of being pregnant, birthing, and becoming a new mother during the pandemic. The data were first analysed by Alys, and then themes were reviewed by Maeve for internal validity. In this chapter, we focus on the three most important themes: knowledge is power; feeling cut off; and fear and choice and COVID-19.

What Is Centred Birth Hypnobirthing?

Centred Birth is a form of small-group antenatal education and hypnobirthing, which was moved into a free, online format at the start of the lockdown in the United Kingdom (U.K.). As facilitators (and midwives), we use our knowledge and experience to return power to parents through shared understanding and techniques for an empowered birth through emphasizing choice as well as maternal autonomy. In this way, the classes are matricentric and are grounded in the belief that "becoming and being a mother shapes a woman's sense of self and how she sees and lives in the world" (O'Reilly 16). The classes discuss the use of this knowledge and these techniques for all kinds of birth, including framing the medical team as a safety net while reinforcing the birthing person as central to the birthing experience and the importance of the birth partner. The techniques offered include information sharing, breathing exercises, language reframing, and hypnotic techniques; decision making, autonomy, and informed consent are all emphasized. The motto of the classes is "Centred Birth, It's All About You."

Access to Expertise

Midwives in the U.K. are the lead professionals for uncomplicated pregnancies and the main coordinators of care for birthing people with medical or obstetric needs. However, during the COVID-19 pandemic, many maternity services restricted access to midwives, reducing antenatal appointments to a bare minimum. All antenatal classes were cancelled. We see this as a sign of medicalization, which runs counter to the social model of care, which provides so many benefits to the mother, partner, and family. Research shows that midwifery activities support time and space for women to share their feelings and identify their needs antenatally; midwives help women exercise self-efficacy during their birth (Wright, Pincombe, and McKellar). Midwifery is a paradoxical profession: Practitioners make an unspoken yet concrete commitment to support women and birthing people (Crowther and Hall), which these authors seem to assume derives from the motivation to be a midwife, yet they are also closely regulated (and often restricted) by law and policy which may limit their ability to provide woman-centred care. The literature identifies that antenatal education, despite being offered pre-dominantly by midwives within healthcare services, can be seen as similarly incongruous; there is a tension between institutional norms and biomedical culture and a philosophy that women should be empowered throughout their birth experience (Brixval, Axelsen, and Lauemøller; Association for Improvement in the Maternity Services). Despite this, having access to expert knowledge is vital.

Our study shows that prior to the pandemic, participants had a good degree of trust in the systems and institutions of birth. Yet when the pandemic forced many of these services to stop, they were left in a state of panic. People had the basic expectation of giving birth in a hospital, as this appears to remain the place that most parents feel is safest. Yet the hospital has changed from a place of safety to a place of risk for many expectant women, and it would seem that this is due to the pandemic. Our classes took on a new meaning, and, for many, they were the only source of extended access to midwifery expertise as part of their preparation for childbearing.

Maternal Ways of Knowing

Mothers' access to knowledge and support in preparing for childbirth helps them feel both confident and safe during birth. Among first-time mothers, fear of the unknown is common. The literature also highlights expectant mothers do not understand what will happen during pregnancy (Borrelli, Walsh, and Spiby) even when they are not birthing during a pandemic. One of our participants had this fear of the unknown, specifically "not knowing how it will go, the signs, [or] what to look out for." This was in response to the question asking them to talk about their feelings about their pregnancy before the pandemic.

Contact with midwives is a vital part of developing the knowledge and understanding of reproduction, which helps women prepare for their birthing and to engage in the practice of mothering (O'Reilly). Developing knowledge and self-efficacy is part of the pregnancy journey. Expectant parents look to the authoritative knowledge of midwives and other healthcare professionals who are viewed culturally as experts. COVID-19 has made it harder for expectant parents to engage with that knowledge and expertise. One participant stated the following: "COVID-19 has exacerbated the fears ... largely because I am now concerned it will be more difficult to access support, from friends and family, healthcare professionals and other support groups that aren't currently running (e.g. breastfeeding groups) if I have any difficulties postbirth." This participant's account seems to suggest that pregnant women and pregnant persons do not have access to knowledge from professionals and peers that would have been usual before the pandemic. But as midwives, we can see that this belief is a side effect of the systems of power that limit maternal ways of knowing. During the pandemic, this lack of access prevents mothers from engaging in the processes of learning, reflection, and exploration that support them to "move away from silence and an externally-oriented perspective on knowledge and truth" to "subjective knowing" where "women become their own authorities" (Belenky, Clinchy, and Goldberger 54).

Midwives, doctors, and healthcare systems have created a system of knowledge that alienates women from their bodies as well as their birth experience. And they have kept that knowledge for themselves, as professionals. As a result, mothers lack a basic understanding of how their birthing bodies work and are denied access to the very healthcare systems that used to reassure them. One participant, for example, was not sure what would happen during the different stages, had never thought of giving birth to the placenta, and had assumed the best position for birth was lying down.

When asked if the classes helped make them feel more prepared for birth, mothers overwhelmingly replied in the positive, but this was frequently linked to access to knowledge relevant to the mother. One participant felt much more prepared after attending the class, as before, she "didn't have a clue about birth plans, placenta, different types of breathing, importance of skin to skin etc." This relationship between knowledge, understanding, and confidence suggests to us that a matricentric model of antenatal education supports mothers' self-efficacy. "I feel more knowledgeable, which, in turn, makes me feel more relaxed and prepared," concluded another participant.

These responses would then seem to reinforce the value of the classes in providing access to information that was otherwise much harder to reach during the pandemic. Regardless of the availability of online pregnancy preparation and birthing support, people still look to the experts and the science that they have been socialized to respect

(Shorey and Valerie) as part of their process of learning their own truths (Belenky, Clinchy and Goldberger). "I originally thought hypnobirthing would be a bit out there for me," one participant said. "But it was good to see it backed up by the science." Many respondents highlighted the value of having qualified midwives teaching the class, one citing the value of "reputable facilitators (lots of courses are private companies with little known about the facilitators)"; another said that "Alys and Maeve were incredibly knowledgeable, professional but approachable." Providing these classes by qualified midwives was, thus, an important factor in parents trusting the information and guidance provided. One nurse participant said it was important for her as a nurse that the classes "were being run by someone who was clearly qualified to be teaching the classes." The nurse also explained that having qualified people run the classes also helped her partner, as he was also a nurse, so he valued evidence-based approaches.

Midwives offer something that these parents otherwise would lack: time to ask questions as part of the process of developing subjective knowledge (Belenky, Clinchy, and Goldberger). The surveys have shown us what parents' key information needs are, and, consequently, we have adapted our classes' content to try to answer these questions before they are asked. What is harder to facilitate is the relationship -building and interpersonal learning that comes naturally from in-person antenatal education, which shall be addressed in our second theme below. Access to knowledge and expertise is a vital part of preparing for birth, and this is clearly lacking for the parents in our study.

Feeling Cut Off

The pandemic has affected the pregnancy and birth preparation experience by limiting social support and connection. People fear being alone in hospital, as family members who would normally be involved in the pregnancy, birthing, and transition into motherhood are no longer allowed to attend the birth. Awareness of this situation has made people reconsider consider home birth as an option. As one participant said, "Home felt safer than hospital during a pandemic." But even at home, there are limitations, which have an impact on the birthing experience: "I can no longer have my partner and my mum there... This is difficult because my mum and partner provide different types of support."

Mothers showed concern that they would have to stay in the hospital and their partners would miss the first few days of their babies' lives. Childbirth is not just the birth of a baby; it is also the birth of a family. It certainly seems that this pandemic has shown that our systems do not regard the psychosocial dimensions of the pregnancy and birth experience as being important, as compared to making sure babies are safely delivered (Lebel et al.).

This is a very medicalized approach. Even in a home birth during the pandemic, extended family will have to be in a different room, so the planned and expected (and needed) social and familial support will not be accessible for the mother. Moreover, for those who already have children, the worry of having childcare available when they have to go into the midwifery led unit (MLU) or a hospital is an added concern. The additional stress that is being piled on to women—through having to spend part of their early labour alone in a delivery suite waiting room or deciding which family members to exclude and send to another part of their home—can reasonably be expected to affect the natural progression of physiological labour (Buckley).

Based on the survey results, the participants associated the pandemic with social isolation and a lack of social support. One respondent expressed how they did not like attending medical appointments without their partner and how they felt cut off from other mothers. Another stated: "I feel that my partner will now be less involved during the birth process."

Considering the impact of pregnancy on mental health, and mental health on pregnancy, it seems absurd not to think of the effect of these restrictions and the pandemic on maternal wellbeing. Women used such words as "concerned," "worried," "nervous," "anxious," and "sad." Others lamented that wider support networks were no longer present. How can we foster a positive birth experience for the whole family if we limit access? These responses evidence the way that power is used in healthcare services, for example, allowing only the birth partner to be present at delivery. As midwives, we fight against the concept that healthcare professionals can allow or not allow things, which leads women to being separated from vital support. The impact of this separation of families during birth will have lasting consequences (Wang et al.).

Pregnant women have once again been required to act for the greater good and for the wellbeing of the wider society at great cost to themselves, and there seem to be no plans to fix this. We cannot allow systems, services, and care providers to continue to ignore the effect of a lack of regular social support on mothers/parents.

Lack of Access to Peer Support

The women in our study lack access to the typical sources of peer and social support that they had prior to the pandemic, which has heightened their existing fears around birth and parenting and has made them feel more isolated. One mother said she feels "cut off from all the other prenatal things [she] was planning on attending, [such as] yoga, prenatal aquatic classes, NCT classes."

These responses speak to our social context as well, which is dominated by individualist philosophy. For many mothers, therefore, peer support and parenting groups are a vital source of pregnancy engagement and part of their process of adjustment to their new identities as mothers. Without these, how will they form those identities?

A matricentric model of maternity care would consider the mother within her context. We should focus on matrifocality in maternity care systems, "in which a mother plays a role of cultural and social significance and in which motherhood is thematically elaborated and valued" (O'Reilly 17). It would appear that the opposite is happening in the U.K. context, which has had a negative impact on maternal identity formation and also on mental health.

Isolation, Lack of Support, and Maternal Mental Health and Wellbeing in the Transition to Motherhood

Perinatal support encompasses both professional support from midwives and peer support; both are linked in the literature to maternal mental wellbeing (Mcleish and Redshaw). Our study highlights the negative impact of COVID-19 restrictions, as participants noted how they felt very isolated and trapped, with no support and no one available for advice. Mothers are feeling lonely and isolated at a time when they need support more than ever. As one respondent said: "I have missed my family and friends and having that close social contact. For me, that is the hardest part."

All roads seemingly lead back to fear, uncertainty, and isolation, alongside what small comfort and empowerment are derived from the classes we offer. Similar findings in research into maternal mental health during the COVID-19 pandemic has also revealed significant increases in anxiety and fear during international lockdowns (Durankuş and Aksu; Mappa, Distefano, and Rizzo). In our study, these fears are predominantly linked to social isolation and support. As one participant said, "I also have new fears about my husband not being able to stay with me in hospital."

We know that the constant presence of a support person enhances the labour and birth experience, which is an important role for the midwife and a vital role for the birth partner (Sosa, Crozier, and Stockl). The research shows that such support enhances the experience and outcomes of birth and that it is best provided by someone with whom the birthing person already has a relationship (Lunda, Minnie, and Benadé). Is it really necessary to restrict partner attendance to this extent? We need a model of birth in which women stay at home until a midwife sees them to ensure they are in labour, so that their partner can stay with them the whole time. We know from personal experience that such a model could work; it would also include additional benefits of reducing unnecessary trips to the hospital in early labour and increase the number of home births. Throughout the pandemic, there have always been home visits, from postnatal community midwives and district nurses. Why is labour and birth considered an expendable community service when other healthcare needs are not?

As midwives, we find this expendability disturbing while appreciating the observable human impact of a terrible situation, being played out with women who are already in a time of change and increased vulnerability as they become mothers. These mothers are also being cut off from extended family, with one participant rhetorically asking, "What effect would not having family and friends around have on my own mental health"?

At least two participants did highlight the benefits of lockdown: more time at home with their partners and time to engage with their pregnancy and their own health (Milne et al.). But these benefits are certainly not available to all, and it is the lowest-paid members of the economy who have had to continue working throughout the pandemic, further entrenching existing heath disparities. The pandemic affects the normative social, familial, and peer-bonding dimensions of the transition to parenthood, which could have long-term effects on the mental health and wellbeing of parents, particularly mothers.

Fear, Choice, and COVID-19

Childbirth in Western culture is seen as fearful, and the roots of that fear are complex and related to our conceptualization of pregnancy, birth, women, and motherhood. Being pregnant during a pandemic—with sudden changes to the provision of maternity services and the awareness of an ever-present risk from a life-threatening virus—is bound to increase fear. It is no surprise that the theme of fear emerged in this study, but the literature also shows that antenatal education can alleviate fears, improve pregnancy outcomes, and improve mothers' knowledge about, and satisfaction with, birth, self-efficacy. and empowerment (İsbira, İnci and Öna; Byrne et al.).

This theme included typical cultural fears around birth in the U.K., particularly the fear of coping and of something going wrong. One participant wondered how she would cope with the pain or how her husband would feel at the birth or whether her baby would be okay. She also feared possible medical interventions, which contrasts with the general cultural assumption that hospital is the safest place to birth a baby (Banks).

COVID-19 has exacerbated fears and brought in new forms of stress, and our classes could not alleviate those fears; they could only offer participants the means to manage their feelings and reactions. As one participant said, "My anxieties have been relieved a lot; however, the anxieties surrounding COVID-19 are still present to some degree." Hypnobirthing classes, such as Centred Birth, focus directly on reducing fear, increasing confidence, and introducing techniques that mothers can use as tools to promote a calm birth. These classes also focus on autonomy, physiology, and choices as well as exercising these choices to optimize confidence in the birthing body.

During this study, women expressed a preference for a calm birth, and many specifically wanted to birth in water. The use of birth pools also promotes social distancing, without affecting the provision of optimal midwifery care, and there is no evidence that their use would present an infection risk (Burns et al.). But sadly, several participants reported that their access to water birth was restricted. By closing MLUs and limiting access to birth pools, pregnant women have fewer options for seeking an empowered birth. Birthing in an MLU is a good option for mothers, resulting in few complications in pregnancy, and can lead to a higher likelihood that these mothers continue with their care, improving the relationship between the midwife and the birthing family. So, it seems that the increased medicalization of birth under this pandemic has resulted in a greater potential for the dehumanization of birth. But there are examples of innovative and person-focused services that have maintained home birth, MLUs, and continuity services throughout the pandemic, which demonstrates that with the appropriate resources and political will, it is possible to support choice during a crisis.

The mothers in our study have a general fear of the future, which combines their fears of COVID-19 with their fears surrounding their transition to parenthood. Other fears relate to overmedicalization, unnecessary interventions, a traumatic birth, or being induced. These may be typical, but given the ways in which responses to the pandemic have resulted in increased medicalization of the birth experience, we wonder if this has accelerated a process of medical control, which the women are feeling. Some participants also feared contracting COVID-19 at the hospital, making women more reluctant to attend their appointments. But this goes deeper. These mothers expressed a real concern for their unborn children and the fear of bringing them into a world of great uncertainty and danger.

Conclusion

COVID-19 has affected important aspects of the maternal experience of pregnancy, birth, and the transition to parenting. Although our classes have helped mothers feel more relaxed, manage their anxieties, prepare for birth, feel confident in their choices, and enhance their knowledge and understanding about birth, they cannot completely alleviate the fears over the virus's impact on what they had come to expect for typical pregnancy care. What does this mean for family life? As we experience increased transmission rates and changing lockdown rules, policymakers and care providers should think how COVID-19 policies have affected the birth experience. If they ignore such concerns, however, it seems obvious they still operate with a mechanized view of birth as something which has to be achieved, regardless of the feelings and relationships of the birthing mother and other partners. At present, all that matters is keeping the baby safe and keeping the mother well enough to give birth, disregarding the humanized dimensions of pregnancy, birth care, and the lived experience of the birthing mother.

We can conclude, however, with a positive note. Despite the difficulties involved in providing parent education and support at a distance, via digital media, the classes seem to have had, overall, a positive impact on these parents' ability to prepare for their births. The classes have built confidence through enhancing knowledge and self-efficacy; they have reassured parents by providing access to expert knowledge and have helped them to reframe birth, even during a time of fear, as a positive, personal experience. The data from this study show that parents feel less nervous and anxious about their birth after having attended the classes. Participants said they felt "a little bit more relaxed" and "less nervous about the actual birth." They also felt "much more prepared," "calmer," and "more empowered." One mother in particular said she felt "really confident" about what her body could do after attending the class.

Despite the pandemic, we have provided a small number of expectant parents (just over two hundred, to date) with some support, information, and tools to take back some measure of pleasure and control as they prepare for birth. Our success underlines the need for midwives to be present during pregnancy so that they may share their knowledge and bolster individual self-belief. We must push back against medicalization to promote maternity care that is more humanised as well as woman centred. If the system does not support this, then it is we, the midwives, who must disseminate models of care that promote positive human contact, nurture relationships, and embody knowledge, which may allow mothers to move confidently into their mothering identity in a supportive space that reduces fear and provides the tools needed to adapt to uncertainty. As one participant said, "I feel more positive about being in control of my birth, have a clear understanding of the ability of my body and have a more positive view of childbirth."

Endnotes

1. In this chapter, we acknowledge that women and people of diverse genders may give birth; however, all our participants appear to be cisgender women, so the terms "women" and "mothers" are used to refer to participants where relevant. Elsewhere we use the inclusive form of "women and birthing people."

Works Cited

Abdoli, Amir, et al. "The COVID-19 Pandemic, Psychological Stress during Pregnancy, and Risk of Neurodevelopmental Disorders in Offspring: A Neglected Consequence." *Journal of Psychosomatic Obstetrics and Gynaecology*, vol. 41, no. 3 2020, pp. 1-2.

Association for Improvement in the Maternity Services. *What Matters to You? A Maternity Care Experience Survey.* AIMSI, 2010.

Banks, Amanda C. *Birth Chairs, Midwives and Medicine.* University Press of Mississippi, 1999.

Barišić, Anita. "Conceived in the Covid-19 Crisis: Impact of Maternal Stress and Anxiety on Fetal Neurobehavioral Development." *Journal of Psychosomatic Obstetrics & Gynecology,* vol. 41, no. 3, 2020, p. 246.

Belenky, Mary F., et al. *Women's Ways of Knowing.* Basic Books, 1997.

Borrelli, Sara E., Dennis Walsh, and Helen Spiby. "First-Time Mothers' Expectations of the Unknown Territory of Childbirth: Uncertainties, Coping Strategies and 'Going with the Flow." *Midwifery,* vol. 63, 2018, pp. 39-45.

Brixval, C.S., et al. "The Effect of Antenatal Education in Small Classes on Obstetric and Psycho-Social Outcomes—A Systematic Review." *Systematic Reviews,* vol. 4, 2015, p. 20.

Byrne, J. et al. "Effectiveness of a Mindfullness-Based Childbirth Education Pilot Study on Maternal Self-Efficacy and Fear of Childbirh." *Journal of Midwifery & Women's Health,* vol. 59, no. 2, 2014, pp. 192-97.

Crowther, Susan, and Jenny Hall. *Spirituality and Childbirth: Meaning and Care at the Start of Life.* Routledge, 2018.

Downe, S, et al. "What matters to women during childbirth: A systematic qualitative review." *PLoS ONE,* vol. 13, no. 4, 2018, doi.org/10.1371/

journal.pone.0194906. Accessed 13 Jan. 2021.

Durankuş, Ferit, and Erson Aksu. "Effects of the COVID-19 Pandemic on Anxiety and Depressive Symptoms in Pregnant Women: A Preliminary Study." *The Journal of Maternal-Fetal & Neonatal Medicine,* 2020, pp. 1-7, doi: 10.1080/14767058.2020.1763946. Accessed 13 Jan. 2021.

Hollins Martin, Caroline J. "A Narrative Literature Review of the Therapeutic Effects of Music Upon Childbearing Women and Neonates." *Complementary Therapies in Clinical Practice,* vol. 20, no. 4, 2014, pp. 262-67.

İsbira, Gözde Gökçe, et al. "The Effects of Antenatal Education on Fear of Childbirth, Maternal Self-Efficacy and Post-Traumatic Stress Disorder (PTSD) Symptoms Following Childbirth: An Experimental Study." *Applied Nursing Research,* vol. 20, no. 32, 2016, pp. 227-32.

Lebel, Catherine, et al. "Elevated Depression and Anxiety among Pregnant Individuals during the COVID-19 Pandemic." 2020, doi:10.31234/osf. io/gdhkt. Accessed 13 Jan. 2021.

Lunda, Petronellah, Catharina Susanna Minnie, and Petronella Benadé. "Women's Experiences of Continuous Support during Childbirth: A Meta-Synthesis." *BMC Pregnancy and Childbirth,* vol. 18, no. 167, 2018, pp. 1-11.

Mappa, Ilenia, et al. "Effects of Coronavirus-19 Pandemic on Maternal Anxiety during Pregnancy: A Prospectic Observational Study." *Journal of Perinatal Medicine,* vol. 48, no. 6, 2020, pp. 545-50.

Mcleish, Jenny, and Maggie Redshaw. "Mothers' Accounts of the Impact on Emotional Wellbeing of Organised Peer Support in Pregnancy and Early Parenthood: A Qualitative Study." *BMC Pregnancy and Childbirth,* vol. 17, no. 28, 2017, https://doi.org/10.1186/s12884-017-1220-0. Accessed 13 Jan. 2021.

Milne, Sarah J., et al. "Effects of Isolation on Mood and Relationships in Pregnant Women during the Covid-19 Pandemic." *European Journal of Obstetrics and Gynecology and Reproductive Biology,* vol. 252, 2020, pp. 610-11.

O'Reilly, Andrea. "Matricentric Feminism: A Feminism for Mothers." *Journal of the Motherhood Initiative,* vol. 10, no. 1-2, 2019, pp. 13-26.

Page, Lesley. "Foreword." *Spirituality and Childbirth: Meaning and Care at the Start of Life,* by Susan Crowther and Jenny Hall, Routledge, 2018, p. xiv.

Shorey, Shefaly, and C.H. Valerie. "Lessons from Past Epidemics and Pandemics and a Way forward for Pregnant Women, Midwives and Nurses during COVID-19 and Beyond: A Meta-Synthesis." *Midwifery,* vol 90, no. 102821, 2020, doi:10.1016/j.midw.2020.102821. Accessed 13 Jan. 2021.

Sosa, Georgina A., Kenda E. Crozier, and Andrea Stockl. "Midwifery One-to-One Support in Labour: More Than a Ratio." *Midwifery*, vol. 62, 2018, pp. 230-39.

Topalidou, Anastasia, Gill Thomson, and Soo Downe. "COVID-19 and Maternal Mental Health: Are We Getting the Balance Right?" *The Practising Midwife*, vol. 23, no. 7, 2020, doi:10.1101/2020.03.30.200479 69. Accessed 13 Jan. 2021.

Walton, Gill. "COVID-19. The New Normal for Midwives, Women and Families." *Midwifery*, vol. 87, no. 102736, https://doi.org/10.1016/j.midw.2020.102736. Accessed 13 Jan. 2021.

Wang, C. et al. "Immediate Psychological Responses and Associated Factors during the Initial Stage of the 2019 Coronavirus Disease (COVID-19) Epidemic among the General Population in China." *Int J Environ Res Public Health*, vol. 17, no. 5, 2020, p. 1729.

Wright, Diane, Jan Pincombe, and Lois McKellar. "Exploring Routine Hospital Antenatal Care Consultations—An Ethnographic Study." *Women and Birth*, vol. 31, no. 3, 2018, pp. e162-69.

Chapter Thirty One

Professional Perceptions of How Women Have Dealt with Pregnancy and Motherhood during the Chaos of the Brazilian COVID-19 Pandemic

Margareth Santos Zanchetta, Marcelo Medeiros,
Walterlânia Silva Santos, Luciana Alves de Oliveira,
Leonora Rezende Pacheco, Paula dos Santos Pereira,
Sheila Mara Pedrosa, Dalva Aparecida Marques da Costa,
and Daiana Evangelista Rodrigues

Sad, crazy or bad / will be qualified / she who refuses / follows such a recipe / the cultural recipe of the husband, of the family / cares, takes care of the routine / only rejects / well-known recipe / who does not suffer without pain / accepts that everything must change

—Francisco, el Hombre[1]

Introduction

Pandemic chaos has begun in Brazil, a country well-known for its inability to overcome health iniquities (Ortega and Orsini). The country has witnessed the resignation of two federal Ministry of Health leaders in a period of three months and, since then, the pro tempore designation of a military person (who is not a health-trained individual) to coordinate nationwide actions to tackle the COVID-19 pandemic. With an average of more than 1,100 deaths per day from June to August 2020, pregnant women—who are in a particular state of social, physical, emotional, and mental vulnerability—are highly at risk. In every segment of society, pregnant women are counted among the dead. Social media widely disseminates information to raise awareness about preventative behaviours against COVID-19 for pregnant women and their significant others. Table 1 displays the nationwide distribution of COVID-19.

Table 1. Cases, Incidence, Death, and Mortality COVID-19, August 31, 2020.

Region	Pop	New cases	Cumu-lative cases	Cumu-lative cases per 100,000	New deaths	Cumu-lative deaths	Cumu-lative deaths per 100,000
North	18,430.980	1,774	537,057	2,914	73	13,476	73
North east	57,067.704	2,643	1,145.097	2,007	162	35,120	62
Centre west	16,281.136	4,313	434,831	2,671	108	9,228	57
South east	88,371.433	3,684	1,355.791	1,534	106	54,572	62
South	29,945.084	33,547	435,496	1,454	104	8,985	30
Total	210,096.337	45,961	3,908.272	1,860	553	121,381	58.0

Source: Ministério da Saúde—Brasil ("Protocolo de manejo clínico do coronavírus")

The pandemic, however, has also unleashed a great amount of illegitimate information (Vasconcellos-Silva and Castiel), limiting the population's ability to decode health information and differentiate reliable from fake news, which has been spread by social media and some professional news outlets. Consequently, any efforts to educate the population about preventative, protective measures were jeopardized, especially among those facing health iniquities due to gender, education, employment, race etc. The low incidence of illiteracy among Brazilian women (7.9 per cent)—as well as their high access to education (women compose 51.75 per cent of students enrolled in presecondary programs and 55 per cent in post-secondary education [Instituto Nacional de Estudos e Pesquisas Educacionais Anísio Teixeira])—resulted in the misleading expectation that they would adhere to COVID-19 information.

To address the frontline situation of pandemic chaos, this chapter explores health professionals' perceptions about women's feelings, expectations, and concerns about mothering and infection prevention during the COVID-19 pandemic while offering guidelines for how to better humanize obstetric care and current infection control protocols and procedures.

Mothering in Brazil

Per the 2010 census, women account for 51 per cent of the Brazilian population. The Brazilian birthrate dropped from 20.14 per cent in 1995 to 13.69 per cent in 2010. Currently, northern Brazil has the highest fertility rate, with 2.51 children per woman (Francisco), and the region also has the highest incidence of COVID-19 (Table 1). However, understanding the social and cultural relevance of motherhood and mothering for Brazilian women goes beyond statistical interpretation. In Brazil, Fábio Fonseca states that pregnancy can be a period that involves paradox, complex sensations, and emotions that can significantly influence women's mental health. Pregnancy can affect the way women establish social relations within their support networks because the awareness of becoming a mother brings intense changes in one's conceptions of motherhood. The meanings of motherhood are grounded in a woman's previous (personal or social) experiences of motherhood.

A mother's role is supported by its lived sociability and the existing modes of mothering in such sociability. An array of feelings is experienced, including uncertainty and a concern about balancing roles, all of which are added to anxiety about living up to the ideals of good motherhood. Such ideals include the idea that a good mother feels guilty for being unable to stay home with her kids. Thus, women's life trajectories are built around choices and meanings about motherhood and mothering, which are influenced by the values, stories, and cultures that shape women's social behaviours (Machado, Penna, and Caleiro).

The process of women's emancipation, which entails the freedom to choose or not to choose stereotypical gender roles, has not freed all women from the role of providing care to their children, husbands, partners, and elderly relatives while performing domestic chores. This lack of freedom, especially in the lives of pregnant women and new mothers, represents a global concern, as an epidemic of domestic violence has unfolded in the home environment during lockdown. This epidemic has only worsened Brazil's negative record of violence against women and further highlighted the country's inability to solve it.

Mothering in Times of COVID-19

Brazil is currently the top country for the mortality of pregnant women due to COVID-19, accounting for 77.5 per cent deaths worldwide from Dec. 2019 to July 2020 (Nakamura-Pereira et al.). An analysis was performed regarding 124 COVID-19 deaths of Brazilian pregnant women and those in puerperium from February 26 to June 18, 2020; these deaths were attributed to COVID-19 because of the presence of a severe respiratory syndrome (Takemoto et al.). The analysis demonstrated that 22.6 per cent of those women did not have access to an intensive care unit. Moreover, 36 per cent were not intubated for artificial respiration. The rate of maternal death from infection was 12.7 per cent. The hypotheses to explain these high mortality rates include low-quality prenatal care, insufficient supply of material resources in the emergency room, and difficulty in accessing health services during the pandemic (Takemoto et al.). It is noteworthy that the Brazilian Ministry of Health published a protocol for the clinical management of

COVID-19, which extended to pregnant women diagnosed twenty-six to forty weeks into gestation; the protocol was based on mothers' and fetuses' actual needs, analysis of safety, risks and benefits, and safe use of medications (Protocolo de manejo clínico).

Table 2 also includes the combined incidence of COVID-19 with dengue, chikungunya, and Zika. (These three are urban arboviruses transmitted by the mosquito called *Aedes Aegypti*). An additional risk for pregnant women is the low rate of vaccinations against other infections (e.g., measles, rubella, and influenza) in other population groups (e.g., children, youth, seniors). Notably, documented concomitant infection rates may decrease due to an under-reporting of cases during the pandemic.

Table 2. Distribution of the Three Top Concomitant Epidemic Tropical Diseases, July 2020.

	Dengue		Chikungunya		Zika	
Region	Cases	Incidence per 100,000	Cases	Incidence per 100,000	Cases	Incidence per 100,000
North	18,771	101.8	902	4.9	373	2.0
North east	108,105	189.4	27,54	48.3	2,936	5.1
Centre west	175,735	1,078.3	680	4.2	482	3.0
South east	294,609	333.4	18,656	21.1	783	0.9
South	276,873	923.6	537	1.8	92	0.3
Total	**874,093**	**415,9**	**48,316**	**23.0**	**4,666**	**2.2**

Source: Boletim Epidemiológico # 51 (Ministério da Saúde—Brasil. "Programa de Humanização no Pré-natal e Nascimento")

Obstetric care in Brazil during the pregnancy-postpartum continuum is delivered according to the Program of Humanization in Prenatal and Childbirth (PHPN) guidelines. This program transformed the philosophy of delivering obstetric and neonatal care in Brazil and aims to improve its quality and capacity. The program's goal is to have fewer technical interventions and implement procedures to better respond to women's social, emotional, physical, moral, cultural, and environmental issues from the prenatal until the puerperium. The PHPN operates in harmony with the principles of the Unified Health System; this system aims to increase access to services and care (Programa de Humanização).

Exploring the Reality in the Context of Obstetric Care

The methodological choice used in this chapter relied on a modified method of rapid participatory appraisal (RPA) of community needs (Annett, Rifkin, and World Health Organization). The RPA is a way of collecting and analyzing information in the field in a short period of time; it involves not only minimal cost and minimal expenditure of professional time but also the high involvement of community members. The results provide an overall map of the situation but no real details. The chosen method for the appraisal was an ethnographic assessment to appraise community beliefs and practices in relation to disease-specific interventions. This method collected only relevant and necessary data in an ethical way while involving the community.

Because it was impossible to physically meet the participants, remote consultations were conducted with professionals about changes in obstetric care due to the pandemic. The consultations were conducted by email, social media, as well as phone calls and messaging for three weeks from May to June 2020. They were asked to answer the following question in one hundred words: How are you perceiving women's attitudes in their experience in being a mother in times of a pandemic? Requests were sent to obstetric nurses, community health nurses, community health agents (CHAs), members of the multidisciplinary health teams, as well as managers and decision makers who freely accepted our invitation to collaborate. The answers were coded following qualitative content analysis of findings and interpretation (Hesse-Biber and Leavy).

Professionals' Perceptions about Mothers' Attitudes and Behaviours

The consulted professionals were mostly in the middle of their careers: Nineteen nurses had an average of ten years of experience in obstetric care (ranging from six months to twenty-nine years); two CHAs had an average of eighteen years of professional experience in primary healthcare; one doula reported eight years of experience; and one lawyer had three years of experience in legal matters relating to healthcare. The data gathered from these twenty-three professionals revealed how they perceived mothers' conceptualization of mothering as it related to COVID-19 uncertainties and how they would better harmonize women's and the healthcare system's demands.

Emerging Meanings of Mothering

The meaning mothers found in mothering seems to be affected by the context of a planned or unplanned pregnancy and its relationship to the timing of the pandemic. Nurses said some women were unhappy that they had become pregnant, saying that, because of COVID-19 it had occurred at the wrong moment. Women who had planned their pregnancy tended to regret it mostly because it was happening in an unappealing context. Women expressed their apprehension about the unknown nature of COVID-19. At the prenatal consultations, nurses often observed women's high emotional fragility due to the fear they had, which tended to be higher than the general population.

During the pandemic, women were forced to abandon months of joyful expectations, plans of breastfeeding, family arrangements to share newborn care, and other dynamics of social support. Women were afraid that they or their baby could become infected by the SARS-CoV-2 virus. (these fears were more concentrated in *primipara* women) through receiving ambulatory care or staying in the maternity ward. Such concerns were also identified by CHAs in their home visits to pregnant women in order to monitor women's self-care for those already living under lockdown. One CHA had this to say: "I saw their insecurity; they feared infection for themselves and their babies. They felt alone, without … help from relatives, especially those who are first-time mothers who are experiencing everything alone." Another

CHA added: "[These women] were very anxious having contact with ... people ... and only leaving home ... for their last prenatal consultations that are mandatory."

In the context of community life, the lockdown increased social isolation for women because they lost their social networks, which was especially difficult for those who had no partner or husband. The lockdown has also increased gender inequity in the family as well as in work relations. Therefore, making mothering more of a social experience, with the participation of family members and friends, remains a priority for women despite the specific demands of the pandemic.

Unsafe Mothering in Time of a Pandemic

Pregnant women and those in the puerperium are concerned about COVID-19 because they do not know its severity, how to treat it, and, mainly, how they will deal with the effects of the pandemic once at home with their babies. After national COVID-19 cases peaked, unsafe attitudes among pregnant women were observed. Nurses reported women's intentions to maintain their labour plan despite it being unsafe (as indicated by the PHPNC). However, this could be understood on the basis of its being a plan that was created at the early stages of the pregnancy, and was not necessarily a denial of COVID-19. In fact, women wanted to have their plan unchanged while acknowledging the pandemic. One nurse said the following:

At the beginning of the pandemic, the fear of having the infection in its severe form was greater than now. They [pregnant women] accepted the rigour regarding the use of masks [even while in labour] and wept a lot when they saw that their children were born well and without infection ...

One CHA also said: "Some are afraid, but others do not see that we are in a pandemic."

Increased fear among women of a low socioeconomic status is related to their inability to stay in a full lockdown. Commonly, these women, or those they live with, have informal work, which they cannot do from home. They are at a greater risk of being infected by the virus. These women travel to the prenatal clinics and maternity ward by bus, but they all wear masks; still, the experience causes them great anxiety. When they see the nurses at the clinics and the maternity ward, however, dressed in their protective gear, they become more relaxed.

Changes Brought to Obstetric Care Practices by the Pandemic's New Order in the Chaos

Changes caused by the pandemic are also relevant for women who were classified as at pregnancy risk and who, thus, required more professional attention and special care. At-risk pregnancy women tend to voice more doubts about care, including delivery, whether their partner will be allowed to attend the birth, the unfolding of intrapartum care, and the possibility of being helped by relatives. Awareness of being an at-risk pregnancy creates a constant fear of developing COVID-19 and its consequences for pregnancy, labour, and the newborn's safety. Alternatively, women who consider themselves at no risk during pregnancy require special professional attention because they may not stay in lockdown and potentially expose themselves to risky situations (e.g., being in crowded spaces). Therefore, feeling they have no risk of being infected with COVID-19 may cause some pregnant women to develop incorrect ideas regarding safety and COVID-19.

Delays surrounding prenatal follow-ups also increased women's fear of the pandemic due to their lack of knowledge about the effects of COVID-19 on the fetus's health. During the first week of the pandemic, prenatal services were interrupted due to the lack of personal protection equipment (PPE). They eventually resumed, but some women initially resisted wearing a mask. Although availability of PPE remains a concern, some organizations incentivize safety by offering masks to those who show up for their prebooked consultations, thus preventing crowding in the waiting rooms.

Due to the growing panic regarding COVID-19 among pregnant women, increased commitment to preventative care and prenatal follow-ups has been observed. The reductions in resources in the public health system make access to laboratorial exams limited. In-person puerperium consultations were suspended as a preventative measure; follow-ups are now supposed to be replaced by CHAs on their monthly home visits.

The new routines in the maternity wards contradict the statement in the Pregnant Woman's Card (a document that displays rights outlined in the PHPN). The main conflict regards the denial of an accompanying person during labour and child birth. For example, currently, it is the mother's exclusive responsibility to care for the newborn during postpartum; however, it is traditionally a grandmother's responsibility to care for the new mother and newborn at their home. As one lawyer said:

> The overlooking of conquered [obstetric care] rights ... has been one of the main complaints: the prohibition of accompanying people in the delivery room; mother-newborn contact in the postpartum and breastfeeding.... The prohibition of mothers to see their babies in the ICU ... the increase in the [unnecessary] number of C-sections and the pressure on women to opt for this type of delivery.

One doula talked about the situation regarding doulas and COVID-19 in relation to pregnant women:

> Prohibitions on the presence of the doula at the time of delivery ... [can lead] to the insecurity of many pregnant women; some have sought legal action to maintain their rights of visitation.... Some women have enjoyed the ban on visits, since they can practice motherhood their way without intrusion.... Some though feel very alone ... a solitary puerperium.... These mothers have remained in social isolation and use tools, such as digital platforms, to communicate with others who are experiencing the same situation.

Mothers' Strategies to Comply with the New Context of Obstetric Care

Women have adapted to the new health services norms during the pandemic, including the need to look for other maternity services, even if they are far from their home. Puerperium home visits performed by the prenatal professionals were also interrupted by the new protocols. As one nurse explained:

[The government] discontinued prenatal care. Maternity wards are overcrowded ... four hundred deliveries per month had to be done in other hospitals, whose situation was already chaotic. Another aspect is the discontinuity of reproductive planning, without . . . contraceptive [methods]. Women are looking for strategies to take care of themselves, using teleservice.

And another nursed added: "Despite some manifestations of anger and frustration regarding the new way of delivering services, women express their gratitude for nurses and physicians who take care of each of them with kindness amid the pandemic."

Women have also changed their behaviour at consultations by asking more questions, potentially decreasing subsequent visits to the clinics. They are using social media through mobile apps and enrolling in online groups with other pregnant women and mothers to help them with any doubts. A nurse working in telenursing also reported a trend of self-medication with over the counter substances in cases of suspected COVID-19, caused by the fear of seeking emergency consultation.

Women's intentions when collaborating with professionals are sometimes unsuccessful in ensuring care continuity, due to two reasons: (a) inconsistencies in home address and phone number make it impossible for professionals to reach out to women for clinical follow-ups or updates about changes in the service's delivery and availability (e.g., blood tests and changes in consultations); and (b) instability in the services' organization limits obstetric nurses from implementing a consistent prenatal and postpartum follow up.

Summary of the Consultation

This RPA highlights opportunities for redesigning services and implementing new collaboration with the clientele in obstetric care. Ignoring women's obstetric rights (still occurring in some regions of the country) was uncovered as the main concern for advocates of humanized obstetric care. In fact, a modified context of obstetric care jeopardizes some advances in the implementation of the PHPN. The consultation's key findings are as follows:

    a.   Professionals face a dilemma between mothers' and newborns' rights that are assured by the PHPN and the implemented COVID-19 infection control protocols;

b. Professionals' advocacy is redirected from the individual (the woman) to the collective (woman, her family, acquaintances, and surroundings, as well as their coworkers);

c. Professionals' care ensures a sense of being cared for, even during the disruption caused by the pandemic in the interpersonal contact during the prenatal period;

d. Mothers lost their protagonist role in the decision-making process due to COVID-19 infection control procedures and new organizational norms;

e. Mothering means being alone and fearing for their children's safety; and

f. Telehealth and social media are helping professionals and mothers to ensure care continuity, safety, and social connectedness.

The RPA was unable to identify the impact of COVID-19-related guidelines on the family-newborn relationship and their repercussions on women's physical, emotional and mental health, social wellbeing, and overall personal safety.

Closing Remarks

In early August 2020, at the time of this chapter's writing, the alarming rate of death among pregnant women led seventeen Brazilian health professional organizations to jointly issue two documents. The first, issued by nursing professional associations, specifically urges the creation of a parliamentary commission of inquiry to investigate the lack of access to emergency care and update the number of women's deaths (Conselho Federal de Enfermagem). The second is a national plan to tackle the COVID-19 pandemic (Associação Brasileira de Saúde Coletiva et al.), which was proposed by a pool of public health associations that emphasized the following:

The emergence of the COVID-19 pandemic accentuates inequities generated by race/colour, class, ethnicity, gender, age, disabilities, geographical origin. and sexual orientation. As the experience of other epidemics shows, in particular women have been strongly impacted by COVID-19. However, all the measures adopted so far by governments have been directed at the population in general, without taking into account the different population segments in the production of data and action strategies.

Moreover, Associação Brasileira de Saúde Coletiva et al.'s plan highlights the absolute need to investigate those who remain neglected or invisible to society (e.g., the homeless and migrants) as well as vulnerable, isolated individuals and groups (e.g., women, seniors, Indigenous, children, LGBTQQIP2SAA) that demand urgent, prioritized, and coordinated action. Therefore, actions are needed to "[trigger a process] for the reconstruction of living and health conditions based on the values of freedom, equality and solidarity, in an effectively democratic Brazil".

The RPA findings provided an important local snapshot of health professionals' perceptions about obstetric care amid the dissemination of fake and inappropriate health information about COVID-19, which created confusion and insecurity among pregnant women. The findings also illuminated a serious primary healthcare issue regarding services' planning and delivery, as well women's health literacy guiding a multidisciplinary reflection for decision making, aiming to increase women's and newborns' protection. The knowledge generated by the RPA can help health professionals as well as women, partners, and families examine the effectiveness of health services and the repercussions of neglecting women's health and obstetric rights. However, the findings can be limited in their transferability because informants did not address women's experiences according to their sexual orientation, ethnocultural belonging, age, and marital and economic status. Still, this RPA has amplified voices from the field— voices of frontline health workers who are heroically battling against a deadly virus amid public health chaos.

Acknowledgment

The authors thank Dr. Maria Antonieta Rubio Tyrrell (Brazilian Association of Obstetric Nurses and Midwives and Federal University of Piauí-Brazil), an obstetric nurse, and Dr. Elyana Teixeira Sousa (Federal University of Mato Grosso), a public health nurse, for their critical review of this manuscript, enhancing its quality. We also express our appreciation to Michael LaPointe for his support for the manuscript development and linguistic editing. Our special "Obrigada" goes to our colleagues, Leonora and Daiana, who despite their maternity leave, resumed their intellectual work and remained engaged in the final phase of this project.

Funding: Editorial support was provided by the Faculty of Community Services, Ryerson University (Toronto-Canada)—Writing Week Initiative 2020.

Endnotes

1. The lyrics are about the meaning of women's life in their family context. Composed by Mexican and Brazilian artists, the song portrays the cultural role of women in their social realm in Latin America.

Works Cited

Associação Brasileira de Saúde Coletiva et al. *Plano Nacional de Enfrentamento à Pandemia da COVID-19.* 2020.

Annett, Hugh, Susan B. Rifkin, and the World Health Organization. "Guidelines for Rapid Participatory Appraisals to Assess Community Health Needs: A Focus on Health Improvements for Low-Income Urban and Rural Areas." *World Health Organization,* apps.who.int/iris/handle/10665/59366. Accessed 14 Jan. 2021.

Fonseca, Fábio. "A constituição do mundo e de si-próprio no enlace existencial mãe-bebê." *Revista abordagem Gestalt,* vol. 23, no. 3, 2017, pp. 326-33.

Francisco, Wagner. "Taxa de decundidade no Brasil." *Mundo Educação,* 2020, mundoeducacao.uol.com.br/geografia/taxa-fecundidade-no-brasil.htm. Accessed 14 Jan. 2021.

Francisco, el Hombre. "Triste, louca ou má." *YouTube,* 5 Oct. 2016, www.youtube.com/watch?v=lKmYTHgBNoE. Accessed 14 Jan. 2021.

Instituto Nacional de Estudos e Pesquisas Educacionais Anísio Teixeira. "Mulheres são maioria na educação profissional e nos cursos de graduação." *Inep,* 2020, inep.gov.br/artigo/-/asset_publisher/B4AQV9 zFY7Bv/content/mulheres-sao-maioria-na-educacao-profissional-e-nos-cursos-de-graduacao/21206. Accessed 14 Jan. 2021.

Machado, Jacqueline, Cláudia Maria de Mattos Penna, and Regina Caleiro. "Cinderella's Shoe Broken: Maternity, No Maternity, and Parenting in

Stories Told by Women." *Saúde em Debate*, vol. 43, no.123, 2019, pp. 1120-31.

Ministério da Saúde—Brasil. "Programa de Humanização no Pré-natal e Nascimento." Portaria 569/2000 Ministério da Saúde; 2020, www.saude.gov.br/images/pdf/2020/July/14/Boletim-epidemiologico-SVS-28-v2.pdf. Accessed 14 Jan. 2021.

Ministério da Saúde—Brasil. "Protocolo de manejo clínico do coronavírus (COVID-19) na atenção primária à saúde." *Ministério da Saúde*, 2020, saude.rs.gov.br/upload/arquivos/202004/14140606-4-ms-proto colomanejo-aps-ver07abril.pdf. Accessed 14 Jan. 2021.

Nakamura-Pereira, Marcos, et al. "Worldwide Maternal Deaths due to COVID-19: A Brief Review. *International Journal of Gynecology & Obstetrics*, vol. 151, no. 1, 2020, 148-50.

Ortega, Francisco, and Michael Orsini. "Governing COVID-19 without Government in Brazil: Ignorance, Neoliberal Authoritarianism, and the Collapse of Public Health Leadership." *Global Public Health*, vol. 15, no. 9, 2020, pp. 1257-77.

Takemoto, Maíra, et al. "The Tragedy of COVID-19 in Brazil: 124 Maternal deaths and Counting." *International Journal of Gynecology & Obstetrics*, vol. 151, no. 1, 154-56.

Vasconcellos-Silva, Paulo, and Luis Castiel. "COVID-19, Fake News, and the Sleep of Communicative Reason Producing Monsters: The Narrative of Risks and the Risks of Narratives." *Cadernos de Saúde Pública*, vol. 36, no. 7, 2020, p. e00101920.

Chapter Thirty Two

Smothered and Era Fever

Victoria Bailey

smothered

walled in i realized all i have done for generations is create
boundaries enforce them patrol them prevent them breaking i
kept a baby inside let it out and i kept it close in a make-safe
place i built each boundary barrier buffer swaddled tucked
padded checked rechecked face up face down don't touch touch
don't put that in your mouth eat turn that off put this on don't
say that repeat after me don't laugh smile don't stare look at
that don't forget to take this put that away do this don't do that
and then i had to say you can't see them stay inside don't go
wash your hands let me smell the soap i thought so wash them
again i enforced new conventions for all of them above me
and below and each one tested me and i was truly smothered

Era Fever

I burnt with anger
because when the façade fell
patriarchy ruled.

Chapter Thirty Three

Trans-cending COVID-19

Catherine Moeller

When COVID-19 struck in March 2020, I was on an eight-hour drive heading home from a professional development training week in Northern Ontario. Our lodgings for the previous week had no television or radio, and we were stunned to suddenly hear the news of all the schools across Ontario closing down due to COVID-19. On our journey home, my colleagues and I laughed a lot and made jokes about how armed guards with gas masks would soon be stopping our cars and spraying disinfectant mist on us. At that point, it was all a silly exaggeration to us.

I woke up the next morning back in Toronto with a terrible case of strep throat and to the sounds of a panicked media. My fifteen-year-old daughter was dancing around the house in delight that her March break had been extended. I had always felt that kids spent too much time in school in the mainstream education system, so I too was happy. With my daughter taking care of my strep throat, I lay in bed watching the news get more horrifying day by day. Prime Minister Trudeau came on the radio to announce that we were in a state of emergency and my wicked Strep throat drew itself out and returned with a vengeance as pneumonia.

Being seriously ill during the early days of the pandemic was deeply unnerving, with the reports of thousands of people fighting for their lives and having to be put on ventilators. In the midst of all of the early hype and terror of the disease, I was paralyzed by having to consider my own mortality. Painful memories of my parents on ventilators when they were passing away from chronic obstructive pulmonary disease kept running through my mind. My daughter brought me food to my bed when I could eat, and I supervised her preparation of many dinners and chores for the family as I lay wheezing and coughing in my bed. As always, when Mom is sick, all things functional in the household grind to a halt and sputter along with jumps and bangs.

I have been bringing up my child while living in a complicated partnership with the man that I call my ex-husband and his dependent brother. My ex suffers from severe and chronic depression, and his brother suffers with schizophrenia and other mental disorders. My brother-in-law is innocent and loyal and has the mind and abilities of an adolescent child; thus, I often feel that I am the only adult in the house.

Our home life is made more complicated, as we rent two of our bedrooms to a revolving array of international students. I schedule their arrivals and departures, support them with any adjustment problems they may have, cook for them, and give them a sense of family in a foreign place. In our house, I am everyone's caretaker and everyone's scheduler. I am the organizer, the cook, the driver, the accountant, the problem solver, the planner, the person who remembers birthdays, holidays, and get togethers, the extended family communicator, as well as the virtual walking catalogue of everyone's likes, dislikes, and preferences. Thus, my child had to take on as much responsibility as she could handle during early COVID-19 when I was sick, but most things just didn't get done.

Very quickly, one student left, leaving a huge hole in our income, and it was only a matter of weeks before the other had to return to his home country before international flights were cancelled. As we are mostly self-employed, we plunged into even more financial hardship, as clients from our other business cancelled services one after another. It felt like a multitude of new problems were popping up daily—all of which I had to solve. I was overwhelmed and was paralyzed in panic for months trying to recover my physical health. From my bed, I began the distressing business of cancelling cell phone plans and calling all of our bill providers and our mortgage provider to defer payments. So many things were happening at once that I felt like I was swimming upstream in a river made of thick mud.

My brother-in-law had been seriously ill, and his surgery was suddenly cancelled due to the pandemic lockdown. From bed, I was managing all of his care, constantly, speaking with 3 different specialists and his family doctor, trying to keep them updated with each other as all in-office appointments had been cancelled. Impossibly, I struggled to meet everyone's needs in the family. At one point the situation became grave when one of his doctors told us to sign power of attorney papers for him and rush him into emergency. Thankfully, he recovered, and we were told he would be okay until surgeries opened up again, so we carried on.

And then there was my teenager to parent and nurture. Only a few weeks before the lockdown, she had come to me with the jarring news that she identified more as a boy than a girl and requested that our family use they/them pronouns when referring to them. This news was a complete surprise and a huge shock; as with COVID-19, there had been no warning. I had been completely in the dark, never imagining or noticing that they had ever had any of these feelings. They had shown no signs of being unhappy with their gender in their childhood, so it was hard for me to understand this sudden change. My reaction to this news was tears. I felt at the time that my first reaction shouldn't be to cry, but somehow it hurt. I am not quite sure why. Of course, I respected their wishes and tried to be as supportive as I could. It was afterwards, privately, that I had to start wrapping my head around this new and unforeseen development in my child's life.

My teenager's announcement immediately felt like one more enormous, laborious project that I somehow had to deal with. I already felt pulled in many directions by working several jobs and trying to help keep our family financially afloat while building a new career. I am generally overwhelmed anyways, and I wasn't ready for a giant new adjustment to add to the top of my pile. There was also the immediate stab of terror to my solar plexus at the thought of losing a daughter, my only daughter. All I had ever wanted while pregnant was to have a baby girl, and I had been delighted when my wish had come true. She was my only child and very loved. Perplexed, I asked myself what this all meant.

After that first talk, I tried ignoring the issue for a time, thinking maybe it would just go away or that it was a phase that they might grow out of. But while I was constantly tripping over and correcting my pronouns, my child's progression along the gender continuum was moving quickly. Soon after their first announcement, they asked me if they could change their name at school to Alex and stop using their feminine name, Sofia. This was initially very distressing to me; it inexplicably felt that somehow, the memory of my cherished, beautiful baby was being damaged. I felt confused and guilty about my feelings. Shouldn't I be celebrating my child's journey in developing their own identity?

It was hard for me to understand what was happening with my kid and why they wanted this change. In the space of one year, I watched them go from wearing lacy bras and cut-off shorts to suddenly dressing in baggy boy clothes, which was confusing for me. As time went on, I began to understand that this gender change was very serious to them. But Sofia was the chubby-cheeked baby in my memories, not someone named Alex. What did this new name do to my baby daughter? Making my distress worse was that Alex started referring to his former name as his dead name. It was disorienting and overwhelming all at once; it also made me feel terribly sad.

But what could I say to him? Of course, I said yes; go ahead and change your name. I would never dream of not respecting my child's wishes. I firmly believed that they and only they have the right to choose their identity, and, after all, it was my job as a mother to support them and help them move towards autonomy. In the meantime, Alex was happily going to school every day and socializing with a new identity and a new name.

One day, I asked Alex if he wanted me to call him his chosen name and refer to him as a boy. The smile I got back was my answer. I will always remember it. Every time I called him Alex in the beginning, I got to see that smile. It made me feel good, and I realized how much this change meant to him. I felt pleased to be able to support him in this way and felt like maybe I was getting the hang of how to be a good mom with this transition thing. I posted his photo on social media on International Transgender Day of Visibility and read him what I had written. He was terribly pleased, and I felt great. Over the next weeks, my new son and I had many conversations on my sickbed about his transitioning. Little by little, I was getting more information about why he felt he wanted to change genders and trying to process it. I was also explaining to him that this transition was a transition for the whole family, that we all had to adjust to in our own way. It would take time for us to catch up to him.

The confusion for me was mainly that he had never shown a sign of unhappiness towards his gender as a child. I felt that there would have been signs, so I somehow didn't trust this sudden change. I had purposely tried to raise my child from a feminist point of view, in more or less a gender-neutral way. I let him take the lead and choose his own way, and it was this approach that saw him spend many years of his early childhood in almost exclusively pink and purple clothes. The feminine stereotype of the colours he had chosen had rubbed me the wrong way at the time, but it was his choice, so I bought what he preferred. When I thought he might like to play hockey as a young child, he chose to learn figure skating because he said that he wanted to skate and wear the pretty dresses.

These childhood choices of his led me to believe that he identified as a girl. His whole adolescence had been like most girls' adolescence and had been about makeup and bras and girly clothes that showed off his emerging women's body. As a young child, he was a talented athlete; he excelled in all of the sports he did. And although I had always encouraged him in his athletic pursuits, I never suffered from the stereotype of athletic girls being tomboys or somehow being perched on the edge of the gender fence. I was labelled a tomboy as a child, but for me, being a tomboy was more about breaking the roles that were expected of me, rejecting stereotypically female clothes, being athletic, getting dirty, and wanting to play rough with the boys. When he was a little girl, I just wanted him to grow up as a happy, strong, and independent person and not be barred by any of the patriarchal barriers usually set for girls and women.

In the beginning of his transition, it was hard for me to think of him as a boy; obviously, he was the same person, just in different clothes. But emotionally, I feared his changing and was afraid of somehow losing him. This made no sense at all intellectually, but emotion and intellect don't always connect. It was a relief for me to realize that he was exactly the same in his new gender role. He still loved makeup and style and was the same kid I had always known. His hair had been in a shortish girl style, which he decided to cut off. My grooming his hair as a girl child was a bond we had shared since he was very young, so it was comforting to continue this tradition with my son. It was early in the lockdown when I shaved all of his hair off into a very short brush cut. It was a happy time for us, and I thought he looked marvellous, like a beautiful, perfect, and elegant androgynous teenager.

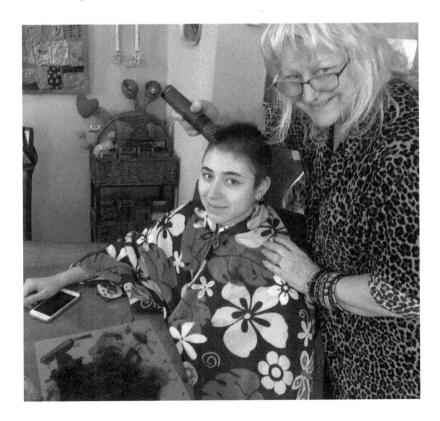

The change in his hairstyle helped me to start seeing him as a boy and to begin to accept his emerging masculinity. Since we were isolated in lockdown and there was no shopping, he began wanting to order different binders to flatten his chest. I hadn't realized he had been wearing tensor bandages to bind; I had just chalked up his evolving baggier fashion look to being artsy. I now realize that the baggier more masculine clothes were the beginning of his transition.

At first, the binding upset me. His young breasts had given me a mother's pride in remembering my own young body, which was once flawless and so similar. Somehow, his not wanting breasts was deleting this motherly pride from my own life. I became strongly aware of how much I identified with my own breasts, which I was previously unaware of. There were a lot of changes for me to process, and time after time, I had to make the separation between myself and my child. Letting go is something all mothers gradually do as their children grow. The process of Alex's transition was forcing me let go sooner than I had expected. I knew I had to accept his rejection of his own breasts, but I felt deeply saddened. I felt I was losing that mother-daughter bond we had enjoyed before, where we could share the joyful celebration of our female bodies. As I had always been empowered by the concept of the goddess, my feminist self felt a great disappointment that my child wanted to leave his feminine, goddess self behind.

As the pandemic went on, we watched Trudeau on television every day at 11:00 a.m. More and more people were dying, and others were going through great economic hardships. In response, the government rolled out financial support plans. Alex spent time making art; he struggled valiantly to apply himself to online schooling and frequently painted his face with theatrical makeup. My health came back, but I still struggled with the extra work of my family and the fears over my mortality, which I now had thanks to COVID-19. The sanitizing of incoming groceries had become a monumental task, which became my job somehow. Keeping everyone in a positive frame of mind seemed to become my job, too. I photographed and catalogued Alex's brilliant face-painting experiments and watched his emerging identity. I wrote a grant and got an online job while I head that Italy had begun using skating arenas for morgues. I continued to organize my brother-in-law's medical imaging appointments. The lockdown eased up a little, and surgeries began to be performed again in hospitals, so we were finally able to get him to his surgery.

Over the months, Alex and I continued a series of conversations about what he was going through and about being trans. I had many supportive conversations with good friends, some of whom are trans. I began to understand that although it seemed like his identity was just emerging to me, these changes had been quietly going on for some time for Alex. I learned a little more from each conversation. I was questioning myself about why I was still feeling so upset about him wanting to be a boy, and I realized that I was being forced to look at my own belief system squarely in the face. I wondered quietly if I was a hypocrite. I had always considered myself to be an LGBT+ ally, and being bisexual myself, I had brought my child up to embrace and accept peoples' differences. I had sent him to an alternative primary school because one of its wonderful core values was LGBT+ positivity and inclusivity. I proudly watched him participate in his school's Gender Splendour Week every year as a child, and I wore pink t-shirts and moustaches to his school in solidarity. I brought him to many Gay Pride parades, and we marched together in Toronto's annual Trans March when he was a young child. Since I had made a point of bringing up Alex to welcome and accept people's differences, then what was the problem? Why was it okay for everyone else to be trans, but when it came to my child, I was not happy?

My therapist introduced me to an LGBT+ parents' group, which was continuing to meet online during the pandemic through Zoom. It had wonderful facilitators, one a mother of a trans child herself. They helped me to accept and validate my own emotions around Alex's transition. I was told that even parents who are trans activists sometimes felt this way about their own trans kids in the beginning, that no emotion was wrong, and that it was normal to worry about our children's choices. They validated for me that my worries about my kid and his future were common for parents of trans kids, which relieved a lot of my guilt and helped me to accept my own feelings. I was reliving my initial reaction to Alex's announcement over and over and wishing I hadn't cried. I felt that I should have said, "Wonderful honey. This is so exciting. Tell me about it." But I will leave the imaginary perfect reactions to the imaginary perfect mothers, who obviously don't exist. In the end, I had to accept that I am just human after all. I felt empowered by being told that I was doing a great job of supporting him, and I could clearly see how happy he was with my support of his new identity.

Alex spent the many hours of isolation we had talking to trans kids on Instagram all over North America. He was gaining more and more knowledge, support, and pride in himself. We had found a paediatric therapist for him to talk to about general anxiety before the lockdown. Now poor Alex had to meet his new doctor over a Zoom call for the first time. I was relieved to find that the doctor specialized in trans issues, and they hit it off right away.

One day while we were obsessively sanitizing our incoming groceries together hoping to eliminate any trace of the virus, Alex started talking about wanting testosterone and a double mastectomy. I felt utter terror but conveyed a positive attitude. Really, I wasn't ready for that. As a mother, I had spent the past fifteen years taking care of his precious body and now he wanted to cut parts of it off? The idea felt like mutilation to me. I knew people who had this type of surgery and was happy for them, but this was my baby! It is not a natural impulse for me, as a mother, to embrace this kind of surgery.

I knew that some trans people never had surgery and hoped that my son would be one of them. Ultimately, I know that it is his body and that he has the right to make decisions about it. I was relieved to hear that it takes a long time for surgery and testosterone treatments to be approved. I felt better knowing that he couldn't just jump into anything and that he would have to spend time exploring and considering his decision.

I know that in time, testosterone and surgery will likely be the way he goes, but I am grateful that I have more time to adjust to the idea. I realize that I have to accept whatever he chooses. I will continue to be supportive. After all, it's my job as a mother. I still entertain a slight hope that he may choose to be a girl again, but deep down, I don't believe that will happen. I have many worries about his future as a trans man, but all parents have many worries about the future for their kids. In the long run, I feel that it doesn't really matter which way his identity takes him, as long as he is happy and feels whole and true to himself. I will support him in whatever direction he chooses. I think I have made my peace with him becoming my son, and the name Alex has taken on a fierce affection for me, as it is the name of my beloved child, of my son.

I have nicknames for him now: Lex, Lexicon, Lexus. We are enjoying our time together during the pandemic, cooped up in the house closer than normal, too close at times. We have regular teenage-parent conflicts but work them out. Even though I still overwhelmed with my many tasks—sometimes feeling like an octopus with my eight tentacles flying in every direction—I am doing my best to respect and adapt to my child's transition. At least I now know that I don't have to obsessively wash all of our groceries anymore—one less problem during these crazy times.

Chapter Thirty Four

Outside

Elsje Fourie

My seven-year-old is not allowed outside, and so
she turns her gaze inwards
leaving intricate miniature tableaus of Lego
around the house.

The kitchen counter has sprouted a Japanese garden,
one-inch figures drinking a bowl of green tea
under blossoming cherry trees
and surrounded by ponds filled with lobsters.

Under her bed yawns a cave,
its entrance guarded by two explorers
lured there by the gemstones and trophies
that glitter in its depths.

On my way to the toilet,
I almost impale my foot
on a party of firemen having a picnic.
Sharing out their tiny plastic baguettes and carrots.

Chapter Thirty Five

Mothering during a Pandemic and the Internalization of Blame and Responsibility

Aleksandra Staneva

Emerging perinatal evidence on the impact of the COVID-19 pandemic on pregnant women and new mothers highlights high rates of depression and anxiety caused by numerous factors, including physical isolation, increased household and childcare duties, relationship conflict, health and financial concerns, as well as an overall fear over the state of the world. This chapter explores the many challenges Australian women face during the COVID-19 global pandemic as they manage multiple roles. I will specifically focus on the maternal experience for women struggling with perinatal mental health challenges prior to the pandemic. This chapter argues that viewed through the lens of an intensive motherhood ideology (Hays), mothering during this global pandemic has been presented as an individual responsibility rather than the collective health crisis that it is. Mothers in our study described mothering as a "personal failure," which was arguably a result of internalized responsibility and individualised self-blame. Taking on personal responsibility is a common imperative in modern motherhood, and during the coronavirus pandemic, mothers have internalized responsibility for the safety, care, schooling, and the emotional and cognitive development of their children as well as for household responsibility and their own career. Mothers have also internalized guilt around their own obstructed path to recovery from mental illness, perceiving it as a personal failure. I will support this argument through examining 1) the challenges the lockdown presented to mothers; 2) mothers' negotiation of their work responsibilities; 3) their mental health challenges; 4) their concerns about their children's development; and 5) the silver linings they have gleaned from the pandemic.

Intensive Mothering and Individual Responsibility

Intensive mothering, as described by the sociologist Sharon Hays, involves a particularly child-centred style of mothering that has three components. First, mothers are the central caregivers; they must use time, energy, money, and expert advice to put their children's needs above their own. Hays writes that intensive mothering is "child-centred, expert-guided, emotionally absorbing, labour-intensive, and financially expensive" (8). This ideology postulates that children are pure and innocent and that childrearing is utterly distinct from the cool-headed and competitive economic and political realm outside the home. Hays argues that intensive mothering supports patriarchy because the benefits of such intensive caregiving are directed at men, who can still work and enjoy a relatively unchanged lifestyle. Such discourse showcases the demands of motherhood, which, in turn, are exacerbated in this pandemic.

Research Context

This research if part of a larger project that explores how mothers attending a peer-support community organization to support their mental health coped during the pandemic lockdown. Peach Tree Perinatal Wellness is an Australian Brisbane-based, non-profit, and peer-led organization that offers support to mums who have experienced any form of perinatal mental health challenges. The author of this chapter is a lived experience researcher at Peach Tree; she designed the study, conducted all interviews, analysed the data thematically, and wrote this manuscript.

Participants, who responded to the research call (between May and

June 2020) were all mothers and self-identified as white Australian. They were aged between twenty-seven and forty-four with children five years of age or younger. They had all also been diagnosed with either perinatal depression, anxiety, psychosis related to becoming a mother, or PTSD as a result of birth. Seventeen mothers took part; five of them had given birth during the lockdown (March and April 2020), and one was pregnant at the time. All but one or the women were parenting with a partner, and some worked from home.

Lockdown Challenges

Belinda Luscombe's May 2020 article for *Time* magazine—"'You Feel Trapped and Overwhelmed': Mothers Understood Isolation before the Pandemic"—argues that the experiences of confinement, remaining homebound and feeling hopeless and displaced, are in reality not new experiences for mothers. She argues that with or without a global pandemic, new mothers are continuously wrapped up in the "enormous and messy emotions of looking after children."

It is not surprising that the mothers in my study found the experience of parenting during a lockdown highly challenging— challenges that were further compounded by their pre-existing mental health issues. (This point will be elaborated on further below.) Practical and logistical challenges included changes in babies' sleeping patterns, disordered routine, as well as no access to health services (such as child health appointments and scheduled IVF treatments). Mothers found their days "dragging and endless" (Allie, a participant pseudonym), and the monotony of childcare, along with the inability to do anything besides parenting, was challenging. Keeping energetic children and toddlers indoors was also a common struggle. The mothers also noted the disruption of plans, the lack of leisure activities, limited access to support, the demand to entertain children, and reduced interactions with adults as other stress sources of stress caused by the pandemic. The lack of routine was the most shared challenge, as noted by Tara: "Any change to my daily routine is a trigger to my anxiety and depression. Many mums like me carve this sort of routine so that we can survive each day, like... in two hours I am going to do this, and then that, and that routine has been completely out." The effective management of postnatal anxiety and depression has been linked to establishing routines and a sense of control over one's daily activities by taking charge of one's health and wellbeing (Ford et al.). As Tara went on to elaborate, a key part for her recovery from postnatal depression has been planning and following a routine. Some mothers adapted by lowering their expectations and prioritizing family routine (with little or no mention of their own needs). As Natasha said, "After the first two weeks I just came to a place of acceptance. I went through the denial and the whole trying to make sense of it all... And then I realized I just had to learn to adapt." The challenges of early motherhood for these mothers were reaching a point of crisis as they tried to manage a tight routine, early motherhood, and their own mental health.

Negotiating Work

Most families took on a heteronormative family dynamics role; mothers mothered children, and fathers worked. Interestingly, fathers' roles were described as "giving mum a break" (Allie) yet usually for no more than an hour and only if asked.

In families where both parents continued to work from home, a fair distribution of domestic chores was possible only after negotiation, which was usually initiated by women who had to set and consistently reinstate new boundaries and rules around housework. Tara explained her situation: "And we all got so completely stressed out.... Anxiety levels were affected.... My relationship with my partner is rockier; we are stuck together, and that's frustrating. Housework—before it was fairly well distributed. But I have had to have a few talks with him about not pulling his weight. He is working from home too, so why isn't he getting to do his bit?" Those who continued to work experienced pulls in different directions. They had home chores to do; they had to parent and to work. And all the while, they felt as if they were failing in every one of their roles. Ellie discussed these feelings:

> My husband had to work extra hours. Initially, it was quite hard. I was working long hours, and not getting any of his support.... I really need the separation [between] work [and] home. When I am at home, I have a lot of pressure to do home things, [like] cleaning.... Initially, I would work, and during my lunch break I would clean the bathrooms. I felt really burnt out.

Ellie's story of burnout is mirrored by Alex's, who was twelve weeks pregnant during the lockdown and was also caring for two toddlers. Alex's partner returned to work, which brought "things back to normal for him"; he stayed late after work and went back to his hobbies during the weekend. Alex had stopped working, parented at home, and felt overwhelmed:

> My mental load was ... oh ... all of a sudden, I was supposed to do so much more than what I always did, and it was just so overwhelming. He would send me a message from work [at] about 3:00 p.m. [asking] "What have you got planned for dinner?" "Nothing cos I have two screaming children who have been on my feet for nine hours." This was ridiculous! We had a big fight. He went back to normal when he went back to work [laughs], but we didn't go back to normal.

Later in our conversation, Alex nonchalantly mentioned that she also had to increase her medication because of COVID-19 and her stressful relationship.

These mothers felt overwhelmed in their daily routine and had little support, falling prey to the intensive mother ideology, in which mothers must do everything for everyone and do it alone. Mothers had to find their own solutions, and because external structures were scarce, they also had to manage their mental health alone.

Maternal Mental Health

Those mothers who already found mothering overwhelming indicated that the pandemic had exacerbated their mental health symptoms. Emma shared the following:

> It has been incredibly draining.... When you are already feeling like shit, not having anything to look forward to, it is just really crushing—to the point [of] just lying in bed [asking] "What's the point of all this; today [will] be just the same as yesterday." All plans got cancelled, and how pointless is all this. Not knowing what's going to happen and no endpoint to it, unable to plan. It doesn't do really good things to your mood and your mind.

The lockdown became a barrier to established support systems. Previously helpful coping strategies—such as socializing, regular playdates, self-care activities, childcare, and support services—were not available. The ability to talk in person with other mothers with lived experience of mental illness, and who normalized their mothering strugglers, was no longer available. Many participants said that digitalized mental health support and online peer support was just not as helpful as in-person support. These mothers said that mothering in isolation increased their depression; they became more impatient and could no longer tolerate their stress levels. They constantly worried about the future. Mothers felt responsibility for their children's uncertain future, as they linked such uncertainty to their own (in)ability to mother. Karla talked about the anxiety she felt "COVID-19 made my anxiety really bad—the fact you had no control, the uncertainty, and everything made my anxiety sky rocket! Feeling stuck at home with a daughter who became more and more irritable. Oh, I snapped, I know. I am sorry. It happened a few times ... not proud of that." Karla's account demonstrates the way in with internalized responsibility heightened her anxiety even further, which also increased her irritability, and her "snapping" was self-referential and unacceptable. Daria shared similar feelings of guilt: "I didn't know how long it would go, how I would raise a baby in the middle of this pandemic. I felt like a bad mum anyway. This definitely delivered a blow to my self-esteem and my confidence in my parenting. Such unknowns... how would I parent him?"

Mothers were running on empty with not much to look forward to. Asking for help and support seemed taxing, too. Yet intensive mothering does not allow mothers to admit they cannot cope. Hence, the mothers in this study downplayed their mental health and were reluctant to seek help during a global pandemic, when people were preoccupied with infection and death rates. Karla expressed this sentiment well: "I felt like my problems aren't big enough. I was thinking nobody would want to listen to me whinge. I feel like I don't deserve to speak about my problems. Similar to my postnatal depression, I felt like I shouldn't be whinging about any of it." Many mothers described that prior to the lockdown they were slowly getting in charge of their mental health after feeling like a bad mother. Those who had worked on taking care of their mental health felt they were moving backwards like Daria: "With the PND I finally got into a routine, going to Peach Tree once a week, seeing family once a week ... and all this stopped. We were only just meeting people, and coffee meet-ups cause I am an introvert anyway, and we finally got into a routine and I opened up, and then all this got interrupted." Allie said something similar: "I was feeling like I was coming out of this postpartum and I was looking into training and moving forward on a path, [but now] I feel like I am going backwards."

Under intensive mothering, aiming to improve one's mental health does not include looking at external factors that could explain why women were finding motherhood difficult. Therefore, when the pandemic restricted the performative and active management of their mental illness, some mothers spoke of "going backwards" on their mental health recovery journey. With only a limited narrative to borrow from within the intensive mother ideology, it is no surprise that mothers experienced their journey at the time as a personal failure. As Eva explained: "I am annoyed at myself because I know how hard I worked, and I just see it go down the drain, and you really can't do anything to change the circumstances that the world is in right now. It is so annoying cos I am trying to push myself to ignore, and just roll with that aspect of things, cos there is nothing I can do." Such a perspective again highlights how taking care of mental health is "hard work."

Before the lockdown, Alex had progressed from postnatal counselling and had started deeper inner work around trauma. Unfortunately, during the lockdown, she regressed and began to feel overwhelmed by parenting again:

> Before COVID-19, I felt like I had moved on and actually had transitioned my counselling from postnatal depression stuff to past trauma counselling. I had moved on, and my day to day was pretty normal and under control. I was able to function and run a business and mother, and I had more good days than bad days. And now I am probably back to that. I had been dealing with the pressure of my expectations now.

Such stories highlight how these mothers dedicated most of their time, energy, and effort solely to their children—and not leaving much for themselves.

What about the Children's Future?

Another area where these mothers internalized self-blame and guilt was the social development of their children. The conditions of the lockdown made the relationship between the mother and child more difficult, as increased resentment and irritability were common. Mothers feared the effect their own mood, which was affected by the pandemic, would have on their children, leading to more self-blame. As Barbara said, "I worry if it [her mood] is going to have an effect on him because I get so angry, frustrated, and he sees that."

Mothers assuming full responsibility over their children's emotional and cognitive development has long been noted in motherhood research. Feminist writing and research have shown how cultural norms can influence mothers to assume all the responsibility when their children struggle, whether emotionally, cognitively, or physically (Maher, Fraser, and Wright; Delany). Consistent with neoliberal ideology, women are responsible for their child's health, regardless of social, biological, or environmental constraints. Once again, the mothers' behaviour determines their children's future.

Some mothers of newborns resented their inability to cope with distress, whereas others had to resort to some ineffective parenting practices, such as allowing their children too much screen time in order to get things done. Again, women judged their parenting as ineffective while trying to "function in the unfunctionable" (O'Reilly 4). They blamed themselves for not coping, and their crucial work remained unacknowledged and unsupported while they struggled with uncertainty, mental illness, and unending work. Because of the influence of intensive mothering, mothers reported spending several hours online, learning new skills and tips on how to entertain and teach their children. I argue that those practices resulted in an increased sense of ambivalence, a pull between distress and increased responsibility to care. Natasha offered the following:

> I feel like the whole time I vacillated between "how lucky are we, and I get to see her all day"... And the opposite end of that is like, "Oh my gosh, she is smothering me and I can't get away, and I am panicking because I can't get away, and I can't have any breathing space." I can't say that I sat in the middle. I feel like I swung all the way from one extreme to the other.

Silver Linings

Despite finding parenting overwhelming, some mothers did acknowledge that spending uninterrupted time with their children for over ten weeks had a positive effect on their bonding. They got to know their babies better and co-created routines by cocooning with the new baby. There were no external pressures to be anywhere or do anything, and that feeling of timelessness allowed them to get away from busy modern life. Interestingly, the mothers whose narratives were focussed on slowing down did not mention an increase in depressive or anxiety symptoms. Arguably, such slowing down stands in opposition to intensive mothering and to the overall modus operandi of neoliberalism, as it disrupts the notion that mothers must always be working and getting things done, which has a positive impact on mothers' mental health.

Conclusion

It is no surprise that the high demands of parenting were exacerbated by the global pandemic and lockdown (Davenport et al.; Herman), especially for women struggling with mental illness. Sheila shared the following: "Just had a baby eight months ago, after I was hospitalized for postnatal psychosis with my daughter ten years ago. So, with COVID-19, I felt like the fears and triggers are back, especially at the start. It was bad. I had very high anxiety, very stressful. Had to be on the phone with my GP regularly. I coped with hoarding food and supplies."

Mothers were the main (and usually the sole) caregivers, whereas fathers "helped out" (nine out of the seventeen mothers used this phrase). Allie's husband would give an hour's break so she could go out for a walk. Fathers in our study also had few domestic responsibilities before the pandemic. Evidence from Canada and Australia also highlights how the pandemic has exacerbated gender inequality regarding childcare obligations, leading to poorer mental health for women than for men (Johnston et al.). In a critical piece for *The Guardian*, Sonia Sodha explores how the COVID-19 pandemic has widened the gender gap, since mothers are assigned responsibility the children and are forced to cut back their working hours, struggling in this dual employment on top of pre-existing mental illness. Jessica

Valenti has also written about how fathers have failed to step up during the pandemic and help their partners with domestic and caregiving responsibilities, forcing them out of the workforce.

Unfortunately, this research also illustrates that mothers blame themselves for not coping with the increased demands of parenting during a lockdown—not their partners. Regrettably, internalized self-blame is not new to mothering, as much research has explored maternal guilt (Staneva and Wigginton). Individualistic ideologies that permeate contemporary society and that powerfully influence mothers continue to significantly contribute to the self-blame mothers experience because of having a mental illness.

This global pandemic and its implications were experienced by most mothers not in a "we-are-all-in-this-together" way but in an internalized one. They felt responsible for all the headaches the pandemic caused and adapted a highly individualistic approach to parenting. This is a symptom of greater and unaddressed social constructs and norms around what it means to mother today, as well as the breakdown of communities, which used to share some responsibility for raising the next generation of people.

Overall, the mothers who participated in this research managed to somehow adapt and cope by deliberately reframing the experience from something completely negative to something with a few positives hidden within. The global challenge of the pandemic has stretched mothers' capacities to new levels of extreme parenting—solo parenting, 24/7, in isolation. Little emphasis is placed on mothers' mental health, particularly for those in precarious situations, including single mothers or those experiencing domestic abuse. Despite evidence that social distancing is the most effective way to manage infectious diseases, the impact of social isolation can increase depressive symptoms and suicide ideation in new mothers (Loades et al.)

This chapter has highlighted that unhelpful social norms around mothering result in further distress for women already struggling with mental health issues and leaves them feeling inadequate. Furthermore, the sharing of domestic and caregiving responsibilities between partners, family, friends, and communities is essential for helping young mothers cope. Specialized perinatal mental health services that are universal, accessible, and safe need to be prioritized in global economic and health pandemic recovery plans. For those mothers that turned away from social pressure to conform to intensive mothering practices, their stress decreased.

This chapter has emphasized the importance of the sharing of responsibilities between partners and of envisioning mothering as a community endeavour. To further disrupt the ideology of intensive mothering, policies must be implemented that tackle inequality and dismantle harmful social norms. If not, mothers will continue to stretch themselves thin between their personal and professional demands. They will experience burnout and internalize all blame. As a result, urgent action is needed on all social, healthcare, and political fronts.

Works Cited

Delany, Toni. *To Entrap and Empower: Maternal Responsibility in an Age of Neo-Liberal Health.* Dissertation, Adelaide University, 2011.

Ford, Elizabeth, et al. "Diagnosis and Management of Perinatal Depression and Anxiety in General Practice: a Meta-synthesis of Qualitative Studies." British Journal of General Practice vol. 67, no. 661 2017, pp.538-46.

Hays, Sharon. *The Cultural Contradictions of Motherhood.* Yale University Press, 1996.

Loades, Maria Elizabeth, et al. "Rapid Systematic Review: The Impact of Social Isolation and Loneliness on the Mental Health of Children and Adolescents in the Context of COVID-19." *Journal of the American Academy of Child and Adolescent Psychiatry* vol. 59, no.11, 2020, pp. 1218-39.

Luscombe, Belinda. "'You Feel Trapped and Overwhelmed': Mothers Understood Isolation before the Pandemic." *Time*, 8 May 2020, time.com/5832733/motherhood-isolation-photos/. Accessed 15 Jan. 2021.

Maher, JaneMaree, Suzanne Fraser, and Jan Wright. "Framing the Mother: Childhood Obesity, Maternal Responsibility, and Care." *Journal of Gender Studies*, vol. 19, no. 3, 2010, pp. 233-47.

O'Reilly, A. "'Trying to Function in the Unfunctionable': Mothers and COVID-19." *Journal of the Motherhood Initiative for Research and Community Involvement*, vol. 11, no. 1, 2020, pp. 4-11

Staneva, A., and B. Wigginton. "The Happiness Imperative: Exploring How Women Narrate Depression and Anxiety during Pregnancy." *Feminism & Psychology*, vol. 28, no. 2, 2018, pp. 173-93.

Valenti, Jessica. "The Pandemic Isn't Forcing Moms Out of the Workforce—Dads Are." *GEN*, 31 July 2021, gen.medium.com/the-pandemic-isnt-forcing-moms-out-of-the-workforce-dads-are-e0cb58e1965b. Accessed 15 Jan. 2021.

Chapter Thirty Six

Context Collapse

EL Putnam

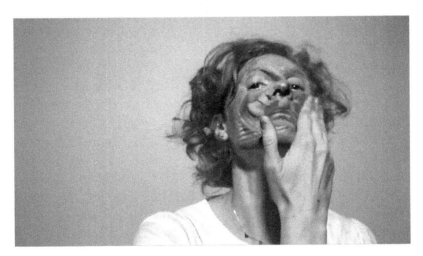

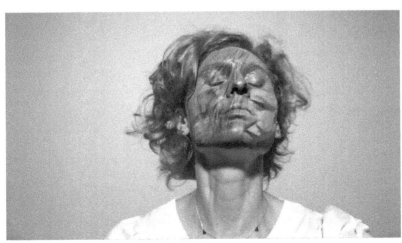

"Context collapse" is a phrase used in digital culture to describe how the boundaries of different communication contexts collapse on social media, as personal, professional, and family spheres coalesce on these virtual platforms. danah boyd coined the phrase to describe how "technology complicates our metaphors of space and place, including the belief that audiences are separate from each other" (Marwick and boyd 2). boyd and Alice Marwick analyze how audiences that have been delegated to different circles of relations offline—resulting in different presentations of self depending on context—are now merged into a single context in social media. Public health restrictions implemented around the globe in response to the COVID-19 pandemic—which have meant the closure of schools, workplaces, and other public spaces as people are encouraged to stay home—have introduced another type of context collapse.

Unlike the online phenomenon, this context collapse is not virtual; personal, professional, and family spheres are now coexisting in the same time and physical space. Although virtual instances of context collapse are difficult to manage and require strategic impression management to keep professional and personal presentations distinctive, the context collapse of COVID-19 is an impossible negotiation of reproductive politics. In response, my artistic practice has become a means of coping with the impact of this context collapse while my work as a performance artist that engages with digital technologies has also been forced to adapt. Like numerous other artists working in performance, I have been experimenting with livestreaming.

In this chapter, I present a series of video stills from these livestreamed performances, discussing the context of how they were produced and how they relate to my ongoing interest in developing a shared aesthetics of interruption of the maternal and digital technologies, which the current pandemic is bringing to the fore. I also talk about how my practice is helping me cope with maternal ambivalence under these circumstances.

Internet livestreaming rose to prominence with the advent of online platforms, such as Justin.tv in 2007 and Twitch in 2011, which could accommodate the technical demands and complexities associated with the medium. It quickly became popular with the e-sports and video gaming communities (Taylor 6). With the development of smartphones, social media livestreaming has also been used for civic activism and engagement as well as a means of broadcasting protests and social justice actions, including capturing the often devastating footage of police brutality and murder (Costanza-Chock 117-18). However, for the arts and performance, livestreaming has been treated as an inferior substitute to "in real life" (IRL) events. Since

COVID-19 lockdowns and public health regulations restricted in-person activities—resulting in the closure of many art and cultural spaces including galleries and theatres—performing virtually gained greater acceptance. It became the most feasible option to present live action, since live video broadcast phenomeno-logically resembles in-person presence to a degree.

I wanted to create livestreamed performances that played with its parameters as a medium, so I experimented with chroma keying. My techniques were inspired by the work of Irish artist Laura O'Connor, who has developed numerous livestreamed performances in which she lays video over her body in poignant, feminist responses to the biopolitics of reproduction in Ireland (Putnam 17-9). In the first performance I livestreamed, I applied green paint to my face, keyed out so a video of my daughter playing with dandelions appeared as the paint layer thickens.[1] In other videos, I interacted with a large piece of blue fabric, keyed out so the video screen becomes a material that I manipulate through a haptic folding. I push and pull the digital image as it becomes a tangible object in the virtual realm, constructing a reality that is entangled yet different from my physical presence.

When I began livestreaming, I quickly came up against the material limitations of inferior technological infrastructure. Our home in the Irish countryside, right at the border with Northern Ireland, had very poor internet connection, as broadband was not available in our area. Even after reducing the quality of the video as much as possible, my streams were regularly interrupted by dropped frames and frozen images. I found these formal challenges related to a topic that I have been researching through my artistic practice and scholarship for several years now—the shared aesthetics of interruption of the maternal and digital technologies. I define the aesthetics of interruption as the sensorial quality of art and media that emerges from interruption, which is similar to the state of the mother as she cares for a dependent child or the formal characteristics of digital technology in the gap, glitch, or lag (Putnam 14-5).

In particular, I am interested in how maternal and digital interruptions intersect through art and aesthetic encounters. These qualities are manifest in the *Context Collapse* livestreamed performances through the lagging images, gaps in action, and pixelated compositions that resulted from poor internet connectivity. This intersection also emerges from the fact that I performed these actions at night after my children went to sleep, meaning there was always a risk of being interrupted by a child crying out for more breastmilk or wanting comfort after a disturbing dream. The content of the work, which involved overlaying videos I created during lockdown with my daughters, dealt with the ongoing interruptions of motherwork and the challenges of producing creative work while in constant close contact with small children. During lockdown, I aimed to produce one performance a week and I presented them over the livestreaming platform Periscope, which links to Twitter. I would not announce when they would take place because I was never certain I would be able to follow through with any scheduled actions, as it depended on my daughters going to sleep.

Through this work, I take advantage of the affordances of livestreaming that are often overlooked or neglected, specifically the distance, difference, and separation of context that the virtual connection attempts to bridge (Hunter 284), as opposed to relying on how the technology alters perceptions of space and time. The use of chroma keying points to the construction and mediation of the virtual performance of the livestream, as moving frames collapse but do not coalesce. I invite a sense of ambiguity and introduce confusion, as I provide no textual description about my actions or the content of the video. I disable the capacity of viewers to interact through text or likes, intentionally distancing myself from the online audience.

The intentional confusion the work invites relates to my struggles with maternal ambivalence, which was heightened in the period of lockdown. Barbara Almond defines maternal ambivalence as "that mixture of loving and hating feelings that all mothers experience toward their children and the anxiety, shame, and guilt that the negative feelings engender in them" (Almond 2), which she describes as stemming from conflicts between the needs of the child and those of the mother. The circumstances of the COVID-19 lockdown intensified the conditions that provoke ambivalence through the context collapse of roles, space, and time, turning the challenging circumstances of raising small children into insurmountable tasks. Rozsika Parker argues how instead of resisting or ignoring maternal ambivalence, it can invite creative mothering, which sparks "the impulse to give, understand, construct and mend" (Parker 111).

I translated these actions into my artistic practice, first through the shooting of videos with my daughters—where the act of performing to camera together with them became gestures of artist-mothering—and then through the incorporation of these videos into my livestreamed solo performances. In the performances, creative mothering is abstracted through artistic negotiation and embodied processing of emotion. At the same time, these videos and performances enable me to entertain a speculative moment regarding the contradictions inherent to my relationship with my children, which Sarah LaChance Adams argues is a significant means of coping with and coming to understand maternal ambivalence (141). In this manner, the series responds to my experiential compression of the COVID-19 lockdown as an attempt to make sense of such extraordinary times. The performances function as acts of agency to counter the incessant grinding down of such an exhaustive state of domestic context collapse while acknowledging and engaging with the interconnectedness of human beings, both online and IRL.

Endnotes

1. To "key out" in video means to mask a section of the image based on colour. Chroma keying enables two or more moving image sequences to occupy the same frame at the same time. In the videos I produced, the parts of my face where green paint is applied are made transparent so the underlying video of my daughter is visible. As I applied and thickened the face paint, the underlying video became more visible. Alternatively referred to as "green screen," it is commonly used in cinema and television, including meteorological reports where it enables a meteorologist to stand in front of an animated weather map.

Works Cited

Almond, Barbara. *The Monster Within: The Hidden Side of Motherhood.* University of California Press, 2010.

Costanza-Chock, Sasha. *Design Justice: Community-Led Practices to Build the Worlds We Need.* MIT Press, 2020.

Hunter, Lindsay Brandon. "Live Streaming and the Perils of Proximity." *International Journal of Performance Arts and Digital Media*, vol. 15, no. 3, Sept. 2019, pp. 283-94.

LaChance Adams, Sarah. *Mad Mothers, Bad Mothers, and What a Good Mother Would Do: The Ethics of Ambivalence.* Columbia University Press, 2014.

Marwick, Alice E., and danah boyd. "'I Tweet Honestly, I Tweet Passionately': Twitter Users, Context Collapse, and the Imagined Audience." *New Media & Society*, vol. 13, no. 1, Feb. 2011, pp. 114-33.

Parker, Rozsika. *Torn In Two: Maternal Ambivalence.* Virago, 2005.

Putnam, EL. "Strange Mothers: The Maternal and Contemporary Media Art in Ireland." *Digital Art in Ireland*, edited by James O'Sullivan, Anthem Press, 2020, pp. 9-28

Taylor, T. L. *Watch Me Play: Twitch and the Rise of Game Live Streaming.* Princeton University Press, 2018.

Chapter Thirty Seven

Smudging My Home and Family: An Anishinaabeg Mother's Response to the COVID-19 Pandemic

Renée E. Mazinegiizhigoo-kwe Bédard

"They say that this is the end of the world.... There's a word they say too—ah...pock ... ah..."

"Apocalypse?"

"Yes, apocalypse! What a silly word. I can tell you there's no word like that in Ojibwe. Well I never hear a word like that from my elders anyway."

Evan nodded, giving the elder his full attention.

"The world isn't ending," she went on. "Our world isn't ending. It already ended. It ended when the Zhaagnaash [white man] came into our original home down south on the bay and took it from us. That was our world. When the Zhaagnaash cut down all the trees and fished all the fish and forced us out of there, that's when our world ended. They made us come all the way up here. This is not our homeland! But we had to adapt and luckily we already knew how to hunt and live on the land. We learned to live here." ...

We've seen what this...what's the word again?"

"Apocalpyse."

"Yes, apocalypse. We've had that over and over. But we always survived. We're still here. And we'll still be here, even if the power

and the radios don't come back on and we never see any white
people ever again."
—Waubgeshig Rice, *Moon of the Crusted* Snow, 149-50

Comparing COVID-19 to an apocalypse is probably a bit of an
exaggeration, but the above quote embodies the thoughts I had when
the pandemic hit. The university I worked at closed; we were told to
stay home and were instructed to stay away from other people. The
world rested. News reports described empty streets and empty
grocery store shelves. Driving around was eerie, and it kind of looked
as though the apocalypse had arrived. After the university closed, I
was left thinking what it means to be Indigenous and survive the
apocalypse. What does it mean to be an Anishinaabeg mother during
a pandemic? I turned to my culture for direction. I reread old stories
and prophecies; I began practicing ceremony daily; and I opened my
medicine bundle and used my women's medicines. I had to revision
my path in life, and it led to a resurgence in cultural awareness for my
role as an Anishinaabeg mother.

In this chapter, I will try to provide insights into how I have been
approaching Anishinaabeg mothering during COVID-19. One
example is through my use of the ceremony of smudging. Smudging
has become a reclamation of ceremony as pedagogy, both as process
and context for mothering in order to nurture my children and family
in those survival skills, knowledge, and values as Kwewag (women). I
also examine the teachings of the Seven Fires Prophecy, which act as
a call to action for Anishinaabeg to return back to our cultural traditions
and teachings in order to revision new pathways forward through these
difficult times foretold by our ancestors. The prophecy teachings were
the reason I took up smudging when COVID-19 became serious
enough for the country to shut down, and they became my anchor for
exploring other similar ethical protocols, such as the teachings of
ayaangwaamiziwin (cautious and careful awareness). I opened my
women's bundle and put in it my maternal medicines or women's
medicines, including white sage along with smudging tools, and I used
those medicines in a daily routine of protecting my home and family.
Sharing the resurgence of smudging in my life in the pandemic is my
way of opening up to other mothers what it is like to live as an
Anishinaabeg mother in a time of great change and upheaval. My hope

in doing so I can reach out to other mothers and form a network of shared experiences of living through COVID-19.

Doodoom: Mother

I am an Anishinaabeg mother, a doodoom to two Kwezensag (little women)—my daughters. The teachings I carry are for them in order to keep them safe, foster their Anishinaabe-Kwezensag identities, and nurture them in the ceremonies of their grandmothers who came before so that someday they can pass this knowledge on to their daughters. What I share in this chapter is the survival knowledge of the ancestral grandmothers, which reaches back thousands of years. We are using their wisdom to endure through this pandemic and keep their teachings alive for those yet to be born to this world, seven generations from now.

When COVID-19 was recognized as a pandemic, it halted my world and sent me to the cupboard to get my medicine bundle. I retreated into my home with my family, held my children close, and used my medicines and smudge to create a safe space emotionally, spiritually, psychologically, and maybe even physically. I worried about keeping my children safe from the dangers of COVID-19. Children in Anishinaabeg culture are critical for the survival of our people and are considered precious gifts. I live for my children and devote much of my daily life to ensuring their happiness, growth, and wellness. In our traditional Anishinaabeg maternal teachings, the mother has to be enduring and strong like a rock (Johnston 25). Anishinaabeg women take many of our teachings on motherhood from the Creation stories of Aki, Mother the Earth, First mother of all of Creation. Anishinaabeg scholar Basil Johnston writes the following: "Mother Earth continues to be bountiful, sustaining all beings. All else changes; the earth remains unchanging and continues to give life. It is a promise to the future, to those yet to be born" (25). The role of mothers in my culture is constancy, drawing on the attributes of the land to understand our role in Creation. I turned to smudging as a maternal practice of constancy, solace, and fortitude in tumultuous times.

Over the months of living through this COVID-19 pandemic, I have learned that even when I didn't feel strong or didn't want to be strong and constant, I did it anyway because my children needed me to be. I became the rock upon which my family could lean. As I turned to my cultural teachings on how to get through hard times, like this pandemic, I knew that I was helping my family to cope with the dark emotions, the changes, and the new life directions we were all experiencing. In terms of the traditional teachings I looked to for clarity, first among them was the Seven Fire Prophecy or Seven Prophets teachings. The prophecy story of the Seven Fires or Seven Gifts describes different eras that the Anishinaabeg would endure and survive. The Seven Fires offers a description of our times as a critical era of upheaval, revisioning, revitalization, and cultural resurgence. We are now in the time of the Seventh Fire, and the knowledge contained in this story can aid all Anishinaabeg to survive if we meet the call to action it contains. The Seven Fire prophecy teachings are my maternal guideposts for the survival of my family.

Entering into the Seven Fires Prophecy: Pandemic Preparedness

Among Anishinaabeg, we know that the pandemic was foretold by our ancestors in the Seven Fire Prophecies. We carried those stories for many generations in preparation for this time period when we would need them again to guide us on how to continue life as Anishinaabeg, how to revision our lives if needed, and how to revitalize what we might have forgotten. Currently, we are said to be living through the Seventh Fire, so I look to what my ancestors foretold in order to cope with my current reality.

I look to the version of the Seven Fires Prophecy story offered by Anishinaabeg Elder Edward Benton-Banai in his 1988 book *The Mishomis Book*. According to Elder Benton-Banai, each of the seven prophets left the Anishinaabeg with seven predictions of what the future would bring. Each prediction pertained to a particular era of time that would come in the future. With regards to the current pandemic, I look at these stories through the lens of a mother, and I find his teachings on the seventh prophet as most instructive, asserting that Anishinaabeg must stay the course of ethical protocols of mino-bimaadiziwin: living well as a human being. As a mother, this teaching is vital to what I want to live, embody, and teach my daughters about living as strong Anishinaabe-kwewag (women).

When I look through a mother's eyes at the Prophecy of the Seventh Fire, I see the pandemic unfolding and the dire choice to either make changes or to suffer. The warnings ring true and stir caution in my heart. Elder Benton-Banai shares the prophecy as follows:

> The seventh prophet that came to the people long ago was said to be different from the other prophets. He was young and had a strange light in his eyes. He said, "In the time of the Seventh Fire a Osh-ki-bi-ma-di-zeeg" (New People) will emerge. They will retrace their steps to find what was left by the trail. Their steps will take them to the elders who they will ask to guide them on their journey. But many of the elders will have fallen asleep. They will awaken to this new time with nothing to offer. Some of the elders will be silent out of fear. Some of the elders will be silent because no one will ask anything of them. The New People will have to be careful in how they approach the elders. The task of the New People will not be easy.... It is at this time that the Light-skinned Race will be given a choice between two roads. If they choose the right road, then the Seventh Fire will light the Eighth and Final Fire—an eternal Fire of peace, love, brotherhood and sisterhood. If the Light-skinned Race makes the wrong choice of roads, then the destruction which they brought with them in coming to this country will come back to them and cause much suffering and death to all the Earth's people.
>
> Traditional Mide people of Ojibway and people from other nations have interpreted the "two roads" that face the Light-skinned Race as the road to technology and road to spiritualism. They feel that the road to technology represents a continuation of the head-long rush to technological development. This is the road that has led modern society to a damaged and seared Earth. (92-93)

In this seventh fire prophecy, the people, the mothers and the fathers, are called again into action to retrace the paths of our ancestors and to turn inwards to our own personal landscape as well as our own families, communities, teachings, and sacred medicines. It is essential for us to take up this course of action on behalf of ourselves, our families, our communities, and all our relations, human or otherwise.

As Anishinaabeg mothers, we need to take care of our families and children by continuing to follow the recommendations of our ancestors and prophets—to stay home, to isolate, to practice appropriate physical distancing, to practice our ceremonies, and to find, harvest, and be vigilant with our medicines around disinfecting and general hygiene. As mothers, we are reminded once again to live with our role in Creation in mind. We must be careful to take up our place as mothers to the next seven generations of Anishinaabeg. We must open our mother's medicine bundles and take out our sacred medicines to heal and protect our families—to teach our children to value the plant medicines offered to us by Aki (Earth; First Mother of Creation on Earth). The Earth teaches all women and girls to remember the role of the mother in the order of Creation; she who provides, nourishes, and heals all her children. Johnston describes Aki as follows:

> There is in addition to constancy in Mother Earth, generosity.... A mother begets a child. She nourishes him, holds him in her arms. She gives him a place upon her blanket near her bosom. A woman may give birth to many children. To all she gives food, care, and a place near her ... the earth is bounteous. Her mantle is wide, her bowl ever full and constantly replenished. On the blanket of Mother Earth there is a place for hunting, fishing, sleeping, and living. From the bowl comes food and drink for every person. All, young and old, strong and weak, well and ill are intended to share in Mother Earth's bounty and magnanimity (25).

We must act to do the same as Aki. Anishinaabeg Elder Art Solomon states the following: "The children represented the future but the women represented the present and the future because without them there could be no future for the nations; the cycles of life could have no continuity; the Creator's plan for human beings would end" (34). In these uncertain times, Anishinaabeg must acknowledge everything that the Earth provides us to survive illnesses and must remember to practice reciprocity with her and among each other.

Recently, Anishinaabeg storyteller, artist, and cultural activist Issac Murdoch (Serpent River First Nation) offered some important Anishinaabeg teachings derived from his own knowledge of the prophecy. In an animate digital video for the Yellowhead Institute, a First Nation-led research centre based in the Faculty of Arts at Ryerson University, Murdoch shared his knowledge of the Onwaachigewinan[1], or prophecies. In the following transcription from his account of the prophecy, he desribes how we are living the prophecy right now:

> For my people, the sicknesses that are happening today were foretold from the prophecies that were passed down from our old ones. We call them *Onwegitchigewin*, meaning things to come. So we know from the old prophecies of the past that there is a lot of traditional practices that can help us add volume of knowledge that's needed for the present time of sickness. For example, it was foretold that people would need to make their own dishes out of wood and never to share them. They were also told of the plant and animal remedies that would be useful during such times. Through the ceremonies and visions of our medicine peoples it was advised that families need to self-isolate on the land. When they did this, they would be okay. This all came from prophecy. This all came from ceremony. Our Elders always remind us, "All of the laws that are being broken right now is what's causing the sickness." Because of this, we have to go back to the old way of life. That's what they always talked about. The Elders are constantly reminding us to go back to the land because it's the biggest and most powerful health care systems we have. The medicines are part of the answer and so is being part of the land. We are the land and the land is ceremony! We are often reminded that hoarding and being greedy is part of what causes the sickness. So if we want the sickness to go away we have to give. We can't hoard anything. This protects us and takes power away from what feeds the sickness. I believe we are in a sacred story now and that a thousand years from now they will be telling this of when the two legged tried to destroy the Earth. I really truly believe that if we follow the natural laws of the land everything will become beautiful again, everything will be okay. I remember years ago, my great-great-grandfather said, "You know what? We need to go home. We have to go back and it's okay to do so because that's where we are going to learn to live again." Naahaw. Miigwech. Thank you. ("COVID-19 | Anishinaabe Pandemic Prophecies")

What I take away from his teachings on the prophecies is that our traditional ways hold the key to our survival in these hard times. The old ways worked to help us survive colonization, and they were not destroyed. If our traditions have survived this long, they can help us survive another seven generations if we trust in them, revitalize them, and use them with the same respect that our ancestors did.

The words and teachings of both Elder Benton-Banai and Murdoch are valuable to our people today as we decide how to live during the pandemic. We must practice reciprocity, and we must be guided by the gifts of kindness, honest sharing, and respect when we take up the prophecy's call to action to return to our old ways to see us through to the future. These are the values, ethics, and beliefs inherent in our maternal teachings about the sacredness of life, which were given to us by our mothers, grandmothers, and great-grandmothers.

Nookweziganoon: Smudging as a Woman's Ceremony

Knowing that the prophecy teachings call Anishinaabeg to take action to preserve and protect our people and culture, I began thinking about Anishinaabeg-centred approaches to dealing with COVID-19. I looked at my medicine bundle and took out the smudging items and the women's medicines. I lay everything out and began the smudging ceremony and the day after that, I did it again and then again the day after that. Nookweigan or smudging became a daily ceremony for many weeks until I felt that we were safe.

Throughout the COVID-19 health crisis, not only has the daily ritual of smudging helped to ground me as a mother in the cultural customs of my ancestral grandmothers—which have provided me spiritual fortitude—but it has also provided specific health benefits in terms of its antibacterial elements. This practice also offers a moment to slow down, seek quiet, acknowledge what I am grateful for, to release tension, and to seek strength to help protect my family. Furthermore, smudging is important to keep me anchored in my personal truth and to help reveal my power as an Anishinaabe-kwe and doodoom. The resurgence of these traditions in my daily life has been a site of cultural empowerment and agency for my family.

I teach my daughters that nookweziganoon is an important ceremony for them as Kwezensag because Kwe resides in the centre of that word. It acts as an anchor within the word, facilitating the making of a moment in time where communication with the divine is possible. Anishinaabeg Elder Richard Morrison shares his knowledge on the meaning of nookwezigan as it relates to the power of it to women and girls:

> Nookwezigan, when we say that noo it means I, me. Kwe is the woman. Kwe is also a moment of time. I, me, in a moment of time. Zig is a life experience. Gan is the object. I am this object in life. I am this object in life in this moment of time. Me and I, my physical and spiritual self comes to a balance; comes to an understanding. There is no thought and there is no feeling about that. So, we learn to focus our energies. There is a total silence inside of us. We breath it in, it smudges us inside and we breath it out. (qtd. in Gitimido)

Kwe's presence in the word nookweziganoon is a loving reminder that all women and girls are at the "center of everything" (Solomon 34) and at "the center of the wheel of life" (Solomon 35). As women, we are the first doorway through which new life enters this world and is welcomed. We provide the first arms to hold it and the first food to nourish it. We are the first teacher to teach it the Anishinaabeg way of life.

As an Anishinaabeg mother, I carry out the nookweziganoon using my mother's medicines. The act of smudging is a sacred act of all Kwewag because it is a ceremony that women can perform at any time during their moon/menstruation cycle. In smudging, Kwewag seek to hold sacredness and respect for all our relations in Creation inside our hearts while we pray. Through prayer, we remember and honour all our ancestors and those yet to be born with only good thoughts. Smudging allows us time to acknowledge the sacred. We state our gratitude for all Gizhew-Manidoo, the first Creator of life, has made and all that Aki, the sacred First mother, has provided on the earth for our survival. As women, we look for these sacred mothers in everything. Kwewag are the embodiment of the Great Spirit's Creation on Earth and through us the gift of birth and maternal leadership, so our women are sacred leaders. Smudging teaches our women and girls that caring for Creation is a woman's responsibility.

The nookweziganoon is an ancient ceremony that has been

performed for generations by the many mothers and grandmothers before me as a tool to teach our children about Anishinaabeg identity and communal responsibility. By smudging with my family, I teach my daughters to understand the importance of their role as Kwezensag to centre the family on what is important: health, family, culture, community, and our role in Creation. They learn through observation and experiential learning-by-doing practices. They watch me and my husband and then mimic our actions. My daughters have learned a lot about living in the time of the Seventh Fire. I hope the smudging ceremony can help them to understand what it means to be Anishinaabe-kwezensag (little women) and revision their place in this new world, which looks so different from the one we lived in just six to seven months ago.

She Smudges Her Home: Performing Nookweziganoon

For me as a doodoom, educating my children on what they need to survive a COVID-19-riddled world is the most important job I have. As the news of COVID-19 was getting worse and worse, I gathered my smudging items—my es (shell) to use as the smudging bowl; my mashkodewashk (white buffalo sage); my ishkodensan (matches); and my migiziwigwan (eagle feather)—to perform the nookweziganoon or smudging ceremony with my girls.

For this ceremony, I set my ceremonial items on my counter in the kitchen, roll my sage into a ball, light it with an ishkodens and let the flame go down naturally to create a soft smoke. I take my migiziwigwan and cleanse it over the smoke, bathing and cleansing it of any negative energy it could have picked up. I then cleanse my hands in the smoke of the smudge, which I clean as if I am cleansing my hands with soap and water over a sink.

As a mother, I do this practice because I hold my children with my hands. I wash my children with my hands. I play with my children and prepare the food that feeds my children with my hands. My daughters mimic my actions, cleansing their little hands. Then I pick up my eagle feather to fan the smoke immediately over all the ceremonial items and the space immediately around the area where I and anyone with me are standing. Fanning distributes the smoke and cleanses the space of negative energies, thus making it safe space to offer prayer and good healing intentions. As we begin this smudging process, I tell my daughters to begin thinking good thoughts, feel love in their hearts, and hold good intentions in their mind as they listen to mommy pray. We take deep breaths, close our eyes, and seek to quiet our whole body and mind.

Next, I lay the feather down and cup the smoke in my hands and bring it over my head and down across my hair as if washing it. I do this so that I will have only positive thoughts, which will help push away the negative thoughts, making room for only my good intentions. I take more smoke and wash it over the heads of my daughters, but they usually push my hands away so they can do it themselves.

I cup more smoke to bring up to cleanse my ears. I do this so that my ears will hear the spiritual truths given by Gizhew-Manidoo. I listen to the truth as it is shared with me by the Creator, the ancestral Grandmothers, the Manidoog (Spirits), the directions—giiwedinong (north), waabanong (east), zhaawanong (south), and epangishimok (west)—as well as all my relations (animals, birds, fish, plants, trees, etc.). I listen to be open to the assistance from manidoowag (spirits as well as other-than-human beings and to hear only the good things, allowing the bad things to go elsewhere. The girls do the same.

Then, I cleanse my face. First, I cup the smoke. I raise it up to my eyes, cleansing my sight so that I will see the truth around me—the beauty of Aki (the First Mother, the Earth), the gifts given us by Gizhew-Manidoo, as well as the love shared with me through my children, husband, friends, and community. I the raise the smoke to my nose and breathe it in deeply. The act of breathing in the medicinal herbal smoke cleanses my insides and draws in good energies to my jichaag (soul-spirit), and breathing out expels the negative energies. Similarly, I cleanse my mouth, breathing in again and exhaling more negative energies. Furthermore, I cleanse my mouth so that all I speak to my children, family, friends, and community will be truthful, positive, kind, loving, and thankful. Little hands wash their face and wait for the next directions.

After the face, we bring smoke up to our hearts and hold our hands over our hearts in a moment of quiet. My children tend to hug themselves for a moment. I cleanse my heart so that my heart will feel the truth and so that it will be good and pure and be open to show compassion, gentleness, and care for others. I also cleanse the bottoms of my feet so that they will seek Anishinaabe-kwe mino-miikana-bimaadiziwin (the good path in life as a woman). It aids me to seek balance and harmony, leads me closer to my family, friends, community, and helps me to walk closer to my loved ones.

Additionally, I smudge my feet to help me in an effort to flee these dangerous times, situations, and locations where COVID-19 is a constant threat, and lead me closer to the land as healer, the Creator as my guide, and my wisdom of my grandmothers. Lastly, I cleanse my chibowmum, or aura (Johnston15), using my eagle feather. I comb downwards over my body, as if combing my hair, brushing the smoke downwards over my arms, legs, and back to brush away any negative energies that are bound up in my chibowmun. I smudge my whole being so that I will portray only the good part of myself through my actions. After my body is cleansed, I begin to cleanse the rooms of the house, including the entryways. Watching my little kids try to wash their feet and body in smoke is usually comical, and the laughter that ensues is often a welcome distraction from the seriousness of living with COVID-19

When I am finally ready to say the prayers, the children quiet down so they can listen to the words. It is time to quiet the mind, focus the heart, and centre ourselves with Creation: Gizhew-Manidoo, Aki (Earth), nibi (sister water), all living things, our families, friends, community, and the world. Anishinaabeg smudge prayers are centred on praying for our relatives in Creation. We send those prayers through the smoke of the smudge to communicate with Creation. Every smudge ceremony is rooted not in "I" but "we." COVID-19 has unveiled to the world an ever increasingly, "toxic individualistic society, a symptom of colonization and capitalism, wherein the status quo has lost its concern for the collective" (Begay, Jade). To think only in terms of "I" is to be egotistical and ignores the important following question: How am I interconnected and inextricably linked to all of my relatives? Anishinaabeg linguist James Vukleich states that we must remember the Anishinaabeg concept of gidinawendimin when praying, meaning "I am all of my relatives and all of my relatives are me" (Vukelich, "Gidinawendimin"). As Anishinaabeg we must pray for people, not exclusively for ourselves. We must always pray for our relations. The idea that a person separate from others does not exist in Anishinaabeg epistemology. Instead, Vukelich explains that through the practice of praying, we understand that we must live as though we are one link in a chain going back through time and also going all the way forwards (Vukelich, "Gidinawendimin"). When I practice my smudging ceremony with my daughters, I feel the closest to those seven generations from the past and those seven generations yet to arrive. When I pray now, I think of the phrase I heard from Vukelich: "Mii sa go geget inawendiyang" ("We truly are all related") (Vukelich, "Gidinawendimin").

To complete the ceremonial process, we let the burnt medicine cool in the vessel and then we return it back to the land, our Mother the Earth. My daughters give back her spent medicine and say miigwech, or thank you, as they place the ashes back on the land, making sure there are no active embers so as not to start a fire. This disposal of the ashes symbolizes that we are cleansed. The negative energies—all bad thoughts, words, and feelings—are not welcome inside the home or our bodies. The ashes can be scattered by the entrance of a home to rid it of negative energies or to act as a barrier against negative energies from further entering the home. Through this ceremony, I can live as a Kwe and live through the COVID-19 pandemic in the same way that my ancestral grandmothers would have lived through their apocalypse. We are all connected through time and space. When we smudge, we draw on their wisdom and powers to keep our family safe.

Ayaangwaamiziwin

To me, smudging is meeting the call to action from the prophets and our ancestors. Smudging changes the mindset from one of fear to one of ayaangwaamiziwin, which refers to a way of thinking that emphasizes having an awareness of your place, your relationships to your relatives, and your role in Creation (Vukelich, "Ayaang-waamiziwin"). Ayaangwaamiziwin tells us that we do not have to accept that the COVID-19 pandemic has to be an apocalypse. The ethical protocols of ayaangwaamiziwin direct that I change my life (aanji-bimaadizi) and reimagine my actions in order to survive: to be cautious and to become more aware of my relationships to everyone in Creation.

There is an old story that Basil Johnston recorded in his book *Ojibway Heritage* about Omagakii (a frog) and Ginebig (a snake). The story embodies the epistemological and axiological mindset of ayaangwaamiziwin that I have tried to embody as a mother as I navigate and explain my use of smudging during the pandemic (39-40). I will offer my own brief retelling here because I have heard this story told from many storytellers across Anishinaabeg territory, but I want to credit Johnston's version as my inspiration. The story begins with a Nookomis (grandmother) and her Kwezens picking blueberries on a summer day. As they pick their berries, they witness an interaction between Omagakii and Ginebig They watch as Ginebig chases Omaagakii into a patch of animikkibag (poison ivy). Ginebig is smart and chooses not to follow Omaagakii into the poisonous bushes but instead waits to see if the frog will come out on its own. He waits and waits a long time, but Omaagakii does not come out. The oils of the animikkibag start to irritate Omaagakii's skin, making it burn and itch, but she does not come out because she knows it will be the end of her. The snake grows bored and leaves to find easier prey. As soon as the area is safe, Omaagakii comes out and hops over to the patch of omakakiibag (jewel weed) growing nearby, and she rubs herself on the plant as the cure for the rash.

The teaching is not just about the cure for poison ivy but a lesson in ayaangwaamiziwin: caution, care, and awareness. Omaagakii was aware of her surroundings and determined the safest place to go. Seeing the danger of dashing out of the ivy patch in fear, she stayed hidden away and was rewarded with safety after Ginebig left. Ayaangwaamiziwin means not to react solely based in fear but to instead be aware and act from a sense of caution and awareness. In the story, Omaagakii teaches us to be aware: "Be aware of what is taking place around you. Be aware of how you are acting in relationship to all of your relatives" (Vukelich, "Ayaangwaamiziwin"). We must think about how our actions affect others and how we can cause the least harm. Omaagakii 's decision to go into the poison ivy did not cause any harm to Ginebig, the landscape, or herself. Omaagakii 's interactions with the plant world teaches us that we are related in Creation, even those who could harm us. The frog learns that the medicines are there for her when she needs them, and they willingly give themselves for others in Creation to use. Omaagakii was gentle with Ginebig, even though the snake intended to kill Omaagakii, and, thus, we learn that how I affect my relatives in Creation is meaningful.

Omaagakii acted with care and kindness and thus was rewarded with freedom. The moment we have awareness of those relationships we can begin to act differently, with less egotism and "toxic individualism" (Begay). The moment our relatives become everyone we have relationships with, and even those we do not, we can act with greater care and in such a way that we are not harming them but rather bringing them peace, harmony, and balance. Therefore, during this COVID-19 pandemic, we wear our masks, we stay home, we social distance, we order things online instead of shopping in stores, and we keep our social bubble of friends and family small. In my ceremonial bundle, along with my smudging items, I place these new teachings and carry them close to my heart.

As I smudge, these teachings extend to my family's lived experiences with COVID-19. I try to think about our sense of resurgent awareness, care, and caution in using smudging to anchor our day-to-day realities within the safety of an Anishinaabeg worldview. I perform this ceremony to connect with the wisdom my ancestral grandmothers. I now know that I chose smudge in order to walk down that "good road of life" that the prophecy tells us to walk: Anishinaabeg mino-miikana-bimaadiziwin. When we walk that road together as a family, we are living the Anishinaabeg way of life, the one our Creator intended us to follow. Anishinaabeg Elder Jim Onaubinsay Dumont of Shawanaga First Nation states: "When you go all the way back to the beginning, the Creator gave us a way of life and that is the way [they[3]] intended for us to live.... There is not any other way of life that will come along and replace it.... Ours is particular to our way of being.... Our responsibility is to keep ours going (qtd in Sinclair 25). With these words in mind, I work hard to remember that my role in Creation as a mother is to ensure that my family keeps our cultural ways of being and living alive.

Michi Saagiig Nishnaabeg scholar, writer and artist Leanne Betasamosake Simpson shares the word "aabawaadiziiwin," which means "togetherness, or the art of being together." She continues: "It means that we must practice good relationships with all living beings around us. This begins in our families and with our children" (122). Simpson explains that the family is a microcosm of our nation, and it is the parents that model the ways we should live as Anishinaabeg (122). We model the values, the leadership skills, and the ways of living in harmony together as citizens in a society. Therefore, this chapter has aimed to model for the readers the ways in which Anishinaabeg mothers live with, deal with, and act in the face of the COVID-19 pandemic. We mother our way through the pandemic by following an Anishinaabe-kwe worldview, which is informed by the teachings, ceremonies, and the wisdom of our mothers and grandmothers who came before us.

Final Thoughts

In closing, we will survive COVID-19. Living through this pandemic has been hard and scary, but we will endure just as our ancestors did long ago when Europeans introduced smallpox, tuberculosis, measles, and other diseases among our people. As the quote from *Moon of the Crusted Snow* shared at the beginning of this chapter states: "Yes, apocalypse. We've had that over and over. But we always survived. We're still here. And we'll still be here, even if the power and the radios don't come back on and we never see any white people ever again (Rice 150). We will endure because our prophecies tell us we will if we stay true to our mino-miikana (the good path).

By the time a vaccine exists for COVID-19, we will have learned so much from living through this moment as mothers. We will remember the teachings of this time and add it to our oral stories; we will share with our children the medicines and ceremonies that saw us through. We will see where our communities, cities, and nation came together to protect our people, our children. When COVID-19 has passed, we will tell our stories to our grandchildren so that they will not forget how the warnings of the prophecies continue to affect our lives and so that they too must hold true to mino-bimaadiziwin if they are to endure the difficult times. This moment feels scary and strange ,but it's moments like these that really make us become strong, innovative, holistic minded, and resilient mothers, women, leaders, and (s)heroes for our children. Miigwech! Thank you!

Endnotes

1. Here I have used the spelling of prophecies (plural) as Onwaachigewinan, which is in the double vowel system. In the quote from Murdoch, he spells prophecy (singular) as Onwegitchigewin. Both are correct, but

dialects, and thus spellings, can vary depending on the person who writes it.

2. This is critical because there are many ceremonies that women cannot perform while on their moon/menstruation cycle[2] due to the uncertainty of their powers during that time of the month. To honour the woman's energies and to not cause a disruption to the lives or sacred objects of others, women usually abstain from any ceremonies during their moon/menstruation time, except smudging.

3. Dumont originally uses the "he" to refer to Gizhew-Manidoo. Regarding the use of pronouns in relation to Gizhew-Manidoo, the Creator has no specific gender. Some Elders, like Dumont, say "he," but they also teach that in the language, there is no preferred gender. It is all genders. I prefer "they" when writing about the Creator so as not to get trapped into a Christian mindset, which automatically uses the pronoun "he." I have replaced "he" with "they" so as to be inclusive of all genders and allow readers who use the pronouns "he," "she," or "they" to be included.

Works Cited

Begay, Jade. "Decolonizing Community Care in Response to COVID-19." *NDN Collective*, 13 Mar. 2020, ndncollective.org/indigenizing-and-decolonizing-community-care-in-response-to-covid-19. Accessed 23 Aug. 2020.

Benton-Banai, Edward. *The Mishomis Book: The Voice of the Ojibway.* University of Minnesota Press, 1988.

Gitimido, Kanzee. "OJIBWE TEACHINGS PART 2 Richard Morrison A K A Geegwegigabooo." *Soundcloud.* 2 Feb. 2016, soundcloud.com/kanzee-gitimido/ojibwe-teachings-part-2-richard-morrison-a-k-a-geegwegigabooo-uniters-media. Accessed 16 Jan. 2021.

Johnston, Basil. *Ojibway Heritage.* 1976. McClelland & Stewart, 2008.

Murdoch, Issac. "COVID-19 | Anishinaabe Pandemic Prophecies." Uploaded by Yellowhead Institute, *YouTube*, 23 Apr. 2020, www.youtube.com/watch?v=5vmDGwfoJH8. Accessed 20 Sept. 2020.

Rice, Waubgeshig. *Moon of the Crusted Snow.* ECW Press, 2018.

Sinclair, Niigonwedom James. *Nindoodemag Bagijiganan: A History of Anishinaabeg Narrative.* 2013. Dissertation. The University of British Columbia, 2013.

Simpson, Leanne. *Dancing on Our Turtle's Back: Stories of Nishnaabeg Re-Creation, Resurgence and a New Emergence.* ARP Books, 2011.

Solomon, Arthur. *Songs for the People: Teachings on the Natural Way.* NC Press Limited, 1990.

Vukelich, James. "Ojibwe Word of the Day Aanji-bimaadizi. 'S/he Changes Her/His Life.'" *Facebook*, 20 Aug. 2020, www.facebook.com/james.vukelich.7/videos/10223003974303440. Accessed 22 Aug. 2020. Accessed 10 Sept. 2020.

Vukelich, James. "Ojibwe Word of the Day Ayaangwaamiziwin. 'Awareness, Caution, Care.'" *Facebook*, 30 July 2020, www.facebook.com/james.vukelich.7/videos/10222871002859237/. Accessed 15 Sept. 2020.

Vukelich, James. "Ojibwe Word of the Day Gidinawendimin. 'We Are Related to Each Other.'" *Facebook*, 23 July. 2020, www.facebook.com/james.vukelich.7/videos/10222804566158361.swet. Accessed 22 Sept. 2020.

Vukelich, James. "Ojibwe Word of the Day Nookwezige. 'S/he Smudges Things Medicinally.'" *Facebook*, 18 Jun 2020, www.facebook.com/james.vukelich.7/videos/10222446426005081. Accessed 4 Sept. 2020.

Chapter Thirty Eight

Futures for Ghosts: Using Traditional Feminized Skill, While Adapting to the Unprecedented, for a Future Unknown

Hillary Di Menna

"I've been thinking," my dad says, his eyes moving towards my daughter's fidgeting hands, as we sit down for dinner, "You were never raised as a teenager." This could sound weird coming from a father, but in our case, he became my father when I was months shy of eighteen. I was a stray. My mom died when I was six years old. I was bounced around relatives and friends, but it was mostly my nonna who continued to raise me until I was twelve, when my biological, and now estranged, father moved me across the country, from BC to Ontario, to live with him and his new family. For four years I lived the kind of life where as soon as you turn sixteen, you grab that black kitten you found outside of a punk show and run, barefoot, to years of sleeping on couches, on coffee shop chairs, in mall basements, in alleyways, and in the arms of friends just as young and scared as you.

My childhood was full of abuse but never at the hands of my mom and nonna. They loved me, and I drew from this love immediately upon learning of the milk and honey swimming in my young belly. I continue to drink from the water of my matriarchs, as if it were Lake Nemi, but

I still wonder where to draw from in order to raise a teenager when my own history is haunted. The space between living with my nonna as a kid and living with my adoptive family as an adult (an adult in that technical, legal document sense) is full of question marks.

"Order whatever you want," he tells my daughter, as grandpas do. At twelve, she can technically still order from the kids section, but she insists she is not a kid anymore, as she wonders aloud how much extra chocolate sauce she can get with dessert. "Is there a term for living in constant grief," I ask. "Like, maybe what older people feel, seeing all their friends die?" It is November 2019.

2018 and 2019 hadn't been great: broken bones, breakdowns, and burials. When I called my brother to tell him my best friend from high school was killed, he answered from his hospital bed. He had received two lifesaving organ transplants in the ward where I saw a family friend for the last time and in the hospital where I recently woke up after passing out from mental exhaustion. In late 2019, friends helped paint our apartment to celebrate new beginnings and that we were making a permanent home. I told myself that I would surround myself with loved ones in 2020, that it would be a year of change.

The dessert arrives. Looking back, I don't remember it tasting so bittersweet.

COVID-19's screaming silence has interrupted my run from past trauma; it howls for me to learn from the past and grow, while keeping me curled up in confinement. Old traditions—crafting, baking, and creating in the way our mothers have taught us to survive strange times—guide me and my daughter. In order to navigate this unprecedented present, I have learned to stop trying to fit into a future that was never healthy in the first place. I don't have time to deal with constructed milestones I am expected to reach. I have a daughter to raise.

Hinting at her arrival late on a February 29, my baby was born on March 2, after a thirty-plus-hour hospital adventure. She came in screaming like a crash cymbal; it was 2008. News of the recession was everywhere: "Grown up stuff," I tell myself, feeling disconnected from it all. It is fitting that she spent her final year as a kid during another explosion of sorts; she coordinates her milestones by taking global temperature.

Twelve Marchs pass.

For us, COVID-19 starts with a call from the school, a usual occurrence, when Mother to a confident and vocal daughter. I finish drying my hands from a regularly scheduled office pizza party—the kind that's supposed to make you forget things like raises and benefits. The office is talking about COVID-19. It seems like I am the only one afraid, as some of my coworkers go as far as to say it is all a hoax. As a certified hysterical woman, I set myself a ground rule: I will not be afraid until the schools shut down. The principal wants to tell me that my daughter had a great day and that she did very well. My cheeks shine bright and proud like Christmas ornaments—until they become white as snow when I hear the schools will be closing. I am allowed to be scared now.

The next day is Friday the 13th March 2020. The subway breaks down on my way home from work; I find myself grateful for the Toronto-life familiarity. I wait in a library for my partner to pick me up. Sitting cross-legged, I eat leftover pizza, listening to the library workers talk about how they may end up closing. It strikes me how dependant I am on the library, which prompts me to list other resources that I depend on which may become unavailable. Everyone is wild about toilet paper, but what about food? What are we supposed to stock up on food wise? Snack Program won't exist while the schools are closed. Why do I never bother with meal prep? Should I be rationing this pizza slice? We will need to get the kid's laptop fixed. She is incredibly social—quick, what do incredibly social people need in times of isolation? I should know this stuff. Why the hell would I know this stuff? My daughter's doctor calls to reschedule her upcoming appointment indefinitely. The job interviews I have lined up are postponed via email. Life is rescheduled indefinitely.

My daughter and I ride the subway together to my work in the mornings, with scarves wrapped around our noses and mouths. I think about the face masks I meant to buy in February, for her birthday present. Face masks became popular among Toronto middle schoolers in January 2020—how did they know; those intuitive middle school wild animals, running from the fire, before the rest of us even know about it. The commute is long, stops punctuate the growing to-do list. Coxwell—Who is going to take care of her while I'm at work? Greenwood—What are the rules around visitations with her dad during a pandemic? Donlands—I guess I'll buy her a bunch of craft supplies and that Batman video game she plays with her uncle. Actually, can Batman be her babysitter? Pape—What am I talking about, Batman is kind of a jerk, wait, what about her medications? Will the pharmacy let us stock up? We eventually get to Castle Frank, that sweet internet reception spot where, on a regular day when the subway is full, phones shine like streetlights. A friend texts me, surprised I am on my way to work, as the Ontario government has just declared a state of emergency. The reception is lost before I can reply. Time is always running out. At the office, we listen to Trudeau's voice from my coworkers' cell phones and computer speakers. All I hear is the clock I set as a six-year-old tick loudly, reminding me of my mortality.

As a child, while other primary school kids focused on adding numbers and understanding proper punctuation, I mastered the art of creating a comforting expression in response to the gasps of grownups saying, "Your mother died at thirty-five years old? That is too young!" As my daughter spends 2020 saying goodbye to her childhood years, I am spending it saying goodbye to all the times I nodded, confused, thinking, "Thirty-five isn't young." Months away from turning thirty-five myself, I now understand that thirty-five does not an all-knowing, fearless grown-up make. My daughter and I are both shedding old skins. As I worry about dying during a pandemic where people are, in fact, dying, the people around me talk about hoaxes, about it only being the sick and elderly dying—awkward mental gymnastics around the justification of deeming any life disposable. My mind can't keep up with what is real or not. As an abuse survivor, living with complex post-traumatic stress disorder, I have grown accustomed to being told I am over-reacting. My mind can't process things fast enough. I am on sick leave by April. People tell me I am lucky for my mental illness.

I used to fantasize about what I would do with time off; I said I would write a book. I want to leave something for my daughter. I want to create and preserve some family history, under the pressure of a self-set ticking bomb. Of course, no writing is done, and of course, in keeping the tradition of all Italian-Catholic moms who came before me, I feel guilty.

I go to the emergency room one night, for the intense pains that come with having a body breaking down from mental exhaustion, the kind of pains doctors try to write off as, "Maybe you are on your period?" and the next morning I am advocating for my daughter's Individualized Education Plan accommodations. There are no breaks in between. I create organizational systems. I keep in regular contact with school staff. I cry at night, from exhaustion. People tell me, "You don't need to be doing this. You don't need to worry about her school experience." When you are someone who has experienced falling through the cracks, you don't let it happen to others. If they could see my baby witchlet's face, when she knows she is not keeping up, that she has spent the majority of her school years being told she is 'different', 'not trying hard enough', that she is 'bad', they would feel the pain from her eyes seep into their own bones. The struggle of advocating for the mental health of a child becomes even more difficult when the world turns upside down and inside out. Learning disabilities and ADHD are no longer just swept under the rug by the school board, they are discarded and forgotten.

I learn dances on YouTube to help her keep up with her musical theatre rehearsals at home. My usually loud daughter doesn't say she is scared, but she seems to be glued to my side. Tears roll down my baby's eyes while participating in virtual funny hat day; her birthday cake hat is a little lopsided. Zoom hangouts have quickly grown tiresome. People freeze; the shapes of their mouths don't match the sounds coming from crackling speakers. Nothing seems real. It is like everything has died and our ghosts are using our bodies to play Pretend Once Was; Zoom calls are the bedsheets we wear to ensure that we continue to be seen—that we aren't all lost.

Still, we maintain a routine. Specialists say to maintain a routine. We make sure to wear clean clothes, go to sleep at bed time, and shower regularly. Our days consist of craft time (including making many an experimental mask as directed by YouTube), Netflix reruns, and Tarot readings—why do I keep pulling the death card?!—virtual doctor appointments, phone calls with counsellors, and coding camps. I used to say, "I can't afford a house, but that's okay, the city is our backyard!" Since that backyard closed, it seems like our apartment shrunk, too. Our apartment isn't huge, but the Wi-Fi never seems to be strong enough to accommodate our new lifestyle.

We make smoothies every morning until we lose two blenders to "Oops, sorry, Mom!" We cook and bake recipes from the recipe cards my daughter's old caregiver gifted her. I fight the landlord as he tries to evict us, as he wants to rent our place at double the rent. I create a better fire escape strategy after a neighbour decided he wanted to burn the building down. Old problems don't disappear with the appearance of COVID-19; they become exacerbated.

No matter how much we do, no matter how much I do, I feel like I am doing nothing.

Knowing how the system is not built to protect us is what both hurts me and gives me strength. My young mother days were not full of showers and cake smashes, but appointments with social workers and meetings at family court. I didn't know about cloth diapers, but I knew about escaping violent homes. I have always done what is needed for us, and, sometimes, tradition does more harm than good. These experiences reinforce my knowing that a premier who famously said his province was "open for business" may not have people's best interests at heart. The stress of these new experiences launch me into a mode I developed to survive past traumas: an intense, exhausting hypervigilance, that was not necessary in this new situation. I don't know what to do or how to properly process anything. I have flashbacks of food bank line-ups and social services waiting rooms. Nothing feels safe. I am no longer facing old dangers, but I am living in an unpredictably dangerous time. In isolation, I have finally been given time to think. I am no longer able to outrun my trauma. I have to face all of it. It hurts. It makes me angry. It makes me rebuild.

Some traditions are great, like mixing pizzelle batter in Pyrex floral pattern bowls. The idea that communities and families should be kept apart but that we can all work for the benefit for a few guys at the top of society's pyramid is not so charming. It isn't bosses checking in on us; it is the friends who fix my daughter's computer and bring us bread, the family who sits outside with us, in the rain, just to make sure they see us, when we aren't able to visit indoors, and the neighbours we have bonded with since our apartment building became its own small town.

The powers that be really want us to keep working towards a bright future, even though such a future was out of reach long before the arrival of COVID-19. Just as I will no longer let my past haunt me, I will not be used to build a future for ghosts. I mourn many things in this time, but a system that makes me feel lucky for being on sick leave is not one of them.

I'm happy to take this opportunity to steal back the time capitalism has tried to keep locked away from us. I will not feel guilty for feeling the same freedom we did when I let her skip school so that we could put stickers on her pink skateboard; or when we went to Hot Topic so that my daughter could spend her birthday money, before seeing *Birds of Prey*, one week before that especially ominous Friday the 13th, as if we knew we needed to sneak in one last movie before the world shut down. We colour together, and I feel relief that I am creating again, without the expectations of capitalism. I feel embarrassment that I stressed so much about a world where my cap and gown would never be as exciting as a wedding gown; my daughter cheers me on when I'm in a ripped-up, floral-slip dress and a leopard print jacket, as I do her when she wears her own vibrancy as she sees fit.

I think a lot of us are scared about talking about COVID-19 grief. We want to be polite. We want to acknowledge that there is someone who has it worse. We are collectively grieving; we are all big-mouthed preteens who have become unusually quiet and glued to the sides of what brings us a feeling of security or, at least, familiarity.

Some days I feel like we are living life as phantoms. Other days I remember to not let myself be haunted by my past. Most days, I am happy to no longer prioritize a future made for dead social constructions. I would be lying if I say that I never crave alone time or that entertaining an only child going through puberty and living with ADHD, while being trapped together in an apartment, is easy. We go on so many walks that even our dog is sick of them. It is very hard at times. I don't know if I will ever have uninterrupted time to write again. But as we move forward into whatever the world ends up looking like, I want to remember what we made work.

My daughter has thrived in virtual school because of the work I did to level the playing field for her. As her psychiatrist tells her, "You know what your mom is? An advocate." Now it's July, and we set her up to work at her nonna's, my mom's, old desk in preparation for the upcoming online school year.

My mom raised me when she had cancer; my nonna raised me while grieving the loss of her daughter. My daughter's whole life has been shaped by the collapse of the system I thought I knew, and she's forever amazing. My crafting a way forwards, with all the complex feelings in between, is keeping with tradition.

In 2021, I'll turn the age too young to die, as my baby turns Lucky 13. And maybe I'll find a quiet place where I can write that book, but in the meantime, I don't mind making early Halloween crafts with my babe and eating too much ice cream.

Chapter Thirty Nine

For the Lockdown Babies

Gráinne Evans

"Sure, you were only a baby," I'll tell her when she asks,
About that time in photographs when everyone wore masks.
"You don't remember the chaos when the world was forced to rest.
You had all you needed in my arms and at my breast."

"You never even noticed," I'll tell her, then I'll say,
"I held you as the weeks went by, we took it day by day.
We were safe and happy, right where we needed to be.
I fed you snuggled in my arms, protecting you was key."

"You were only a tiny baby," I'll tell her and explain,
Why so many people were afraid, anxious and in pain.
"It wasn't always easy, those isolating newborn days,
But feeding you flooded me with love, got me through the haze."

"You were a lockdown baby," I'll tell her when it's time.
"I was your whole world back then, just as you were mine.
And now, though it's just a memory, I still smile when I see,
A rainbow in a window, put there for you and me."

Chapter Forty

Are We Not the Heroes? Racialized Single Mothers during the COVID-19 Lockdown

Punam Mehta

In this critical feminist photovoice chapter, I blend visual images with written text to explore how I coped as a single racialized mother during the COVID-19 lockdown. More specifically, I explore how I un/coped as a racialized single mother during the COVID-19 lockdown. I use feminist standpoint theory to occupy a position that incorporates both conscious knowing of the world and the ways the world is shaped by our material circumstances (Hekman 342). I draw awareness to the issues of power dynamics based on my own lived experiences with the understanding that knowledge is socially situated (Hekman 342). This understanding made it possible to bring attentiveness to specific factors and ask critical questions more than it was for nonsingle mothers.

In this chapter, I argue that the COVID-19 lockdown brought to light the injustice faced by me and many other racialized single mothers, which some feminists have been pointing out for decades. I explore the closing the playgrounds, the practice of feminist-informed yoga, the endless baking, keeping my day job, and gendered racism. Finally, to break the cycle of misogyny, which values the morals of the traditional family unit (Connell and Pearse 198), society must recognize single-mother families as families that challenge the traditional family unit.

More specifically, I examine the hidden labour that I did in the context of the COVID-19 lockdown, which included becoming a homeschool teacher, a full-time cook, an entertainer, and more while maintaining two part-time jobs and completing a doctoral dissertation. The thematic photographs speak to specific subjects, whereas the narrative text focuses on the story I am telling the reader about the difficulties of life in lockdown. Finally, I reflect on the broader gendered and racialized irregularities of power as a consequence of heteropatriarchal social arrangements that expose the hidden labour women do in traditional family structures.

I argue that the context of COVID-19 did not create this labour disproportionateness but intensified it, revealing gross inequalities about who performs most household labour. For too long, the unequal carework done by single mothers has been excused as a labour of love—or that caregiving comes naturally to women—despite an extensive history of feminist mothers fighting their exploitation. Furthermore, critical feminist writing attends less to the challenges faced by racialized single mothers. Using feminist standpoint theory allowed me to increase my own awareness of the factors that nonsingle mothers and/or nonracialized mothers often do not always recognize, particularly the stigma of racialized single motherhood.

Playgrounds

I took this picture of my daughter on the first day of the lockdown, which was also her last day at the playground. I remember the panic I felt about the uncertain fear of living with the new reality of a COVID-19 lockdown. Children's playgrounds have been a central part of our daily lives since she was born, and now they were off limits. Playgrounds benefit us in immeasurable ways, as they offer freedom to meet other kids and parents and they are available at no cost to me as a single mother. During the lockdown, the loss of access to free community playgrounds did tremendous harm to our overall health and wellbeing. The loss of free places to play exposed the unfair burden of poverty that many racialized single mothers face and the need for increased financial support (Little 662).

Yoga

During the lockdown, we deviated from the homeschool agenda and moved into a daily yoga practice. In this photo, my daughter is sitting on a yoga mat, and I talked to her about consciousness and our connection to the cosmic consciousness. I spoke to her about the kinds of happiness that plug into your consciousness—the direct consciousness of a person, a sensation, or a dream. I introduced her to the ancient yoga traditions of the Indus Valley civilization as she moved in and out to the flow of breath to stillness. The COVID-19 lockdown was an opportunity for us to investigate the spiritual dimensions of our preindustrialized civilization, which humanity tends to undervalue. I explained that women, particularly women of her cultural identity (she is both Jain and Sikh), carry the strength and power of these traditions through her ancestors. I explained to her how the yogic traditions are carried on through her yoga practice. I talk to her about the problems with yoga in the modern world, as it is rooted in an obsession with the body. I encourage her to start practicing yoga at her young age and to learn about ways to live within the ancient yoga traditions. Sharing these teachings with my daughter were some the most enjoyable moments of the COVID-19 lockdown.

Baking

This is a picture of my daughter baking some muffins. We both learned to bake during the COVID-19 lockdown. There was so much time, and I saw baking as a learning opportunity to do more teaching. This picture looks like a picture-perfect moment, but it was, in fact, stressful for me. We ended up baking every night. This image relates to my life, as it reveals all the cooking and cleaning that I had to do in order to amuse my daughter. Although my child did love baking, I do wish these moments were more joyful for me. During the COVID-19 lockdown as a single mother, I was continuously on call to teach and please my daughter. I did not want my daughter glued to her iPad and I compared myself to other parents on social media sharing pictures of their beautiful baking. This inspired me but since the lockdown ended, we have never baked again.

My Day Job

This is me taking a nap with my daughter after waking up at 3:00 a.m. to work my day job. The isolation of the COVID-19 lock-down demonstrates the need for single mothers to have inexpensive childcare and modifiable work hours (Werner et al. 101). I fell asleep on the bed. I wake up everyday at 3:00 a.m. Even at 3:00 a.m., I feel guilty. I feel guilty for not doing more. Before the pandemic, life was busy enough, as I was working on my

PhD, teaching many courses, coordinating other people's research, and taking care of my child. It was an impossible balance before the lockdown and insane to expect single mothers to endure the most work. After the pandemic, I was completely burnt out in a way that I had never experienced, and I was left with nothing to give.

Gendered Racism

This is a picture of my mother, my daughter, and me a few years ago. I get my work ethic from my tireless mother. I argue that second-generation women of colour mothers, like myself, have been taught that survival means working as hard as possible without complaining or making time for self-care. As a child growing up, I observed my own racialized mother, who was a refugee to Canada, had been forcibly married as a teenage bride, and later became a single mother; she worked her fingers to the bone, regardless of the costs to her physical, emotional, mental, and spiritual health. My mother coped with racism, discrimination, and micro-aggressions by overachieving and always thinking positively. Prior to the COVID-19 lockdown, I had already experienced a lifetime of racism and discrimination growing up in my Canadian community neighbourhood and later as I entered into the world of academia. The lockdown made the simultaneous experiences of both racism and sexism in my life as a racialized single mother more difficult. For example, I have been teaching for several years at a university and I now understand how important it is to show students of colour that there are teachers who look like them. It is equally important for a teacher who is affected by gendered racism, such as myself, to learn to practice self-care in ways that are different from my own mother. On a basic level, self-care includes sleeping properly, eating nutritious food, and having a group of trusted friends with whom you can share your lived experiences of gendered racism and single motherhood. On a deeper level, self-care means healing that is centred on physical, emotional, mental, and spiritual wellbeing.

On the last day of lockdown, the school bus came and took my daughter to her school, where I pictured her back in her classroom. I went inside my house and locked the door, and I arranged myself on my yoga mat, feeling a bit like a lump of coal. My feet hurt. They are cracked, bloody, and sore. I needed to rest. Heroes need rest.

Conclusion

This critical feminist photovoice essay provided me with a chance to take stock of the personal cost of being a racialized single mother. It presented an opportunity to reimagine nontraditional family futures and prioritize social actions that may get us there, particularly the social action of valuing of mothers' work as paid work. The text and images speak to the many challenges of being a single racialized mother in lockdown. The COVID-19 lockdown brought to light the injustices I face as a single racialized mother. I explored the negative consequences of closing the playgrounds, as they are some of the few free spaces that single mothers who are financially burdened can rely on for play and socialization. I showed how yoga was a way of introducing spirituality into my daughter's life, whereas the endless baking I did emphasized the pressure and expectations I had placed on myself. I highlighted the work I did to keep my job, as becoming unemployed is simply not an option for a racialized single mother. Finally, my discussion of gendered racism underscored my need to learn to better care for myself in the context of the COVID-19 lockdown. Empowering single motherhood involves breaking the patriarchal discourse that values the morals of the traditional family unit (Connell and Pearse 198). It also involves recognizing the necessity of guaranteeing that racialized single mothers and their children do not live in poverty (Little 662). We need to increase the number of women in government who are committed to improving the lives of racialized single mothers. We also need racialized single mothers to rally around activism that recentres our rights and our children's rights in feminism itself.

Works Cited

Hekman, Susan. "Truth and Method: Feminist Standpoint Theory Revisited." *Signs: Journal of Women in Culture and Society*, vol. 22, no. 2, 1997, pp. 341-65.

Little, Margaret Hillyard. "The Leaner, Meaner, Welfare Machine: The Harris Government's Ideological and Material Attack on Single Mothers." *Making Normal Social Regulation in Canada*, edited by Deborah Brock, Nelson, 2003, pp. 235-58.

Werner, Marion, et al. "Conceptual Guide to the Unpaid Work Module." *Gender and Women's Studies: Critical Terrain*, edited by Margaret Hobbs and Carla Rice, Canadian Women's Press, 2016, pp. 96-104.

Chapter Forty One

The Invisible Frontline Workers: Narratives of Indian Mothers' Experiences through the Pandemic

Ketoki Mazumdar and Pooja Gupta

With physical distancing, work from home, and new parenting challenges, COVID-19 has created a new reality for parents worldwide and brought about significant stress for parents, especially mothers. Mothers in India and elsewhere have been caught in an entanglement of roles—parent, partner, employee, employer, sibling, caretaker/guardian, friend/ peer, and teacher—throughout the early months of the pandemic. Along with adjusting to being at home all day with their young ones, mothers in India are also walking the fine line of balancing working from home, taking care of household chores, and attending to their children, without the usual support systems, for example schools, daycares, domestic help, and family members. Most of these resources disappeared once India went into a nation-wide lockdown as a preventive measure against COVID-19. Studies conducted in the light of the pandemic have pointed towards the stress experienced by mothers globally (Adams-Prassl et al. 19; Davenport et al. 30; O'Reilly 12). The more visible frontline workers in the public sphere have been praised; however, as Andrea O'Reilly reflects, most are forgetting what mothers are facing and accomplishing, both at home and work, as frontline workers.

In this chapter, our goal was to explore the mothering experiences of a cohort of Indian mothers under the challenging times of COVID-19 and to focus on the meaning they found from mothering during pandemic and how they coped. In particular, these mothers had an increase in their workload, both of the physical and the emotional kind; they also had to adapt to new challenges, which often lead to heightened stress levels, affecting their psychological well being. The mothers in our study played a multitude of roles under stressful conditions. Despite this, they still sought to achieve self-care—carving time out for themselves, drawing professional, and personal boundaries, and being vocal about their needs. Their narratives reflected that their self-care practice, including becoming more self-compassionate towards themselves and their immediate family members, helped to make their mothering journeys a little less strenuous during the lockdown. In their stories, one could see that the mothers were in the process of negotiating the space between intensive mothering (Hays 8) and being a mother who puts on her own oxygen mask first before helping others. The mothering experiences of these Indian mothers during the pandemic were not much different from the experiences of other mothers worldwide, primarily because these mothers were located within a sociocultural space that was both patriarchal and individualistic. These urban mothers could share their personal narratives of maternal agency while still being rooted to their culture.

Mothering in India

The need to be a good mother and be great at it is a result of deeply rooted social and cultural expectation that women often experience throughout the course of their lives (Chrisler 118). These expectations are certainly true in the lives of Indian mothers, as society has naturalized childcare as women's primary responsibility and as intrinsic to their identity. For Indian mothers, raising children is often seen as a matter of pride and contentment and as an activity that earns them a respectable position in society (Nandy and Dutta 44). Motherhood is idealized in Indian society through the brave, self-sacrificing ideals represented through history and popular media (Bagchi 20; Sarkar). Mothers who remain in the domestic sphere are idealized, which gives them glory but not empowerment (Krishnaraj; Sinha 3).

This status of the mother in Indian society is often found to dovetail with the idea of "good mothering," which is indicative of mothers who are primary caregivers, who devote all their time and energy towards their child and their wellbeing, and who almost always put their family before their own wellbeing. Additionally, the desire to be considered as a good mother, which is an essential contributor to their worth and respectability in Indian society, can be a source of stress. The experience of mothering in India is similar to the concept of "intensive mothering" proposed by Sharon Hays (8), which centres the mother as the primary caregiver of her children.

Thus, being self-compassionate (Neff 87) and practicing self-care take on a unique relevance in motherhood because when one forgets to take care of themselves, their mental health and wellbeing are negatively affected along with their personal and professional identity (Hays 14). Furthering this idea Divya Pandey states that in India, women experience motherhood as a multilayered process, which is dictated by their family, faith, religion, customs, specific practices, and superstitions (295). Thus, researchers must give each of these experiences a voice and make them part of the overarching psychological and sociological discourses in the field. This chapter will reflect upon the diversity of experiences of a cohort of urban Indian mothers. These mothers negotiated their mothering journeys and tried to cope with the unprecedented situation of mothering through a pandemic by employing self-care and self-compassionate practices in their daily lives.

Methodology

This chapter is an excerpt from a study exploring the experiences of mothers in India during the COVID-19 pandemic. It examines the narratives of ten Indian mothers and looks at the interplay of self-compassion and self-care in how these mothers navigated the stressful and uncertain realities of the pandemic. Qualitative interviews were conducted between May and July 2020; respondents were selected through purposive sampling by locating prospective participants.

The participants consisted of urban Indian mothers who had children aged ten years and younger. Their personal and sociocultural contexts were explored through one-on-one interviews. This allowed the mothers to speak, think, and deliberate on their lived experiences of mothering through the pandemic and to be heard and to feel acknowledged without the boundaries and constraints of structured questionnaires and interviews. The mothers were aged between thirty and thirty-eight years of age. Out of the ten participants, seven had completed graduate degrees (two of them had attained doctorate degrees); the remaining three participants held bachelor degrees. All of the participants were in heterosexual marriages and lived with their spouses, except two participants, whose spouses lived away from home due to work. The participants' children were aged between two and six years. Of the ten participants, two were stay-at-home mothers, whereas the remaining eight were employed in a full-time or a part-time capacity, with their work having moved from the office to the home. They were working an average of eight hours daily. Of the participants, seven mothers belonged to a nuclear family, and four of the ten had children who attended online classes regularly.

Themes

Adapting

The task of maintaining a sense of normality in their lives and those of their children during the pandemic required mothers to evolve and adapt in order to face these new challenges. Most mothers felt that the drastic increase in their household workload was the most significant change experienced during lockdown. Before the lockdown, almost all the participants had external support in the form of domestic help, who would take care of the household chores of cleaning and cooking; others had a nanny working for them or had the support of other people who would help them with certain chores, such as paying bills or grocery shopping. With the lockdown enforced, these service providers were also restricted to their own homes, and most mothers found these responsibilities landing squarely on their shoulders. One of the participants, Anupriya[1] said, "I have always got some kind of domestic help. Apart from that, I also used to have a cook, who used to cook once in a day. So, basically during lockdown, that was the major game changer because we had no help."

The mothers felt that their routines drastically changed; they worked longer hours, completed many more tasks, and experienced a significant drop in their personal time. Their parenting also changed, as they had to take a more hands-on approach with regards to their children's schooling by supervising their online classes. All these changes made it important for the mothers to plan their days and ensure that everything worked with clockwork precision. Vrinda[2] shared how she felt, "everything started to be placed like dominoes. If you don't do the work ... then your child does not get time to spend with you. So, everything in motion had to be in place."

Most of the mothers noted that reducing their own expectations for themselves and their children vastly helped them in successfully navigating the challenges they faced. Accepting that doing everything every day is not possible and acknowledging the limitations imposed by the pandemic helped the mothers take some pressure off themselves. Some mothers allowed themselves to be unproductive for some time in the day, and a few others scheduled specific time slots to rest and recover. Nisha[3] said the following: "The only thing which has helped me in keeping myself out of stress is to let things go. So, I say to myself that if someday cleaning the house is not done, then it's not done. Sorry, I did not find time and energy to do that. I, too, need to rest and relax."

Whereas some mothers involved their children in small household tasks to keep them occupied and keep an eye on them, others encouraged their children to be independent and taught them how to keep themselves occupied. In some cases, mothers found it helpful to be more lenient towards their children as compared to before the pandemic, when it came to accessing the children's screen time and their daily routines. Mothers also dedicated time to spend with their children, when they would do an activity together that helped both of them connect. Archana[4] shared the following: "We spend a good fifteen minutes talking to each other in the morning; whatever conversation she wants to have, I have those conversations with her."

Challenges of Mothering

Mothering in any context is a challenging experience; however, the drastic and sudden changes brought on by the pandemic created unique challenges in the lives of the mothers in this study. Whereas some mothers felt guilty for not being able to spend time with their children, for not being able to concentrate and fulfil their professional duties, and not being able to dedicate some time for themselves, other mothers found themselves worrying about the impact of the pandemic on the children. Specifically, when mothers were asked about their feelings, they worried about not being able to give their children enough time, feeling responsible for the children's emotional and behavioural wellbeing, and being lenient with their children, which all gave rise to feelings of guilt. Some mothers confided that taking some time off to just unwind made them uncomfortable. Sneha[5] said: "When I get time, I am actually physically exhausted, but when I have the time and I do something else to relax, instead of finishing the to-dos, I feel guilty." Other mothers spoke about how their stress from trying to balance too many things—such as family life, work responsibilities, and household chores—affected the way they interact with their child.

The mothers tried to ensure that their children remained comfortable during the lockdown, yet they also worried about what the long-term consequences of this period would be on their children. Some mothers were concerned that the drastic reduction of social interaction with peers (which they had to work hard at even before the pandemic) would make their children become more reclusive, hurting their socio-emotional development. Swasti[6] shared the following: "I think he is getting comfortable being by himself, which makes me worried. This pandemic will definitely get over, [but] I want my family members to be without much change, so that [isolation] I think it is impacting him. He is getting more aloof, and that makes me feel extremely guilty."

Work Challenges

Working from home was a whole new experience for the employed mothers of this study, as they had to juggle their professional and personal lives all within the four walls of their homes, attending to work and childcare responsibilities. Although some of the mothers were thankful for the flexibility their workplace afforded them, they also felt this flexibility caused their work to spill into their home commitments. Some mothers set boundaries so as not to do work tasks in the time they had reserved for their children. Anuradha[7] said the following: "If it's a trade-off between giving time to my kid or giving time to emails which are sitting in my inbox, I'd choose my priorities, in this case, my son. So, if it is nine in the night, I will sit and read a story to my son because that is his time, and I will not respond to any email, even though I may get ten reminders to do it."

Most of the mothers, however, found themselves splitting their time between household chores and work demands, multitasking being their only option. Lata[8] explained the following: "I used to keep the laptop on the kitchen slab while I cooked the meals for the day all while … attending meetings and being responsive at times as well." Her experience was similar to the experience of many mothers, as they had to find ways to complete two tasks at once if they wanted to ensure that their house functioned without any glitches.

Almost all mothers shared that they have had to ensure that their child kept busy with some activity—such as playing, watching something, studying, or napping—while they were working or finishing their household chores. Since most respondents had young children who needed supervision, they had to carefully monitor their activities, which caused a reduction in their productivity, resulting in their having to work late into the night or on the weekends. The narratives of the mothers highlighted they had to make quick decisions about whether to prioritize their paid work or their household work. For instance, Lata said "If I am cooking, I will not take a call because that is also a priority for me. In fact, now I can say in front of my director that I was cooking and I couldn't take the call, as I have my mother to take care of along with my child. I have to cook, and that is also a very critical part of my role." On the other hand, mothers who prioritized work demands, found themselves feeling guilty over lost time with their children. This was well illustrated in Swasti's narrative. "Playing with my son has become an effort now, it has to be included in the plan otherwise it will not happen. My focus is my job, when I think my focus should be my son."

Support

Some of the mothers felt that they were not being adequately supported through the unprecedented times of COVID-19. They shared how they were expected to finish all the household tasks on their own and were finding it difficult to cope with the responsibilities of parenting alone. The burden of planning and managing their own and their family's schedules for the day largely fell on the mothers; additionally, mothers also felt frustrated by the lack of external support, such as domestic help, cooks, and nannies. A few mothers struggled with the feeling that their husbands would not understand their point of view or support their decisions and activities through the day; they said their husbands did not feel responsible for household and childcare responsibilities. One respondent noted how although her husband was understanding, he almost never did any household chores, as he believed that this was the responsibility of women. Adding to their troubles was the unsolicited advice that they had to face from their extended family members concerning their childrearing practices. Some mothers shared how they found themselves in situations where they felt that others would not understand their unique difficulties, and, thus, they felt hesitant to seek help or even just a patient listening ear. This was similar to Omika's[9] experience: "On Sundays, when I have my parents around and I want to do something on my own, they constantly ask me to spend time with the baby. So, it meant that the mother has to be completely attached to the baby for the whole day for the baby to feel good."

The situation of a few of the other mothers seemed to change for the better, as a few of them reported that they felt emotionally supported by their husbands, who would lend a patient ear to their problems and help them work through their moments of emotional distress. One of the mothers also shared how her husband would take their child out every time she had to join a meeting at work. Another important source of support for mothers was grandparents. The mothers referred to both maternal and paternal grandparents as pillars of support when it came to looking after the children; they helped to ensure that the children were being taken care of and helped to complete other household chores.

Self-Compassion and Self-Care

Although each mother followed her own unique path through the lockdown, they all faced similar challenges and had similar coping strategies. At the start of the lockdown, many mothers shared how they could not break through the shackles of feeling guilty. It was only as the weeks went on that most of the mothers realized that they were not alone in their struggles. Lata shared how after a few weeks she thought that "All of us are in a situation, which is a helpless one, so the entire globe is struggling with it, and I am not alone here." With this sense of being connected to others around them, most mothers started being kinder to themselves. Some mothers would just check in with themselves, similar to Nisha who shared how she would take some time to understand what was bothering her: "Is it my husband or my daughter, or is it with myself that I am not able to manage stuff or I am not able to take out time for me?"

Along with this, mothers became more mindful of themselves in their daily lives and in their interactions with their children, as they began to include elements of self-compassion into their lives. The mothers defined self-care as taking care of their own physical and psychological health. Most of them reported taking time off to watch movies and videos, treating themselves to ice-cream and chocolate as well as to more sleeping and reading. A few of the mothers mentioned how they ensured some personal time by either getting up earlier than their family members to plan the day or by taking weekends off from household responsibilities and sometimes even drawing clear boundaries regarding the tasks they would do. Sometimes, they consciously chose their own wellbeing over their other responsibilities. Some mothers would stay up late, after their children had gone to bed, to spend time with themselves and process the day they had by either making mandala art or just by sitting and doing nothing. Roopa[10] also added that this time of the day was nice and pleasant: "No one [is] calling you for something; you are not needed anymore." A significant concern among almost all of the mothers was that they did not have enough time for themselves. As Anupriya said, "Monday to Friday we don't have that much time to think whether we are happy or not."

Conclusion

The mothers in this current study were urban, and educated; they hailed from middle- or upper-middle-class societies and had young children. They recounted their experiences mothering during the COVID-19 pandemic and discussed how they had to shoulder increased professional and household duties. They endured parenting stress while making sure everything ran like clockwork. These narratives gave a chance to look at lived experiences of mothering through a lens that offered a picture beyond prevailing patriarchal discourses in India. They had to perform their role as mothers in a changing landscape, yet it provided them an opportunity to express their maternal agency. They constructed and performed their own versions of motherhood, even though the trope of being an ever-present mother was ubiquitous. They resisted some of these demands through being more self-compassionate, drawing boundaries, seeking help, and taking time for self-care.

Despite their difficulties, the mothers' agency was the nucleus around which the family revolved. Although the mothers were clearly in the driver's seat when it came to running the day, their agency as a key stakeholder of the family was not recognized by the sociocultural structures surrounding them. The integral role they played in maintaining their homes, as well as a semblance of normality, highlights how they, too, acted as frontline workers for their families. It is worth mentioning that this study only looked at mothering at a particular segment of India's population. The country has great vast regional and cultural diversity as well rural-urban divisions and class and caste differences. Thus, ideas concerning motherhood, as well as the experiences of mothers, differ widely within the country.

In conclusion, the mothers walked a fine line between handling all of their new responsibilities under the pandemic while carving an identity for themselves. The Indian mothers in the study were frontline workers for their families during the pandemic, and this study was an endeavour to highlight their work and place it within the larger global motherhood discourse.

Endnotes

1. Anupriya is a thirty-four-year-old experienced IT professional living with her husband and her four-year-old child. During the time of interview, her full-time employment required her to work from home for six hours a day. Please note that pseudonyms are used throughout this chapter.

2. Vrinda is a thirty-two-year-old MBA graduate, who works part-time. She lives alone with her five-year-old child, as her husband lives away from home due to work.

3. Nisha, a thirty-three-year-old MBA graduate; she is a stay at home mom who lives with her five-year-old child and her husband.

4. Archana is a thirty-eight-year-old banking professional, who had also started her MBA program during the lockdown. She lives with her six-year-old child and her husband; she also has the support of a full-time nanny.

5. Sneha is a thirty-year-old PhD scholar, who lives with her three-year-old child and her husband.

6. Swasti is a thirty-five-year-old banking professional, who lives with her seven-year-old child and her husband.

7. Anuradha is a thirty-four-year-old mental health professional. She lives with her husband and her two-year-old child.

8. Lata is a thirty-five-year-old, working full-time as a program coordinator. During the time of the interview, she was living with her six-year-old child and her mother. Her husband was away due to work.

9. Omika is a thirty-six-year-old associate professor at a premier business management institute, living with her three-year-old child, husband, parents and in-laws, as well as a live-in nanny.

10. Roopa is a thirty-five-year-old qualified teacher, who had two children, aged four and two years. She lived with her husband and her mother. Her children were not attending online classes regularly, and she worked from home for an average of three hours a day in her part-time job.

Works Cited

Adams-Prassl, Abi, et al. "Inequality in the Impact of the Coronavirus Shock: Evidence from Real Time Surveys." CEPR Discussion Paper 14665, 2020, pp. 1-55.

Bagchi, J. "Foreword: Motherhood Revisited." *Janani: Mothers, Daughters, Motherhood*, edited by R. Bhattacharya, Sage Publications, 2006, pp. 11-21.

Chrisler, Joan. "Womanhood Is Not As Easy As It Seems: Femininity Requires Both Achievement and Restraint." *Psychology of Men & Masculinity*, vol. 14, no. 2, 2013, pp. 117-20

Davenport, Margie H., et al. "Moms Are Not OK: COVID-19 and Maternal Mental Health." *Frontiers Global Women's Health*, vol. 1, no 1, 2020, pp. 1-6.

Hays, Sharon. *The Cultural Contradictions of Motherhood*. Yale University Press, 1996.

Krishnaraj, Maithreyi, ed. *Motherhood in India: Glorification without Empowerment?* Routledge, 2010.

Nandy, A., and D. Dutta. "On Women's Back: India Inequality Report." *Oxfam India*, 2020, www.oxfamindia.org/sites/default/files/2020-01/Oxfam_Inequality%20Report%202020%20single%20lo-res%20%281%29.pdf. Accessed 30 Oct. 2020.

Neff, Kristin. "Self-Compassion: An Alternative Conceptualization of a Healthy Attitude toward Oneself." *Self and Identity*, vol. 2, 2003, pp. 85-102.

O'Reilly, Andrea. "'Trying to Function in the Unfunctionable': Mothers and COVID-19. Maternal Health and Well-Being." *Journal of the Motherhood Initiative*, vol. 11, no 1., 2020, pp. 7-24

Pandey, Divya. "Motherhood: Different Voices." *Motherhood in India: Glorification without Empowerment?* Edited by Maithreyi Krishnaraj, Routledge, 2010, pp. 292-320.

Sinha, Chitra. "Images of Motherhood: The Hindu Code Bill Discourse." *Economic & Political Weekly*, vol. 42, no. 43, 2007, pp. 49-57.

Sarkar, Sucharita. "Why Mothers Need to Laugh at...Mothering." *Academia*, 2015, www.academia.edu/32811165/Why_Mothers_Need_to_Laugh_at_Mothering. Accessed 18 Jan. 2021.

Chapter Forty Two

Everyday Stories on Extraordinary Times: History, Relationality and Indigenous Women's Experiences during the COVID-19 Pandemic

Jaime Cidro, Mary Jane Logan McCallum,
Wendy McNab, Roberta Stout, and
Lorena Sekwan Fontaine

Introduction

Many times, we have heard that this pandemic is unprecedented, and in many ways, it is. A group of five Indigenous women, who are longtime friends, gathered to explore how the pandemic has affected our lives. For us, the pandemic shut down our workplaces, shut down our kids' schools, and brought our work into our homes full-time; in that, the pandemic swiftly changed our everyday lives to a greater or lesser extent, depending on the ages of our kids. But much of what marks this pandemic—anxiety about our health and the health of our families and those around us, frustration with isolation and immobility, and regularly confronting obstacles in the undertaking of our daily lives—is not new for us.

Likewise, our responses to the pandemic draw from our relations, both human and nonhuman, and we survive by drawing on our past, our relationship to the land, and our inner sense of authority and direction. Although our experience of COVID-19 has been marked by significant change, it has not been a complete break; rather for Indigenous women, history continues to live and breathe in our daily lives, and it is both vexing and a source of strength, especially during times of stress. For us, both the histories of colonialism and the extraordinary beauty of our cultures and our ways of relating to the world around us have come into sharp relief in our everyday lives during the COVID-19 pandemic. In this chapter, we describe our experiences of living in this pandemic, paying specific attention to the ways in which our history and our cultures shape our experiences.

After a brief review of literature on Indigenous women, this chapter analyzes one primary theme drawn from a conversation between five Indigenous women held in the late summer of 2020. The main theme that became clear from this conversation was loss and grief—the loss of opportunities to meet with infrequently visited friends and colleagues at professional conferences; the loss of regular connections to our families and communities; and the loss of access to our culture and ceremonies. This sense of loss was felt as something qualitatively different from mere disappointment; rather, it compounded an underlying sense of the importance of such meetings for our sense of who we are and how we work, particularly in light of our histories of loss, displacement, and our struggle for authority in our work. Another theme that emerged but is not included in this chapter was relationality—how we struggle and how we maintain relations with the world around us even in the context of self-isolation and instability. This theme was uncovered not only in parent-child and grandparent-grandchild relations but also in relations with our own parents. Moreover, during a time when we were told to stay inside, many of us went outdoors and turned to the world around us for help. For the purposes of this chapter, we will focus solely on the theme of loss and grief.

Scholarly writing on Indigenous mothers and women often fails to capture the substance of our everyday lives. Oftentimes, Indigenous motherhood is depicted as a dualistic foil that is meant to capture all that may be remarkably wonderful and extraordinarily terrible about the worlds we inhabit and our place within them. A significant portion of the writing is ethnographic in quality and focuses on defining Indigenous women's supposed traditional timelessness and our so-called proper place in society. These roles are often described in various ways: esteemed, autonomous, influential, and respected. Another portion of this scholarly writing attempts to locate the decline of the state of motherhood using primarily the tools of policy analysis. Yet this literature often depicts a similarly brittle trope of exploited, Indigenous womanhood under colonialism ever in danger of losing its life, kids, and community. Such renderings often take explicitly and obvious sexist federal Indian policy as the singular and monolithic agent in all lives of Indigenous women for all time. This dichotomy is often narrated in an oversimplistic accounting of our history in three essentialist stages—starting with traditional, ideal Indigenous womanhood, followed by colonialism and its dangers, and then finishing with a triumphant, resurgent, and resilient Indigenous womanhood. A newer wave of women writers is critical of these essentialist and often heterosexist portrayals of strong Indigenous women; these writers ask whether these tropes can in fact silence our vulnerabilities, our diversity of experience, and the changes to our material realities over time (Vermette; Simpson). Our existence is multiple, interwoven, and told in relation to one another. We tend in these analyses to forget the everyday lived experiences of Indigenous women and the ways that our history lives and breathes in our daily lives, echoed in the way we talk to each other about our experiences.

Scholars and policy analysts from around the globe are highlighting the disproportionate impact of COVID-19 on Indigenous communities, which often already face inequitable service provision, food insecurity, crowded housing, and poverty (Curtice and Choo; Markham, Smith, and Morphy; McLeod et al.; Meneses-Navarro; Monchalin; Thompson, Bonnycastle, and Hill). There is also the potential for an increase in domestic violence due to self-isolation and quarantine. Furthermore, the pandemic has posed a threat to Elders—who are repositories of knowledge, language, and culture—and has stretched the capacity of already under-resourced education systems for Indigenous peoples. Finally, the pandemic has had not only health and cultural impacts but also economic ones, which imperil communities with existing tenuous economies (Swaikoski). It is within this context that Indigenous women are engaging in the labour of mothering. COVID-19 has underscored the differences, contradictions, and complexities of Indigenous motherhood in the Western neoliberal system. With these nuanced intricacies in mind, we engaged in conversations about the lived experiences of Indigenous mothers during this time of pandemic. The past returns to us in these times in our resistance to and engagement with public health measures, in our fear for our Elders' experience of systemic racism in Canadian hospitals during the pandemic, in our value of the past and our connections to it. How do we respond when our work in Indigenous education and healthcare is often obstructed by new responsibilities outside of our choice, the heightened public interest in healthcare, and an inability to regularly visit?

Methodology

From its inception, through to engagement with methodology, data gathering, and analysis, this project has been entirely embedded in a COVID-19 context of social isolation, including increased domestic labour and childcare and other carework; the closure of our workplaces and decreased outputs; and increased risk as well as anxiety related to the health of family and communities. This project has been equally influenced by the deep desire of five friends to visit, discuss, and document our distinct experiences. It is within that context that we make meaning of our lives. The participants—Jaime Cidro, Mary Jane Logan McCallum, Wendy McNab, Roberta Stout, and Lorena Sekwan Fontaine—are long-time friends and mothers. We all have careers in academia and health and are at the similar stage of midlife. Each has been affected by the legacy of residential schools and colonial violence, and each engages in multiple areas of caregiving (such as children, grandchildren, and aging parents). Before the pandemic, we would regularly gather to bead, celebrate birthdays and other special occasions, and attend ceremonies and other cultural events. Our families and lives are centred in Winnipeg, and our friendships have become fundamental. Prior to meeting for this project, we developed approximately forty questions that we wanted to discuss. In addition, we each brought four to five items which helped us to think about stories we wanted to tell about our experience. This list is included in the appendix. Likewise, we use some images of these items to retell the stories here. The conversation transcripts were shared with participants to allow them to clarify, add, or delete content prior to analysis. We applied thematic analysis to identify themes in relation to what we recalled most about the conversation and what appeared most clearly to us in review of the transcripts. The remainder of this chapter will focus on the primary theme, which is loss and grief.

Loss and Grief: Our Colonial Past Returns to Us in a Pandemic

As part of our experiences, we identified a generalized feeling of loss and grief due to the cancellation of professional activities, such as conferences, family events, like funerals and birthdays, and cultural activities, like feasts and powwows. The following excerpts from our conversation describe how we individually as women, as well as collectively as friends and mothers, have experienced these losses. Lorena describes the loss of gatherings, both birthdays and funerals. She also describes the creative ways she and her family have tried to create joyful and memorable spaces to celebrate life and lives past. Jaime discusses the losses she felt for her daughter and the cultural activities they had participated in along with Roberta and Mary Jane's daughters, such as powwow club, and how these activities have left a gap both for her and her daughter. Wendy's reflections on the cancellation of cultural gatherings—such as the annual Nibi (water) gathering, Sundance, and the Winnipeg Folk Festival—have left her with a loss of spiritual connection to the land. Roberta talks about the cancelling of activities and events, such as graduation and birthdays, and the ways she had to get creative in the home to ensure that her daughter was comfortable and happy.

Jaime describes her sadness at the loss of participating in her regular powwow club and the connection she and her daughter felt through an inherited jingle dress:

I had gotten this from a friend [pulls out a jingle dress], for my daughter. I was trying to get some moccasins to match because I was thinking, "Surely, we'll be going to the spring powwow at the university, so she can wear this and have a matching baby shark barrette." My friend had given this to us at

Christmas because my daughter was going to the powwow club and because Mary Jane's daughter was dancing, she was okay to dance now. She was building up to it. She's not doing a great job of dancing, but she was doing it more than she was previously. I was thinking, "Now she's got a really nice dress that was given to me by a friend," and she was doing dancing by electric powwow [Tribe Called Red]. She really likes that, and then now she would wear it. She didn't like the dress when I first gave it her cause it's heavy and it was too big for her in December. By April, it now fits her. Now she's wearing it cause ... she sees when she dances, it makes noise. Now it's of interest to her. I've actually had it hanging in my bedroom on a rack. Because in my mind, I thought well maybe the spring powwow's not happening at the university, but surely there will be powwows that'll happen this summer, right? I'll just leave it out. I haven't put it away I'm just waiting for this magical time. Powwow season seems basically done, and here I have this dress still sitting in my room for this time that ... is not going to happen. This dress which did not fit her, now fits her. By the time the powwow club starts, by the time she can wear it, she might not fit this dress that I was really grateful to receive. My friend made this herself and gave it to us. She might not even get a chance to wear this really lovely dress that I ... always wanted her to wear. I was always so mad that she wouldn't dance at the powwow club, so then I would bring her brother. I had to pay my son ten dollars every week to take her dancing so I can visit because I'm there to visit Mary Jane and Roberta. That was my main interest in going was to visit with my friends and let her dance with Roberta's daughter and Mary Jane's daughter. She's kind of into it, and now, nothing. All my build up and hope for this little girl that I waited for so long for. Now that was taken away from us.

As a group of women, we would gather often to eat on a Sunday afternoon and bring out our beading projects. The most skilled beader of the group, Roberta, reflects on how the loss of this time together doing cultural-based activities left her with a sense of loss, especially of that time to decompress and share our experiences as women and mothers:

Beadwork reminds me of prepandemic gatherings. I associate it with feasting with women, sharing news, be it mundane or surprising. Those real-time get-togethers for dumping and decompressing was part of our collective wellbeing, self-care, and caregiving. None of us could have known how deeply we'd be affected, as Indigenous mothers and grandmothers, when our faces went from 3D to 2D and our celebrations of one another included drive by round dances and horns instead of hugs and potlucks.

Wendy also misses engaging in cultural activities and gatherings because they provided a place and space to ground her. For Wendy, she really missed participating in cultural learning through regular spring and summer events, including Nibi:

Every year starting in May, or even April, right up until August, we're out of the office. We're out on the land. We're doing something, whether it's for work or personal. Two or three years ago, when we had the Canadian Institute of Health Research. Pathways Annual Gatherings, it was in the Blackfoot territory, and we did a land-based event. It was the most powerful, amazing, fun experience that I had. It made an imprint on me. We asked permission of the people who were on their territory if we could go on their land and create this event. They were all society leaders. They were ceremonial people, and they helped us with the planning. One of the things they said at the end was "When we have our Sundance, we want you to come." Everybody was welcome to come. I took that really seriously because they let us come, and they showed us these places that are not open to the public. Nobody knows about them unless these Elders take you there. There are so many places in their territory. It's just amazing. You can feel the energy, too. It's really powerful. I took it very seriously. They let us into these places, and we got to see these things that are not even documented. One of the Elders who is a very good friend of ours now, like a family member, took us somewhere special. He had found another buffalo jump or harvesting area, and he took us there. It was amazing. Then we went the following year, and we were able to do it as a work event. We were there for two weeks. We camped, and we stayed in a teepee for two weeks. The other special thing that I missed was a family feasting area in Cowesses. It is special because that is where the ashes of my two uncles and auntie were placed. As kids, we would slide down these hills in the winter. We would spend the summers and some of the winters there as a family. We would go swimming in the lake that's at the bottom of the hill. It's kind of become our family plot. That's where we go feast. On the way back from Alberta, we stopped there. My uncle passed away four or five years ago, and last year was the first memorial that they were having, so we stopped for that. What I absolutely love is looking at the earth. Using a camera or a drone and zooming in and looking and seeing things. There are images that you can see from only those perspectives.

Our histories of dispossession and removal also influenced how we made meaning of the pandemic. One of the most devastating moments of the early pandemic for Mary Jane was seeing an image and reading the associated media article about mass burials in New York City in early April 2020. The burial site was an island off the Bronx, used as a potter's grave:

So, this was an article, like picture me, 10:30 at night, scrolling through my phone reading the news before bed, which is terrible, and I know that, and I still do it. They scooped up a whole huge trench, and they were going to put the people who had died, in that wave in New York where they didn't have any place for them. They needed them to be away, and people could come back and claim them, so they had names on their coffins, and they all had wood coffins. They weren't all together, it was kind of organized generally, but it was like a mass grave. It's on Lenapehoking [Lunaape territory], right? Those are my ancestors under there, too, right? Then you think, "Oh, these pandemics that our people have experienced and survived," but also huge losses. There could be mass burials too of our people under there from the seventeenth century, and the eighteenth century.

In thinking about the stay-at-home directive, Mary Jane kept thinking about the multiple places called home to her and how this directive reinforced simply one of them:

I kept thinking, if I was going to say, stay at home, where is home to me? 'Well, it's Winnipeg. But it's sort of Ontario, too, still. Munsee is my band, that's where our collective, whatever it is; a mile or two squares that's left is Munsee land. That's kind of home, too; that's where we've been doing [our language and history] workshops every couple of months and meeting with relatives and other friends from the band, and also who live there [and nearby]. That all stopped too, so it was like disconnected from that. Then I thought, well, is New York sort of a home, too? We're all told to not travel anywhere, so we couldn't go to those other homes to be in. I thought about that, the assumption of where your home is, and where you should stay was, yeah, it was probably pretty hard on lots of people because we move so much, right? I was thinking, is there something settler colonial about the directive to stay home? And death, and what mass deaths do to communities? Or mass removals or evacuations. You lose your ways of telling stories; there's communication that stops between generations. Those big things that happen to communities have all kinds of other social repercussions, and even remembering things, and telling history, right? So, yeah, that was just like a "wow" moment.

Our shared history of federal regulation, forced assimilation, and systemic racism came back to bite us during the pandemic as well. For example, Jaime at first hated being told to wear a mask as it gave her the sense that she was being infantilized:

I see in the [United] States, all of these groups of people refusing to comply with anything. I find that outrageous, but then a part of me, a small part but still a part of me, is like, 'I kind of get that…. I don't need to be policed. I'm not following these; don't tell me what to do.' You know, even though I know it's in my best interest. Intellectually, I know all those things. We're all smart—I know those things—but there's this part of me that always wants to go rogue.

In considering health regulations, Mary Jane agrees with Jaime's resistance and the sense of being overly regulated: "We're also health researchers! When I look back over public health laws and Indigenous communities, there has been an awful lot of regulation to the effect that those communities are becoming poorer, becoming less sovereign. So, what is the other side of this regulation?" Wendy also agrees with this tension between public health regulation and resistance: "Historically, we've been controlled, so that resistance makes total sense. That's what I mean when I say my choice has been taken away. That's always been something that has to do with that historical piece. It's about resistance." Roberta reflects on the impact of these regulations on our perceptions of time. Our usual markers of time were lost. The marker of when kids went to school, for example, was taken away when the schools shut down for the year. Having these demarcations in our day-to-day experiences taken away was jolting. Roberta shares the following:

> Those first few months of the pandemic are memorable only in that many of us couldn't see straight, nor could we remember day to day or week to week what had happened. We simply learned how to follow the dots on the floor. Even if we didn't have the virus, it had somehow infected all of us. It did so by playing with time. All of the markers that give structure, meaning and memory to time had been displaced. It has marked the lives of Indigenous women who were at home, trying to make bannock out of sourdough.

Despite the impact of regulations, some communities took control. Roberta finds it interesting that over half of First Nations communities took control and shut down very quickly. Wendy argues that the First Nations communities had learned this because of their experience with H1N1:

> Because of all the training that they went through because of H1N1, they already had those plans in place. That is why they immediately shut down. In some cases, there's nobody allowed in their community. At my work, we had this list every day where it showed each First Nation community that was shut down. We learned who was locked down, what was open in those communities and if there was a case of H1N1 or not.

Mary Jane further discusses how First Nations communities contended with the pandemic: "The roads were blocked; they had security right on the road. These roadblocks blocked ambulance access, mail access, and access to commerce on the reserve. This was the extent communities were willing to go to protect the membership."

To Lorena, this experience taps into "historical memory, about our grandparents' generation, or our great-grandparents' generation, [those who] had to get a pass to leave the reserve and that's familiar in a sense. Restriction of movement, being told where we could go, where we can't go, having the looks, like, 'What are you doing out of your place?' I was wondering how my mother was feeling. Is it familiar? Is it more traumatizing? Is it, intuitively, does she already know this?" Jaime further explains:

> That "going rogue" piece, for some people, you can kind of understand it if you layer on that historical component around it, like segregation, all of those pieces, you can see why lots of people are just [like] "Forget this. Don't tell me what to do." Even though you know it's in your best interest, like there's all this public health information, but also, who does public health information benefit? There's just a lot of factors that go into how you emotionally respond to this. Even though I get all that, but there's a part of me that's just irritated by that and wanting to go rogue.

In late May of 2020, Lorena's aunt became sick and was medivacked out of her community for treatment, staying there until June 10. From the moment she got on the plane up until her return, her treatment was frightening and negligent. She was ignored, made uncomfortable, not given any comfort, had procedures she did not consent to, and was put in a dirty room. No one talked to her, and she couldn't get any answers. Lorena says:

> It's racism. But we're in the middle of a pandemic. That hospital is full of Aboriginal people. I was seeing some pretty awful things in there with patients because I could go in part of the way. I'd go in every night and bring her food because she wouldn't have survived off of what they were giving her. My aunt would go in the morning to give her breakfast, and [the hospital staff] would run it up to her, but we couldn't see her.

She really needed somebody there to be her advocate. The hospital advocate didn't do anything for her because they don't have the authority, and the second offered only naïve platitudes.

When Lorena's aunt started to voice her opinions, doctors ignored them, as if she were not qualified to understand her own health: "She was really traumatized," Lorena explains. But her family was able to fight for her, which was not the case for most Indigenous people in the hospital, as Lorena describes:

I was so worried about the other Aboriginal people I saw in there. A lot of them don't have family members in this city, so they're there by themselves. And, I worried, I worried about people in the hallways. I worried about people in the emergency room, and so, it was traumatizing going in there. The racism my aunt was experiencing in the hospital consumed me during the pandemic, and it still is now.... We're still in the middle of the pandemic, and so many people in the hospital are still really vulnerable. So, it's COVID, but it's also a larger issue. Systemic racism in the healthcare system is embedded in our history of racial segregation and white settler priority in Canada; and this history continues to haunt us in the present. [There are Indigenous patient advocates in the hospital].

As Indigenous women, our experience with racism, exclusion, and loss, as well as with intense surveillance as professionals in healthcare and education is extensive. Our histories preclude and influence our experience with the pandemic in illuminating ways, and this became clear in Mary Jane's and Jaime's work lives as well. As women who work in a vastly under-represented environment—academia—both became anxious about who would care for their students and how their work may continue, or become erased, in their absence. McCallum explains:

Being an under-represented faculty, I feel like I need to especially support them [her students] because I feel like they deserve to have an educator who is going to at least understand some aspect and not be a racist, right? They don't get that very often. Then you're just exhausted because you can't do that to everybody and then you don't have any time for yourself at the end of the day. It was this fear that other people were going to do this work not us, well, and not as caring, right? It just felt like there was more pressure at that time than there is normally. We need to sit on that committee cause otherwise, no one's going to represent this perspective. Then it was just like, "Oh my gosh. I'm not there and I don't know who's doing that. With the chair position, when they're doing a search for a job, if it's not done correctly, I feel upset about it. Indigenization sort of got dropped. It is the first thing to go because everybody's now worried about the university and keeping the lights on basically. I feel like this danger, and then I feel responsible to intervene. It feels like if I'm not there, I don't know what's happening. It's a matter of numbers, right?

Jaime agrees about the impact on efforts around Indigenous education: "I don't have the time and I can't participate at that level that I would normally have more availability and interest in doing so. Then our concern feels like its now kind of superfluous, like its shallow for us to bring it up now during a pandemic." Jamie has similar concerns around her productivity. As a career-driven academic and administrator, her inability to do her research (including work on doulas, removals for birth, as well as ongoing harmful practices in healthcare) and to make it publicly available greatly weighed on her.

Conclusion

As five women, we are undoubtedly overwhelmed. The pandemic has exacerbated the lack of definitiveness between home and work life, and our careers have suffered as we continue to feel isolated from all the things that gave us meaning. The impact on our identity not only as carers but also as women with careers that place an emphasis on output and productivity has been debilitating.

As a group of women our experiences have been different but have some profound similarities. We are grieving the loss of what was a normal existence, which has included travel, professional development activities, and participation in cultural activities and ceremonies, which provide these important cultural ties to our Indigenous identities. We are grieving the onslaught of cancellations to the point of despair. Our few outlets to take care of ourselves as women have been cancelled, and we are left with a gaping hole and loss in our lives. This is the missing year! The year we miss one another! We miss beadwork and being in real time with one another. We miss not knowing what is to come and how to plan for it. We miss the opportunities our children once had. We miss seeing familiar faces. We miss faces. We miss the mundane and the surprises. And we miss shared caregiving.

We are also dealing with caring for our families, as parents for our children, as spouses, grandmothers, and as children of our aging parents. Although this carework was underway prepandemic, the stressors of isolation, homeschooling, and dealing with aging parents has put strain on this work. We are delirious with the strain of caring for all those around us—supporting them in their own grief and loss in the cancellations of their normal lives. Writing this chapter has provided for some catharsis. We were compelled to participate because of our intrinsic need to visit, document, and make meaning of our lives with one another. The importance of friendship has never been made more apparent as during this pandemic. While we may not be washing our clothes together like our ancestors, we support ourselves in ways that are rich and full of laughter and tears.

Appendix A

The following is a list of items that each of us brought to our gathering. They represent our experiences during our pandemic, including things we did and things we missed doing.

Lorena: Party hat to make her daughter's birthday special; the special gifts Roberta gave her at an event created for her fiftieth birthday; a place mat—part of the way that she and her daughter made dinners a special escape; a twenty-two-page document tracking the racist treatment her aunt went through at a Winnipeg hospital during lockdown; laptop—friends, meetings, social life, funeral/wake.

Jaime: Beading/beadwork—baby shark barrette for daughter; daughter's jingle dress for spring powwow; old photographs of the ChiChiMaun; grandparents' English china.

Wendy: Video of grandson and family echoing each other ("expressive response"), "berry pour" (see description in Appendix B) art making and interpreting (art therapy).

Roberta: Photo of road trips with Roberta's daughter, having fires outside, photo of camping in back yard, daughter's graduation T-shirt that says, "Conquered the pandemic," little x-ray, card from Lorena and her daughter Sarah—with plants.

Mary Jane: Mass grave in NYC, Muncey; language and history courses cancelled; Zoom calls with online research and chief; research what has changed—university asks; photo of Scobie Logan in the news; daughter's homeschooling material; doll diaper.

Appendix B: Berry Pour "We Carry and Hold with Love" (see below for the image)

After I got home from our visit, I put this painting beside me (smudged it) as I worked daily on other art pieces for my art therapy program. I would look over at it whenever I could. I would turn it every so often so I could look at it from different angles. The green area is what I saw first. I turned it until I felt in my body where I should start. I prepared my water colour paints and sat with them until I felt a pull towards the first colour and so on. I continued to turn it. As I painted, I observed.

Green. I saw the turtle and the heart of the turtle. She carries us on her backs; she helped birth this land we sit on. Just as women, we have birthed those who walk on this earth. Life Giver.

The yellow is the shining of sun that provides nutrients and energy. It is what connects us to the sky.

The blue is the water. Water is our medicine. It is what connects to the land and earth. Our babies grow in water, and we birth our babies from the waters. The waters around us connect us to land.

The berry paint has turned into a tree. It is strong and fragile. It provides us with oxygen. It allows us to make fire, tools, and to hold ceremonies.

The tree in this image is just barely holding the turtle above the water with the sunshine blanketing it all. The sun, water, and tree are all connected and held.

This image reminds me of the strength and power of women and how spiritual our bodies are and how much we hold even in both our weakest/tears/hurt moments and also in the strongest/doing it all/

tears/adapt/ moments. We are powerful and strong. Supported. Held. Strong. Related. Seen. Loved. Medicine.

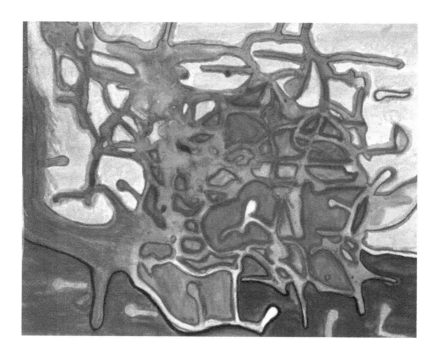

Works Cited

Curtice, Kaitlin, and Esther Choo. "Indigenous Populations: Left behind in the COVID-19 Response." *The Lancet*, vol. 395, no. 10239, 2020, p. 1753.

Guy, Batsheva, and Brittany Arthur. "Academic Motherhood during COVID-19: Navigating Our Dual Roles as Educators and Mothers." *Gender Work and Organization*, vol. 27, no. 5, 2020, pp. 887-99.

Markham, Francis, Diane Smith, and Frances Morphy, eds. *Indigenous Australians and the COVID-19 Crisis: Perspectives on Public Colicy.* Centre for Aboriginal Economic Policy Research, 2020.

McLeod, Melissa, et al. "COVID-19: We Must Not Forget about Indigenous Health and Equity." *Australian and New Zealand Journal of Public Health*, vol. 44, no. 4, 2020, pp. 253-56.

Meneses-Navarro, Sergio, et al. "The Challenges Facing Indigenous Communities in Latin America As They Confront the COVID-19 Pandemic." *International Journal for Equity in Health*, vol. 19, 2020, pp. 1-3.

Monchalin, Renée. "Novel Coronavirus, Access to Abortion Services, and Bridging Western and Indigenous Knowledges in a Postpandemic World." *Women's Health Issues*, vol. 31, no. 1, 2020, pp. 5-8.

Simpson, Leanne Betasamosake. *As We Have Always Done: Indigenous Freedom through Radical Resistance*. University of Minnesota Press, 2017.

Swaikoski, Dylan. "Leisure in the Time of Coronavirus: Indigenous Tourism in Canada and the Impacts of COVID-19." *World Leisure Journal*, vol. 62, no. 4, 2020, pp. 311-14.

Thompson, Shirley, Marleny Bonnycastle, and Stewart Hill. "Poor Housing 'Wash Hands Frequently' and 'Self-Isolate' Akin to 'Let Them Eat Cake' in First Nations with Overcrowded Homes Lacking Piped Water." *Canadian Centre for Policy Alternatives*, 2020, www.policyalternatives.ca/publications/commentary/fast-facts-%E2%80%9Cwash-hands-frequently%E2%80%9D-and-%E2%80%9Cself-isolate%E2%80%9D-akin-%E2%80%9Clet-them-eat. Accessed 19 Jan. 2021.

Vermette, Katherena. *The Break*. House of Anansi, 2016.

Chapter Forty Three

What Are the Ties that Bind? Mothering and Friendship across Difference and Distance

Natasha Steer and Jen Vasic

Friendships between mothers play a seminal role in developing collective and individual identities (Cronin). We believe this to be true for our friendship, too. Natasha is racialized and is a single-lone mother parenting her sixteen-year-old son. Jen is white and is a mother through adoption, who is parenting her five-year-old son with her husband. During the pandemic, Natasha has entered into a new phase of motherhood as a parent to an adolescent who is actively asserting his independence while Jen waits to adopt a second child.

In this chapter, we examine our friendship in the context of our overall experiences of mothering and, more recently, during the COVID-19 pandemic. Following from this, our dialogue below is guided by the following research questions. How have we most leaned on each other during the pandemic? In what ways has this been similar and different to before the pandemic? To answer these questions, we engaged in a duoethnographic process, a back-and-forth dialogue about the phenomenon of focus. In considering what it means to be a mother and a friend while navigating very different mothering experiences prior to and during the COVID-19 pandemic, we conclude that our friendship serves as a landing place for us through overwhelming times and exists in multiple virtual sites. We realize, though, that we are early on in our discussions regarding race in our friendship. This article provides one example of how friends can have conversations across difference and distance that are individually supportive and promote consciousness raising (different mothering journeys and race in our particular case), thus having ripple effects that may influence broader social change.

Method

Duoethnography is a research method in which multiple researchers occupy the space of researcher and participant and use their subjective experiences to engage in a broader analysis of organizations and society (Johanson and Jones), typically through exchanging text. This method is unique because it contributes to knowledge and raises consciousness in ways that can have transformative effects on the researchers themselves (Norris and Sawyer). This approach is appropriate for examining our friendship and mothering experiences before and during the COVID-19 pandemic for two reasons. First, it mirrors our typical patterns of communication; we regularly engage in a fluid back and forth exchange about a range of issues. Second, we typically filter our individual experiences through social analysis.

There are three sources of data for this article. These include our direct Facebook messages; early on in the pandemic, we sent messages to each other almost daily. Now that our children's schools are running again, we message each other less frequently, though still regularly. A second source of data is a Google Doc we started for this project in order to respond to our research questions. We engaged in this exchange approximately five times, asynchronously, over the course of one month in the summer of 2020. A third source of data comes from our "autobiographical notes" (Johanson and Jones), in which we locate ourselves overall and as mothers as well as provide an overview of our friendship.

Given time constraints related to the pandemic and our otherwise full lives, we engaged in a rapid thematic analysis of each data source. We each coded larger sections of data and then came together to discuss our codes to codevelop themes and consider their meanings in the context of our friendship and each of our respective lives (Vindrola-

Padros and Johnson).

This article is written in a hybrid model, which is similar to other duoethnographic studies we have encountered to date. Similar to Marjana Johannson and Sally Jones and Steven Camicia and Juanjuan Zhu, we provide some context and discussion. As with Evans and Darren Lund, as well as Lund and Marryam Navabi, who rely exclusively on their exchanges to discuss their phenomenon of study, we also lean on our dialogue to tell our story.

Autobiographical Notes

Natasha

I became a single mother at the age of nineteen. I immediately felt the pressure of navigating stereotypes and was determined to be empowered in my journey. I was successful in this largely because of the incredible support I had from friends and family, including Jen.

I am racialized and still working through the part that race has played in my motherhood journey and my life as a whole. Still, identities are complex, and although my identity as a biracial single teen mother cannot and should not be ignored, there are other aspects as well. I am privileged through my education, class, sexuality, ability, nationality, language, profession in education, and gender identification.

My single-lone motherhood has become an integral part of my identity as I seek to share stories that disrupt mainstream narratives of single motherhood, which fail to portray the fully complete, loving, and healthy single-mother families that exist, including the life my son and I have built together.

Jen

I am an adoptive mother after a three-year infertility journey. My experience of motherhood is shaped by various privileged identities. I am white, middle class with a working-class and immigrant background, hetero, cisgender, able bodied, employed as a city councillor, and as a current PhD candidate, highly educated. In motherhood, however, I am—despite all attempts by others to legitimate our family unit by telling us how much our kid looks or acts like my partner and me—an outsider in a world that reveres fertile bodies and the so-called miraculous work fertile, often assumed to be women's bodies, do to create life and bear children.

Our passing as a biological two-parent family combined with our race and socioeconomic status affords us many privileges and the social capital to accrue yet more benefits. We navigate the world with our differences not fully embraced but instead negotiate expectations and others' hopes that we may present as a biologically related family, which is an exhausting and lonely project.

Our Friendship

Although our relationship began in person—we knew each other in elementary school and became good friends in high school—most of our friendship has been at a distance. This began when Jen moved to Waterloo to start university, the same year Natasha became pregnant. This distance was amplified when Natasha and her child later moved to China for four years. Our shared experiences include our parents and/or grandparents being settlers in Canada; we share many privileges, and we are both mothers. We also share a worldview oriented towards social justice. Yet our experiences are marked more by differences that shape how we each navigate societal expectations about our mothering identities and trajectories. Natasha must do this more substantially and overtly because of looking and being younger when she first became a mother, her race, and job precarity as the sole provider for her family.

Google Doc Excerpt

Natasha: I'm at a point in my life—and this was true prepandemic—in which the family I have built for myself and for my kid seems to have dwindled. As a single mother at nineteen, I instinctively knew that without having another adult in our core family unit, I would need to lean on others for support. That support felt strong when my child was younger, but it has since petered out in various ways as he has gotten older. As a fellow single mom recently told me, "You've lost your village." This is especially hard when, in many ways, I now feel I need much more support than I needed when I was parenting a small child.

It has been noted that two-parent nuclear families tend to shift their focus inwards. I don't know what this is like personally, having been raised in a female-headed household myself. But you didn't do this, Jen. When you got married and then became a mother yourself, you did not turn inwards—or if you did, you folded us in along with you. I don't know what it's like to have a partner parenting alongside me. But I do know what it's like to have someone commit to being there and then show up for you in ways that you don't encounter elsewhere.

Facebook Excerpt

Natasha: Today mostly sucked

Jen: Oh no :(Why?

Natasha: But my kid saw I was lonely and came for a walk with me, which was nice

Natasha: It is really, really lonely with just him.

Natasha: It's good I have things to do, but it's also just sad.

Jen: Yes :(This is really exacerbating the separation from him too. I'm sorry :(

Natasha: Yeah, thanks. It is fine. Just something to adjust to I guess.

Natasha: Anyhow, would love to write tomorrow...

Jen: Ya, like you need another thing to adjust to right now. And great! I'll try to get up too because I think I could work a bit on my own writing tomorrow!

Jen: This is interesting because in her book *Girl Talk: What Science Can Tell Us about Female Friendship*, Jacqueline Mroz notes motherhood can act as a turning point in friendships between those who identify as female. She describes motherhood as a catalyst for altered female friendships—most notably around the time people become new moms when they spend less time with each other than they did before.

However, when you became a new mom, our relationship strengthened. This is in contrast to my other friendships with those who became parents around the same time as me. All are in partnerships. Was it your unconscious though intentional network building that kept me around, begging the question of how much more work lone moms really have to do?

We are also at transition points in mothering. Your kid is finishing high school, and mine just started school. Yet it seems we anticipated this transition—and dare I say it, the sheltering in place that was to come—by starting a twice-weekly distanced writing practice. I like to imagine that our friendship transcends practicalities and we share some deeper connection that cannot be explained.

Facebook Excerpt

Natasha: I just feel like so many parenting things are out the window right now.

Jen: All your work is in there.

Jen: You did the main thing, which is make him think critically.

Natasha: We can't do this for a year and a half.

Jen: We won't do this for a year and a half.

Natasha: It's interesting to think about how motherhood at different stages/ages affects relationships. I think noting our origins is relevant here because we transitioned from two close friends in high school to creating close-knit family ties in early adulthood right around the time that you moved farther away.

Close female friendships such as ours often depend on reciprocity for the survival of their relationship: "Time and energy is *given* to others rather than invested in the self'" (Skeggs quoted in Cronin 674). Do you think this applies to us? I think it does, but I believe that we both strive to invest in ourselves as well. I also know that I have always leaned on you more than my other relationships. I sometimes worry about this, if it is too much.

To your last point, it's true that we set ourselves up perfectly for the hardship of navigating a pandemic together. I can honestly say that creating a routine—and ensuring that we had at least two times a week to dedicate to ourselves, our writing, and our friendship—helped ground me through the intense lows of navigating the deep isolation that the pandemic brought into my life.

Jen: Reciprocity in friendships is such an interesting topic because reciprocity can mean different things to different people, and this can change within particular relationships and over time. We've spent more time talking about your motherhood journey, but that's because you've been a mother longer. The balance is shifting, and we've added conversations about my journey. You have also provided the space for me to process situations and make decisions, and you have an uncanny empathy and understanding about why I may feel conflicted in any particular situation.

Facebook Excerpt

Jen: My family went out to pick up some groceries. We ordered them. They'll shop for us; we just have to pick it up, and I'm shockingly worried.

Natasha: Does N have gloves?

Jen: He has his winter gloves. They have hand sanitizer. We'll put the gloves in the wash. He'll get a treat if he touches nothing, and I don't know if we'll wipe everything down. I guess we should?

Natasha: Some people are.

Natasha: You can soap it and leave the soap on for five minutes.

Jen: Oh man.

Jen: This is all a lot!

Natasha: These are great things in place for N!

Natasha: It's a lot.

To your first point, Anne Cronin talks about a "domestic partnership," which is built on the shared relationship of motherhood and where the relationship is less about fulfilling individual needs and more externally oriented in that it supports another person. Our friendship seems to both focus on the external (i.e., the domestic partnership) and be internally oriented (i.e., our relationship supports our individual development and goals of self-actualization). In this way, we are in reciprocity with each other; moreover, our friendship helps us to be in reciprocity with the world.

Natasha: It's interesting to think about how different people need different things in relationships and how our understandings of reciprocity don't always match up neatly. Even if we were perfectly in sync with this concept of reciprocity, it wouldn't guarantee that we both felt supported. I like to think that we haven't needed our relationship to look like any one thing. Although our support has been constant over the years, our relationship has continuously shifted, and we have shifted along with it. Is it possible that our relationship is just bigger than both of us? That we feel a sense of commitment not only to each other as people but to the relationship itself? Perhaps we are simply used to this constant evolution, so the pandemic merely brought about another shift—a deeper commitment—in our relationship.

Jen: You're right. It wasn't the pandemic that brought us to this level of commitment. Maybe it is a commitment to the relationship itself. When I was doing one of my social work internships, my supervisor who did lots of couples counselling told me that he asks couples to focus on their relationship rather than their individual needs. Perhaps when oriented towards the relationship itself rather than the individuals, relationships are stronger and each individual's needs get met, even if at different times.

Findings

Throughout the pandemic, relationships have had to adapt to physical distancing, with significantly fewer opportunities to spend in-person time with those we care about. Although distance relationships may not be our first choice, the pandemic has necessitated this distance. In this section, we reflect upon our above texts to share three findings: our relationship is a place where we provide each other support through life's most overwhelming and intense times; our friendship exists in varied spaces; and our relationship is marked by differences, especially concerning race.

Support through Overwhelming and Intense Times

This duoethnography has illuminated that our relationship is a constant in each of our lives and has sustained us through various intense and overwhelming situations related to motherhood, work, other relationships, and now COVID-19. Our friendship provided us each with much needed reprieve through the height of the pandemic as we navigated quarantine, motherhood, and other competing priorities and life events. For Natasha, this reprieve came in the form of support she does not otherwise have, as she spent the majority of her energy ensuring that her son had his own supports to navigate this especially challenging time to be a teenager. For Jen, this relationship was a go-to outside of her immediate family, with whom she was stuck. She found, as she always does, solace in the act of messaging and knowing that whether or not Natasha responds immediately, she will have read and empathized with the experience. We note that we each find strength in our relationship's stability and longevity and in knowing we can rely on each other to be there when needed, which we both feel is not characteristic of our other friendships.

Varied Sites of Friendship

There are many sites where we engage in dialogue, with each serving a different purpose (e.g., phone, video, social media, text, and a Google Doc). In Facebook messenger, one of our primary methods of communication, we dialogue with each other synchronously and asynchronously as we process our day-to-day identities and experiences as mothers, workers, and people in lockdown during a pandemic. We also video conferenced two mornings a week. Although we sometimes checked in with each other or provided support, we primarily used this space to separately and together—and quietly—find ourselves and our identities as writers.

Participation in each of these sites has informed our ever-evolving individual identities and also consistently remade our friendship. At times, the multiplicity of the sites we use to connect with each other can feel overwhelming itself. Yet this awareness that we have for each other in multiple spaces provides what feels like a safe landing space for wherever we may find ourselves. We believe our relationship serves as a model for other relationships now currently forced to remain at a distance due to the COVID-19 pandemic; it suggests that various platforms of engagement can be used to people's advantage.

Friendship across Race

There are many differences between us that we often discuss, most notably our different mothering identities (i.e., lone and adoptive). We notice that the content of our discussions—and what we support one another through—is often deeply tied to our differences. Nonetheless, the difference of race does not often surface in our discussions, although we both use an antioppressive and antiracist lens in our work and advocate against oppression in both our personal and professional lives. Although Natasha deeply understands the racism that occurs in the world and how being racialized affects how one navigates that world, she was raised not to see her race. As a consequence, she believes this is one reason why the topic of her race does not show up in her closest relationships or conversations. To this effect, we wonder who the onus is on to talk about race in an interracial friendship. In what ways, and to what extent, can we sit with one another through these conversations? What fears, if any, may be getting in the way of having these conversations between friends?

Conclusion

Although our friendship is not dependent on our motherhood, motherhood seems to have been a turning point that strengthened and deepened our relationship. Despite our physical distance from each other both before and during the pandemic and our differences, we continue to nurture each other's individual growth and tend to our relationship across fragmented, largely virtual, sites. Ultimately, this exploration has raised more questions for us than it has answers, which have implications for our own, as well as other, friendships across distance and difference. How ought reciprocity be measured in relationships? How might we wholeheartedly allow a friend to live their experiences and walk alongside them, regardless and perhaps because of our differences? What are the ties that bind?

Works Cited

Camicia, Steven P., and Juanjuan Zhu. "Synthesizing Multicultural, Global, and Civic Perspectives in the Elementary School Curriculum and Educational Research." *The Qualitative Report*, vol. 17, no. 52, 2012, pp. 1-19.

Cronin, Anne. "'Domestic Friends': Women's Friendships, Motherhood and Inclusive Intimacy." *The Sociological Review*, 63, no. 3, 2015, pp. 662-79.

Giroux, Henry. *Theory and Resistance in Education: Towards a Pedagogy for the Opposition.* Bergin & Garvey, 2001.

Johansson, Marjana, and Sally Jones. "Interlopers in Class: A Duoethnography of Working-Class-Women Academics." *Gender, Work & Organization*, vol. 26, 11, pp. 1527-45.

Lund, Darren, and Marryam Navabi. "A Duo-Ethnographic Conversation on Social Justice Activism: Exploring Issues of Identity, Racism, and Activism with Young People." *Multicultural Activism*, vol. 15, no. 4, 2008, pp. 27-32.

Mroz, Jacqueline. *Girl Talk: What Science Can Tell Us about Female Friendship.* Seal Press, 2018.

Norris, Joe, and Richard Sawyer. "Toward a Dialogic Methodology." *Duoethnography Dialogic Methods for Social, Health, and Educational Research*, edited by Joe Norris, Richard D. Sawyer, and Darren E. Lund, Routledge, 2016, pp. 9-39

Vindrola-Padros, Cecilia, and Ginger Johnson. "Rapid Techniques in Qualitative Research: A Critical Review of the Literature." *Qualitative Health Research*, vol. 30, no. 10, 2020, pp. 1596-1604.

Chapter Forty Four

"A Wise and Well-Informed Person"–Australian Mothers during the Pandemics of 1918–1919 and 2020

Belinda Robson

Introduction: Remembering the Flu Pandemic of 1918 and 1919

This dispatch is from Australia's COVID-19 lockdown, where I have sought respite in researching the flu pandemic of 1918 and 1919—"the single greatest demographic shock mankind has ever experienced ... since the black death" (Porter 484) resulting in approximately fifty million deaths worldwide (Johnson and Mueller). As the global death toll for COVID-19 soars, I have found this historical perspective serves as a counterpoint to the current bewildering circumstances and enables me to untangle threads from my own family narrative. In late January 2020, as south-eastern Australia was engulfed by terrifying smoke haze from bushfires, my family nursed my eighty-six-year-old mother through her final days. In our grief, we barely registered the reports of a mysterious virus in Wuhan, which at the time seemed a long way away from Melbourne, Australia, a city traumatized by climate change. But by March, Australia had closed its state and international borders and had introduced social distancing measures not seen since the 1918–1919 flu pandemic. As I retraced the details of my mother's life after her death, I found myself recalling a conversation with her about the deaths of both of her maternal grandparents during the flu pandemic. In the pre-COVID-19 world, I had not thought to dig any deeper when I had the chance. Now, I want to understand what happened, how it happened, and what it meant for mothers.

My focus on the role of mothers during these two pandemics is a way of identifying continuities and contradictions in the role of the mother, despite a century of social and economic transformations. I also seek to contribute to the burgeoning field of motherhood studies in Australia by drawing on feminist and social historical understandings of the sacrificial mother and bereavement in Australian wartime (Damousi) as well as more recent Australian scholarship on mothering (Leahy and Bueskens). What more can we learn about the values associated with mothering by the way Australia has navigated two of its worst pandemics?

To answer this question, I use the experiences of mothers as reported by Melbourne's media, which offer an opportunity to consider how language and imagery shaped cultural assumptions. There are three themes I propose to structure this approach. First, I look at the place of the good mother in public health responses to the pandemics. Second, I consider the emotional burdens and pressures on mothers during both pandemics. Third, I will explore the complex needs of mothers balancing paid work with their role as mothers. I conclude that, although white, middle-class women have made significant economic gains over the past century, both pandemics drew on public health measures that disproportionately affected poor and marginalized mothers.

A Tale of Two Pandemics

Almost as soon as it struck, COVID-19 drew comparisons with the 1918–1919 flu pandemic for health agencies seeking precedence and guidance. It is estimated the 1918–1919 flu pandemic affected up to 40 per cent of Australia's population and led to 3,561 deaths in Victoria and up to 20,000 deaths across Australia (Parliament of Victoria). The pandemic had two waves in Victoria—February to April 1919 and then May to June 1919—before being declared over on September

15, 1919. The mortality rate was highest amongst men aged twenty-five to forty years,—the years often associated with starting a family—and over five thousand children lost one or more parent to the flu (Parliament of Victoria). Yet Australia was spared the worst ravages of mortality, with 233 deaths per 100,000, compared to 430 in England and five hundred for non-Maori in New Zealand (McQueen).

In contrast to the wrangling between states and the Commonwealth government during the 1918–1919 flu pandemic, policymakers had the benefit of history to help understand the levers they could use to control the contagion in 2020 (Moloney and Moloney). The Australian government established a national cabinet of all the states and territories and formulated a "go now, go hard, go smart" policy based on advice from a cross-section of experts advising on quarantine and the likely acceptance of strategies to enforce civic compliance with various degrees of lockdown measures. Included in the expert group was Alison Bashford, a medical historian and quarantine history specialist. Social historians, such as Janet McCalman, also drew on the history of pandemics to contribute to public debate about recovery following COVID-19 (Dawson and McCalman).

Responses to both pandemics reflected prevailing assumptions about family, nation, and motherhood. These included an implicit acceptance that mothers would carry the emotional burden of dealing with children's anxieties. In both periods, there were few resources and supports available to address the specific needs of mothers. Although it was more common for mothers to be in some form of paid work in 2020, class and race differences affected the forms this employment took. Many lost their jobs, whereas others who worked in industries such as retail, healthcare, construction, abattoirs, and other essential services faced an increased risk of infection. This situation created different experiences of the pandemic, as some mothers could work remotely from home, whereas others lost work or had to make sacrifices to perform work out of the home that was seen to contribute to the social good.

The Competent and Good Mother

The public health response to both pandemics relied on so-called good mothers being able to manage the pressures at home. As Australian historian Stuart Macintyre notes, the flu pandemic in Australia "revealed the hollowness of the national identity proclaimed during the war" (188). The First World War had highlighted the need for national strength and efficiency—to be measured by the good health of its people. In 1919, white, middle-class mothers were central agents of public health, with "the discovery that preventative medicine must begin with the mother and her child" (*The Age*, 11 July 1919, 6). At the same time, this period saw "contradictory outcomes for gender relations" (Grimshaw et al. 218). Motherhood was a site for measuring competence, and there were standards to meet: "Unhappily, there are a large number of mothers, in all grades of society, who are not in any sense competent to help in their child's education" (*Argus*, 3 July 1918, 12).

The child welfare movement, reaching fruition in the nascent baby health centre movement in 1917, conceptualized the white mother as central to public health because she embodied the potential of disease prevention and racial purity among the next generation. A mother needed to fulfil a number of requirements: "[She] needs to be a very wise and well-informed person and, at the same time, a very practical and cheerful person" (*Argus*, 3 July 1918, 12). Her bond with the child was irrefutable: "No standard ought to be tolerated which fails to regard mother and child as an indivisible unit throughout early infancy" (*Horsham Times*, 26 Sept. 1919, 12).

But it was not clear whether all mothers had the skills necessary to raise and educate their children to the standards required during the flu pandemic. When Victorian schools were closed for weeks in February and March 1919 and closed again later in the year, there was concern about the children who missed out on education because mothers might not act in the best interests of their children. Victorian mothers were warned about the following:

> Education is far too important justify parents in keeping their children away from school ... but no amount of preaching on my part will induce them to send their children to school while another mother in the neighbourhood keeps her offspring at

home. I must tell these people that they are under a sacred obligation to their children to have them sufficiently educated, so that they may in the race of life be able to take their stand alongside other children. (*Albury Banner and Wodonga Express*, 21 Feb. 1919, 12)

The "race of life" was even harder for Aboriginal mothers and children. This period saw a systematic policy of forced adoption—now known as the Stolen Generation—where between 10 and 30 per cent of Aboriginal children were forcibly removed from their families because Aboriginal mothers were deemed to lack the qualities desired in good mothers (Australian Human Rights Commission).

There are few records on how Aboriginal mothers in Australia responded to the flu pandemic. In 1919, Victoria's White Australia Policy meant that Aboriginal mothers were not given citizenship status and were excluded from the Commonwealth's Maternity Allowance Act 1912, unsurprisingly producing a largely race-blind approach to public health.

Special measures were taken by the Board for the Protection of Aborigines to prohibit visits to their communities in recognition of their increased physical risk (*Geelong Advertiser*, 25 Feb. 1919, 6). A similar approach was taken in 2020 when Aboriginal-run health services rapidly took control of infection within their communities in the face of the pandemic by swiftly closing them to visitors. Social isolation measures disrupted formal and informal support systems, affecting mothers especially, as travel became restricted, and it became difficult for mothers to get the assistance they needed.

Mothers under Pressure

During the COVID-19 pandemic, Victorian parents were advised to "try to remain calm and positive when talking to your child [and to] avoid talking in a way which could make your child feel more worried" (Victorian Government). This echoes advice to Australian mothers in 1919 when they were advised to maintain a calm vigilance over children: "Keep calm and unafraid.... Remember that most patients recover. Take all precautions but think as little as possible about the epidemic and try to keep the home cheerful and the children happy and occupied" (*Argus*, 12 Feb. 1919, 10).

But mothers were also expected to monitor the progress of the pandemic:

> It is like trying to go on with your work, with half your mind waiting for a ring on the telephone ... it seems to me that those who can "keep smiling" and make themselves and their households into cushions or shock-absorbing buffers against the jars and jangles of the great shunting going on in world affairs are doing some of the most useful work in their power. A calm person not easily worked up is a blessing and a boon— and lucky the children who have a mother of that pattern. (*The Observer*, 26 Apr. 1919, 41)

The pandemic naturally exacerbated the anxiety mothers felt about their own health and that of their families. This anxiety was intensified by media reports of mothers who made sacrifices to keep children alive, such as the Collingwood mother of three children who lost her husband to the flu and collapsed in the street from fatigue trying to get the money to feed her children (*The Age*, 4 Mar. 1919, 5) and a woman who had died with a small child still suckling her breast (*Yackandandah Times*, 13 Feb. 1919, 2). Similarly, Catherine Beckman, aged fifty-seven, was found dead on the farm she had been managing on behalf of her blind husband. Her twenty-one-year-old daughter, Sophie, and seventeen-year-old son, Carl, were also found dead, with the newspaper reporting that Sophie had become frightened at the death of her mother and withdrew to the shed to die (*Ballarat Star*, 7 May 1919, 1). Readers were also exposed to the plight of a native Indian from Montreal, breaking the ice on the river to paddle her canoe thirty miles to meet her husband, with one child dead of influenza beside her and her second child dying in her arms (*The Age*, 31 May 1919, 4).

Middle-class women were recruited to offer material assistance during the flu pandemic to those left with few resources. The Melbourne District Nursing Society, which at the peak of the pandemic was helping over one hundred patients a day in their homes, found the following:

> ... whole families prostrated, with no one to look after them ... mother, father and children congregated and huddled in one room, a room which has become dirty through forced neglect....

In another house, the nurses find a mother in a serious condition while the young children, unable to help themselves, are living in filth and rags.... In [another] house when the mother died, no one could be persuaded to lift the dead woman from the floor. (*Herald,* 22 Apr. 1919, 7)

Such tragic stories capture the self-sacrificial mother endeavouring to hold her family together and the shock when a mother can no longer care for her children.

Mothers also carried a similar burden during the COVID-19 pandemic, especially when reports drew attention to the poor management of lockdown within marginalized communities and the central role played by the mother in dealing with the consequences. In July 2020, it was reported that Hannah Muhumed—one of the three thousand residents of nine high-rise public housing towers in Melbourne who were placed in hard lockdown due to a concern about the cluster of cases—became separated from her prematurely born baby, Hanen, who was still hospitalized (Paul). Although authorities organized an esky of breastmilk be transported to her baby, the image of a desperate mother separated from her baby echoed the stories from 1919 of a mother's desperation to keep her baby alive.

In October 2020, a Melbourne mother sent her five-year-old back to school at East Preston Islamic College after a period of isolation, with a note from the state Department of Health and Human Services that he was clear of COVID-19, only to find that he was in fact positive. The authorities had given confusing advice, which meant the specific recommendations about each family member had not been clear to the family, and the mother's decision led to a further lockdown of up to three hundred people, including 120 in a public housing block (*ABC News*).

Mothers of children with a disability also lost access to school-based supports. Melbourne mother Leanne Haynes felt "at breaking point" as she attempted to homeschool her two children with autism, demonstrating the challenging circumstances faced by many mothers whose children had special needs (Hermant, Campanella, and Kent).

It is little wonder then that mental distress among mothers increased from 9 per cent to 22 per cent during the COVID-19 pandemic (Melbourne Institute), a higher rate of increase than experienced by childless women. Mental health issues for mothers received little attention during the COVID-19 pandemic, even though 45 per cent of women felt "that everything was an effort" compared to 36 per cent of men (Australian Bureau of Statistics). Women losing paid work rose five times more than that of men while their hours doing unpaid work also increased at a greater rate than men's (Workplace Gender Equality Agency; Craig). As reports of family violence increased and children were more vulnerable to abuse in a locked-down home, the pandemic accentuated the risk of violence in the home.,

Australian and Victorian governments introduced responses to the economic and social disruptions faced by women, including additional funding for family violence and mental health supports, but they struggled to develop policies that met the diverse needs of mothers, including those from culturally diverse backgrounds or of children with a disability. In 2020, the 26 per cent of Victoria's population who spoke a language other than English were over-represented in precarious employment, suffered disproportionately from health and economic disparities, and faced language barriers, insecure incomes, as well as increased racism (Walsh). Socioeconomic disadvantage was associated with higher risk of sickness and death from COVID-19. For working-class and migrant mothers, protecting children and themselves became difficult, as face-to-face support services closed and public transport became a site of infection risk. The advice to keep calm during lockdown was perhaps of limited use when it did not speak to the needs of families forced to engage in paid work or to balance the multiple needs of family members.

Mothers and Economic Independence

In 1919, during the second wave of the flu pandemic in Victoria, the labour movement stressed the importance of economic independence for mothers to recognize their true value to society: "How far are we still from the proper realisation of the value of a child as an asset of the State, and how little we realise the true position the mothers of the community would occupy in a properly-organised social system where the economic independence of women was fairly recognised and assured!" (*Labor Call*, 26 June 1919, 9). Not all mothers had access to economic security, and, indeed, the flu pandemic exacerbated the economic and social vulnerability of mothers. Studies of the experience of mothers, especially single-parent families, during this period suggest they had little access to economic resources (Swain and Howe). The numbers of single mothers increased between January and September 1919, when 1,173 children were committed to the Children's Court of Victoria. The *Victorian Year Book 1919-20* attributed this increase from the previous year to the deaths of their fathers from the flu (396). A father leaving a mother entailed blame, whereas a widow was not to blame. In cases of children committed to the care of the state, the poverty of the mother following desertion by the father accounted for 339 out of the 589 blameable cases. The same source also reported that poverty following the death of the father accounted for 885 of the 1,330 blameless cases (395). A loss of the main income earner meant mothers had an even heavier load to carry.

Prior to the 1919 pandemic, creches had been established for working-class mothers for decades when they needed income from paid work outside the home. In the Melbourne suburb of Prahran, a creche had been running for over twenty-nine years before the pandemic "for the benefit of mothers who find it incumbent to engage in outside daily work in order to assist in obtaining a livelihood." But the creche was not a charity: "The creche is not a charity.... Mothers have to pay for leaving their children there, and this fact imbues a spirit of independence into the minds of mothers" (*Malvern Standard*, 27 Sept. 1919, 17).

A mother's spirit of independence was also tested when the COVID-19 lockdown compounded poverty and social isolation. Women from multicultural backgrounds who worked in low-paid but essential jobs—such as elderly care, food manufacturing, and cleaning—had poor access to information and suffered from an increased risk of infection from working in high-risk industries (Multicultural Centre for Women's Health). The lockdowns most affected those who were not able to enjoy the privileges of remote working and those mothers who had lost paid work due to industry closures. These systemic inequities in employment were barely acknowledged in the public health response that struggled to provide immediate supports to mothers to ensure they could cope (Duckett).

With the closure of schools during the COVID-19 pandemic, advice to parents about homeschooling assumed that mothers in paid employment would have the resources to work from home or to access paid leave. In fact, this thinking only applied to privileged mothers and excluded those in casual employment or who had lost their jobs and now faced financial insecurity. Those mothers who could draw on resources to support their role at home as well as maintain paid employment had a different experience than other mothers.

The struggle for economic independence for mothers continues, and victories have primarily advantaged white, middle-class women. The pandemics have amplified the fault lines in public health responses and redrawn the parameters of a mother's duty to include managing her own health as well as of the health of children while fulfilling the new emotional demands arising from social isolation and economic insecurity. In this way, both pandemics tell us a lot about a mother's role, despite their occurring one hundred years apart.

Conclusion

In formulating public health responses to pandemics, policymakers often assume that there is a mother at home to nurture her children as well as to comply with public health measures. The ideal mother was white and middle class. She was also required to maintain a cheerful homelife for her children and comply with the public health instructions.

In 2020, the ideal mother was still seen as white and middle class, but now she was also expected to maintain any paid employment that could be performed remotely while balancing homeschooling her children. As the pandemic goes on, mothers from multicultural backgrounds still receive little support and continue to be marginalized by working in high-risk industries. Mothers of children with a disability experience additional strains looking after their children at home. Despite social and economic transformations over the past century, both pandemics have exposed how complex and varied a mother's duties can be.

The historical comparisons of these debates illuminate tensions and contradictions within the role of the mother. But these comparisons also have their limitations. Media reports often reveal prevailing ideologies and not necessarily objective truth, and the actual experience of COVID-19 is still emerging. Although greater policy attention is being given to the stresses of balancing paid work (or the financial hardship following a loss of income) and raising children in 2020, the 1918-1919 flu pandemic and COVID-19 have both accentuated deep structural class and race inequalities.

Living through COVID-19 has shown me the importance of documenting the experiences of mothers to capture their complex worlds. It has also given me insights into circumstances that I could never have imagined at the start of 2020. But above all, this project has allowed me to continue a connection with my own mother as a way of dealing with the trauma of this moment.

Works Cited

ABC News. "East Preston Islamic College Closes After Student Tests Positive to COVID-19, Surrounding Suburbs Alerted." *Australian Broadcasting Commission*, 21 Oct. 2020, www.abc.net.au/news/2020-10-21/victoria-coronavirus-case-in-east-preston-melbourne-school/12800092. Accessed 20 Jan. 2021.

"Aborigines Do Not Suffer." *Geelong Advertiser*, 25 Feb. 1919, 6.

"A Pathetic Case. Family Practically Starving. Neglect by Benevolent Societies." *The Age*, 4 Mar. 1919, 5.

Australian Bureau of Statistics. "Household Impacts of COVID-19 Survey: Insights into the Prevalence and Nature of Impacts from COVID-19 on Households in Australia." *Australian Bureau of Statistics*, Aug. 2020, www.abs.gov.au/statistics/people/people-and-communities/household-impacts-covid-19-survey/latest-release. Accessed 20 Jan. 2021.

Australian Human Rights Commission. "Bringing Them Home. Report of the National Inquiry into The Separation of Aboriginal and Torres Strait Islander Children from Their Families." Australian Human Rights Commission, 1997, humanrights.gov.au/our-work/bringing-them-home-report-1997. Accessed 20 Jan. 2021.

"By Love Serve One Another." *Herald,* 22 Apr. 1919, 7.

Craig, Lyn. "Coronavirus, Domestic Labour and Care: Gendered Roles Locked Down." *Journal of Sociology*, vol. 56, no. 4, 2020, journals.sagepub.com/doi/full/10.1177/1440783320942413. Accessed 20 Jan. 2021.

Damousi, Joy. *The Labour of Loss. Mourning, Memory and Wartime Bereavement in Australia*, Cambridge University Press, 1999.

Dawson, Emma, and Janet McCalman. *What Happens Next? Reconstructing Australia After COVID-19*. Melbourne University Press, 2020.

Duckett, Stephen. "Waves of Inequity in the Coronavirus Pandemic." *Grattan*, 24 Aug. 2020, grattan.edu.au/news/waves-of-inequity-in-the-coronavirus-pandemic/. Accessed 20 Jan. 2021.

"Editorial." *The Age*, 11 July 1919, 6.

Grimshaw, Patricia, et al. *Creating a Nation 1788-1990*. McPhee Gribble, 1994.

Hermant, Norman, Nas Campanella, and Lucy Kent. "Parents of Children with Disabilities are Struggling to Teach Their Children During COVID-19." *Australian Broadcasting Commission*, 6 May 2020, www.abc.net.au/news/2020-05-06/coronavirus-parents-need-help-teaching-students-disabilities/12211664. Accessed 20 Jan. 2021.

Hygeia. "Our Babies." *Horsham Times,* 26 Sept. 1919, 12.

"Indian Mother's Tragedy." *The Age*, 31 May 1919, 4.

"Influenza in New Zealand." *Yackandandah Times*, 13 Feb. 1919, 2.

Johnson, Niall P A S, and Juergen Mueller. "Updating the Accounts: Global Mortality of the 1918–20 'Spanish' Influenza." *Bulletin of the History of Medicine*, vol. 76, no. 1, 2002, pp. 105-115.

Leahy, Carla Pascoe, and Petra Bueskens. *Australian Mothering: Historical and Sociological Perspectives*. Palgrave Macmillan, 2020.

Locke-Burns, Lilian. "State Provision for Mother and Child." *Labor Call*, 26 June 1919, 9.

Macintyre, Stuart. *The Oxford History of Australia. Volume 4. The Succeeding Age 1901–1942*. Oxford University Press, 1997.

McQueen, Humphrey. "The Spanish Influenza Pandemic in Australia 1912–19." *Social Policy in Australia. Some Perspectives 1901-1975*, edited by Jill Roe, Cassell, 1976, pp.131-47.

Melbourne Institute. "Behind Closed Doors. The Surge in Mental Distress of Parents." *Melbourne Institute*, melbourneinstitute.unimelb.edu.au/__data/assets/pdf_file/0011/3456866/ri2020n21.pdf. Accessed 20 Jan. 2021.

Moloney, Kim, and Susan Moloney. "Australian Quarantine Policy: From Centralization to Coordination with Mid-Pandemic COVID-19 Shifts." *Public Administration Review*, vol. 80, no. 4, 2020, pp. 671-82.

Multicultural Centre for Women's Health. "Submission to the Public Accounts and Estimates Committee Inquiry into the Victorian Government's Response to the COVID-19 Pandemic." 31 July 2020,

Multicultural Centre, www.mcwh.com.au/submission-to-the-public-accounts-and-estimates-committee-inquiry-into-the-victorian-governments-response-to-the-covid-19-pandemic/. Accessed 20 Jan. 2021.

Parliament of Victoria. "Epidemics and Pandemics in Victoria: Historical Perspectives." *Parliament of Victoria*, May 2020, www.parliament.vic. gov.au/publications/research-papers/category/36-research-papers. Accessed 20 Jan. 2021.

Paul, Margaret. "Parents Caught in Melbourne Public Housing Coronavirus Lockdown Stopped from Visiting Baby." *Australian Broadcasting Commission*, 9 July 2020, www.abc.net.au/news/2020-07-09/corona virus-public-housing-lockdown-stops-parents-visit-baby/12439778. Accessed 20 Jan. 2021.

Porter, Roy. *The Greatest Benefit to Mankind. A Medical History of Humanity from Antiquity to the Present*. Harper Collins, 1997.

"Shocking Discovery at Ballark. Three Victims to Pneumonic Influenza. Mother, Daughter and Son." *Ballarat Star*, 7 May 1919, 1.

Swain, Shurlee, and Renate Howe. *Single Mothers and their Children. Disposal, Punishment and Survival in Australia*. Cambridge, 1995.

Reiger, Kerreen M. *The Disenchantment of the Home. Modernizing the Australian Family 1880-1940*. Oxford University Press, 1985.

"The Flu and the Schools." *Albury Banner and Wodonga Express*, 21 Feb. 1919, 12.

"The Prahran Creche. A Well Managed and Necessary Institution." *Malvern Standard*, 27 Sept. 1919, 17.

Tomes, Nancy. "Destroyer and Teacher: Managing the Masses During the 1918–1919 Influenza Pandemic." *Public Health Report*, vol. 125, no. 3, 2010, pp. 48-62.

Vesta. "The Education of Children. First Steps at Home." *Argus*, 3 July 1918, 12.

Vesta. "Influenza Epidemic. What to do." *Argus*, 12 Feb. 1919, 10.

Victorian Government. "Talking to Your Child About Coronavirus (COVID-19)." *Victorian Government*, 2020, www.coronavirus.vic.gov. au/talking-your-child-about-coronavirus-covid-19. Accessed 20 Jan. 2021.

Victorian Year Book 1919–20. Australian Bureau of Statistics, www.abs.gov.au/ AUSSTATS/abs@.nsf/allprimarymainfeatures/48267BBA5D74598 FCA2577750018066D?opendocument. Accessed 20 Jan. 2021.

Walsh, Michael. "Here's What You Told Us About Racism in Australia During the Coronavirus Pandemic." *Australian Broadcasting Commission*, 14 May 2020, www.abc.net.au/news/2020-05-14/racism-in-australia-during-the-coronavirus-covid-19-pandemic/12234832?nw=0. Accessed 20 Jan. 2021.

Workplace Gender Equality Agency. "Gendered Impacts of COVID-19." *Workplace Gender Equality Agency*, 11 May 2020, www.wgea.gov.au/topics/gendered-impact-of-covid-19. Accessed 20 Jan. 2021.

Chapter Forty Five

No Room for Family: COVID-19 Fatigue

Fiona Joy Green and Tracey Farrington

> Be Calm. Be Kind. Be Safe.
>
> —Dr. Bonnie Henry, provincial health officer
> for British Columbia, Canada

The above advice given by Dr. Bonnie Henry during her daily briefings in the first months of the COVID-19 pandemic became something of a welcome and guiding mantra to many. Her focus on empathy and collective understanding rather than on restrictions and criticism has been commended and acknowledged for successfully flattening the curve of infections in the first month of the pandemic outbreak and for keeping the subsequent number of cases, and thus deaths, low (McElroy). Saluted as a hero by many, the *New York Times* recognized Henry as "one of the most effective public health officials in the world, with lessons for nations struggling to emerge from lockdowns" (Porter). And we're two of those fans.

The onset of COVID-19 meant people retreated to their homes (for those who have them). Schools, daycares, and workplaces closed, putting many mothers out of work or into the position of working from home and simultaneously into the role of educating and caring for their children and elderly family members. Essential frontline workers in health services, law enforcement, public safety and emergency response, food and agriculture, transportation, industry and manu-facturing, sanitation, communications and information technology, and financial institutions were both quickly identified and praised.

Yet mothers—who predominantly took on the added responsibility and burden of the work as teachers and elements of work associated with the essential services listed above while they kept themselves and family safe—remained unseen and ignored as indispensable to the wellbeing of children, the elderly, and the economy.

"No Room for Family: COVID-19 Fatigue" sketched by Tracey Farrington exemplifies the devastation of this invisibility, seclusion, and exhaustion for mothers. Outsiders are often blind to the chaos within the walls of the home, where mothers and families are at a breaking point, emotionally, physically, financially, and mentally. Mothers have been muted, muzzled into silence, while the lives of their family implode around them at home as they struggle to be calm, to be kind, and to be safe.

Works Cited

McElroy, Justin. "Why 'Be Kind, Be Calm and Be Safe' Is More Than Just a Catchphrase in B.C.'s COVID-19 Fight." *CBC News*, 25 Apr. 2020, www.cbc.ca/news/canada/british-columbia/bc-covid-new-normal-activities-social-anxiety-1.5544951. Accessed 9 Aug. 2020.

Porter, Catherine. "The Top Doctor Who Aced the Coronavirus Test." *New York Times*, 12 June 2020, www.nytimes.com/2020/06/05/world/canada/bonnie-henry-british-columbia-coronavirus.html. Accessed 7 Aug. 2020.

Artist, Tracey Farrington

Notes on Contributors

Gillian Anderson, PhD, is a mother, professor, and chair of the Sociology Department, at Vancouver Island University. Her research and teaching interests focus on gender and familial relations, mothering, motherwork, and the sociology of home. She is a member of a research team investigating the gendered impact of COVID-19 on mid-island mothers' caring labour. Recently, she coedited *Sociology of Home: Belonging, Community and Place in the Canadian Context* (2016) published by CSPI.

Victoria Bailey is currently completing a PhD in creative writing. Her feminist-focused work has been included in a variety of academic, creative writing, and nonfiction publications.

Renée E. Mazinegiizhigoo-kwe Bédard is of Anishinaabeg (Ojibwe/Nipissing/Omàmiwinini) and French Canadian ancestry. She is a member of Okikendawdt (Dokis First Nation). She holds a PhD from Trent University in Indigenous studies. Currently, she is an assistant professor at Western University in the Faculty of Education. Her areas of publication include practices of Anishinaabeg motherhood, maternal philosophy, and spirituality, along with environmental issues, women's rights, Indigenous Elders, Anishinaabeg artistic expressions, and Indigenous education.

Maya Bhave is an adjunct professor at St. Michael's College in Vermont. Her latest research has focused on female soccer players as well as mothers and child loss. She is currently working on a new manuscript examining mothers' shifting identities when their children leave for college. She lives with her husband and two sons near Burlington. Her latest book is entitled *War and Cleats: Women in Soccer in the United States.*

Jennifer L. Borda (associate professor, University of New Hampshire) researches mediated ideologies regarding social norms about gender, work, and family to advance political and public policy reform. She is author of *Women Labor Activists in the Movies* (McFarland, 2010), coeditor of *The Motherhood Business: Consumption, Communication, and Privilege* (University of Alabama Press, 2015), and has published a variety of scholarly articles and book chapters. She also addressed strengthening institutional family-friendly policies as an NSF-funded ADVANCE fellow at the University of New Hampshire.

Grace Ellen Brannon PhD, is an assistant professor in the Department of Communication at the University of Texas at Arlington. Dr. Brannon's research focuses on intersections of family, health, and privacy, especially related to patient experiences. She is also interested in how issues related to (dis)ability are communicated about within families and in the workplace, and how these communication patterns affect health outcomes.

Rebecca Jaremko Bromwich is a lawyer, legal academic, mother of four, one-time Green Party parliamentary candidate, and long-time environmental activist.

Elizabeth Brulé is an assistant professor in the Department of Gender Studies at Queen's University with a research focus in critical pedagogical approaches to learning, including Indigenous feminist, antiracist, anticolonialist, and critical disability theory and activism. She is of Métis and Franco Ontarian heritage.

Susie Burpee is a professional contemporary dance artist with a twenty-five-year career, which includes choreography, performance, teaching, and mentorship. She holds an MA in theatre, drama, and performance studies from the University of Toronto and is guest faculty at postsecondary dance training programs across Canada. Susie lives in Tkaronto/Toronto, with her husband and two daughters.

Olaf Kraus de Camargo is a developmental paediatrician and associate professor in the Department of Pediatrics at McMaster University and is a researcher at the CanChild Centre for Childhood Disability Research and MacART (McMaster Autism Research Team).

Mar Dieste Campo has a master's degree in gender studies from the University of Zaragoza, Spain. Her main research interests include gender studies, the social construction of motherhood as well as the collectivization of care and community participation.

Jaime Cidro (Anishnaabe) is a professor of anthropology at the University of Winnipeg and a Canada Research Chair in health and culture. She is the mother of two boys and one girl. Her research focuses on Indigenous social determinants of health and Indigenous maternal and child health.

Haile Eshe Cole is an assistant professor at the University of Connecticut. She received her PhD in anthropology with a concentration in African Diaspora Studies from The University of Texas at Austin. Her scholarly interests include Black feminisms, community-engaged/social justice research methodology, motherhood, and health disparities. Her most recent projects explore Black birth work and the reproductive health of Black women in the United States.

Ana Lucía Hernández Cordero, PhD, is professor at the University of Zaragoza, Spain. Her main research interests include feminist studies, public policies from a gender perspective, the social construction of motherhood, female migrations, and the sociological study of family and kinship networks in global care chains. Her doctoral thesis won first prize in the III Spanish National Contest of Doctoral Theses on Migrations in 2019.

Dalva Aparecida Marques da Costa, PhD, RN, is faculty member at the Municipal School of Public Health, Municipal Secretary of Health (Goiânia). Her clinical expertise is in the area of intensive care, and she teaches public health management. Ethnography is her main research method of interest. She is a member of the Group of Qualitative Studies in Health and Nursing (*Nequase*)—Federal University of Goiás (UFG; Goiânia)-Brazil National Council of Technological and Scientific Development.

Molly Wiant Cummins received her PhD from Southern Illinois University. Currently, she is a lecturer in the Department of Communication at the University of Texas at Arlington. Dr. Wiant Cummins's research centres on (intensive) motherhood and feminism as they relate to pregnancy, birth, and mothering discourses. She is also interested in critical communication pedagogy.

Perlita R. Dicochea is the Communications Associate and a Program Coordinator at the Center for Comparative Studies in Race and Ethnicity at Stanford University and is a commissioner with the Historical Heritage Commission of Santa Clara County. Having earned her Ph.D. in ethnic studies from U.C. Berkeley, she served some years as a professor and more recently as a museum curator. Currently, Perlita is working on a children's story about her toddler son's experiences in dance classes.

Hillary Di Menna has been a teenage runaway, an academic, and overall troubled girl. The only identity she truly understands is that of mother to a wild-haired, whirlwind of a daughter. Together, they live among black cats, eat raspberries for communion, and write love letters to the moon.

Alys Einion-Waller is associate professor of midwifery at Swansea University. She is an equalities activist and a researcher in the fields of midwifery, motherhood, narrative, gender, LGBTQIA equalities, and inclusive education. She is the author of two novels: *Inshallah* (2014) and *Ash* (2018) (Honno) and is the coeditor of *Bearing the Weight of the World, Exploring Maternal Embodiment* (Demeter Press). A Fellow of the Royal College of Midwives, she is also the founder of Centred Birth Hypnobirthing.

Gráinne Evans is a thirty-seven-year-old Irish mother of four, living with her Canadian husband in the North of Ireland. An accredited La Leche League leader, she works as a volunteer breastfeeding counsellor in her hometown of Maghera. A passionate advocate for birth, breastfeeding, and attachment parenting, Gráinne enjoys writing poems and rhymes on these subjects for her blog *The Breast of Rhymes* in her spare time.

Tracey Farrington is a contemporary, interdisciplinary artist who has wheat in her heart and saltwater in her soul. A graduate from Vancouver Island School of Art, she holds a master of photographic arts (MPA) and is an international photographic judge. She has a unique career path breaking down gender barriers and advocating for equality. A mother of two, and a certified dream coach and Reiki master, she is unapologetically known as the Princess of Awesomeness. www.TJFarrington.com

Lorena Sekwan Fontaine (Cree-Anishinaabe) is a single mother to a teenage daughter and a caregiver to aging family members. She is also a professor at the University of Winnipeg, whose research focus is on the legacy of residential schools, cultural genocide, and Indigenous language rights.

May Friedman's research looks at unstable identities, including bodies that do not conform to traditional racial and national or aesthetic lines. Most recently, much of May's research has focused on intersectional approaches to fat studies, considering the multiple and fluid experiences of both fat oppression and fat activism. May works at Ryerson University as a faculty member in the School of Social Work and in the Ryerson/York graduate program in communication and culture.

Elsje Fourie is an Assistant Professor of Globalization and Development in the University of Maastricht's Faculty of Arts and Social Sciences. Her research and teaching have focused on Africa's role in debates around foreign development assistance and political modernity, with a special emphasis on Ethiopia. She is also increasingly interested in projects such as this volume, which connect the humanities and social sciences in innovative ways. She has two young daughters.

Brooke Harris Garad is a research scholar and chair of the Equity, Diversity, and Inclusion Committee at the Indiana Institute on Disability and Community, Indiana University-Bloomington. Harris Garad has international experience as a teacher educator and holds a PhD in global, multicultural, and equity studies in education from Ohio State University. Equity issues are central to Harris Garad's academic line of inquiry, and she values the importance of community -oriented and culturally sustaining pedagogies.

Paula González Granados is a social worker and has a PhD in social and cultural anthropology from the University Rovira i Virgili (Tarragona, Spain). She currently works as a full-time professor at the University of Zaragoza. Her interests and publications have to do with audiovisual anthropology, gender, motherhood, care, different family models, and family and work conciliation.

Fiona Joy Green, PhD, is a feminist mother and professor of women's and gender studies at the University of Winnipeg, who believes in the power of revolutionary feminist motherwork. She's interested in the agency of children and parents, in gender identities, and in the ability of matroreform and feminist motherlines to contribute to feminist parenting, feminist theorizing, and feminist praxis. Fiona has authored *Practicing Feminist Mothering* (ARP, 2011), and coedited four Demeter Press collections addressing the areas of maternal pedagogies and evolving feminist parenting practices. As coauthor of *Family Blog Lines: Tal[k]ing Care* (familybloglines.com/), she collaborates in exploring parenting and families in relation to the everchanging digital world.

Pooja Gupta is a registered clinical psychologist, Mumbai, India, with a MPhil in clinical psychology. Her areas of interest include parenting interventions, including compassion and mindfulness-based practices.

Lynn O'Brien Hallstein (PhD Ohio State University) is a professor of rhetoric and an affiliated faculty of the Women's, Gender, and Sexuality Studies Program at Boston University. As a motherhood scholar who employs a communication lens, her research explores the various ways that contemporary motherhood is constructed rhetorically. She has published two single-authored books, four coedited books, and twenty-two peer-reviewed journal articles and/or book chapters, while also presenting conference papers regularly at both communication and motherhood conferences.

Zaje A. T. Harrell, PhD, is a health psychologist with a passion for integrating theory and praxis. She holds a joint doctorate in psychology and women's studies with content expertise in coping, mental health, and community change. She descends from the activist, justice-seeking tradition of Black clubwomen. She is a married Black feminist mother of three children, ages eleven, nine, and seven and lives in the greater Baltimore area.

Sara Hayden, PhD, is professor of communication at the University of Montana. Her research focuses on the rhetoric of motherhood and has been published in journals, including *Quarterly Journal of Speech*, *Women's Studies in Communication*, and *Communication and Critical/Cultural Studies*. She has coedited two books, *Mediated Moms:*

Contemporary Challenges to the Motherhood Myth (2016) with Heather Hundley and *Contemplating Maternity in the Era of Choice: Explorations into Discourses of Reproduction* (2010) with Lynn O'Brien Hallstein.

Stevie Lang Howson (they/them) is a mother, PhD student, and union organizer living in Sydney, Australia. Prior to COVID-19, they were working as a casual academic, teaching sociology and gender studies. Their PhD research examines the impacts of sentencing decisions and imprisonment on mothers. Stevie is the sole parent of one five-year-old child, and their research interests are mothering, vulnerability, and care under neoliberalism. They are transgender, bisexual, and nonmonogamous and have been hanging out for the revolution for quite a while now.

Saba Karim Khan is an author, award-winning documentary film-maker, and educator. She received an MPhil in social anthropology from the University of Oxford and works at NYU Abu Dhabi. Her research focuses on South Asia and the Middle East, the politics of sexual harassment, radicalism, social movements, diasporas, and using qualitative methods. Saba writes for *the Guardian*, *the Independent*, *Wasafiri*, *Sentio*, *Excursions*, and *Huff Post*, among other international publications. Her debut novel, *Skyfall*, was published by Bloomsbury in December 2020.

Sylvie Lafrenière, PhD, is a mother, grandmother, and stepmother. A sociologist with the Sociology Department at Vancouver Island University, she is currently working for the university's teaching and learning centre, assisting faculty in the switch to online teaching. Her research interests are typically centred around official-language minority groups in Canada—specifically Francophones outside Québec—culture, media, and communication theory. Her teaching centers on incorporating lived experiences and creating inter-disciplinary experiential learning opportunities for students.

Hakyoon Lee is an assistant professor in the Department of World Languages and Cultures at Georgia State University. She has been teaching Korean at Georgia State University since the fall semester of 2013. Her research interests are at the intersection of sociolinguistics, language and gender, bilingualism and multilingualism, and Korean transnational families.

Jennifer Long is a Canadian artist, curator, and arts administrator. Her artwork draws inspiration from the quiet moments and rituals of everyday life in order to explore the complexities of women's experiences. Long's lens-based practice has been exhibited and published internationally and awarded funding by all levels of the Canadian arts councils. Long is a founding member and administrator of the Feminist Photography Network.

Lidia Ivonne Blásquez Martínez has a PhD in socioanthropology from EHESS, France (2007). Since 2011, she has held a professor-researcher post at the Metropolitan Autonomous University-Campus Lerma, Mexico, and she is currently head of PSPI research area. Her work has focused on interdisciplinary approaches to socio-environmental conflicts, sociocultural change, violence, and politics of the commons, as well as feminist political ecology. As a result of her own experience, she has developed an interest in women's career paths to better understand gender inequalities in academia.

Ketoki Mazumdar PhD, is an Assistant Professor at the School of Human Ecology, Tata Institute of Social Sciences, Mumbai, a psychotherapist and a mother. Dr. Mazumdar's research interest lies in the areas of maternal mental health, parenting, self-compassion, as well as mindfulness, compassionate, and trauma-informed therapeutic practices. She is also continually endeavouring to understand how young and established adults create meaningful lives and to help people flourish and achieve well-being.

Mary Jane Logan McCallum (Munsee) is a professor of history at the University of Winnipeg, a Canada Research Chair in Indigenous peoples, histories, and archives. Her research focuses on modern Indigenous histories in health, education, and labour, with a recent focus on Indigenous histories of tuberculosis in Manitoba. She is the mother to one daughter.

Wendy McNab (Cree) is a First Nations health researcher as well as a marriage and family therapist student at the University of Winnipeg. She is a mother of one adult son and a Kookum to one grandchild.

Marcelo Medeiros, PhD, RN, is a full professor at the Faculty of Nursing (UFG). He is the editor of the *Electronic Journal of Nursing*, the research lead of the *Nequase*, and a visiting researcher at the

Daphne Cockwell School of Nursing–Ryerson University, Toronto, Canada. He is a research supervisor for multidisciplinary master and PhD programs at UFG. His qualitative research expertise is in community health nursing, social risks, and vulnerabilities as well as violence against children, adolescents, and women. His current works are in global nursing. He is the researcher lead of the Group of Qualitative Studies in Health and Nursing (*Nequase*)—Federal University of Goiás (UFG; Goiânia)-Brazil National Council of Technological and Scientific Development.

Punam Mehta is a feminist teacher-scholar who took the long path into academia. She finished her doctorate during the COVID-19 pandemic on feminist-informed yoga for marginalized mothers in Canada. Her emerging research is centred on the (re)contextualization of historical perspectives on yoga and the yoga traditions in the modern world through a cultural-feminist lens, particularly the application of the yoga traditions as an approach to healing for marginalized mothers. She has completed degrees in women's studies, biology, and community health sciences.

Catherine Moeller is a Toronto artist. She is employed in the community arts field and is the proud mother of a trans teenager. She works with students, seniors, multigenerational groups as well as newcomers, refugees, and sex workers. Catherine facilitates art, community building, and supports for folks coping with social barriers and the lived experience of poverty. During COVID-19, she also does art and wellness visits for the isolated and those with mental health challenges for Jumblies Theatre and Arts.

Andrea O'Reilly is a professor in the School of Gender, Sexuality and Women's Studies at York University, editor of the *Journal of the Motherhood Initiative*, and publisher of Demeter Press. She is editor of twenty-three books, including *Feminist Parenting: Perspectives from Africa and Beyond* (2020) and *The Routledge Companion to Motherhood* (2019) and is author of three monographs, including *Matricentric Feminism: Theory, Activism, and Practice* (2016). She is twice the recipient of York University's Professor of the Year Award for teaching excellence and is the 2019 recipient of the Status of Women and Equity Award of Distinction from OCUFA (Ontario Confederation of University Faculty Associations).

Luciana Alves de Oliveira, PhD, is an assistant professor at the Institute of Biological Sciences (UFG). She is a member of the Academic Integrity Committee (UFG) and oversees best practice in research, including matters of bioethics and ethics. Her area of interest is qualitative studies in public health. She is a member of the Group of Qualitative Studies in Health and Nursing (*Nequase*)— Federal University of Goiás (UFG; Goiânia)-Brazil National Council of Technological and Scientific Development.

Lucia Montes Ortíz is a PhD candidate in Ecology and Sustainable Development at El Colegio de la Frontera Sur (Mexico). Her work centres on the ecology and taxonomy of zooplankton. Besides her research area, she has a broad interest in gender equality in science due to her own experience as an academic mother, which has led her to engage in science from a feminist perspective and to participate in programs to empower young girls to bridge the gender gap in science.

Kate Orton-Johnson is a senior lecturer in digital sociology at the University of Edinburgh. She is co-director of the master's in digital society at Edinburgh and co-convenor of the British Sociological Association Digital Sociology study group. Her research focuses on intersections between technology, culture, and everyday life. She has published on the ways in which motherhood is articulated, represented, and resisted online and on how we can understand motherhood as digitally mediated.

Leonora R. Pacheco, PhD, RN, is an associate professor at the Faculty of Nursing (UFG). As an obstetric nurse, her area of expertise is gender and violence, violence against children, violence and quality of life, immigrant and refugee populations, social vulnerabilities, family health, and qualitative research (mainly ethnography). She is a member of the Group of Qualitative Studies in Health and Nursing (*Nequase*)—Federal University of Goiás (UFG; Goiânia)-Brazil National Council of Technological and Scientific Development.

Sheila Mara Pedrosa, PhD, RN, is an assistant Professor at the Faculty of Nursing, Unievangélica (Anápolis, Brazil), and its lead researcher at the Centre of Studies on Violence and Social Vulnerability. Her academic interests are violence against women, violence in the school, and violence and quality of life. She is a member of the Group of Qualitative Studies in Health and Nursing

(*Nequase*) – Federal University of Goiás (UFG; Goiânia)-Brazil National Council of Technological and Scientific Development.

Paula dos Santos Pereira is a PhD candidate, a psychologist, and a coordinator of the Health Services to Population in Situations of Violence and Health in the Socioeducational System Program—State of Goiás Secretary of Health (Goiânia). She is an instructor at the Multiprofessional Residency, university-affiliated hospital (UFG). Her research interests include gender and intergenerational violence, public health policies, and violence prevention in vulnerable populations. She is a member of the Group of Qualitative Studies in Health and Nursing (*Nequase*)—Federal University of Goiás (UFG; Goiânia)-Brazil National Council of Technological and Scientific Development.

Barbara Philipp created her Knock Down diary during lockdown. As a mother-artist, she observes the damage in societies when care is not valued in laws and in political commitments.

Kinga Pozniak is a sociocultural anthropologist and a postdoctoral researcher at CanChild Centre for Childhood Disability Research at McMaster University. Her research focuses on the experiences of parents who have children with disabilities.

Cali Prince is a Community Cultural Development practitioner, poet, practice-led researcher, academic tutor, and doctoral candidate at the Institute for Culture & Society, Western Sydney University, Australia. Her body of work focuses on creativity, collaboration and transformation. She has published in peer reviewed journals as well as practitioner focused platforms and publications. As a mother, her creative writings often come in the silence that falls after midnight.

EL Putnam is lecturer in digital media at the National University of Ireland Galway, where she is director of the master's program in digital media. She is an artist-philosopher working in performance art and digital technologies. Her forthcoming book, *Strange Mothers: the Maternal, Digital Subjectivity, and the Aesthetics of Interruption*, is being published with Bloomsbury. She is a member of the Mobius Artists Group (Boston) and holds a PhD from the Institute for Doctoral Studies in the Visual Arts.

Maeve Regan is a research Midwife at Birmingham Women's and Children's NHS Foundation Trust. She is passionate about equality in perinatal services and family-centred care. She has been teaching Centred Birth Hypnobirthing online throughout the pandemic.

Belinda Robson is a freelance historian who has also worked in women's policy roles across state government and community services for over thirty years. In addition to writing commissioned histories, she has published several articles relating to her PhD on the history of psychiatry and the development of art therapy in mental health services. She is currently researching the historical evolution of services for mothers and children and lives in Melbourne, Australia.

Daiana Evangelista Rodrigues. PhD, RN, is an associate professor in the Department of Nursing, Federal University of Rondônia, Porto Velho-Brazil. She coordinates the Multiprofessional Health Family Residence and coleads the Center of Studies in Collective Health. Her academic interests are teaching and conducting qualitative research on primary healthcare and vulnerable populations (e.g. women, adolescents, and children). She is a member of the Group of Qualitative Studies in Health and Nursing (*Nequase*)—Federal University of Goiás (UFG; Goiânia)-Brazil National Council of Technological and Scientific Development.

Walterlânia Silva Santos, PhD, RN, is an associate professor in nursing at the Faculty of Ceilândia, University of Brasília, Brazil and a visiting Researcher at Daphne Cockwell School of Nursing–Ryerson University, Toronto, Canada. She is a community health specialist, whose scholarly interests are global nursing and evidence-based community nursing. She is a member of the Group of Qualitative Studies in Health and Nursing (*Nequase*)—Federal University of Goiás (UFG; Goiânia)-Brazil National Council of Technological and Scientific Development.

Helen Sargeant is a visual artist based in West Yorkshire, England. Her work is autobiographical and focuses on the representation of the maternal body. She has developed a collaborative practice with her own family and other artists with the aim of widening the representation of the maternal subject. www.helensargeant.co.uk

Emily Satterthwaite's research explores areas of the tax law, in which tax choices and taxpayer compliance obligations may have regressive equity implications. Her focus is on vulnerable taxpayer populations, including subsistence entrepreneurs, self-employed individuals, and paid domestic workers. She is a member of the faculty at the University of Toronto Faculty of Law.

Aleksandra Staneva, PhD, is a lived experience researcher at Peach Tree Perinatal Wellness, Brisbane, Australia. Her work focusses on exploring maternal mental health from peer-support and lived-experience frameworks. She employs feminist critical-realist approaches and applies mixed-methodologies, such as participatory action research, poetry and visual methods, alongside traditional quantitative approaches. Aleksandra is a mother of a twelve-year-old son, and she is also a counsellor in private practice.

Natasha Steer is the author of *Great Lakes to Great Walls: Reflections of a Single Mom on Young Motherhood and Living Overseas* (2016). She became a single/lone mother at the age of nineteen and has travelled to over fifty countries with her teenage son. Empowering students by day and writing by night, Natasha has a BA in English literature and an MEd in social justice education. www.natashasteer.com.

Roberta Stout (Cree) is a mother to a teenage daughter while providing in-home care to her parents. She has been involved in Indigenous health research and advocacy for over twenty years.

Jen Vasic is a social worker with more than ten years of experience in the nonprofit and academic sectors. She has worked as a youth worker, program coordinator, and researcher. Currently, she is a city councillor in Waterloo and a PhD candidate at Wilfrid Laurier University. She is studying the connection between poverty and education as well as the ways that significant adults stand in solidarity with youth who help their families make ends meet.

Margareth Santos Zanchetta, PhD, RN, is an associate professor at the Daphne Cockwell School of Nursing–Ryerson University, Toronto, Canada. Her scholarly interests are gender as a social determinant of health (SDH), health promotion, individual and community health literacy, global nursing, global health and equity, as well as the social development of socially deprived communities.

She collaborates with Brazilian scholars to transfer knowledge on SDH. She is a member of the Group of Qualitative Studies in Health and Nursing (*Nequase*)—Federal University of Goiás (UFG; Goiânia)-Brazil National Council of Technological and Scientific Development.

Dara Herman Zierlein is a political artist, illustrator, and painter who continuously uses her art to advocate awareness in the world. Dara's work has been exhibited internationally, and she has been published in among others, *Mom Egg Review, Resist Grab Back, the Earth Issue, Lunch Ticket,* and *the Nation OPPART.* She is currently illustrating for *The Rumpus,* a literary forum. Her first children's book, *Don't Eat the Plastic,* will be published Spring 2021. motherstime.blogspot.com/.

Holly Zwalf's past research has focused on feminism, queer theory, and the erotic maternal. She's the editor of *Mothers, Sex, and Sexuality* (Demeter Press) and has presented at the American Anthropological Association AGM, the San Francisco National Sexuality Resource Centre Summer Symposium, and at the Australian Association of Research into Mothering conference in Brisbane. She's also the coordinator of Rainbow Families Qld, an organization that supports and advocates on behalf of LGBTQIAP+ parents in Queensland, Australia.